REGIME INTERAC
INTERNATIONA

This major extension of existing scholarship on the fragmentation of international law utilises the concept of 'regimes' from international law and international relations literature to define functional areas of legal specialisation and institutional activity. Responding to prevailing approaches, which focus on the resolution of conflicting norms between regimes, it explores the way in which norms and institutions from disparate regimes overlap and interact. Leading scholars reflect on how, in situations of legal pluralism and concurrent activity, such interaction shapes and controls knowledge and norms at the domestic, transnational and international level, in often hegemonic ways. The contributors draw on topical examples of interacting regimes, including climate, trade, intellectual property and investment regimes, to argue for new methods and understanding of regime interaction. Together, the essays combine historical, doctrinal, critical and sociological forms of legal analysis to provide important insights into an issue that continues to challenge international legal theory and practice.

MARGARET A. YOUNG is a senior lecturer at the Melbourne Law School, University of Melbourne, Australia. She was formerly based at the University of Cambridge, where she was the inaugural Research Fellow of Public International Law at the Lauterpacht Centre for International Law and Pembroke College.

REGIME INTERACTION IN INTERNATIONAL LAW

Facing Fragmentation

Edited by

MARGARET A. YOUNG

CAMBRIDGE
UNIVERSITY PRESS

CAMBRIDGE
UNIVERSITY PRESS

University Printing House, Cambridge CB2 8BS, United Kingdom

Cambridge University Press is part of the University of Cambridge.

It furthers the University's mission by disseminating knowledge in the pursuit of education, learning and research at the highest international levels of excellence.

www.cambridge.org
Information on this title: www.cambridge.org/9781107521780

First published 2012
First paperback edition 2015

A catalogue record for this publication is available from the British Library

ISBN 978-1-107-01048-2 Hardback
ISBN 978-1-107-52178-0 Paperback

CONTENTS

CONTRIBUTORS

JAMES CRAWFORD SC, FBA, is Whewell Professor of International Law, University of Cambridge and a Fellow of Jesus College. He was Director of the Lauterpacht Centre for ten years between 1995 and September 2010. He was a Member of the United Nations International Law Commission from 1992 to 2001 and Special Rapporteur on State Responsibility from 1997 to 2001. In addition to scholarly work on statehood, self-determination, collective rights and international responsibility, he has appeared frequently before the International Court of Justice including in the Advisory Opinions on Nuclear Weapons (1996) and the Israeli Wall/Barrier (2004). He has also appeared before other international tribunals, and is actively engaged as an international arbitrator.

JEFFREY L. DUNOFF is Professor of Law and Director, Institute for International Law & Public Policy at Temple University Beasley School of Law. He has served as Visiting Professor at Harvard Law School and Princeton University, a Visiting Fellow at the Lauterpacht Centre, a Law and Public Affairs Fellow at the Woodrow Wilson School, a member of the Warwick Commission on the Future of the Trade System, a consultant for the World Bank, and on the editorial board of the *Yearbook of International Environmental Law*. His scholarship focuses on public international law, international regulatory regimes, and interdisciplinary approaches to international law. Recent publications include *Ruling the World? Constitutionalism, International Law and Global Governance* (with Trachtman) and *International Law: Norms, Actors, Process* (with Ratner and Wippman).

JAMES FLETT works in the World Trade Organization (WTO) and Trade Policy team of the European Commission Legal Service. He has represented the European Commission in 120 cases before the European Court of Justice, and the EC in 90 proceedings before the WTO. He regularly advises the Commission on WTO law. Before joining the Commission Legal Service in 1995 Mr Flett spent several years working for the international law firms Clifford Chance and Van Bael & Bellis, in London and Brussels, with a particular emphasis on international trade law.

STEPHEN HUMPHREYS is Lecturer in Law at the London School of Economics. Prior to joining the LSE in 2009, he was Research Director at the International Council on Human Rights Policy in Geneva. He previously acted as publications director for the Open Society Justice Initiative in New York, and before that oversaw a project monitoring minority rights and discrimination in ten EU accession countries for the Open Society Institute in Budapest. He conducted research on climate change and the Kyoto mechanisms with ENDA Tiers Monde in Dakar, Senegal. He is the editor of *Human Rights and Climate Change* (2009) and the author of *Theatre of the Rule of Law* (2010).

PETER KORTH is an Associate at Hengeler Mueller, Berlin. His recent writings include *Dritthaftung von Ratingagenturen* (2010) and 'Quasivertragliche Expertendritthaftung und "soziologische Jurisprudenz"' in Gralf-Peter Calliess (ed.), *Soziologische Jurisprudenz – Festschrift für Gunther Teubner* (2009).

MARTTI KOSKENNIEMI is Professor of International Law at the University of Helsinki and Global Professor of Law at New York University. From 2008 to 2009 he was the Arthur Goodhart Visiting Professor of Legal Science at the University of Cambridge. Professor Koskenniemi was appointed as a member of the United Nations International Law Commission in 2002 and he was Chair of the Study Group on the *Fragmentation of International Law: Difficulties arising from the Diversification and Expansion of International Law*, which produced a report and recommendations to the General Assembly in 2006. From 1997 to 2003 he served as a judge of the Administrative Tribunal of the Asian Development Bank. He was counsellor for legal affairs at the Finnish Ministry for Foreign Affairs from 1978 to 1994. His main publications include *From Apology to Utopia. The Structure of International Legal Argument* (1989), *The Gentle Civilizer of Nations. The Rise and Fall of International Law 1870–1960* (2002) and *La politique du droit international* (2007).

ANDREW LANG is a Senior Lecturer in Law at the London School of Economics. Formerly, he was the Gott Research Fellow in Law at Trinity Hall, at the University of Cambridge. He is a co-founder, with Colin Picker, of the Society of International Economic Law. He sits on the Editorial Boards of the *Modern Law Review*, the *Journal of International Economic*

Law and the *Law and Development Review*, and is a Book Review Editor for the *International and Comparative Law Quarterly*. He is the author of *World Trade Law After Neoliberalism: Re-imagining Global Economic Governance* (2011).

NELE MATZ-LÜCK is Professor for the Law of the Sea, University of Kiel, Germany. Formerly, she was a Senior Research Fellow at the Max Planck Institute for Comparative Public Law and International Law in Heidelberg. From 2005 to 2007 she was a research fellow at the German Federal Constitutional Court where she was mainly engaged in cases related to public international law. She is author of the book *Wege zur Koordinierung völkerrechtlicher Verträge* (2005) and co-author of *Conflicts in International Environmental Law* (2003).

PENELOPE NEVILL is in practice at the Bar of England and Wales at 20 Essex Street Chambers, London, where she specialises in public international law and related areas before domestic and international courts and tribunals. She is a Visiting Tutor in public international law at King's College, London, and a former Fellow of the Lauterpacht Centre for International Law and Law Fellow of Downing College in the University of Cambridge. She is a graduate of the Universities of Auckland (BA, LLB (Hons)) and Cambridge (LLM) and a Barrister and Solicitor of the High Court of New Zealand. She is currently completing professional qualifications in the United Kingdom at 20 Essex St Chambers, London, with a view to continuing her work in public international law and international arbitration.

CHERYL SAUNDERS is a laureate professor at the University of Melbourne, with a personal chair in law. She has specialist research interests in public law and comparative public law, with particular reference to intergovernmental relations, constitutional design and comparative constitutional method. In 2005/06, she held the position of Arthur Goodhart Visiting Professor of Legal Science at the University of Cambridge and in 2009 was a visiting fellow at Corpus Christi College, Oxford. She is President Emeritus of the International Association of Constitutional Law, a Fellow of the Australian Academy of Social Sciences and a member of the Advisory Board of International IDEA. In 1994 she was appointed an officer in the Order of Australia, for services to the law and to public administration.

GUNTHER TEUBNER is Professor of Private Law and Legal Sociology, Goethe Universität Frankfurt and Professor, International University

College, Torino. He was Centennial Professor, London School of Economics, from 1998 to 2009. His research fields include social theory of law and comparative private law. He is the author of *Networks as Connected Contracts* (2008); *Regime-Kollisionen: Zur Fragmentierung des Weltrechts* (2006); *La cultura del diritto nell'epoca della globalizzazione: L'emergere delle costitzioni civili* (2005); *Il diritto possibile* (2005); *Direito, Sistema, Policontexturalidade* (2005); *Diritto policontesturale* (1999); *Droit et réflexivité* (1994); *Law as an Autopoietic System* (1993) (translated into nine languages). He is the editor and co-author of *Contractual Networks* (2008); *Nach Jacques Derrida und Niklas Luhmann* (2008); *Paradoxes and Inconsistencies in the Law* (2006); *Transnational Governance and Constitutionalism* (2004); *Global Law Without A State* (1997); *Environmental Law and Ecological Responsibility* (1994); *State, Law and Economy as Autopoietic Systems* (1992); *Paradoxes of Self-Reference in the Humanities, Law and the Social Sciences* (1991).

MARGARET YOUNG is Senior Lecturer of the Melbourne Law School, University of Melbourne, Australia. She was the inaugural Research Fellow in Public International Law at Pembroke College and the Lauterpacht Centre for International Law, University of Cambridge from 2006 to 2008. Her fields of research and teaching include international and domestic public law and she is the author of *Trading Fish, Saving Fish: The Interaction between Regimes in International Law* (2011).

ACKNOWLEDGEMENTS

This book is the product of much collaboration, the most significant of which was a conference at the Lauterpacht Centre for International Law, the University of Cambridge, in June 2009. The conference was both an examination and an exercise of 'regime interaction', bringing together international law scholars and practitioners, adjudicators from international tribunals, secretariat staff and advisors to states and non-governmental organisations. Several people who are distinguished by their generosity and academic rigour (and their general resistance to any one 'functional specialisation') have made significant contributions throughout this project, and I wish to express my deepest thanks to Georges Abi-Saab, James Crawford, Françoise Hampson, David Kennedy, Martti Koskenniemi, Sol Picciotto, Cheryl Saunders, Joanne Scott, Eleanor Sharpston and Gunther Teubner. I am equally indebted to the other speakers at the conference who have each contributed chapters to this volume.

At Cambridge, Anita Rutherford, Tara Grant and Karen Fachechi of the Lauterpacht Centre were indispensable in organisational matters, and I am also grateful to my former college, Pembroke College, for co-hosting the event. Thanks are also due to the lively conference participants and especially to Sophie Chapman, Yseult Marique, Francesco Messineo, Brendan Plant and Chris Thomas for their assistance with note-taking. At Melbourne Law School, the Institute for International Law and the Humanities provided encouragement and support, and I am grateful to its Director, Anne Orford. Alissa Sputore and her staff at the Law Research Service provided excellent editorial and research assistance at the final stages of the book production. Finally, I wish to thank the two anonymous peer reviewers from Cambridge University Press as well as Finola O'Sullivan for her continuing support.

Margaret Young

Introduction: The Productive Friction between Regimes

MARGARET A. YOUNG

Defining regimes and theorising their interaction is a risky undertaking for international lawyers. Acknowledging the boundaries and relationships between fields of functional and professional specialisation – such as international trade law, human rights law and the law of the sea – may be read as a repudiation of international law's systemic nature, and of the common governing principles that are essential both to the discipline and to the idea of international law. At the same time, however, there is an urgent need for international lawyers to understand how different branches of norms and institutions overlap on issues of global concern. This extends from the problem of conflicting legal norms – which has already garnered broad attention – to novel explorations of the way in which, in the default situation of diversity and concurrent activities, norms and institutions from disparate legal regimes interact.

An understanding of regime interaction requires engagement with specialised regimes and with the often unseen interaction between them, as well as with key existing and emerging principles of international law. It demands a flexibility of approach that draws on legal, historical, doctrinal, institutional and sociological forms of analysis. It is grounded in real global issues that traverse regimes, such as marine pollution, trade in services, indigenous guardianship of biological diversity and the protection of foreign investors. It requires investigation into different stages of international law-making and adjudication – because regime interaction is not simply a matter for international judicial tribunals who seek to interpret conflicting norms, but is a constant feature in the setting of agendas for new negotiations, the ongoing norm elaboration within regimes and even the domestic policy coordination between state ministries and departments. It combines a critical awareness of the perils of conceiving of regime interaction – which include the reification of 'regimes' – with a constructive commitment to the potential for productive friction and growth of set institutional and normative arrangements. In short, it needs to 'face' the complex issues that arise from the fragmentation and diversification of international law. This prodigious challenge is at the heart of this volume.

This introductory chapter provides a brief background to the phenomenon of the fragmentation of international law and its seminal literature, a tentative typology of the meanings of the term 'regimes', which has differed within international law and international relations scholarship, and a brief preview of the chapters.

A. The fragmentation of international law

The recognition that international law is made up of fragments of normative and institutional activity is not new. Notwithstanding the ambitious hopes represented by the United Nations system, there has never been a single global legislature or appellate court to mould a unified body of international law. Nor has there ever been a uniform will for such a system by sovereign states. Instead, states have implicitly or explicitly conceived of particular issues and problems – often at key historical moments of transition and often strategically – and responded by agreeing to new laws and supporting international organisations. So besides the wealth of laws stemming from treaties agreed under the auspices of the United Nations and its specialised agencies, there are additional branches of international trade law, human rights law, investment law and so on. And unlike the rapid increase in regulatory frameworks and agencies within domestic states – which has also happened at key moments of strategic and ideological change – there has been no hierarchical order to resolve normative and institutional conflicts. In recent times, this expansion of international treaties and associated international organisations and tribunals has generated a burgeoning interest in the effects of fragmentation: what it means and whether something ought to be done about it.

At the turn of the century, the International Law Commission of the United Nations (ILC) directed its attention to the fragmentation phenomenon, and later convened a 'Study Group' of ILC members. The ILC Study Group, chaired by Martti Koskenniemi, released a consolidated study into 'The Fragmentation of International Law' in 2006,[1] followed by

[1] ILC Study Group, 'Fragmentation of International Law: Difficulties arising from the Diversification and Expansion of International Law', Report of the Study Group of the International Law Commission finalized by Martti Koskenneimi (A/CN.4/L.682 and Corr.1) (13 April 2006).

a set of conclusions by way of 'practical guidelines to help thinking about and dealing with the issue of fragmentation in legal practice'.[2] Its terms of reference were to focus on situations where multiple international norms co-existed in relationships of interpretation or conflict.[3] This focus augmented existing literature that has been preoccupied with the potential that conflicting norms could lead to disarray and disorder within the international legal system.[4] Amongst that literature are calls for unity and coherence.

The ILC Study Group's findings, although underpinned by a systemic understanding of international law, are modest, contextual and heterogenous. Its recommendations aim to be 'concrete' and 'practice-oriented'.[5] For example, the Study Group discusses the rule of *lex specialis derogat legi generali*, which is based on the primacy of the specific over the general, and observes that a more specific treaty will usually trump the general treaty.[6] The Study Group also discusses the principle of *lex posterior derogat legi priori*, which gives primacy to a more recent treaty over an earlier one,[7] and a 'principle of harmonization', according to which international norms are interpreted 'so as to give rise to a single set of compatible obligations'.[8] The Study Group points to peremptory norms, norms 'accepted and recognised by the international community of states as a whole from which no derogation is permitted',[9] such as the prohibition of slavery or genocide, and emphasises that such norms will trump all others in an event of conflict.[10] Special treaty clauses that set out the priority of

[2] ILC Study Group, 'Fragmentation of International Law: Difficulties arising from the Diversification and Expansion of International Law, Conclusions of the Work of the Study Group' (A/CN.4/L.702) (18 July 2006).

[3] See, e.g. ILC, 'Conclusions', Conclusion (2), 7–8 (distinguishing between situations where one norm assists in the interpretation of another and where the application of two norms would lead to incompatible decisions).

[4] See the discussion in Martti Koskenniemi and Päivi Leino, 'Fragmentation of International Law. Postmodern Anxieties?' (2002) 15 *Leiden Journal of International Law* 553; see also Georges Abi-Saab, 'Fragmentation or Unification: Some Concluding Remarks' (1999) 31 *New York University Journal of International Law and Politics* 919, and associated writings in the influential journal symposium on 'The Proliferation of International Tribunals: Piecing Together the Puzzle'.

[5] ILC, 'Conclusions', p. 2.

[6] Ibid., Conclusion (5), pp. 8–9.

[7] Vienna Convention on the Law of Treaties (VCLT) Art. 30. See ILC, 'Conclusions', Conclusions (24)–(30), pp. 17–19.

[8] ILC, ibid., Conclusion (4), p. 8. Note also the Study Group's reference to the harmonising effect of treaty interpretation under VCLT Art. 31(3)(c), which the Study Group calls a principle of 'systemic integration': Conclusions (17)–(23), pp. 13–17.

[9] VCLT Art. 53.

[10] ILC, 'Conclusions', Conclusion (32), p. 20.

conflicting norms, such as the provision in the United Nations Charter for Charter obligations to prevail over members' obligations under any other international agreement, are also supported.[11] The offered techniques are non-exhaustive, flexible, and not always in harmony themselves, given the possibility, for example, that the application of a *lex specialis* and *lex posterior* principle to actual or potential conflicts of norms could lead to different results.

The recommendations of the ILC Study Group were offered without regard to the institutional dimension of fragmentation. That the Study Group's mandate expressly excluded an analysis of the relations between various international institutions is understandable, given the ILC's position within the United Nations system, which may have precluded any substantive recommendations about institutional practices or hierarchical relations between international organisations. Notwithstanding the restricted nature of its mandate, however, the Study Group was well-aware of the growth in 'quasi-autonomous normative sources' arising at the international level,[12] and of the complexity associated with non-governmental participants and other actors.[13] Indeed, it concludes its pioneering study by calling for further work to be done on 'the notion and operation of "regimes"'.[14]

B. A typology of 'regimes'

'Regimes' is a short-hand, non-legal term that has multiple and overlapping meanings in diverse literatures, including public international law and international relations (IR). These meanings are often qualified with adjectives such as 'self-contained' or 'special', as described in the following typology.

The International Court of Justice (ICJ) used the term 'self-contained regimes' to describe the rules of diplomatic law, in order to emphasise that the consequences of breach were contained within the prescriptive content of the primary rules.[15] Although the ILC once drew upon this

[11] Such priority was based on UN Charter Art. 103 and the special character of the UN: see ibid., Conclusion (36), p. 22.

[12] ILC, 'Analytical Study', p. 249.

[13] Ibid., p. 252.

[14] Ibid., p. 249.

[15] *Consular Staff in Tehran (USA* v. *Iran)* [1979] ICJ Rep 7 (para. 86). See further Bruno Simma, 'Self-Contained Regimes' (1985) 16 *Netherlands Yearbook of International Law* 111, 115 and 117 (self-contained regimes as a limited sub-category of subsystems of international law, which embraced 'a full (exhaustive and definite) set of secondary rules'). For

'misleading doctrine', it was subsequently abandoned.[16] The ILC Study Group concludes that the term was a misnomer, and cautions against its use, although it concedes that groups of rules and principles concerned with a particular subject matter could be labelled as 'special regimes'.[17]

The concept of 'special regimes' was useful for the ILC Study Group in conceptualising the operation of *lex specialis*. The Study Group identifies three possible understandings of the term:[18]

> (i) [narrowly, where] violation of a particular group of (primary) rules is accompanied by a special set of (secondary) rules concerning breach and reactions to breach [ie the diplomatic law as conceived by the ICJ in *Tehran*];
> (ii) [more broadly, where there is] a set of special rules, including rights and obligations, relating to a special subject matter. Such rules may concern a geographical area (eg a treaty on the protection of a particular river) or some substantive matter (eg a treaty on the regulation of the uses of a particular weapon). Such a special regime may emerge on the basis of a single treaty, several treaties, or treaty and treaties plus non-treaty developments (subsequent practice or customary law); and
> (iii) [most broadly, where] all the rules and principles that regulate a certain problem area are collected together so as to express a 'special regime'. Expressions such as 'law of the sea', 'humanitarian law', 'human rights law', 'environmental law' and 'trade law', etc give expression to some such regimes. For interpretative purposes, such regimes may often be considered in their entirety.

These definitions of 'special regimes' contain differing assumptions, some of which are mirrored in other literature on 'regimes', including from IR scholarship. These differing assumptions deserve greater attention, affecting as they do the utility of the definitions for the current study of regime interaction.

There are four principal sets of assumptions that diverge in the definitions of regimes offered in the ILC and other literature. These relate to the actors, institutions, 'stages' of legal development and, finally, the possibility of systems-based or emergent practices within regimes. In short,

criticism of the Court's use of the term, see James Crawford and Penelope Nevill in Ch. 8 of this volume, p. 259.

16 Pierre-Marie Dupuy, 'The Danger of Fragmentation or Unification of the International Legal System and the International Court of Justice' (1999) 31 *New York University Journal of International Law and Politics* 791, 797, and sources cited therein.

17 See ILC, 'Analytical Study', pp. 65–101 (esp 82); 492.

18 See ILC, 'Conclusions', pp. 11–12 (para. 12).

they are assumptions about the 'who', 'what', 'when' and 'why' inherent in 'regimes'. Articulating the differences in these four sets of assumptions provides for a better understanding of the conceptions of 'regimes' and the associated study of regime interaction in this volume.

The first set of assumptions relate to the actors that make up regimes. Two of the ILC's three conceptions of 'special regimes' rest on international norms and practices propagated by a single set of actors – namely, states. According to a positivist conception, some regimes apply to all states (for example, when treaties enjoy universal membership) while other regimes apply only to some (most commonly, because only a group of states have consented to be bound by a treaty). State participation and consent is the same foundation underpinning the notion of 'regimes' developed in international relations scholarship (notwithstanding the marked deviations in some of the other fundamentals of the discipline founded by Morgenthau as compared to international law). In contrast, states are *not* the sole influences operating in the ILC Study Group's third conception of 'special regimes'. This is akin to scholarship on private law and transnational arrangements, which consider the operation of 'private regimes' that coalesce around issues of functional specialisation but that are not necessarily motivated by – and may even exclude – the interests of states.[19]

'Regimes' in IR scholarship have been defined as 'sets of implicit or explicit principles, norms, rules, and decision-making procedures around which actors' expectations converge in a given area of international relations'.[20] Given the background realist assumptions of the IR discipline, it is fair to imply that it is the intentions of states that are paramount in establishing regimes, as defined.[21] The idea of 'regimes' in IR literature has spawned a massive literature that has sought to study discrete groups

[19] See further Gunther Teubner and Peter Korth in Ch. 1 of this volume. A further distinction may be made in public law, where the term 'regime' has been used to emphasise both formal arrangements as well as the 'temper and manner' of sovereign rule: see Martin Loughlin, *The Idea of Public Law* (Oxford University Press, 2003) 31.

[20] Stephen Krasner, 'Structural Causes and Regime Consequences: Regimes as Intervening Variables' in Stephen Krasner (ed.), *International Regimes* (Cornell University Press, 1983) 1, 3. See also Oran Young, *International Cooperation: Building Regimes for Natural Resources and the Environment* (Cornell University Press, 1989).

[21] For example, discussions of the 'club model' of multilateral cooperation emphasise that different international regimes are made up of specialised state bureaucrats and officials: see e.g. Robert Keohane and Joseph Nye, 'The Club Model of Multilateral Cooperation and Problems of Democratic Legitimacy' in Roger Porter et al. (eds.), *Efficiency, Equity, and Legitimacy: The Multilateral Trading System at the Millennium* (Brookings Institution Press, 2001) 264.

of norms under the rubric of 'regime theory'[22] – a normative turn that preceded current constructivist accounts.[23] 'Regime theory' has tended to analyse single regimes rather than regime interaction, although there is a growing body of work on 'regime complexes'.[24] The IR definition of 'regime' has also been influential in international law scholarship.[25]

Other conceptions of 'regimes' seek to include actors besides states within the term. The broadest of the ILC Study Group's three notions of 'special regimes' emphasises a body of 'functional specialization or teleological orientation', such as environmental law or trade law.[26] This may imply that the ideals, objectives and activities of other actors, besides states, are formative to the regimes. If so, it requires one to consider the influence of 'professional mindsets' on regime interaction.[27] Technical experts, non-governmental organisations, secretariat staff, tribunal members, and other actors become part of the definition of regimes and thus essential to a study of regime interaction.

Such awareness underpins a sociological understanding of fragmentation – and the Weberian idea of functional specialisation – and informs the approach of scholars who acknowledge that the conflict between regimes in international law reflect wider societal conflicts. The associated studies of 'discursive networks' seek to demonstrate certain biases and preferences within regimes that preclude efforts at harmony or conflict resolution.[28] Fields of functional specialisation also underlie the conception of

[22] See Krasner, *International Regimes*. The term 'regime' has other connotations within the wider political science literature, where it is sometimes used to denote governments or other systems of power (as reflected in the popular genteelism 'regime change').

[23] See e.g. Anne-Marie Slaughter, 'International Law and International Relations Theory: A Dual Agenda' (1993) 87 AJIL 205, 206; see also, on the tensions between early IR conceptions of law and the normativity of regime theory, Crawford and Nevill in Ch. 8 of this volume, pp. 258–259.

[24] See e.g. Kal Raustiala and David Victor, 'The Regime Complex for Plant Genetic Resources' (2004) 58 *International Organization* 277; Robert Keohane and David Victor, 'The Regime Complex for Climate Change' (2011) 9 *Perspectives on Politics* 7.

[25] E.g. Krasner's definition is adopted by Jeffrey Dunoff in Ch. 5 of this volume, p. 139.

[26] ILC, 'Analytical Study', para. 136, p. 72.

[27] On the influence of experts on international law, see Martti Koskenniemi, 'The Fate of Public International Law: Between Technique and Politics' (2007) 70 *Modern Law Review* 1; David Kennedy, 'The Mystery of Global Governance' (2008) 34 *Ohio Northern University Law Review* 827. See also Koskenniemi in Ch. 10 of this volume. See also Andrew Lang in Ch. 4 and Margaret Young in Ch. 3 of this volume.

[28] Andreas Fischer-Lescano and Gunther Teubner, 'Regime-collisions: The Vain Search for Legal Unity in the Fragmentation of Global Law' (2004) 25 *Michigan Journal of International Law* 999; Oren Perez, *Ecological Sensitivity and Global Legal Pluralism: Rethinking the Trade and Environment Conflict* (Hart Publishing, 2004).

'regulatory regimes' governing particular activities, such as taxation or finance arrangements.[29] Moreover, an awareness of the role of an expanded set of actors is central to IR scholarship on 'epistemic communities'.[30]

That 'regimes' are *not* dependent on states is fundamental to the study of global, private legal relations identified as 'transnational regimes'.[31] The problem of regime interaction is especially challenging in this context: the 'private' legal regimes, though not based on the interests of states as articulated in international fora, still seek a global, unifying reach. Like regimes in international law, transnational regimes such as *lex digitalis* are motivated by sectoral differentiation, but they are removed from any state-based political articulation. The resulting legal pluralism presents known and emerging challenges for governance,[32] especially in the context of interacting regimes. Techniques from private international law are being offered in both the transnational and international context in an increasingly fluid and dynamic way.[33]

The second set of assumptions inherent in the differing conceptions of 'regimes' relates to institutions. The role of international organisations is not apparent in any of the ILC's conceptions of 'special regimes', although arguably the two broader conceptions implicitly rely on some kind of institutional background to the relevant rules and principles. For example, intergovernmental rules relating to a geographical area have historically depended on administrative bodies.[34] The normative influence of such institutions on matters of international governance has received renewed attention in legal and interdisciplinary literature,[35] and has animated studies on 'linkages', 'global administrative law' and 'new

[29] Sol Picciotto, 'Constitutionalizing Multilevel Governance?' (2008) 6 *International Journal of Constitutional Law* 457, 463, and Sol Picciotto, *Regulating Global Corporate Capitalism* (Cambridge University Press, 2011) 22ff.

[30] See e.g. Peter Haas, 'Introduction: Epistemic Communities and International Policy Coordination' (1992) 46 *International Organization* 1.

[31] See Teubner and Korth in Ch. 1 of this volume. The ILC Study Group calls for greater attention to transnational regimes (as well as international regimes) in its conclusions: see ILC, 'Analytical Study', p. 253.

[32] See generally Christian Joerges, Inger-Johanne Sand and Gunther Teubner (eds.), *Transnational Governance and Constitutionalism* (Hart Publishing, 2004).

[33] Ralf Michaels and Joost Pauwelyn, 'Conflict of Norms or Conflict of Laws? Different Techniques in the Fragmentation of International Law' in Tomer Broude and Yuval Shany (eds.), *Multi-Sourced Equivalent Norms in International Law* (Hart Publishing, 2011) 19; see also Alex Mills, *The Confluence of Public and Private International Law* (Cambridge University Press, 2009).

[34] See e.g. reference to the Danube regime established by Danube riparian states discussed in Crawford and Nevill in Ch. 8 of this volume, p. 258.

[35] See e.g. José Alvarez, *International Organizations as Law-Makers* (Oxford University Press, 2005).

governance', as well as fragmentation.[36] Examples of institutional interplay, particularly in the environmental sphere, enhance understanding of particular legal arrangements.[37]

Regimes may well include or depend upon an 'institutionalized system of dealing with a particular field of behaviour'.[38] A combination of approaches would thus adopt a definition of regimes that includes institutions. Accordingly, regimes are sets of norms, decision-making procedures and *organisations* coalescing around functional issue-areas.[39]

The third set of assumptions that deviate as between different regime definitions relate to what are loosely described here as 'stages' of legal development and application. International law is constantly made, implemented and enforced. These 'stages' are not always temporally sequenced; especially as law may be 'made' before it is formally negotiated or implemented.[40] Yet the literature on fragmentation has so far concentrated mainly on the resolution of conflicting norms,[41] which occurs after laws are negotiated or have otherwise become custom. Such a focus is apparent in the first two of the ILC Study Group's conceptions of 'special regimes'. Yet its broadest conception allows for a more dynamic understanding of

[36] For a sample of the limitless references, see, on linkages, the symposium in (2002) 96:1 *American Journal of International Law*; on global administrative law, the symposium in (2005) 68 *Law and Contemporary Problems* 1–377; on new governance, the collection by Gráinne de Búrca and Joanne Scott (eds.), *Law and New Governance in the EU and the US* (Hart Publishing, 2006); on fragmentation of institutional authorities, the collection by Tomer Broude and Yuval Shany (eds.), *The Shifting Allocation of Authority in International Law* (Hart Publishing, 2008). For a focus on the role of dispute settlement bodies see e.g. Chester Brown, *A Common Law of International Adjudication* (Oxford University Press, 2007); Yuval Shany, *The Competing Jurisdictions of International Courts and Tribunals* (Oxford University Press, 2002).

[37] See e.g. Olav Schram Stokke (ed.), *Governing High Seas Fisheries: The Interplay of Global and Regional Regimes* (Oxford University Press, 2001); see also Sebastian Oberthür and Thomas Gehring (eds.), *Institutional Interaction in Global Environmental Governance: Synergies and Conflict among International and EU Policies* (The MIT Press, 2006). On the 'cognitive openness' of particular legal institutions to ecological issues, see Perez, n. 28 above.

[38] Crawford and Nevill in Ch. 8 of this volume, p. 259 ('We would define a regime as a more or less institutionalized system of dealing with a particular field of behaviour, often associated with the governance of territory, which claims a substantial measure of comprehensiveness and exclusivity.') See also Steven Ratner, 'Regulatory Takings in Institutional Context: Beyond the Fear of Fragmented International Law' (2008) 102 *American Journal of International Law* 475, 485.

[39] As adopted in Young in Ch. 3 p. 86 and Nele Matz-Lück in Ch. 7 of this volume, pp. 204–205.

[40] As implicit in Lauterpacht's judicial function: see Hersch Lauterpacht, *The Function of Law in the International Community* (Clarendon Press, 1933).

[41] But note the consideration of multi-sourced equivalent norms (MSENs): Tomer Broude and Yuval Shany (eds.), *Multi-Sourced Equivalent Norms in International Law* (Hart Publishing, 2011).

legal processes, because a field of functional specialisation in its entirety, such as trade law, is subject to ongoing normative development and change, especially with respect to multilateral negotiations but also due to state practice.

The IR regime definitions – with their emphasis on the convergence of principles, norms, rules and decision-making procedures – also seem to accommodate different stages of legal development, although sometimes at the risk of ignoring issues of juris-generative power. Specialised legal knowledge, however well-organised, is not the same as a regime. A flexibility of understanding of stages of legal development within regimes must combine, in studies of regime interaction, a legal sense for the cross-fertilisation between relevant stages.[42]

The fourth set of assumptions inherent within the current definitions of regimes relate to the possibility of systems-based or emergent practices. One of the dangers of discussions about 'regimes' is that they risk essentialising certain bodies of laws and principles. When a broad definition is used, such as the ILC Study Group's third conception, the danger is particularly great, because the multiplicious and often conflicting perspectives and preferences within professional circles may be reduced to a single set of ideas.[43] In addition, notions of 'regimes' obscure the generality of international law and may distort our understanding about the overall international legal system.[44] It makes the use of metaphors in the regime literature – such as 'ships', 'islands', 'arenas' and 'platforms' – seem rather imprudent.

Yet notwithstanding the problems with reification of regimes, it remains the case that there is a certain 'stickiness' within particular bodies of laws, institutions and professional specialisations, especially those that are constituted by specialist courts and tribunals.[45] The unwieldy and intransigent nature of regimes is often intentional, and may reflect a wish by powerful states to protect their dominance.[46] Moreover, functional

[42] As adopted especially by Dunoff in Ch. 5, Young in Ch. 3 and Matz-Lück in Ch. 7 of this volume.

[43] This was noted early in the 'linkage' literature surrounding 'trade and …' issues: see e.g. Jeffrey Dunoff, 'Rethinking International Trade' (1998) 19 *University of Pennsylvania Journal of International Economic Law* 347, 384; see also by Andrew Lang, 'Reflecting on "Linkage": Cognitive and Institutional Change in The International Trading System' (2007) 70 *Modern Law Review* 523, 538; see also Koskenniemi, 'The Fate of Public International Law', n. 27 above, 27 (warning about the dangers of reducing a 'trade' or 'environment' regime to a single policy upon which to ground cooperation).

[44] Crawford and Nevill in Ch. 8 of this volume, pp. 258–259.

[45] Ibid, p. 257.

[46] Eyal Benvenisti and George W. Downs, 'The Empire's New Clothes: Political Economy and the Fragmentation of International Law' (2007) 60 *Stanford Law Review* 595. Conversely,

differentiation leads to path dependency, higher transaction costs, 'tunnel vision'[47] and even 'solipsistic and imperial' tendencies within regimes.[48] Awareness of these issues allows for a hybrid definition of 'regimes' which combines many of the approaches and insights of international law, transnational law and international relations literature: regimes are sets of norms, decision-making procedures and organisations coalescing around functional issue-areas and dominated by particular modes of behaviour, assumptions and biases.

Clearly, engagement with the concept of 'regimes' requires a critical understanding of the strategic dimensions of fragmentation. Such engagement must be undertaken in tandem with an awareness of international law as an emergent system – and with an ongoing attempt to understand how the different elements of international law and governance interact. Whether and how regimes are removed from their social embeddedness[49] is a crucial question which underscores further and lasting questions about whether and how international law can reflect international society.[50] It requires an understanding of a range of law-making processes, including domestic legal systems,[51] as well as other phenomena. It is particularly urgent in confronting global problems that are 'wicked' in nature, where there can be no definitive formulation or bounded solution.[52] The productive friction of 'regime interaction' may lead to a more responsive and effective international legal system than the sum of the constituent regimes.

the rhetoric of 'fragmentation' may be strategically used in order to support efforts at international law reform: Anne-Charlotte Martineau, 'The Rhetoric of Fragmentation: Fear and Faith in International Law' (2009) 22 *Leiden Journal of International Law* 1.

47 See Teubner and Korth in Ch. 1 of this volume (contrasting the 'tunnel vision' of global regulatory regimes with the broader objectives of national legal systems, which are instead conceived by the dominant political principle of territory and carried out, at least in theory, with public interest aims).

48 See Koskenniemi in Ch. 10 of this volume, p. 318.

49 See further Teubner and Korth in Ch. 1 of this volume; cf. Dunoff's conception of 'law-making communities' within regimes in Ch. 5 of this volume.

50 As posed, for example, by Philip Allott's *Eunomia: New Order for a New World* (Oxford University Press, 1990). Cf. Dunoff's discussion of redemptive narratives in this volume, endorsed also by Crawford and Nevill in Ch. 8 of this volume, and related questions of legitimacy raised by Young in Ch. 3 and Matz-Lück in Ch. 7 in this volume. Such issues also enliven current research forays into the constitutionalisation of international law.

51 See especially Cheryl Saunders in Ch. 2 of this volume. See also André Nollkaemper, 'The Power of Secondary Rules to Connect the International and National Legal Orders' in Tomer Broude and Yuval Shany (eds.), *Multi-Sourced Equivalent Norms in International Law* (Hart Publishing, 2011) 45.

52 See further Young in Ch. 3 of this volume, p. 101.

C. Themes and structure of the book

The deviating assumptions within the concept of 'regimes' make the task of 'facing fragmentation' a particularly challenging one. They animate the core research questions of the present volume, which is structured around the themes of contexts, communities and control.

The first research theme explores the 'contexts' of regime interaction. What concepts of 'regimes' are assumed within a national, transnational and international legal perspective? How are 'transnational' and 'international' regimes estranged from the state? What are the effects when the regimes interact, both with each other and with domestic legal processes? This theme requires drilling down into a domestic legal setting, to ask how the interaction of regimes plays out *within* a state, and how state processes affect regime interaction at the transnational or international level. Legal pluralism *within* a state, as exists especially with respect to indigenous communities, brings further complexity. At an international level, the apparently unified position provided by states at various international fora may mask conflicting views in order to fit with the objectives and rationalities of the relevant international regimes. What legal framework exists, or should exist, for regime interaction to reflect the views of those affected by international law?

The second research theme investigates 'regime communities'. Who makes up regimes, and what is the effect of drawing boundaries around regime communities? What are their aims, objectives and knowledge-claims (and hegemonic quests)? How does this relate to our concept of society outside the modern state, especially given discussions about the 'constitutionalisation of international law'? Is international law bereft of a 'redemptive narrative'?[53] If international law is a system, do meta-principles exist, such as the idea of cooperation between international jurisdictions? These debates tie in with the 'contexts' of regime interaction, and further problematise the definition of regimes.

The third research theme investigates 'control' in issues of regime interaction. Such 'control' is often jurispathic in nature[54] – one 'regime' asserts that a particular law prevails over another. This is part of the exercise of interpreting the terms of international law, and gives rise to questions of legitimacy. On what authority does treaty interpretation within a regime draw upon other sources from other regimes, especially if the

[53] See further Dunoff in Ch. 5, pp. 149 ff and Crawford and Nevill in Ch. 8, pp. 252 ff.

[54] See further Dunoff in Ch. 5, p. 146.

constituent membership of the relevant regimes is not uniform? Even more vividly, on what basis do judicial tribunals proclaim the law – a task bestowed more often within regimes with compulsory dispute settlement procedures such as the World Trade Organization (WTO) – and how do the techniques used by such tribunals impact upon international law as a system or even more broadly as 'law'? These questions relate to the issues surrounding the communities and contexts of regimes, and especially the risk of managerialism in regime interaction. Is it possible that regime interaction is a process where the whole and the sub-set are always acknowledged, and the hidden aims for global order are open and contested? Rather than an effort at integration or harmonisation, can regime interaction lead to productive frictions?

The book is structured in three parts which reflect these three research themes, although the following previews of the chapters demonstrate that the issues overlap between each part. Part I considers regimes in their international, transnational and domestic contexts, and includes foundational thinkers in private law and comparative constitutional law, as well as an empirical account of interacting international regimes. Part II builds on these contexts to consider more expressly the fraught question of 'regime communities', and identify the different actors, vocabularies and objectives that influence regime interaction. Part III demonstrates with a range of examples the high stakes of treaty interpretation, litigant strategies and judicial techniques. It concludes with a strong warning about the hegemonic attributes of regimes and a consequential critique of the problem-solving tendencies of regime interaction.

1. Contexts

In 'Two Kinds of Legal Pluralism: Collision of Transnational Regimes in the Double Fragmentation of World Society', Gunther Teubner and Peter Korth extend the idea and consequence of functional differentiation of society – which at a global level has led to the creation of 'transnational' regimes addressing specific issue-areas – by considering potential collisions between a variety of modern and indigenous legal systems. Drawing on examples of private law disputes relating to cybersquatting and biopiracy, they argue that such potential collisions reflect the double fragmentation of world society and its law: trademark infringement across national borders risks conflicts not only between national legal systems, but also between domestic laws and private transnational rules that seek to govern the internet; patent protection for the commercial exploitation of certain traditional products results in conflicts between modern legal norms and the rules and customs of indigenous peoples (some of which are now recognised in public international law). By extending the metaphor of fragmentation from law to social systems and principles, they demand attention to the question of how social norms become embedded as *legal* norms, and suggest that formal methods of inquiry are deficient in this regard (especially given the interconnectedness within indigenous societies between religious, political and other knowledge-based systems of interaction). Whether clashes between the global regimes and other legal norms can be addressed by known conflict-rules within public and private international law, or must be resolved by other principles and protections, is the subject of their chapter.

Implicit in Teubner and Korth's conclusions about the need to compensate for the 'tunnel vision' of global regulatory regimes and transnational regimes during norm interaction is the idea that domestic legal systems are, by contrast, fairly balanced in their pursuit of a broader ideal of 'common welfare' and that individual domestic norms are thus usually mutually restricted. This leads to a further question as to how such domestic coordination and balancing impacts upon, and is impacted by, the interaction of global regimes. A domestic constitutional and political perspective is thus useful.

In 'International Regimes and Domestic Arrangements: A View from Inside Out', Cheryl Saunders examines the internal legal arrangements that allow for the coordination (although never complete) of norms *within* a state. Drawing on examples from one country, Australia, she considers how key domestic institutions support coordination across policy areas. This includes political coordination and adjudication of policy areas that are already subject to regime interaction at the international level, such as the relationship between the International Covenant on Civil and Political Rights (ICCPR) and other core human rights treaties.[55]

At a domestic level, the federal nature of the Australian system gives rise to additional layers of legal norms, as do the customary laws of Australia's indigenous people. Saunders demonstrates how the potential collision between laws from the central body (the Commonwealth) and

55 Consider Saunders' example of new statutory procedures to examine Australia's compliance with seven human rights treaties, as well as her discussion of interpretative principles for rights-protections applied by Australian courts; cf. the High Commissioner for Human Rights' proposal for a single treaty monitoring body in the OHCHR: see, e.g. Françoise J. Hampson, 'An Overview of the Reform of UN Human Rights Machinery' (2007) 7 *Human Rights Law Review* 7, 12ff.

each of the Australian States is at least partly rectified by savings clauses within federal statutes, by comity between State courts and by the idea of a single common law (and the practical reality of an apex court). The impact on these arrangements of norms from international regimes is of increasing importance, both for the development and implementation of the law itself, and for those seeking to enforce it. This issue is especially vital when the relevant international law is itself situated within multiple regimes.

In 'Regime Interaction in Creating, Implementing and Enforcing International Law', Margaret Young considers the international and domestic implications for the creation, implementation and enforcement of international law whose subject matter spans more than one established international regime. Using empirical evidence from fisheries governance, she discusses the major impediments to regime interaction, including the flawed twin ideas that international law is made up of regimes with set and exclusive competences and mandates, and that interacting regimes should be constituted by identical state parties. In contrast, she demonstrates that regime interaction is often based on institutional arrangements for information sharing and normative development that are dissociated from the consent of member states.

Young argues for a 'legal framework of regime interaction', where inter-regime scrutiny is constant and continuous, without any hierarchy between regimes, and where there are procedural safeguards to ensure the accountability of regime participants. Such a framework has major implications for international institutional law, such as the doctrine of implied powers of international organisations, and is relevant in addressing the risk of managerialism inherent in the meeting between experts within regimes. The alternative sources of legitimacy within such a framework – depending as they do on the inclusion of a range of state and non-state actors – may well demonstrate the convergence of transnational and international law, and promote the possibility of political engagement over regime struggles by those affected by international law.

2. *Communities*

In 'Legal Regimes and Professional Knowledges: The Internal Politics of Regime Definition', Andrew Lang claims that understanding how biases and preferences are embedded *within* regimes is crucial in efforts to understand regime interaction. Otherwise, there will be a tendency in scholarship of regime interaction to reify regimes. He therefore adopts an internal perspective and uses the international trade law regime, and specifically its constructed concept of a trade barrier, to identify processes by which normative biases and 'principles of vision' become embedded in regimes.

For Lang, technical experts have been central to the processes of regime definition in the trade law context. This expertise has been especially significant at moments of reclassification and redefinition within the trade regime – for example, when telecommunication services formerly governed by the International Telecommunications Union were liberalised under the auspices of the General Agreement on Trade in Services (GATS). If apparently objective core concepts within an international regime are the product of communications between experts – located in commercial and domestic regulatory groupings as well as within international organisations – rather than collective political engagement, there will be major structural limits to the transformative potential of regime interaction in international law. Arguably, this is especially the case when such interaction is formative to regime definition.

In 'A New Approach to Regime Interaction', Jeffrey Dunoff argues that the methodology in exploring the interaction between international legal regimes has been skewed towards processes and pronouncements within international judicial fora. A methodology that is more reflective of common scenarios of regime interaction would, he argues, embrace the ongoing normative and institutional relations between international regimes in a variety of settings – operational, regulatory and conceptual – and not just during litigation.

This broader attention to 'relational interactions' also incorporates a wider set of actors, including non-state actors. Dunoff uses Robert Cover's influential concept of 'nomos', with which Cover described the cohesive self-governing orders of particular (non-state) social groups in the United States, to analyse the practices and influences of participants within international regimes. Supported by a range of examples that include interactions between the international human rights regime and the international trade regime, Dunoff's new model of regime interaction demonstrates how these actors influence dynamic and evolving encounters between regimes, even as they operate without an overarching 'redemptive narrative' of the international legal system.

In 'Structural Ambiguity: Technology Transfer in Three Regimes', Stephen Humphreys takes us directly to the terms within international regimes. He shows how specific terms may be found across several regimes: 'technology transfer', as an example, currently appears in at least the climate, trade and investment regimes. Structural ambiguity exists because the shared terms are not themselves semantically unambiguous and because the regimes that accommodate them do not cohere.

Humphreys's investigation into the role and effect of ambiguity on interacting regimes takes in and tests the ILC's seminal study. At issue for Humphreys is the ILC Study Group's staging of international law's fragmentation: its consideration of fragmentation's timing, sources and causes, and its receptiveness to judicially-applied notions of hierarchy. By contrast, Humphreys demonstrates that the political and ideological differences over the term 'technology transfer' occur notwithstanding that the encapsulating regimes are contemporaneous and largely ratified by the same states. 'Technology transfer' either requires or renders unlawful redistribution by the state, depending on the regime in which it appears (and, even more complexly, the view of the relevant expert or management group *within* the regime), suggesting a range of implications for regime interaction and for international law.

3. *Control*

In 'Norm Interpretation across International Regimes: Competences and Legitimacy', Nele Matz-Lück continues the consideration of treaty terms by examining the role of treaty interpretation in situations when international regimes interact. Underpinning her conception of such interaction is support for a certain degree of coherence and formalism within the international legal system. This is similar to the position of the ILC Study Group, which pointed to Article 31(3)(c) of the Vienna Convention on the Law of Treaties (VCLT) as a central tool in promoting 'systemic integration' when norms came into conflict.[56] Matz-Lück shows how even aside from situations of direct conflicting norms, the factual and legal overlap between regimes can benefit from tools of treaty interpretation.

Matz-Lück considers different contexts of interpretation: when conducted by states as members of regimes – either individually or collectively through plenary organs – or when conducted by compliance or adjudicatory bodies. She shows, with examples from the regulation of marine pollution and other areas, how norms within one regime can mould and adapt to factual situations in other regimes. However, at issue is the existence and degree of state consent to the results of this interpretative exercise. Although desirable from the perspective of an increasingly systemic vision of international law, Matz-Lück argues that methods of

[56] ILC, 'Conclusions' conclusion (17), pp. 13–14; see also ILC, 'Analytical Study', pp. 206–244.

treaty interpretation that are too open to cross-regime fertilisation are a challenge to legitimacy, and calls for caution in this regard.

James Crawford and Penelope Nevill's chapter, 'Relations Between International Courts and Tribunals: The "Regime Problem"', focuses attention on the adjudicatory process within public international law. Resolving disputes is central to the role of law as a professional and technical practice, and when such disputes relate to conflicting norms or more general interacting regimes, international lawyers, unlike domestic lawyers, must advise on a landscape that lacks a court of general jurisdiction (although the ICJ comes close).

Crawford and Nevill argue that when such cases arise, the decisions made by judges, acting without clear rules, can offer insight into the idea of international law as law. Drawing on cases from international investment law, trade law, environmental law and fisheries law, as well as private international arbitration, they offer a non-exhaustive list of nine techniques to deal with regime and rule conflict. In doing so, they remind us that specific rules are based upon and *depend upon* the general law, and, like Lang, warn that the terminology of 'regimes' threatens to obscure the generality of public international law.

Moving from a judges' to a litigator's perspective, James Flett reviews a range of WTO disputes in his chapter, 'Importing Other International Regimes into World Trade Organization Litigation'. With a 'practitioner's eye' for strategies to assist a client's case, he argues that panels and the WTO Appellate Body are open to norms from other areas of international law, even if this is not recorded in their final reasoning and must instead be understood from the record – although often not publically available – of party submissions. In addition, he shows that a number of agreements within the WTO regime expressly sanction the use of norms from other areas of international law.

If the WTO dispute settlement is drawing upon international regimes so often and so heavily, Flett posits that the security and predictability of the trade system may be disrupted. For Flett, a necessary corrective to such interaction occurs when panels and the Appellate Body invoke detailed reasons for their decisions to 'import' from other regimes. Such a requirement for dispute settlement bodies and other decision-makers who invoke norms from other regimes can be contrasted with other ideas offered in the volume concerning the legitimacy and legal framework for regime interaction.

Decrying the tendency to label regime interaction as 'natural' or rational, Martti Koskenniemi, in 'Hegemonic Regimes', provides a forceful critique of the apparent problem-solving attitude in the idea of regime interaction. He analogises the interaction between states (which has generally found a middle ground between war and integration) and the integration of regimes. States have historically assumed a hegemonic stance in which they claim that their own interests have universal application; this has been perfected latterly through the use of economic, technical and scientific vocabularies. Koskenniemi argues that regimes, too, seek to 'implement' expertise as if it is self-evident and normal.

Koskenniemi claims that in their imperialist dealings, interaction between regimes becomes a question of which regime is likely to succumb or be co-opted. While efforts to correct the hegemonic influences of regime interaction may be found in such areas as the 'constitutionalisation of international law' and 'global administrative law', Koskenniemi considers that these, too, tend to the managerial. Smoother coordination and coherence is *undesirable* if it further facilitates an unjust international legal order. Provocatively, Koskenniemi provides a matrix that sets out the risks of greater coordination. For him, ideas about what is best for international society may be better advanced by a refusal to accept regime interaction, or at the very least a strategic awareness of the dangers it represents.

PART I

Contexts

Two Kinds of Legal Pluralism: Collision of Transnational Regimes in the Double Fragmentation of World Society

GUNTHER TEUBNER AND PETER KORTH*

A. GlobalSantaFe[1]

In September 2001, Global Marine Inc. and Santa Fe International Corp. announced their merger. The new enterprise would operate under the name 'GlobalSantaFe Corp.'. Immediately after the announcement was made, Park, a Korean citizen, registered the domain name 'globalsantafe.com' with the Korea-based domain name registrar Hangang. Following the registration, Park did not make active use of the website. It only said 'under construction'.

In October 2001, GlobalSantaFe Corp. asked the United States District Court, Eastern District of Virginia, Alexandra Division, to compel Hangang and the Virginia-based domain name registry VeriSign, which was responsible for the administration of the top level domain '.com', to transfer the domain name 'globalsantafe.com' to it. GlobalSantaFe Corp., referring to the Anticybersquatting Consumer Protection Act ('ACPA'),[2] claimed that Park had violated its trademark rights. On 1 April 2002, the court entered judgment in favour of GlobalSantaFe Corp.

On 9 April 2002, Park filed an application for an injunction in the District Court of Seoul, requesting the court to prohibit Hangang from transferring the domain name as ordered by the US court. The District Court of Seoul granted this injunction, finding that the US court lacked jurisdiction over the matter. Hangang accordingly refused to transfer the domain name to GlobalSantaFe Corp.

* We wish to thank Andreas Fischer-Lescano for his valuable contributions.

[1] *GlobalSantaFe Corp* v. *Globalsantafe.com*, 250 F Supp 2d 610 (ED Va, 2003).

[2] 15 USC § 1125(d) (1999).

But GlobalSantaFe Corp. did not give up. It asked the US court to direct VeriSign to cancel the domain name until transferred. On 5 February 2003, the court gave judgment in the plaintiff's favour. The court found that ACPA's jurisdictional requirements were met because VeriSign was located in Virginia. Further, concerns of 'international comity' did not dictate deference to the injunction issued by the Korean court. On the contrary, the 'Princess Lida doctrine', according to which the first court that asserts jurisdiction in a case requiring control over property may exercise that jurisdiction to the exclusion of any other court, would militate for its jurisdiction.[3]

B. Neem tree

True miracles are ascribed to the neem tree (*Azadirachta indica*), particularly in India, where the tree is worshipped as being holy. Extracts from its leaves are used to fight against fourteen different types of fungus and against bacteria found in burn tissue, as well as against typhoid pathogens. The extract is used to prevent viral infections, and is implemented against small pox, chicken pox, hepatitis B and herpes. All parts of the tree are used in ayurvedic medicine.

The natural product has become an object of commercial exploitation by transnational companies. US company W.R. Grace & Co. acquired a whole series of patents in the US and Europe in connection with the production of a stabilising Azadirachta solution for fighting fungi.[4]

This attempt by transnational companies to obtain exclusive rights on 'natural' knowledge prompted considerable resistance by indigenous peoples. Activists of various non-governmental organisations (NGOs) filed legal remedies against these patents – successfully in Europe. European patent no. 0436257, which had been granted by the European Patent Office (EPO), was revoked following the activists' objection because it did

[3] See *Princess Lida of Thurn and Taxis* v. *Thompson*, 305 US 456 (1939).

[4] Literature on the neem tree patent is extensive; especially instructive: Shalini Randeria, 'Rechtspluralismus und überlappende Souveränitäten: Globalisierung und der "listige Staat" in Indien' (2006) 57 *Soziale Welt* 229, 237; Vandana Shiva and Radha Holla-Bhar, 'Piracy by Patent: The Case of the Neem Tree' in Jerry Mander and Edward Goldsmith (eds.), *The Case Against the Global Economy: And For a Turn Toward the Local* (Sierra Club Books, 1996) 146, 148. Cf. further Murray Lee Eiland, 'Patenting "Traditional Medicine"' (2007) 89 *Journal of the Patent and Trademark Office Society* 45; Anja V. Hahn, *Traditionelles Wissen indigener und lokaler Gemeinschaften zwischen geistigen Eigentumsrechten und der public domain* (Springer, 2004) 279.

not meet the novelty of invention standard, as laid down in article 52 (1) and article 54 (1) and (2) of the European Patent Convention[5] (EPC).[6]

C. Two kinds of legal pluralism

What is it that connects these two *causes celèbres*? They are examples of situations in which new kinds of collisions of legal norms are at issue forcing the law to develop new conflict rules.

Both cases are of relevance for conflict law. This is evident at first sight in GlobalSantaFe. Here the issue was clearly the collision of US law with Korean law, for which the respective national conflict of law rules would have to choose between two national legal orders – hopefully driven by the goal to achieve international legal harmony. However, analysed more carefully, GlobalSantaFe is not only about the collision of two national legal orders. Instead, taking into account that the case transcends both national legal orders, that it can be 'localised' in the world wide web, the question whether GlobalSantaFe should be governed by the autonomous laws of the internet, by the rules agreed on by the Internet Corporation for Assigned Names and Numbers (ICANN) on assigning domain names, becomes central. According to these rules, the principle of priority applies unless the domain name has been registered in bad faith.[7] Or should the case alternatively be decided on the basis of a hybrid mixture of the participating national legal orders and the ICANN policies?

But what is the collision in the neem tree case? At first glance, the case only raises substantive law issues, namely the question whether the European patent no. 0436257 has been rightfully issued under the EPC, more precisely whether the invention registered by W.R. Grace & Co. passes the novelty test of article 54 of the EPC. However, is it not more adequate to describe the material problem of the neem tree case as a conflict between norms which govern the modern globalised world and habitual rules rooted in a local culture? The patent protection which was granted excludes indigenous groups from an important and, up to this point, free use of the

[5] Agreement on the Issue of European Patents of 5 October 1973, revised version of EPC art. 63 (17 December 1991) and the decisions of the European Patent Office's Administrative Council of 21 December 1978, 13 December 1994, 20 October 1995, 5 December 1996, 10 December 1998 and 27 October 2005, as well as the preliminary applicable clauses of the file of revisions of the EPC of 29 November 2000.

[6] EPO, *Rescission* (13 February 2001), bill no. 90250319.2–2117, patent no. 0436257; petition against this ruling was rejected by the EPO on 8 March 2005 (file no. T 0416/01–3.3.2).

[7] The 'bad faith' exception follows from ICANN, *Uniform Domain Name Dispute Resolution Policy* (26 August 1999), [4(a)], at www.icann.org/udrp/udrp-policy-24oct99.htm.

neem tree's healing medicinal powers. Hence, the question is whether the patent protection regime collides in a legally relevant sense with a right of indigenous groups to use their traditional knowledge freely.

In relation to the traditional understanding according to which only national legal orders can be in conflict with each other, the two cases clearly pose new problems for the law. So how can their characteristics be more precisely described? One aspect of GlobalSantaFe is the clash between rules claiming global reach with norms limited to a territory. At the same time it seems to be relevant that national legal rules, which emerge from political processes of legislation and are, therefore – at least idealistically – aimed at promoting the public interest, meet with rules which are exclusively oriented towards the particular interests of the internet. And the novelty of the collision in the neem tree case may lie just in the fact that intellectual property rights, which are essential for the functioning of modern societies' 'knowledge economies', clash with traditional rules for the protection of ancient medicinal cultures.

But do the two cases really represent a problem for the law of conflicts which exclusively deals with collisions of *legal* norms? Social norms, i.e. expectations of behaviour which emerge from processes of spontaneous interactions, are in principle not relevant for the law of conflicts. They only gain legal significance when legal norms, if only implicitly, incorporate them into the system of law, for example by making reference to them. ICANN policies and rules for the protection of indigenous cultures are, therefore, only relevant to the law of conflicts if they actually possess legal quality.

This short description of problems has already shown that the conflict rules of private and public international law are not suited to dealing with the new types of norm collisions. The policies enacted by the board of directors of the private law corporation ICANN – incorporated under the California Nonprofit Public Benefit Corporation Law – which, pursuant to section four of the *Registrar Accreditation Agreement*,[8] are to be observed by the domain name registrars – private law corporations responsible for the worldwide allocation of domain names – are not on their radar. And exploring rules of indigenous cultures has mostly been left to law anthropologists doing fieldwork in Western Sumatra and other places.

Five theses are to be developed:

(1) In their differences the two types of collisions at issue in GlobalSantaFe and the neem tree case reflect the *double fragmentation* of

[8] ICANN, *Registrar Accreditation Agreement* (29 May 2009), at www.icann.org/registrars/ra-agreement-17may01.htm.

world society and its law. The fragmentation is a double one because, firstly, the functional differentiation of modern society causes collisions between different social functional systems and the legal norms coupled to them. Secondly, differences between social organisational principles cause clashes between the formal law of modern society and the socially embedded legal systems of indigenous societies.[9]

(2) Both cases are about the conflict of *legal* norms – albeit of a very different kind. In GlobalSantaFe, national legal orders collide with the transnational regime law of the *lex digitalis*. In the neem tree case, international intellectual property law collides with legal norms of indigenous cultures.

(3) Until now, the rules on the conflict of laws of neither public nor private international law offer an adequate solution for these new types of collisions. They have been constructed for coping with collisions of national legal orders and not for solving conflicts between national laws and transnational law or the law of indigenous cultures, respectively.

(4) With regard to transnational regimes, collision rules have to be developed which take their character as 'self-contained regimes' into account. Here, the *substantive law approach* which has been developed in private international law seems to be most suitable.

(5) With regard to indigenous cultures, the collision rules to be developed must respect the social embeddedness of the legal norms. In this case, the *model of the institutionalised and proceduralised protection of basic rights* seems to be the most promising.

D. Collisions of transnational regimes: cybersquatting

1. Collisions of rationalities in the functionally differentiated global society

GlobalSantaFe is exemplary for a new type of conflict of legal norms – for the conflict between the law of transnational regimes and the law of nation states. The law of the private internet regulation authority ICANN collides with both US and Korean law, respectively. What is new about

[9] To avoid misunderstandings: the description of a social sector as 'indigenous' does not refer to a formation of society as penned by a nation state (in our example the state of India) but to segments of indigenous forms of society. These can be found almost everywhere in world society regardless of national borders.

this type of collision is that one of the colliding entities is not a national legal order, as the traditional doctrine would require, but instead a transnational regime law. This collision reflects the first fragmentation of global society: its fragmentation into autonomous global functional systems.

To gain a more precise understanding of this, one must proceed from the assumption that law, following the logic of functional differentiation, has established itself globally as a unitary social system beyond national laws. A unitary global law reproduces itself through legal acts which are guided by different programmes but are in the end oriented towards the binary code legal/illegal. The unity of global law is just not, as in the nation state, based on the consistency of legal norms structurally secured by the hierarchy of courts; rather, it is process-based, deriving simply from the modes of connection between legal operations, which transfer binding legality between even highly heterogeneous legal orders.[10] The operative unity of law is also achieved on the global level. This unity is not a normative unity of law but is characterised by a multitude of fundamental contradictions of legal norms. Legal unity within global law is redirected away from normative consistency towards operative 'interlegality'.[11] Interlegality does not only mean the existence of a static variety of normative systems which are strictly separated from each other, as described in the classic legal sociology of Eugen Ehrlich, Santi Romano, Maurice Hauriou, Georges Scelle and Georges Gurvitch,[12] but also of a dynamic

[10] For the system-theoretical concept of a world legal system see Niklas Luhmann, *Law as a Social System* (Oxford University Press, 2004); see also Gunther Teubner, 'Global Bukowina: Legal Pluralism in the World Society' in Gunther Teubner (ed.), *Global Law Without A State* (Dartmouth, 1997) 3; Andreas Fischer-Lescano, 'Die Emergenz der Globalverfassung' (2003) 63 *Zeitschrift für ausländisches öffentliches Recht und Völkerrecht* 717; Anthony D'Amato, 'International Law as an Autopoietic System' in Rüdiger Wolfrum and Volker Roeben (eds.), *Developments of International Law in Treaty Making* (Springer, 2005) 335; Klaus A. Ziegert, 'Globalisierung des Rechts aus der Sicht der Rechtssoziologie' in Rüdiger Voigt (ed.), *Globalisierung des Rechts* (Nomos, 2000) 69; Mathias Albert, *Zur Politik der Weltgesellschaft: Identität und Recht im Kontext internationaler Vergesellschaftung* (Velbrück, 2002) 203; Gralf-Peter Calliess, 'Reflexive Transnational Law: The Privatisation of Civil Law and the Civilisation of Private Law' (2002) 24 *Zeitschrift für Rechtssoziologie* 185.

[11] Boaventura de Sousa Santos, 'State Transformation, Legal Pluralism and Community Justice: An Introduction' (1992) 1 *Social and Legal Studies* 131; Marc Amstutz, 'Vertragskollisionen: Fragmente für eine Lehre von der Vertragsverbindung' in Marc Amstutz (ed.), *Festschrift für Heinz Rey* (Schulthess, 2003) 161.

[12] Eugen Ehrlich, *Grundlegung der Soziologie des Rechts* (Duncker & Humblot, 1913) 81; Santi Romano, *L'ordinamento giuridico* (Sansoni, 2nd edn, 1918) § 12; Maurice E. Hauriou, *Aux sources du droit: le pouvoir, l'ordre et la liberté* (Presses universitaires de Caen, 1933) 11; Georges Scelle, *Précis de droit des gens, Band 1: Principes et systématique*

variety of normative operations, in which 'parallel norm systems of different origin stimulate each other, interlock and permeate, without coalescing into united super-systems that absorb their parts, but permanently coexist as heterarchical formations'.[13]

In other words, what is characteristic for post-modern interlegality is not only the collision of grown local customary laws with legal acts of parliamentary provenance, but also a new confusedness in the legal in-between-worlds of global society that has to live with contradictory individual case decisions, with colliding settings of rules governing the same social field and with masses of laws that do not give rise to a single 'ultimate rule of recognition'.[14] Instead of a generalisation of expectations by means of an authoritative final decision, unity of legal texts and homogeneity of methods of cognition, the post-national constellation is characterised by the juxtaposition of a number of structurally closed legal systems, all of which principally claim to be applied pre-eminently within their respective realms. Neither a hierarchical construction of the law nor a *Grundnorm* nor a common point of final reference can hold these heterarchical systems together.

Here, a new kind of internal differentiation of law is noticeable. For centuries its internal differentiation had followed the political logic of nation states and was manifest in the multitude of national legal orders, each with their own territorial jurisdiction. Even public international law, which regarded itself as the contract law of the nation states, did not break with this form of internal differentiation of the law. The final break with such conceptions was only signalled in the last century with the rapidly accelerating expansion of international organisations and politically initiated regulatory regimes,[15] which, in sharp contrast to their genesis

(Recueil Sirey, 1932) 6; Georges Gurvitch, *The Sociology of Law* (K. Paul, Trench, Trubner & Co, 1947) 181.

[13] Marc Amstutz, 'Zwischenwelten: Zur Emergenz einer interlegalen Rechtsmethodik im europäischen Privatrecht' in Christian Joerges and Gunther Teubner (eds.), *Rechtsverfassungsrecht: Recht-Fertigung zwischen Privatrechtsdogmatik und Gesellschaftstheorie* (Nomos, 2003) 213.

[14] Andreas Fischer-Lescano and Ralph Christensen, 'Auctoritatis interpositio. Die Dekonstruktion des Dezisionismus durch die Systemtheorie' (2005) 44 *Der Staat* 213.

[15] For the concept 'regime' in public international law, see Nele Matz, *Wege zur Koordinierung völkerrechtlicher Verträge: Völkervertragsrechtliche und institutionelle Ansätze* (Springer, 2005) 358; Christian Walter, '(Inter)national Governance in verfasungsrechtlicher Perspektive: Überlegungen zu Möglichkeiten und Grenzen der Entwicklung eines "Internationalen Verfassungsrechts"' in Adrienne Héritier, Michael Stolleis and Fritz Scharpf (eds.), *European and International Regulation after the Nation*

within international treaties, established themselves as autonomous legal orders. The internal differentiation of law along national boundaries is now overlain by sectoral fragmentation.

In contrast to constantly reiterated claims, the appearance of global regimes does not entail the integration, harmonisation or, at the very least, the convergence of legal orders; rather, it transforms the internal differentiation of law thereby not producing unity but a new fragmentation of law. The fragmentation of society affects the law in such a way that success-oriented political regulation of differentiated societal spheres causes a parcelling of issue-specific policy arenas, which, for their part, juridify themselves. The traditional differentiation in line with the political principle of territoriality into relatively autonomous national legal orders is thus overlain by a sectoral differentiation principle: the differentiation of global law into transnational legal regimes, which define the external reach of their jurisdiction along issue-specific rather than territorial lines, and which claim a global validity for themselves.[16] It is important to emphasise that this does not mean that the old differentiation along national legal orders disappears. It is not argued that the nation state will be disposed of in the course of globalisation. One kind of internal differentiation is not replaced with the other, rather two different principles overlap: territorial-segmental and thematic-functional differentiation.[17] This overlap creates a new type of collision of norms which can be observed in GlobalSantaFe – the conflict between the national laws of Korea and the US on the one hand, and the rules of the internet governance ICANN on the other.

State: Different Scopes and Multiple Levels (Nomos, 2004) 31, 38; Christian Tietje, 'The Changing Legal Structure of International Treaties as an Aspect of an Emerging Global Governance Architecture' (1999) 42 *German Yearbook of International Law* 26.

[16] Martti Koskenniemi, *Global Legal Pluralism: Multiple Regimes and Multiple Modes of Thought* (5 March 2005), at www.helsinki.fi/eci/Publications/Koskenniemi/MKPluralism-Harvard-05d[1].pdf. Especially with regard to ICANN as 'Global Regulatory Regime' see Dirk Lehmkuhl, 'The Resolution of Domain Names vs. Trademark Conflicts: A Case Study on Regulation Beyond the Nation State, and Related Problems' (2002) 23 *Zeitschrift für Rechtssoziologie* 61, 71; Milton Mueller, *Ruling the Root: Internet Governance and the Taming of Cyberspace* (Massachusetts Institute of Technology, 2002) 211; Christian Walter, 'Constitutionalizing (Inter)national Governance: Possibilities for and Limits to the Development of an International Constitutional Law' (2001) 44 *German Yearbook of International Law* 170, 186f.

[17] See also Michael Stolleis, 'Was kommt nach dem souveränen Nationalstaat? Und was kann die Rechtsgeschichte dazu sagen?' in Adrienne Héritier, Michael Stolleis and Fritz Scharpf (eds.), *European and International Regulation after the Nation State: Different Scopes and Multiple Levels* (Nomos, 2004) 17.

However, GlobalSantaFe also illustrates that in order to understand the new types of norm collisions, it is not sufficient to consider only the global regulatory, i.e. politically initiated, regimes. Global regulatory regimes certainly give us a picture of the fundamental transformation of global law from territorial to a sectoral differentiation, but only to the degree that it is induced by those forms of legal regimes which derive from international agreements. No light whatsoever is shed upon the equally rapid growth in the numbers of non-statal 'private' legal regimes. It is these regimes that give birth to 'global law without the state',[18] which is primarily responsible for the multi-dimensionality of global legal pluralism.[19]

2. *Legal quality of ICANN policies*

How the law should deal with conflicts between national laws and legal pluralistic systems of norms, such as the transnational regimes, is a largely unanswered question.[20] Controversially discussed is specifically the problem whether norms of sectorial private regimes possess legal quality at all. In GlobalSantaFe it is hence questionable whether there really is a tripolar collision of *legal* norms, that is, whether not only the national legal orders of the US and Korea collide but whether the transnational regime law of the ICANN policies has any claim to be considered as the legal order on which the decision should be based. Are the ICANN policies part of a *lex digitalis*, understood as an autonomous legal order on one level with the *lex mercatoria*,[21] the *lex sportiva*[22] or the *lex constructionis*?[23]

[18] Gunther Teubner (ed.), *Global Law without a State* (Dartmouth, 1997).

[19] Topical discussion in Emmanuel Melissaris, 'The More the Merrier: A New Take on Legal Pluralism' (2004) 13 *Social & Legal Studies* 57; Paul Schiff Berman, 'The Globalization of Jurisdiction' (2002) 151 *University of Pennsylvania Law Review* 311, 325; Carol Weisbrod, *Emblems of Pluralism: Cultural Differences and the State* (Princeton University Press, 2002) 5, 68; Surya P. Sinha, 'Legal Polycentricity' in Hanne Petersen and Henrik Zahle (eds.), *Legal Polycentricity: Consequences of Pluralism in Law* (Dartmouth, 1995) 31.

[20] See the discussion in Ralf Michaels, 'The Re-State-ment of Non-State-Law: The State, Choice of Law, and the Challenge from Global Legal Pluralism' (2005) 51 *Wayne Law Review* 1209; Andreas Fischer-Lescano and Gunther Teubner, *Regime-Kollisionen: Zur Fragmentierung des globalen Rechts* (Suhrkamp Verlag, 2006); Paul Schiff Berman, 'Global Legal Pluralism' (2007) 80 *Southern California Law Review* 1155.

[21] Cf. only Alec Stone Sweet, 'The New Lex Mercatoria and Transnational Governance' (2006) 13 *Journal of European Public Policy* 627.

[22] Cf. for *lex sportiva* Florian Becker and Dirk Lehmkuhl, 'Multiple Strukturen der Regulierung: Ursachen, Konflikte und Lösungen am Fall des Leichtathleten Baumann' in Adrienne Héritier, Michael Stolleis and Fritz Scharpf (eds.), *European and International Regulation after the Nation State: Different Scopes and Multiple Levels* (Nomos, 2004) 225.

[23] See also generally Milos Vec, 'Das selbstgeschaffene Recht der Ingenieure: Internationalisierung und Dezentralisierung am Beginn der Industriegesellschaft' in

In opposition to contrary positions,[24] the way in which this question is answered is of great importance. The law is dependent upon criteria by which it can determine its own boundaries. Not all of the normative behavioural expectations produced within society – those of morals,[25] for instance – can be relevant as legal norms for the law, since the law's societal boundaries would otherwise be blurred. The law would lose its ability to fulfil its societal function of providing a way to decide conflicts by transforming them into an answerable *quaestio iuris*. If the ICANN policies were simply social norms, there would be no real conflict of laws necessitating the development of a new collision of rules whose starting point must be the assumption that all legal norms colliding are in principle equally valid.

If there is a 'collision' of legal norms with mere social norms, the legal norms have absolute priority. Social norms are only of relevance for the law when the law opens itself towards them, for example by making reference to societal conventions.[26] This is also true for the transnational arena, in which social norms are factored in by techniques of reference established in law. Ralf Michaels mentions in this context three methods of private international law: incorporation, deference and delegation.[27] In the absence of such referring rules, social norms become only subcutaneously relevant in the process of interpreting legal norms. This does not mean to deny the substantial influence which social norms exert on the law. However, if there is a true conflict between legal and social norms, the legal norms prevail.[28]

If, on the other hand, the ICANN policies possess legal quality, then their claim to be applied is of equal force to that of the US and Korean legal systems. In this case, a collision of legal norms exists and the rules on the conflict of laws have to be rethought from conflicts between national

Adrienne Héritier, Michael Stolleis and Fritz Scharpf (eds.), *European and International Regulation after the Nation State: Different Scopes and Multiple Levels* (Nomos, 2004) 93.

24 Cf. Berman, above n. 20, 1179.

25 For the relationship between law and morality, see Luhmann, above n. 10, 78f.

26 Cf. for many Jan Busche, '§ 157' in Franz Jürgen Säcker and Roland Rixecker (eds.), *Münchener Kommentar zum Bürgerlichen Gesetzbuch, Band 1: Allgemeiner Teil, 1. Halbband*: §§ 1–240, ProstG (C. H. Beck, 5th edn, 2006) § 157 Rn. 16.

27 Michaels, above n. 20.

28 For the priority of legal rules over social rules see BGHZ 10, 228 (232), to § 138 para. 1 BGB. See also Christian Armbrüster, '§ 138' in Franz Jürgen Säcker and Roland Rixecker (eds.), *Münchener Kommentar zum Bürgerlichen Gesetzbuch, Band 1: Allgemeiner Teil, 1. Halbband*: §§ 1–240, ProstG (C. H. Beck, 5th edn, 2006) § 138 Rn. 14.

legal orders to conflicts between transnational sectorial regimes themselves and – as in our case – with national legal orders. Such an adjustment from territoriality to 'affiliation to a functional regime' means that the legal parameters cannot simply be taken from the particular territorial legal system.[29] A decision cannot be reached by mechanically subsuming the rules of whichever forum state happens to be addressed, but is at the same time dependent on the particularities of the respective functional regime.

What is the criterion by which the law decides whether a norm possesses legal quality? This question, too, is highly controversial. It should be clear by now that the sought-after criterion cannot be found in whatever connection between a nation state and the norm. It is necessary to give up the popular assumption that global law exclusively derives its validity from processes of state law-making and from state sanctions, be these derived from state internal sources of law, or from officially sanctioned international sources of law.[30] The fragmentation of society requires us to extend the concept of law to encompass norms lying beyond the legal sources of nation state and international law. As Paul Schiff Berman's formulation indicates, one of the central and as yet unsolved future tasks of international law will be:

> recognizing and evaluating non-state jurisdictional assertions that bind sub-, supra-, or transnational communities. Such non-state jurisdictional assertions include a wide range of entities, from official transnational and international regulatory and adjudicative bodies, to non-governmental quasi-legal tribunals, to private standard-setting or regulatory organizations.[31]

'Transnational communities', or autonomous fragments of society, such as the globalised economy, science, technology, the mass media, medicine, education and transport, are developing an enormous demand for regulating norms, which cannot, however, be satisfied by national or

[29] Following this argument Graeme B. Dinwoodie, 'A New Copyright Order: Why National Courts Should Create Global Norms' (2000) 149 *University of Pennsylvania Law Review* 469; Berman, above n. 20.

[30] As still proposed by Dieter Reuter, 'Das selbstgeschaffene Recht des internationalen Sports im Konflikt mit dem Geltungsanspruch des nationalen Rechts' (1996) 6 *Deutsche Zeitschrift für Wirtschaftsrecht* 1, even though he asks for new solutions when it comes to international law.

[31] Berman, above n. 20, 325; See also T. Alexander Aleinikoff, 'Sovereignty Studies in Constitutional Law: A Comment' (2000) 17 *Constitutional Commentary* 197, 201f.

international institutions. Instead, such autonomous societal fragments satisfy their own demands through a direct recourse to law.

As extensively argued elsewhere, the norms enacted by these 'transnational communities' do not already possess legal quality simply because they adhere to the binary code of legal/illegal in judging behaviour.[32] Rather, what is decisive is the institutionalisation of processes of secondary rule-making. Autonomous law (with or without a state) only exists when institutions have been established which systematically assess all first order observations that use the code legal/illegal by means of second order observations on the basis of the code of law. Transnational law detached from state law should, accordingly, be defined as follows:

> *Transnational law* identifies a third category of autonomous legal orders beyond the traditional categories of national and international law. Transnational law is created and developed by the law creating powers of global civil society, it is based on general principles of law and their concretisation in social practice, its application, interpretation and development are – at least primarily – the responsibility of private dispute resolution providers, and it is codified – if at all – in general catalogues of principles and rules, standardised contract forms or codes of conducts which are set up by private rule-making bodies.[33]

Judged against the criterion of the establishment of processes of secondary rule-making, the *lex digitalis* and with it the ICANN policies are genuine legal norms.[34] Their sources are the secondary rules governing the private autonomous acts of internet users, the Rules for Uniform Domain Name Dispute Resolution Policy (UDRP),[35] the respective supplemental rules of

[32] Teubner, 'Global Bukowina', above n. 10; Andreas Fischer-Lescano, *Globalverfassung: Die Geltungsbegründung der Menschenrechte* (Velbrück, 2005) 129.

[33] Gralf-Peter Calliess, 'Transnationales Verbrauchervertragsrecht' (2004) 68 *Rabels Zeitschrift für ausländisches und internationales Privatrecht* 244, 254f.

[34] Cf. for *lex digitalis* Henry H. Perritt, 'Dispute Resolution in Cyberspace: Demand for New Forms of ADR' (2000) 15 *Ohio State Journal on Dispute Resolution* 675, 691f. Explicitly stating the legal substance: Gralf-Peter Calliess, 'Globale Kommunikation – staatenloses Recht: Zur (Selbst-)Regulierung des Internet durch prozedurales Recht' in Michael Anderheiden, Stefan Huster and Stephan Kirste (eds.), *Globalisierung als Problem von Gerechtigkeit und Steuerungsfähigkeit des Rechts* (Franz Steiner Verlag, 2001) 61; Vagios Karavas and Gunther Teubner, 'www.CompanyNameSucks.com: The Horizontal Effect of Fundamental Rights on "Private Parties" within Autonomous Internet Law' (2005) 12 *Constellations* 262; Karl-Heinz Ladeur and Lars Viellechner, 'Die transnationale Expansion staatlicher Grundrechte: Zur Konstitutionalisierung globales Privatrechtsregimes' (2008) 46 *Archiv des Völkerrechts* 42, 64.

[35] See especially Section 4 lit a. UDRP.

the dispute resolution providers accredited by ICANN[36] and, finally, the rulings of the provider panels.

Consequently, there is a tripolar collision of laws in GlobalSantaFe. There are no rules as yet for deciding conflicts of legal orders involving transnational laws. Such rules need to be created.

3. *New collision rules*

On what principles are the new collision rules to be based?

The principle of territoriality which was regarded as decisive by the US court in GlobalSantaFe and pursuant to which the decision to apply US law was made on the ground that the domain name registry VeriSign was located in the US is not satisfactory. Its application is not convincing on a theoretical level because of the genuine aterritorial character of the internet and its rules. And on a practical level it is not convincing to regard the principle of territoriality as decisive because its application not only leads to a fragmentation of the law of the internet but may also cause conflicting rulings should other courts – as in our case the Korean court – find that the territorial basis of the case lies in their jurisdiction.

A better solution would be achieved if the development of the collision rules was oriented on the rules of referral established in private international law. Then, the question would not be to which national territory the case has its closest link but in which of the competing national and functional legal orders the 'location of the legal relationship' – aterritorially understood – lies. The primary question for collision law would be on which regime of law (local, national or transnational) the legal relationship is mainly based. It would have to be answered by making use of the criterion of 'primary coverage', which Trachtman has developed from the perspective of the economics of institutions in order to solve the problem of overlapping jurisdictions.[37] The determination of the applicable national or transnational legal order would depend on the answer to the question in which social sector the legal relationship is located, and the case would have to be decided pursuant to the substantive rules of the legal order which has the strongest structural

[36] A list of accredited Dispute Resolution Providers as well as their supplement rules are accessible at ICANN, *List of Approved Dispute Resolution Service Providers* (13 August 2010), at www.icann.org/en/dndr/udrp/approved-providers.htm.

[37] Joel P. Trachtman, 'Institutional Linkage: Transcending "Trade and …"' (2002) 96 *American Journal of International Law* 77, 90f.

connection to that social sector and which, therefore, can claim to have the strongest 'interests' in being applied.[38]

If the 'primary coverage' lay in the transnational regime even the national courts would have to apply the legal norms of that transnational regime. If, on the other hand, it lay in the national legal order, even the transnational regime's panels would have to apply the respective national law. This clear-cut solution reached by making use of rules of referral would offer two advantages: it would reduce the danger of conflicting court rulings in one and the same case; and it would, by using the criterion of 'primary coverage', consider material, i.e. case-adequate, aspects instead of basing the decision on the existence or non-existence of an arbitrary link between the legal relationship and a specific territory.

If this collision rule was used in GlobalSantaFe it would, due to the inescapable transnationality of the world wide web, be most plausible to regard its 'primary coverage' as resting with ICANN's policies for the assignment of domain names. The collision rule would point to the global *lex digitalis*, the rules of which would have to be applied by the national courts. Pursuant to the ICANN policies, in a first step, the principle of priority would be applied – hence Korean citizen Park would prevail. However, in a second step, GlobalSantaFe Corp. would, according to § 4 lit. a UDRP, be granted the opportunity to establish that:

(1) the domain name Park registered was identical or confusingly similar to its company trademark;
(2) Park did not have a right or legitimate interest in respect of the domain name 'globalsantafe.com'; and
(3) Park had registered and used the domain name in bad faith.

However, the question is whether a simple analogy to the rules of referral of private international law adequately grasps the particularities of a collision between national law and transnational regime law. Is there not a major difference between national legal orders, with which private international law has traditionally dealt, and transnational regimes that demand a more complex solution?

The main difference is probably that national legal orders are comprehensive legal systems in the sense that even highly specialised regulations are embedded in a tight web of legal norms. Consequently, in national

[38] Similar thoughts can be found in the 'governmental interest approach', developed by Brainerd Currie, which formulates rules for the solution of interlocal collisions in US law: Brainerd Currie, *Selected Essays on the Conflict of Laws* (Duke University Press, 1963) 183 f; Brainerd Currie, 'Comment on *Babcock v. Jackson*' (1963) 63 *Columbia Law Review* 1233, 1242f.

law, an 'inner balance' is achieved between the various legal norms, principles and policies applicable in the respective nation state. In contrast, transnational legal orders, as specialised 'self-contained regimes',[39] only set rules for those functional sectors of society to which they are structurally coupled. Their legal norms reflect exclusively the rationality criterion of a particular social sector. They are not oriented towards achieving the 'public welfare' of a comprehensive polity as are the contextualised norms of a nation state's legal order.

This difference needs to be taken account of when developing a new collision law. If the 'primary coverage' of the case at hand is found to lie with an issue-specific transnational regime, collision law must compensate the regime's 'tunnel vision' by incorporating contextualising elements which allow for the consideration of competing or opposing principles. In particular, the following come to mind:

- Adherence to the '*ordre public transnational*': as in private international law, a referral to the respective legal order to be applied is not unconditional. Any result which would be obtained by exclusively applying the law of the regime would have to be measured against an 'ordre public transnational' as to its acceptability. It is important to notice that the 'ordre public transnational' would not be a uniform and globally valid *ius non dispositivum*. Instead, different regimes have different concepts of what constitutes the indispensable fundament of a normative order. Consequently, a regime specific 'ordre public transnational' would have to be considered.
- *Comitas* towards other global regimes and their eigen-rationality: as a second contextualising mechanism one would have to demand that when producing their legal norms the transnational regimes must consider the eigen-rationalities of other regimes and their legal orders.

But even if mechanisms which compensate for the one-sidedness of 'self-contained regimes' were successfully incorporated into collision law, the question remains whether an analogy to techniques of referral established in private international law takes sufficient account of the particularities

[39] For the concept of 'self contained regimes', see Martti Koskenniemi, *Outline of the Chairman of the ILC Study Group on Fragmentation of International Law: The Function and Scope of the Lex Specialis Rule and the Question of 'Self-Contained Regimes'* (2003) 9, at http://untreaty.un.org/ilc/sessions/55/fragmentation_outline.pdf: 'A regime is a union of rules laying down particular rights, duties and powers and rules having to do with the administration of such rules, including in particular rules for reacting to breaches. When such a regime seeks precedence in regard to the general law, we have a "self-contained regime", a special case of lex specialis.'

of the new collision types. The challenge of these does not only lie in the fact that they are 'trans-national' but also that they are 'trans-institutional' in character. This means that both national legal orders and transnational legal regimes can claim with equal force that their respective laws be applied. Faced with the double challenge of a simultaneous and equally valid claim for application, private international law seems to fail because it only refers to one of the participating legal orders.

In modern society, many parts of social life are indeed already subject to multiple and partly inconsistent rules of behaviour, simultaneously dictated by numerous different legal orders. It does not seem very adequate, then, to address this situation by simply favouring one legal order over the others. Instead of artificially separating the colliding legal orders, a solution which aims to achieve a balance, a compromise, a synthesis between the competing regimes should be found.

For this, it seems plausible to make use of the *substantive law approach*, which has mainly been developed by Arthur Taylor von Mehren and which has been influential in US private international and inter-local collision law.[40] In order to decide a case characterised by the new types of collision of laws it would, accordingly, be necessary to create a new rule of substantive law which integrates elements of all competing legal orders.[41] Considering the 'material law solution' of the 'adjustment' or 'adaptation problem',[42] German private international law is – despite the differences to the proposed *substantive law approach*[43] – no stranger to the development of special and independent substantive law rules.

[40] See Arthur Taylor von Mehren, 'Special Substantive Rules for Multistate Problems: Their Role and Significance in Contemporary Choice of Law Methodology' (1974) 88 *Harvard Law Review* 347, 356 f; Arthur Taylor von Mehren, 'Choice of Law and the Problem of Justice' (1977) 41 *Law and Contemporary Problems* 27, 38f. For a more recent use of the substantive law approach, see Luther L. McDougal III, '"Private" International Law: Ius Gentium Versus Choice of Law Rules or Approaches' (1990) 38 *American Journal of Comparative Law* 521, 536f. See also Friedrich K. Juenger, *Choice of Law and Multistate Justice* (M. Nijhoff, 1993) 236f.

[41] Dinwoodie, above n. 29, 543f., also argues for a substantive law approach regarding problems of international intellectual property law. For a substantive law approach as a method of dealing with collisions of legal norms, see also Berman, 'Global Legal Pluralism', above n. 20, 1218.

[42] For 'adjustment' or 'adaptation', see Gerhard Kegel and Klaus Schurig, *Internationales Privatrecht* (C. H. Beck, 9th edn, 2004) 357; Jan Kropholler, *Internationales Privatrecht* (Mohr Siebeck, 6th edn, 2006) 234. See also Ernst Steindorff, *Sachnormen im internationalen Privatrecht* (Klostermann, 1958) 17f., 26.

[43] Differences are, firstly, that the 'adjustment' or 'adaptation problem' only arises in the case of a 'contradiction of norms' (accumulation of norms or lack of norms) and, secondly, that the substantive law rule to be created pursuant to its 'material law solution' is

The main advantage of this approach as opposed to the referral technique of classic private international law is that it compensates for the 'tunnel vision' of 'self-contained regimes' whilst at the same time recognising the inevitable trans-institutionality of the new collisions.[44]

Thus, GlobalSantaFe would require the creation and application of a legal norm which combines elements of US law, Korean law and ICANN policies. This rule would be identical to the above-mentioned rule of the *lex digitalis*. The decision would not be in favour of the cybersquatter.

E. Collisions of organisational principles of society: biopiracy

1. *Functional differentiation v. segmental/stratificatory differentiation*

In the neem tree case the collision problem presents itself differently.[45] It is true that, here, as in GlobalSantaFe, regime collisions representing conflicts between social systems are at work.[46] They express themselves in the numerous attempts to address the problem of the granting of exclusive rights to use traditional knowledge on the global level.[47] Partial

primarily based on the legal order referred to, thus does not represent a true synthesis of the rules of the colliding legal systems.

[44] For a similar approach for collision of rules in a European multi-layer context, see Amstutz, above n. 13, 216f.; Christian Joerges, 'The Impact of European Integration on Private Law: Reductionist Perceptions, True Conflicts and a New Constitutional Perspective' (1997) 3 *European Law Journal* 378; Christian Joerges and Christine Godt, 'Free Trade: The Erosion of National, and the Birth of Transnational Governance' (2005) 13 *European Review* 93.

[45] Detailed elaboration of the collision problems and their possible solutions is given in Andreas Fischer-Lescano and Gunther Teubner, 'Cannibalizing Epistemes: Will Modern Law Protect Traditional Cultural Expressions?' in Christoph Beat Graber and Mira Burri-Nenova (eds.), *Intellectual Property and Traditional Cultural Expressions in a Digital Environment* (Edward Elgar, 2008) 17.

[46] Cf. Saskia Sassen, *Territory, Authority, Rights: From Medieval to Global Assemblages* (Princeton University Press, 2006).

[47] See Convention on Biological Diversity, opened for signature 5 June 1992, 1760 UNTS 79 (entered into force 29 December 1993) arts 8(j), 10(c). See also *Ministerial Declaration*, WT/MIN(01)/DEC/1 (20 November 2001, adopted 14 November 2001) para. 19. See further the drafts compiled and discussed by the the World Intellectual Property Organization (WIPO) Intergovernmental Committee for the Protection of Traditional Knowledge, *Intellectual Property and Genetic Resources, Traditional Knowledge and Traditional Cultural Expressions/Folklore*, WIPO/GRTKF/INF/1 (2006) www.wipo.int/

rationalities of global society collide with each other: economic, scientific, medical, cultural and religious principles are in conflict regarding access to traditional knowledge and its restriction. Greatly simplified, this means when using traditional knowledge, economic, scientific and medical utilisation interests collide with claims of integrity and diversity of cultures, religions and ways of life. As a consequence, related regulatory projects react to these conflicts in very different ways.

Seen from this perspective, traditional knowledge rightly qualifies as a problem of colliding rationalities in modern society. However, it is necessary to go a considerable step further, beyond the current discussions on legal fragmentation. Colliding rationalities do not adequately describe the problem of traditional knowledge, as it only does justice to the simple rather than to the *double fragmentation* of global society. Although it makes clear how stocks of traditional knowledge are subjected to diverging demands from functional regimes worldwide, it does not take into account the second level of fragmentation – the cultural polycentrism, the conflict between various world cultures.[48] However, the traditional knowledge conflict arose precisely from this double fragmentation of functional global systems on the one side and regional cultures in global society on the other.[49] By re-rooting the conflicts alone, it becomes possible to give the search for legal norms sociological directions that deal with the conflict more adequately.

The decisive factor is the distinction between global and regional cultural principles of society: functional differentiation of 'modern' knowledge stocks versus the social embedding of traditional knowledge. This distinction gives the conflicts of traditional knowledge their idiosyncratic colouring. It is not modern society as such, as a capitalist society, as an organisational society or as a knowledge society that is involved, but individual, highly specialised action centres, emerged from internal differentiation – functional systems, formal organisations, networks, epistemic communities – each of which is participating in the disintegration of knowledge production in regional cultures in their own special

export/sites/www/tk/en/consultations/draft_provisions/pdf/draft-provisions-booklet.pdf.

48 See Sinha, above n. 19.

49 Cf. Rudolf Stichweh, 'Strukturbildung in der Weltgesellschaft – Die Eigenstrukturen der Weltgesellschaft und die Regionalkulturen der Welt' in Thomas Schwinn (ed.), *Die Vielfalt und Einheit der Moderne: Kultur- und strukturvergleichende Analysen* (VS Verlag für Sozialwissenschaften, 2006) 239.

way. If these modern institutions, that are specialised in one function each, meet with diffuse structures in segmented or stratified societies, they have no choice but to tear traditional knowledge generation out of its context in which it has been embedded and transform it into their own metabolisms.

> To divorce 'science' from 'religion' and to tear away the 'cosmological' or spiritual gloss from an allegedly 'practical' core will undermine many forms of traditional knowledge.[50]

Monocontextural 'self-contained' regimes utilise 'integrated' traditional cultural connections for their specialised goals by detaching them from the reproductional connection on which traditional knowledge relies for its further development. In short: the multi-directional traditional institutions are undermined by the uni-directionality of modern hyperstructures.

It is about the maximisation of the inherent rationality of hyperstructures inside global society in its enhanced need for information – of functional systems, formal organisations, of networks and epistemic communities – tearing stocks of knowledge of regional cultures out of their vital context and inexorably drawing them into their wake. This becomes particularly evident by the way in which globalised science treats traditional knowledge.[51] The scientifically legitimate claim that knowledge belongs in the public domain necessarily destroys structures of communal ownership of knowledge in regional cultures. The principle of general access to knowledge violates spheres of confidentiality motivated by religion. Scientifically specialised methods of controlled verifiability necessitate the deletion of dependence on religion, culture and habitat, which, however, are necessary for traditional knowledge to survive in the first place.

[50] Rosemary J. Coombe, 'Protecting Cultural Industries to Promote Cultural Diversity: Dilemmas for International Policy-Making Posed by the Recognition of Traditional Knowledge' in Keith E. Maskus and Jerome H. Reichman (eds.), *International Public Goods and Transfer of Technology Under a Globalized Intellectual Property Regime* (Cambridge University Press, 2005) 559, 606.

[51] See, e.g. International Treaty on Plant Genetic Resources for Food and Agriculture, opened for signature 3 November 2001 (entered into force 29 June 2004) arts 1.1, 12.3. For Daes' criticism of well-meaning projects protecting traditional knowledge by a global database and thus subdue it to the principles of modern sciences, see Erica-Irene Daes, 'Intellectual Property and Indigenous Peoples' (2001) 95 *American Society of International Law Proceedings* 143, 144.

2. *Basic rights as models for rules on the collision of laws*

These particular conflicts cannot adequately be met by conventional rules on the collision of laws, as they were developed for conflicts between 'Western and Non-Western Law'.[52] Rules of collision which are suitable for the clash of constitutive principles of society have to be designed to restrict the expansion of global society's hyperstructures into regional cultures, to ensure the best possible compatibility with the integrity of traditional knowledge. It is necessary to start with the individual expansive institutions of modernity and demand that they regulate themselves by exerting pressure on them from the outside. The formula is: externally enforced self-restriction of the destructive expansion into socially embedded stocks of knowledge. The hyperstructures of globalised, modern society need to be coerced into respecting the indisposability of regional cultures.[53]

The sociological theory of basic rights developed by Niklas Luhmann will be categorically useful in regard to issue framing. It has shown that destructive aspects of functional differentiation have been successfully counteracted by social countermovements in other contexts, in which those countermovements coerced expansive social systems to self-restriction. Additionally, however, the theory needs to be adjusted to apply to different types of conflict between functionally differentiated 'globalness' and knowledge embedded in regional cultures.

Seen from a sociological perspective, basic rights are not just the judicially protected rights of individuals against state power that lawyers usually see. They are the social counter-institutions that exist inside individual subsystems and restrict their expansion from within. From the point of view of systems theory, the historic role of basic rights is not exhausted by protecting individual legal positions, but primarily consists in securing the autonomy of social spheres against tendencies to usurp them.[54]

[52] Roeland Duco Kollewijn, 'Conflicts of Western and Non-Western Law' (1951) 4 *International Law Quarterly* 307.

[53] With regard to the difficulties, subsuming traditional self-conceptions in modern categories, especially in judicial categories, see Coombe, above n. 50, 611.

[54] Regarding the system theoretical approach to basic rights as institution, see Niklas Luhmann, *Grundrechte als Institution: Ein Beitrag zur politischen Soziologie* (Duncker & Humblot, 1965). See also Gert Verschraegen, 'Human Rights and Modern Society: A Sociological Analysis from the Perspective of Systems Theory' (2002) 29 *Journal of Law and Society* 258. Regarding its elaborations in various societal contexts, see Gunther Teubner, 'The Anonymous Matrix: Human Rights Violations by "Private" Transnational

In reaction to the emergence of autonomous spheres of action in modern society, basic rights have historically emerged, especially in response to the matrix of autonomised politics. As soon as expansionist tendencies became evident in the political system that threatened the integrity of other autonomous areas of society, turbulent social conflict ensued. The positions attained in the course of these conflicts have been formulated as basic rights and institutionalised in politics as counter-institutions. Such expansionist tendencies have manifested themselves historically in very different constellations: in the past, mainly in politics; today, mainly in economics, science, technology and other sectors of society.

Such collision rules which are created by using the model of institutional basic rights protection are structurally different from the collision rules of private and public international law in that they do not regulate the collision of national legal orders but collisions of social spheres. Initially it was about the collision of politics with autonomous social spheres, later about the collision among autonomous social spheres themselves, and finally, as in our context, about the collision of constitutive principles of society. Strengthening the autonomy of spheres of action as a countermovement against usurping tendencies constitutes the general, reactive mechanism that works in the conventional, vertical dimension of political basic rights as well as in the contemporary horizontal dimension in which basic rights are deemed to have a 'third-party effect' on other expansive subsystems. If the core task of political basic rights was to protect the autonomy of spheres of action from political instrumentalisation, then securing the chance for the so-called non-rational action logic to articulate against the matrix of the dominant social trends towards rationalisation has become the central task of 'social basic rights'.[55]

Biopiracy is a good example of today's expansionist tendencies in diverse subsystems elsewhere, namely on the problematic border between globalised modern-day society and traditional regional culture. The primary issue is actually a problem of the horizontal effect of basic rights:

Actors' (2006) 69 *Modern Law Review* 327; Karl-Heinz Ladeur, 'Helmut Ridders Konzeption der Meinungs- und Pressefreiheit in der Demokratie' (1999) 32 *Kritische Justiz* 281; Christoph Graber and Gunther Teubner, 'Art and Money: Constitutional Rights in the Private Sphere' (1998) 18 *Oxford Journal of Legal Studies* 61.

[55] For continuative analyses, see Calliess, above n. 10; Ralph Christensen and Andreas Fischer-Lescano, *Das Ganze des Rechts: Vom hierarchischen zum reflexiven Verständnis deutscher und europäischer Grundrechte* (Duncker & Humblot, 2007); Ladeur and Viellechner, above n. 34.

> In the fields of cultural protection and biopiracy, however, the key actors are not states but private entities, such as universities, museums, and business corporations.[56]

Thus, a further generalisation with regard to the basic rights theory becomes necessary; this time in the other direction. If the matrix of functional differentiation not only threatens the integrity of areas of autonomy within modern society, but also the integrity of traditional knowledge in regional cultures, then it would correlate with the institutionalised logic explained here to expect that external conflicts, protests, organised resistance and social movements of modern-day hyperstructures all coerce the institutionalisation of basic rights so as to internally restrict their inherent urge to expand. And institutional imagination is required to realise the coerced self-restriction of functional systems, organisations, networks and epistemic communities in effective policies and legal norms.

Consequently, rules on the collision of laws that are to be unfolded in the context of a modified theory of basic rights need to aim at the development of hybrid legal forms within modern law that represent a peculiar compromise between regional cultural identities and modern-day legal mechanisms of protection. The compromise has to find a way past modern institutions' sensitivity to regional-cultural specialities on the one side and the operability of modern law on the other since only by using the language of modern law is it possible to effectively protect the particularities of regional cultures.

3. *Re-entry of the 'extrinsic' into the 'intrinsic'*

This would imply that institutions of the modern age ought to be encouraged with the help of collision rules to reconstruct the interests of indigenous cultures within modern law. Does this then mean that protecting traditional knowledge has to be facilitated using modern law that refers to 'customary law'? In the past, policy-makers influenced by anthropology have actually supported this option.[57] But that confronts the attempt to express the relation between global modernity and regional cultures as

[56] Daes, above n. 51, 148.

[57] Ibid.; Anthony Taubman, 'Saving the Village: Conserving Jurisprudential Diversity in the International Protection of Traditional Knowledge' in Keith E. Maskus and Jerome H. Reichman (eds.), *International Public Goods and Transfer of Technology Under a Globalized Intellectual Property Regime* (Cambridge University Press, 2005) 521; Coombe, above n. 50.

a question of basic rights with the fundamental problem of whether the extrinsic can authentically be reconstructed to be intrinsic.

If the goal is to limit the expansion of modern-day institutions, there is no way around reconstructing extrinsic factors using intrinsic concepts in order to erect internal barriers in the appropriate positions. Otherwise, external protest and resistance in the name of regional cultures will rebound off them without any effect at all. But there are more and less responsive, more and less environmentally sensitive types of reconstructions, which is all that counts. These are always 'reconstructions', since 'indigenous law' does not 'actually' exist as formal law in the way in which it would have to be constructed in the modern age. It is a sheer construct of its modern inventors. Modern law picks out the elements of factual usages and customs of the regional cultures that it needs, drawing them together into a collage that it presents as 'customary law', that is, as normative ownership positions and obligations to act, that are supposed to be created by the regional culture. Modern law's reading of regional cultures is thus based on a single huge misunderstanding – possibly a creative misunderstanding. It is only creative, however, where it does not project new discoveries out of the blue and where it succeeds in tracing and transforming actually existing foreign cultural material into modern law. As the Portuguese legal sociologist Boaventura de Sousa Santos, who is staging a post-modern theory of legal pluralism, says: 'Law. A Map of Misreading'.[58]

When the collision law of global modernity refers to the 'customary law' of indigenous cultures, it systematically misunderstands certain communications within regional cultures as legal acts, capable of creating legal norms, and indeed has to misunderstand them if they are to become effective barriers to the expansion of modernity, notably not only as legal acts through which law judges with the help of norms produced elsewhere, but as legal acts that produce norms themselves. Using this real fiction, law creates a new legal production mechanism in the institution of 'indigenous law' that is capable of counteracting modern expansionist tendencies by implementing prohibitions and other legal sanctions. This is where the opportunities lie for a global system to protect basic rights for indigenous peoples to develop responsiveness. The attempt at understanding how these cultures see themselves appears promising, in order to reconstruct this understanding as restrictions in the respective

[58] Boaventura de Sousa Santos, *Toward a New Legal Common Sense: Law, Globalization and Emancipation* (Butterworths LexisNexis, 2003) 417.

language of the fragmented systems of the modern age. The way in which the bearers of traditional knowledge perceive themselves – 'the principle of indigenous self-determination' – should be the normative centre of gravitation.[59] It is therefore not about an abstract protection of traditional knowledge as such, but about protecting the cultural conditions in which traditional knowledge is produced.

4. Recourse to 'customary law'

Instead of a substantive global approach, it appears to be more appropriate to link up with and recognise existing cultural practices, and acknowledge in the context of a conflict-of-law approach 'that traditional knowledge must be acquired and used in conformity with the customary laws of the peoples concerned'.[60]

As part of the United Nations Human Rights Framework, articles 19 and 27 of the International Covenant on Civil and Political Rights (ICCPR) apply. Furthermore, General Comment no. 17 of the Committee on Economic, Social and Cultural Rights notes for article 15(1)(c) of the International Covenant on Economic, Social and Cultural Rights (ICESCR):

> With regard to the right to benefit from the protection of the moral and material interests resulting from any scientific, literary or artistic production of indigenous peoples, States parties should adopt measures to ensure the effective protection of the interests of indigenous peoples relating to their productions, which are often expressions of their cultural heritage and traditional knowledge. In adopting measures to protect scientific, literary and artistic productions of indigenous peoples, States parties should take into account their preferences. Such protection might include the adoption of measures to recognize, register and protect the individual or collective authorship of indigenous peoples under national intellectual property rights regimes and should prevent the unauthorized use of scientific, literary and artistic productions of indigenous peoples by third parties. In implementing these protection measures, States parties should respect the principle of free, prior and informed consent of the indigenous authors concerned and the oral or other customary forms of transmission of scientific, literary or artistic production; where appropriate, they

[59] Coombe, above n. 50; Taubmann, above n. 57, 46; Daes, above n. 51, 146.

[60] Four Directions Council, *Forests, Indigenous Peoples and Biodiversity: Contribution of the Four Directions Council* – Submission to the Secretariat for the Convention on Biological Diversity (1996).

> should provide for the collective administration by indigenous peoples of the benefits derived from their productions.[61]

These considerations suggest the development of rules on conflict of laws between specialised modern law and holistic institutions in traditional society. At this point, the usual suggestions for a law of collision demand recourse to 'the acquisitions and use of indigenous people's heritage according to the customary laws of the indigenous people concerned'.[62] As mentioned above, direct recourse to customary law is, however, impossible, because making reference to local customary law already means looking at holistically organised forms of society through the lens of functional differentiation and functional coding. The law of collision in this sense presupposes a modern counterpart for autonomous law. As this does not exist here, it is necessary to follow the approach described above as 'productive misunderstanding': the modern, transnational institutions will each have to develop their own norms of referral and simultaneously create substantive law rules of self-restraint. This duplication – recourse to the extrinsic and restriction of the intrinsic – forms the main difference in comparison to the referral technique of private international law.

If we follow this institutionalist point of view, it becomes apparent that it is not enough, as the referral technique of private international law would suggest, to make reference to 'indigenous law' and to protect traditional knowledge as a mere store of knowledge, such as some authors suggest for digital evaluation, documentation and securing of traditional knowledge.[63] Of course, this may serve better its use by modern economy and science. It may also help to prevent illegitimate patenting practices, as the qualification of a discovery as being a novelty becomes impossible due to its prior digitalisation. However, it fails to protect and to facilitate the necessary conditions for traditional knowledge production, because the development of such knowledge depends mainly on the context in which it is produced, i.e. the preservation of the regional cultures' general conditions. At this point, the conflict between the highly specialised

[61] Committee on Economic, Social and Cultural Rights, *General Comment No. 17: The Right of Everyone To Benefit from the Protection of the Moral and Material Interests Resulting from Any Scientific, Literary or Artistic Production of which He or She is the Author*, 35th sess., UN Doc E/C.12/GC/17 (12 January 2006) paras 15(1)(c), 32.

[62] WIPO Intergovernmental Committee on Intellectual Property and Genetic Resources, Traditional Knowledge and Folklore, *Composite Study on the Protection of Traditional Knowledge*, 5th sess., WIPO/GRTKF/IC/5/8 (28 April 2003) para. 105, at www.wipo.int/edocs/mdocs/tk/en/wipo_grtkf_ic_5/wipo_grtkf_ic_5_8.pdf.

[63] Justified criticism in Daes, above n. 51.

modern-day concept of knowledge and holistic traditional knowledge becomes apparent again, as does the conflict between the specialised law of the modern age and the socially embedded law of regional cultures. Can modern law do justice to this conflict? 'Globalize diversity holistically' – this is one suggested paradoxical response.[64] It is not only the result, but the entire process of knowledge production, which has to be included in the basic rights' protection. Basic rights' protection must include both the knowledge as such and its social embedding.[65]

5. *Proceduralised rules of collision*

It becomes apparent that such a concept of autonomy should not merely aim at preserving culture reservations in their existing form. Solely introducing a species' protection policy is insufficient, as it targets structural rather than procedural autonomy. The protection of basic rights needs to create a framework in which indigenous cultures can develop independently and in conflict with modernity, either by restricting specific invasions through modernity or, in compensation, stipulating a resource transfer to indigenous segments of society. There are a number of useful approaches with regard to the realisation of this aim, to which the law of collision protecting traditional knowledge can connect and which provide first indications for further advancement of global basic law protection.

This applies for the attribution of communal-collective rights. Who is the beneficiary of such procedural rights? As discourse rights, these rights serve trans-subjective goals. Identifying the range of beneficiaries is not an ontological problem. Rather, it is about the question: who is to be entrusted with the legal enforcement of discourse rights? This does not necessarily have to be a personified collective. Instead, a whole series of techniques can be used to attribute rights to an entity that can help to implement these rights. This is important not only for the rights themselves, but also for the procedural standing. For instance, the Australian Court stated in *Onus* v. *Alcoa of Australia Ltd.* that:

> the members of the [Gournditichjmara] community are the guardians of the relics according to their laws and customs and they use the relics. I agree ... that in these circumstances the applicants have a special interest in the preservation of these relics, sufficient to support locus standi.[66]

[64] Taubman, above n. 57, 525. [65] Ibid., 540.

[66] *Onus* v. *Alcoa of Australia Ltd* (1981) 149 CLR 27, 43 (Mason J).

A broad definition of the term 'community' that reflects the contingencies in the formation of epistemic groups is required,[67] but simultaneously enables the protection of the discourse rights and the effective determination of the circle of addressees. As an example, a Brazilian law which has been enacted to implement the Convention on Biological Diversity (CBD) describes a local community in article 7(3) as being a

> human group, including descendants of Quilombo communities, differentiated by its cultural conditions, which is, traditionally, organized along successive generations and with its own customs, and preserves its social and economic institutions.[68]

Enabling these groups to participate in the decision to access traditional knowledge is the central challenge of the process of making the legal norms compatible. To the extent that authors criticise this challenge as a desideratum of the bureaucratisation of traditional knowledge,[69] they tend to ignore that the logic of *altera pars* requires reciprocity. Doing without it ultimately means accepting fatalistically the mono-directional usurpation of global society, and to give in to global deregulation instead of striving for constitutionalisation. It also means misjudging the various legal obligations, which particularly urge parties to observe the concept of 'prior informed consent' (PIC) and 'benefit sharing'.[70] Developing both mechanisms further is the condition of the possibility to effectively protect traditional knowledge.

[67] Benedict Anderson, *Imagined Communities: Reflections on the Origin and Spread of Nationalism* (Verso, 1991).

[68] Provisional Act No. 2, 186–16, 23 August 2001 (English translation at www.biodiv.org/doc/measures/abs/msr-abs-br-en.pdf).

[69] Hanns Ullrich, 'Traditional Knowledge, Biodiversity, Benefit-Sharing and the Patent System: Romantics v. Economics?' (Working Paper No 2005/07, European University Institute – Department of Law, May 2005) http://ssrn.com/paper=838107.

[70] See also Commission on Human Rights, Sub-Commission of Prevention of Discrimination and Protection of Minorities, Working Group on Indigenous Populations, *The Mataatua Declaration on Cultural and Intellectual Property Rights of Indigenous Peoples* (June 1993) para. 2.5 www.wipo.int/export/sites/www/tk/en/folklore/creative_heritage/docs/mataatua.pdf: 'Develop in full co-operation with indigenous peoples an additional cultural and intellectual property rights regime incorporating the following: collective (as well as individual) ownership and origin, retroactive coverage of historical as well as contemporary works, protection against debasement of culturally significant items, cooperative rather than competitive framework, first beneficiaries to be the direct descendants of the traditional guardians of that knowledge, multi-generational coverage span.'

Via PIC[71] it has to be ensured that communal groups participate in the decision-making processes that affect them,[72] and in relation to which they should be given the right to deny access to their resources and knowledge, if necessary.[73] Article 5 of the 'African Model Legislation for the Protection of the Rights of Local Communities, Farmers and Breeders, and for the Regulation of Access to Biological Resources' endeavours to put this concept into words:

> (1) Any access to biological resources, knowledge and or technologies of local communities shall be subject to the written prior informed consent of: (i) the National Competent Authority; as well as that of (ii) the concerned local communities, ensuring that women are also involved in decision making.
> (2) Any access carried out without the prior informed consent of the State and the concerned local community or communities shall be deemed to be invalid and shall be subject to the penalties provided in this legislation or any other legislation that deals with access to biological resources.
> (3) The National Competent Authority shall consult with the local community or communities in order to ascertain that its/their consent is sought and granted. Any access granted without consultation with the concerned community or communities shall be deemed to be invalid and in violation of the principle and requirement for prior informed consent as required under this Article.[74]

The various legal consequences that are available in response to a usage of traditional knowledge without valid agreement are addressed here. As such, they are hardly noticeable in the proposed European Commission's

[71] See Marc-Antoine Camp, 'Wer darf das Lied singen? Musikethnologische Anmerkungen zum rechtlichen Status traditioneller Musikkulturen' (2005) 9 *Sic! – Zeitschrift für Immaterialgüter-, Informations- und Wettbewerbsrecht* 307 http://musicandcopyright.beyondthecommons.com/Camp2005Deutsch.pdf.

[72] Commission on Human Rights, Sub-Commission on the Promotion and Protection of Human Rights, Working Group on Indigenous Populations, 22nd sess. (19–23 July 2004) 5: 'Free, prior and informed consent recognizes indigenous peoples' inherent and prior rights to their lands and resources and respects their legitimate authority to require that third parties enter into an equal and respectful relationship with them, based on the principle of informed consent.'

[73] See Ulrich Brand and Christoph Görg, *Postfordistische Naturverhältnisse. Konflikte um genetische Ressourcen und die Internationalisierung des Staates* (Westfälisches Dampfboot, 2003) 75.

[74] Organisation of African Unity, *Model Legislation for the Protection of the Rights of Local Communities, Farmers and Breeders, and for the Regulation of Access to Biological Resources* (2000) www.wipo.int/tk/en/laws/pdf/oau_modellaw.pdf.

Directive of 26 April 2006 on Criminal Measures to Enforce Rights of Intellectual Property, aimed at tightening the Commission's Directive 2004/48/EC,[75] which restricted itself to product piracy. Questions of biopiracy remain unaddressed. The reference to the creation of consensus according to the customs of the respective epistemic community is particularly relevant with regard to the question of PIC and secondary liabilities in cases of omission, and the resulting penalisation or restitutionary obligations.[76] Work on certifying origins in order to secure prior consent and ensure that usage is allocated effectively is decisive.[77] The obligation to disclose the origin of knowledge helps not only to guarantee 'that only really new discoveries are patented',[78] but also opens up a contact point for communication on controlling established rights of procedure.

To the extent that norms regulating profit distribution to indigenous groups are designed to facilitate usage of traditional knowledge for economic purposes by the usufructuary, contractual agreements regulating usage seem to be least suitable. By integrating the culture into Western exchange-economies and destroying cultural-religious content contracts would do the opposite of protecting cultural autonomy. From an intercultural point of view, a solution using funds may therefore be more suitable and less difficult to implement than other regulatory norms, and therefore possibly most promising. The fund solution offers the option of diffuse monetary compensation, which could compensate for the lack of direction in these highly specialised intrusions. UNCED Agenda 21[79] of the World Summit for Sustainable Development in South Africa in

[75] COM(2006) 168 final, 26 April 2006.

[76] Hence liability regimes regularly refer at the same time to customary law. See Jerome H. Reichman and Tracy Lewis, 'Using Liability Rules to Stimulate Local Innovation in Developing Countries: Application to Traditional Knowledge' in Keith E. Maskus and Jerome H. Reichman, *International Public Goods and Transfer of Technology Under a Globalized Intellectual Property Regime* (2005) 337; Carlos Correa, *Protection and Promotion of Traditional Medicine – Implications for Public Health in Developing Countries* (South Centre, 2002).

[77] See lately CBD Ad Hoc Open-Ended Working Group on Access and Benefit-Sharing, *Report of the Meeting of the Group of Technical Experts on an Internationally Recognized Certificate of Origin/Source/Legal Provenance*, 5th mtg, UN Doc. UNEP/CBD/WG-ABS/5/7 (20 February 2007).

[78] Gregor Kaiser, 'Biopiraterie: Der neue Kolonialismus' (2006) 51 *Blätter für deutsche und internationale Politik* 1172, 1175.

[79] *Report of the United Nations Conference on Environment and Development*, A/CONF.151/26 (Vol. I) (12 August 1992) annex I www.un.org/documents/ga/conf151/aconf15126-1annex1.htm.

September 2002 offered strong support for this regulatory technique. It has led to the call to 'negotiate within the framework of the Convention on Biological Diversity (CBD), bearing in mind the Bonn Guidelines, an international regime to promote and safeguard the fair and equitable sharing of benefits arising out of the utilization of genetic resources'.[80] In response to this demand, the Eighth Conference of the Parties to the CBD of March 2006 in Curitiba has preliminarily systematised these efforts in its Decision VIII/4.[81] It seems to be a promising start for making the contradictory logic described above compatible, to the extent that it culminates in the establishment of an international regime under the umbrella of the CBD that will introduce the concepts of PIC and 'benefit sharing' as effective regulations.

Conclusions

The preceding considerations have led to the following conclusions:

(1) When national law is in conflict with the laws of transnational regimes and the norms of indigenous cultures, respectively, the question is whether a collision with genuine legal norms or rather with social norms is at issue. Contrary to divergent legal pluralistic positions, it is important not to ascribe legal quality to all social norms. If a legal norm clashes with a social norm, an 'asymmetric collision rule' applies: the legal norm always prevails. By contrast, in the case of a conflict between genuine legal norms, collision law has to start from the assumption that the clashing entities claim equal priority. Both cases presented above, cybersquatting and biopiracy, are about collisions of genuine legal norms. Cybersquatting represents an example of a conflict between national legal orders and transnational private regimes. In cases of biopiracy, norms of national or international intellectual property law collide with real-fictive indigenous legal norms on the protection of traditional knowledge.

(2) Despite their equality as laws, all three colliding legal orders – transnational regime law, national law and indigenous law – are different from the point of view of collision law. They, of course, firstly differ

[80] *Report of the World Summit on Sustainable Development*, A/CONF.199/20 (2002) para. 44(o).

[81] CBD, Eighth Conference of the Parties, *Decision VIII/4: Access and Benefit Sharing*, at www.cbd.int/decision/cop/?id=11016.

in their scope (global, national, local). However, for our purposes, it is more important that they also differ in the degree to which they are socially embedded. It is this difference that has to be taken into account when developing new collision rules:

- The social embedding is the weakest in transnational regime law. Transnational regimes produce their own autonomous law. Coupled to only one functional sector of global society, they occur as 'self-contained regimes', their highly specialised legal norms only reflect the eigen-rationality of a single social sector. Transnational regime law is disconnected from processes which relate to society as a whole, from processes that aim at achieving the 'common welfare'.
- Modern national law is autonomous, formally enacted law and as such not embedded in social contexts any more, either. However, as opposed to transnational regime law national law is characterised by processes of 'internal contextualisation' in the sense that its legal norms, no matter how specialised, are always forced to interact. The legal norms of national law are caught in a relationship of permanent mutual (self-) restriction.
- Contrary to formal-autonomous national and transnational law, indigenous law is comprehensively socially embedded. The reason for this is to be found in the segmental/stratificatory differentiation as the organisational principle of society that dominates in traditional cultures and which stands in harsh contrast to the principle of functional differentiation. Their legal norms are genetically and structurally inseparably interwoven with religious, political, economic and traditional knowledge-based systems of interaction.

(3) These differences have consequences for the solution of norm collisions. If a transnational legal regime claims its law to be applied, collision law must ensure that the 'tunnel vision' of the 'self-contained regime' is broadened and made receptive to opposing principles. Since these collisions are not only trans-national but also trans-institutional in character, making use of the referral techniques of private international law is generally not the appropriate method. For most cases, the *substantive law approach* seems to be the most promising as elements of each of the colliding legal orders are taken into account and reflected in the new substantive law rule that is to be created. This leads to a hybrid law in the sense that, seen from the perspective of the deciding panel, the new substantive law rule absorbs extrinsic elements into its law while at the same time leaving the autonomy of the extrinsic intact.

(4) If the collision is characterised by the participation of an indigenous legal order it should be dealt with pursuant to the *model of the institutionalised and proceduralised protection of basic rights*. Self-restrictions need to be imposed upon the legal norms of modern society. In the interest of a (path-dependent) further development of the indigenous culture this collision method has to be shaped not in a static-absolutist but rather in a procedural-dynamic way.

Translation by Anna Furness revised by Anne Emert.

2

International Regimes and Domestic Arrangements: A View from Inside Out

CHERYL SAUNDERS

Introduction

The purpose of this chapter is to examine the phenomenon of international regime interaction from the perspective of the state, operating in accordance with the theories, principles and practices of domestic constitutional law.

This perspective has the potential to contribute to the understanding of the subject matter of this volume in several ways. First and most obviously the institutional and legal organisation of a state provides a contrast with the relative absence of hierarchy and coordination that characterises the international sphere and to that extent helps to explain the conditions that make international regime interaction a subject for inquiry. The concern of the state with coordination and some of the mechanisms through which coordination is achieved are examined in the next section. As that section shows, the contrast should not be overdrawn.[1] The task of coordination within a state is too complex ever to be complete, even if completion were desirable. The common condition of multi-level government in any event assumes a degree of diversity and intra-state autonomy. Nonetheless, the contrast is obvious and may be instructive. Equally significantly, the expectation of coordination and its link with the constitutional values of democracy, accountability and the rule of law further distinguish the organisation of the state from that of the international sphere.

Secondly, this perspective draws attention to the implications of the organisation of the international sphere for the project of coordination within the state. International law and international relations necessarily

[1] Jack Goldsmith and Daryl Levinson, 'Law for States: International Law, Constitutional Law, Public Law' (2009) 122 *Harvard Law Review* 1791.

impact on states. States in turn have institutions, principles and practices that structure their engagement in international activity and moderate the relationship between international and domestic law. In many cases, these arrangements are old-fashioned, reflecting ostensibly simpler times. In some cases they may contribute further to the fragmentation of international law, by enabling differences in the understanding and application of international legal principles between states. In any event, as part B shows, the proliferation of international law, including the elaboration of quasi-autonomous international regimes, places pressure on such arrangements and further complicates intra-state coordination. One consequence is to hamper any impact that coordination within a state might otherwise have had on the relationship between international regimes. Insofar as these developments suggest a growing autonomy of the international sphere as a whole, moreover, they diminish the force of theories of state legitimacy as explanations for the derivative legitimacy of international law.[2]

States differ in their internal organisation, their willingness to acknowledge pluralism, their receptiveness to international law and their degree of influence in the international order. This chapter uses one country, Australia, as a case study, through which to explore the themes of the book from the standpoint of domestic law and practice. Australia has certain characteristics that make it useful for this purpose. The Australian political culture attaches considerable importance to coordination and the Australian system of law and government make a high degree of coordination feasible, notwithstanding the federal form of the state. Australia continues to insist on dualism in the relationship between domestic and international law including, probably, customary international law.[3] It is possible to generalise from the Australian experience, to the extent that all functioning states have a capacity for coordination and all manage the relationship between domestic and international law. On the other hand, in some significant respects, Australia also is distinctive. As a middle-level, relatively efficient, stable and moderately wealth state with a population of only 20.7 million people, which also is geographically remote from much of the rest of the world, Australia is better placed than many other states to demand a high level of internal coordination and to maintain a

[2] José Alvarez, *International Organisations as Law-makers* (Oxford University Press, 2005) 630ff.

[3] In relation to treaties see, e.g. *Minister of State for Immigration and Ethnic Affairs* v. *Ah Hin Teoh* (1995) 183 CLR 273; in relation to criminal offences under customary international law see *Nulyarimma* v. *Thompson* (1999) 165 ALR 621.

degree of distance from international law. The implications of these differences should be borne in mind in applying conclusions from this chapter in other contexts.

Finally, something should be said about the concept of a regime for the purposes of this chapter. In its report on *Fragmentation* the International Law Commission canvassed three possible understandings of special regimes: those with a 'special set of secondary rules … that claims primacy to the general rules concerning consequences of a violation'; those in which there are 'interrelated wholes of primary and secondary rules' that 'cover some particular problem differently from the way it would be covered under general law'; and those constituted by 'whole fields of functional specialization … in the sense that special rules and techniques of interpretation and administration are thought to apply'.[4] Of these three, the first holds particular interest from the standpoint of the state, insofar as the design of such regimes makes them less susceptible to state monitoring and control. But each raises some questions for intra-state coordination, and the chapter has been written to encompass all three.

A. The state in relief

1. *Theory*

All functioning states exercise considerable authority over their respective territories through a combination of policy and law. To a greater or lesser degree, all attach value to the coordination of both means and ends. Their reasons for doing so range from considerations of political accountability and control on the one hand to efficiency, equity and predictability on the other. Coordination involves at least the minimisation of inconsistency or overlap and may extend further to complementarity, formal equality and uniformity. Coordination is theoretically feasible through the hierarchical structure of the organs of state and the framework of state law within which they operate, whatever the shortfall in practice.

The emphasis on coordination differs between states in accordance with a variety of factors. The history of a state, its contemporary circumstances and the diversity of its people may encourage a state to embrace pluralism, to be tolerant of it or at least to become resigned to it. Some forms of governance suggest a lesser attachment to coordination. Most obviously,

[4] International Law Commission, *Fragmentation of International Law: Difficulties arising from the Diversification and Expansion of International Law* A/CN.4/L.682, [128], [129].

multi-level government assumes some autonomy of the respective spheres, at least where the arrangements are constitutionalised. Even separation between the legislature and the executive in a form that accepts an autonomous decision-making capacity for each complicates coordination and suggests that it is less likely to be valued for its own sake.

For reasons of history and institutional design, Australian political culture places considerable emphasis on coordination, in the deepest sense. Australia has a parliamentary form of government in the British tradition in which the legislature is supreme in theory but is dominated by the executive for most practical purposes, resulting in the 'fusion' once celebrated by Walter Bagehot.[5] Australia departed from the British prototype in several respects that suggested a greater diffusion of power, including the adoption of a federal form of the Australian state, accompanied by an entrenched, justiciable Constitution. The progressive centralisation of the Australian federation marks the diminishing significance of the former, however, while the significance of the latter was minimised from the outset by the 'thinness' of a Constitution confined to the horizontal and vertical organisation of power within the state.[6] Neither the highly distinctive culture of Australia's indigenous population nor the increasing diversity of the Australian community as a result of successive waves of immigration appears to have prompted official enthusiasm for pluralism.

The remainder of this section examines the mechanisms for coordination of law and policy in Australia, both to enable comparison with the international sphere and as a necessary foundation for analysis of the impact of international law in part B. In the interests of clarity it begins by considering the operation of coordinating mechanisms within a single sphere of government, using the Commonwealth or national sphere, for the purpose. The segments that follow examine the mechanisms for coordination within the Australian federation and between Australia and the neighbouring state of New Zealand, with which it enjoys a close relationship that is no longer purely international in character.[7]

[5] Walter Bagehot, *The English Constitution* (New York: Garland Pub., 1978; Reprint of the 1872 edn. published by H. S. King, London).

[6] Joseph Raz, 'On the Authority and Interpretation of Constitutions: Some Preliminaries' in Larry Alexander (ed.), *Constitutionalism* (Cambridge University Press, 1998) 152.

[7] Cheryl Saunders, 'To Be or Not to Be: The Constitutional Relationship between New Zealand and Australia' in David Dyzenhaus, Murray Hunt, Grant Huscroft, *A Simple Common Lawyer* (Oxford: Hart Publishing, 2009) 251.

2. *Practice*

(a) Unitary

Within each Australian jurisdiction, the organising principle for the coordination of policy, including proposals for new legislation and the exercise of inherent executive power, is provided by the principles and practices of parliamentary government in the form sometimes known as 'responsible' government.

Under these arrangements, the key institution is the cabinet,[8] which in the Commonwealth involves the ministers responsible for each 'portfolio' area. Ministers outside cabinet are co-opted if and when their areas of responsibility are under discussion. The portfolios are allocated by an executive Administrative Arrangements Order, on the advice of the Prime Minister, when a government is formed. Typically, such an order identifies the legislation to be administered by each minister and the subject areas handled by the department(s) for which each minister is responsible. In early 2010 there were nineteen such departments, most of which dealt with particular government services, although some were 'central' agencies that also play a coordinating role.

One of the functions of the cabinet is to 'resolve potential conflicts within government' (which may take a variety of forms).[9] Coordination may be achieved in full cabinet, through cabinet committees, or through the role of the Prime Minister, as the cabinet chair, supported by the cabinet secretariat. The coordination role of cabinet is reinforced by the doctrine of collective ministerial responsibility, which requires all participating ministers to take responsibility for all cabinet decisions. To that end, elaborate arrangements are made for the timely distribution of supporting information before and after meetings. In preparing a submission for cabinet, ministers are under an obligation to consult 'among departments that have a proper interest in the subject matter (ie where the issues impinge upon a department's core functions)'.[10]

Not all matters are dealt with through the 'cabinet system'. Each government can organise the business of cabinet as it pleases. Typically, however, cabinet is likely to consider at least significant new policy proposals and proposals requiring legislation. Legislation is drafted by a centralised

[8] See generally Department of the Prime Minister and Cabinet, *Cabinet Handbook* (Commonwealth of Australia, 6th edn., 2009).

[9] Ibid., 1. [10] Ibid., 18.

drafting office, with an eye to the rest of the Commonwealth statute book. There has been a tendency for the drafting of instruments of a delegated legislative character to become more centralised as well.[11] Matters not handled through the cabinet system are dealt with by individual ministers. Even here, however, there is some potential for coordination through the body that formally advises the Governor-General in the exercise of the executive power, the Federal Executive Council.[12]

Despite these elaborate arrangements, coordination between subject areas may well be imperfect. Particularly where legislation is not involved, ministers may handle matters unilaterally, with limited consultation, in ways that are not picked up by the cabinet system. Reliance on cabinet committees as the primary decision-makers may also reduce the range of effective consultation.[13] Coordination inevitably is more difficult in areas that are subject to regulation or administration by bodies established at arm's length from the traditional departmental structure, particularly where these are corporatised or partly privatised and thus subject to less or no ministerial and departmental control. The finding of the Cole Inquiry that neither the Department of Foreign Affairs and Trade (DFAT) nor relevant ministers had actual knowledge that the privatised Australian Wheat Board (AWB) was making unlawful payments in association with the Iraqi oil-for-food programme illustrates the difficulties of maintaining oversight of the activities of such bodies, even when significant international obligations are at risk.[14] While DFAT passed on the short-form contracts between the AWB and the Iraqi Grain Board to the UN, it was apparently unaware of the collateral arrangements under which unlawful payments were made.

Techniques of a different kind are used for the purposes of coordination of the interpretation and enforcement of law and the development of the common law. Consistently with the tenets of a common law legal system, the adjudication of most legal disputes in Australia is handled by

[11] Legislative Instruments Act 2003 (Cth), s. 3.

[12] Department of the Prime Minister and Cabinet, *Federal Executive Council Handbook* (Commonwealth of Australia, September 2009).

[13] *Cabinet Handbook*, above n. 8, paras 84, 85: 'Cabinet's endorsement of committee minutes is a formal process not usually involving the re-opening of discussion'.

[14] *Report of the Inquiry into Certain Australian Companies in Relation to the UN Oil-For-Food Program* (Cole Inquiry), 2006, Chapter 30, at www.offi.gov.au/agd/WWW/unoilforfoodinquiry.nsf/Page/RWPD51F1BDC6A077710CA2572650017A3A6#_ednref106 (viewed 8 July 2011); Jürgen Kurtz, 'A Look Beyond the Cole Inquiry: AWB Ltd, Bribery and Australia's Obligations Under International Law', Democratic Audit of Australia, Discussion Paper 16/06, 2006.

the ordinary courts, organised in a hierarchical structure with the High Court of Australia at its apex. Well-understood rules of priority, aided by an array of common law interpretive techniques, are used to resolve conflicts between the common law and statutes, between Commonwealth statutes, or between the Constitution and ordinary law.[15] Generally, there is no distinction between functional or 'special' areas, although specialist tribunals or other institutions may lead to the emergence of 'regimes' of sorts, with a distinctive culture of their own.[16] In an example of another kind, in resolving conflict between common law and statute one interpretive presumption favours common law rights that are deemed to be 'fundamental', by requiring Parliament to express its intention to override such rights with 'irresistible clearness'.[17] In addition to these essentially adjudicative techniques, other types of conflict between laws or between policy and law may be managed through the exercise of discretions exercisable within the executive branch, to refrain from taking action to enforce a public right or to prosecute for an alleged offence. Executive capacity to manage such conflict is eroding, as the rules of standing to defend public rights become more flexible. A series of arguments for retaining it, based on the 'public interest', nevertheless were put forcefully by one Justice of the Australian High Court, as recently as 1998.[18]

Objection may be taken to this focus on state law to the exclusion of other norms that govern the way in which people live their lives. In the Australian context, such norms include bodies of aboriginal customary law that retain considerable significance for many of Australia's indigenous people. Religious and other cultural norms affect the behaviour of other groups as well. These social facts offer an important corrective to a tendency to exaggerate the effective power of the state over those who are subject to its authority. But, equally, it is a mistake to underestimate the

[15] Simon Evans and Cheryl Saunders, 'Overlap, Inconsistency, Conflict and Choice: Reconciling Multiple Norms in the Australian Federation' in Hans-Peter Schneider, Jutta Kramer and Beniamino Caravita di Toritto (eds.), *Judge made Federalism? The Role of Courts in Federal Systems* (Baden-Baden: Nomos, 2009) 131.

[16] In *Kirk* v. *Industrial Relations Commission* (2010) 239 CLR 531, the High Court reasserted the authority of generalist superior courts to review significant error by courts or tribunals occupied with 'special problems' in order to avoid the development of 'distorted positions': [64].

[17] *Saeed* v. *Minister for Immigration and Citizenship* (2010) 84 ALJR 507, [15], French CJ, Gummow, Hayne, Crennan and Kiefel JJ, describing the presumption as a 'working hypothesis' that 'is an aspect of the rule of law'.

[18] *Bateman's Bay Local Aboriginal Council* v. *Aboriginal Community Benefit Fund Pty Ltd* (1998) 194 CLR 247, [83]–[86], per McHugh J.

significance of state law in the Australia of the twenty-first century. At the time of European settlement, formal claims of sovereignty notwithstanding, it might accurately be said that many indigenous peoples were governed solely by their own laws. In some cases, they were not aware of the existence of any other source of law for more than 100 years. There is evidence, also, that the very concept of sovereignty differed at the time of settlement and that the law of the new occupiers tolerated a degree of pluralism at that time.[19] The position has long since changed, however, and it is now highly unlikely, to say the least, that there are indigenous Australians unaffected by state law, although many may have limited knowledge and understanding of it. In the event of overt conflict, there is no doubt that state law will prevail. And if anything, at least vis-à-vis customary law, the authority of state law is consolidating. In one unsettling illustration, legislation enacted in 2006 severely restricts the authority of a Court to take 'any form of customary law or cultural practice' into account in making decisions about bail and sentencing, thus removing one of the few remaining ways in which indigenous tradition affected the operation of Australian law.[20]

(b) Federal

Further dimensions are added to the task of coordination where, as in Australia, the state is organised as a federal system in which power is divided between spheres or levels of government under an entrenched Constitution that is supreme law. In such a case, the usual techniques for coordination apply within each jurisdiction, but there is additional potential for inconsistency, overlap and conflict between jurisdictions on either the vertical or a sub-national horizontal plane, in relation to both policy and law. The extent of these difficulties may depend on the design of the federation. In Australia the problem appears to be magnified by a dualist structure in which the Commonwealth and each State has an almost complete set of institutions, enabling it to make, execute and enforce its own laws. The judiciary is a partial exception, insofar as the High Court is the final appeal court for both the federal and State court hierarchies and State courts may be invested with federal jurisdiction.[21] The signifi-

[19] Lisa Ford, 'Before Settler Sovereignty and After Aboriginal Sovereignty' in Bain Attwood and Tom Griffiths (eds.), *Frontier, Race, Nation* (North Melbourne: Australian Scholarly Publishing Pty Ltd, 2009) 185.

[20] Now Crimes Act 1914 (Cth) ss 15AB, 16A.

[21] Constitution of the Commonwealth of Australia, ss 73, 77(iii) respectively.

cance for present purposes of these features of the Australian judicature is elaborated below.

The Constitution itself contemplates and provides a mechanism for resolving vertical inconsistency of law, between the Commonwealth and the States. The Constitution of the Commonwealth prevails over the Constitutions of the States, and a valid Commonwealth law prevails over inconsistent State law.[22] Inconsistency is understood broadly, to include circumstances in which the Commonwealth intends to 'cover the field' even when no direct inconsistency arises.[23] To guard against the application of the covering the field test where State laws are intended to coexist with a Commonwealth law unless they are directly incompatible, it is now common for a 'savings' provision to be included in Commonwealth statutes to deny an intention to 'exclude or limit the operation of a law of a State ... that furthers the objects of the [Act] and is capable of operating concurrently' with it.[24]

It is not possible either to 'save' a State law in this way from direct inconsistency or to retrospectively cure an inconsistency created by a Commonwealth Act that has been interpreted as covering the field. In reaching this latter conclusion, in *Metwally*, Deane J pointed to the wider significance of the provision recognising Commonwealth supremacy over an inconsistent State law, when he observed that the section:

> is not concerned merely to resolve disputes between the Commonwealth and a State as to the validity of their competing claims to govern the conduct of individuals in a particular area of legislative power. It serves the equally important function of protecting the individual from the injustice of being subjected to the requirements of valid and inconsistent laws of Commonwealth and State Parliaments on the same subject.[25]

The Constitution does not expressly anticipate other forms of legal inconsistency and conflict within the Australian federation. As such issues have arisen they have been resolved by the courts in a manner that unmistakably favours a high degree of coordination. The potential for inconsistency between the laws of two States is kept in check largely by the threat

[22] For an example see *Croome* v. *Tasmania* (1997) 191 CLR 119, in which a Commonwealth law enacted in response to a view adverse to Australia by the Human Rights Committee overrode the provision of the Tasmanian criminal code that formed the basis of the Communication to the Committee.

[23] *Ansett Transport Industries (Operations) Pty Ltd* v. *Wardley* (1980) 142 CLR 237.

[24] The Sex Discrimination Act 1984 (Cth) s. 11 is one of many examples.

[25] *University of Wollongong* v. *Metwally* (1984) 158 CLR 447. See now also *Dickson* v. *The Queen* (2010) 84 ALJR 635 [19].

that constraints on the power of State Parliaments to make laws with extraterritorial effect might be invoked should the need to do so arise.[26] The principles that govern conflict or, as it is now termed 'choice' of law to determine which law applies to resolve a tortious dispute that has links to two or more States have been modified to provide 'certainty and uniformity of outcome no matter where in the Australian federation a matter is litigated'.[27] The structure of the judicature has been interpreted to require a single 'Australian' common law, obviating the possibility of divergent streams of the common law within the several States.[28] Most remarkably of all, the rules of precedent have been developed, in the interests of 'comity', so that 'intermediate appellate courts … should not … depart from decisions … in another jurisdiction' unless they are 'convinced' that the decision is 'plainly wrong'.[29] In consequence, State courts are now effectively bound to follow each other, even in relation to the interpretation of relevantly similar State legislation. The similarity of much State legislation, moreover, has provided the platform for recent suggestions by the High Court that it remains possible in some circumstances to derivatively adapt the single common law to 'common themes' of Australian legislation.[30]

The design of the Australian federation leaves scope for diversity between States in areas of State authority governed by legislation or executive policy. In practice, however, diversity has progressively diminished and continues to do so with accelerating speed. One of several causes is the expansion of Commonwealth power through the interpretation and application of the Constitution by the High Court. While this process is not particularly relevant for present purposes, it may be noted in passing that the Commonwealth power in section 51(xxix) to implement treaties to which Australia is a party has been one of the principal contributing factors to the expansion of Commonwealth power overall, fuelled by the proliferation of treaty law. Another explanation for diminishing diversity, which merits further elaboration, is the vast network of Australian intergovernmental arrangements, operating both horizontally and vertically and securing levels of coordination between the orders of government

[26] *Mobil Oil Australia Pty Ltd* v. *Victoria* (2002) 211 CLR 1.

[27] *John Pfeiffer* v. *Rogerson* (2000) 203 CLR 503 [43], [44].

[28] *Lipohar* v. *R* (1999) 200 CLR 485 [50].

[29] *Farah Constructions* v. *Say-Dee Pty Ltd* (2007) 230 CLR 89, 152. At the same time, it was held that an intermediate court should not depart from 'seriously considered dicta' of a majority of the High Court.

[30] *Imbree* v. *McNeilly* (2008) 236 CLR 510 [129], Gummow, Hayne and Kiefel JJ.

that range from simple information exchange to deep uniformity of legislation, its interpretation and administration. Occupying an intermediate position between these two extremes is the Australian scheme for the mutual recognition of standards for goods and occupations by all participating jurisdictions, which in turn is predicated on a substantial degree of homogeneity.[31]

The drivers of intergovernmental relations in Australia are more than forty ministerial councils, which bring together ministers with similar portfolios across jurisdictional lines in meetings that are held at least annually and sometimes more often.[32] Such councils have a variety of tools at their disposal to achieve the desired degree of coordination, most of which are underpinned by an executive agreement of some kind. The commitments made in intergovernmental agreements generally suggest that they are not intended to be contractually enforceable, although there are signs of growing willingness on the part of the High Court to scrutinise their constitutionality.[33] Sanctions for breach are typically political or fiscal or both; much intergovernmental activity in the Australian federation depends on fiscal incentives offered by the Commonwealth to the States in circumstances of extreme vertical fiscal imbalance. The control exercisable by governments over their respective legislatures in consequence of the operation of the principles of responsible government ensures that all such agreements generally can readily put into effect, even where legislation is required to do so.

Arrangements of this kind are capable of giving rise to 'special regimes' within the domestic sphere. Ministers with similar responsibilities meet in a specialist council; they agree to a programme of action; the funding often comes from the corresponding Commonwealth portfolio area; the resulting arrangements may involve regulatory and monitoring institutions, techniques for self-enforcement and systems of primary and secondary rules. Regimes that in this sense are distinct can be identified in Australia in functional areas ranging from river management to food standards to the regulation of gene technology to corporations and securities regulation. In theory, within each jurisdiction, the processes of cabinet government enable the coordination of activities across functional

[31] Agreement relating to Mutual Recognition, 1992 and implementing Commonwealth and State legislation.

[32] Ministerial Councils Compendium, 2009, www.coag.gov.au/ministerial_councils/index.cfm (viewed 8 July 2011).

[33] For example, *Arnold* v. *Minister Administering the Water Management Act 2000* (2010) 240 CLR 242.

areas. In practice, once an intergovernmental element is introduced, coordination becomes much more difficult. Quite apart from the greater complexity of the exercise, the ministerial council system is relatively unstructured and the manner in which meetings are prepared does not necessarily enable cabinet deliberation within each jurisdiction on the issues that are likely to be raised.

Spasmodic attempts have been made to deal with this difficulty in recent decades. From the early 1990s, ministerial council procedures were progressively revised in an attempt to enhance the coordination of decision-making within jurisdictions. The current protocols, for example, require ministers to 'ensure they are in a position appropriately to represent their governments at Council meetings' and require the circulation of agendas and papers at least three weeks before meetings.[34] The problem of 'cross-portfolio' issues is acknowledged and attempts made to resolve it by, for example, liaison between council chairs many, although not all, of whom are Commonwealth portfolio ministers. Ministerial council secretariats (most, although again not all, of which are located in Commonwealth departments) have reporting obligations to the Department of Prime Minister and Cabinet.[35]

More recently still, the Council of Australian Governments (COAG), comprising the heads of all Australian governments, has begun to develop greater capacity for coordination. COAG is chaired by the Prime Minister and thus is serviced by the department to which ministerial councils report. Its formal functions include 'consultation on … major whole-of-government issues arising from Ministerial Council deliberations'.[36] It appears now to have a hierarchical relationship with other Councils: the COAG website describes the function of Councils as to 'develop policy reforms for consideration by COAG, and oversee the implementation of policy reforms agreed by COAG'.[37] It is assisted in oversight of the implementation of intergovernmental arrangements by a COAG 'Reform Council', appointed by COAG itself to 'strengthen accountability for the achievement of results through independent and evidenced-

[34] *Broad Protocols for the Operation of Ministerial Councils*, June 2004, at www.coag.gov.au/coag_meeting_outcomes/2004-06-25/index.cfm (viewed 15 July 2010).

[35] Council of Australian Governments, *Ministerial Councils*, www.coag.gov.au/ministerial_councils/index.cfm (viewed 8 July 2011).

[36] *Ministerial Councils Compendium*, above n. 32, 8.

[37] Council of Australian Governments *Ministerial Councils* www.coag.gov.au/ministerial_councils/index.cfm (viewed 8 July 2011).

based monitoring, assessment and reporting of the performance of all governments.'[38] This tightening of the COAG framework has taken the coordination of intergovernmental relations within Australia to a level that has not hitherto been achieved and is an illustration of the significance attached to the value of coordination in, at least, one state.

(c) Supra-national

Against this background, the relationship between Australia and New Zealand highlights the added complication of attempting coordination outside the confines of a single, albeit federated, state. The two countries enjoy a very close relationship, many aspects of which are subsumed under the broad umbrella of the creation of a single economic market. Nevertheless, they are independent states. Elsewhere such a relationship might be developed in a way that is described as supra-national. The epithet is less appropriate in this case, however, because of the absence of any distinctive, shared institutional structures. Their absence is attributable to the fact that this is a bilateral relationship and to the relative size of New Zealand compared to Australia. Instead, New Zealand has been incorporated into many of Australia's internal intergovernmental arrangements, including the ministerial council network headed by COAG, and the mutual recognition scheme.[39]

Even so, the independent status of the two countries affects the operation of intergovernmental arrangements in which New Zealand is involved in a range of ways.[40] There is no sovereign authority available to make arrangements such as the mutual recognition scheme legally binding, as has occurred between the Australian States. The different interests of the distinct populations of the two states make New Zealand wary of deep arrangements that commit it to, for example, uniformity, as opposed to harmonisation and give it a degree of leverage in negotiations that is not available to the Australian States. New Zealand retains a veto, even when, as in relation to the mutual recognition arrangements, other participants make decisions by weighted majority voting.

Certain matters are also excluded from the ambit of agreements between Australia and New Zealand that are deemed to raise 'nation

[38] Council of Australian Governments, *COAG Reform Council* http://www.coag.gov.au/crc/index.cfm (viewed 8 July 2011).

[39] Trans-Tasman Mutual Recognition Arrangement 1997 and implementing Commonwealth, state and New Zealand legislation.

[40] These are examined in greater detail in Saunders, above n. 7.

state' issues. Taxation is an example, but arrangements are also necessarily designed so as not to compromise any differing international obligations undertaken by the respective states.[41] Further, disputes for which adjudication would otherwise be appropriate cannot be resolved through a single court or tribunal, in consequence of restrictions imposed by the Australian Constitution. In these circumstances, dispute resolution relies on other techniques: comity, information exchange, reciprocity and some shared personnel.[42]

B. Accommodating international law

1. *Theory*

This section considers the impact of international commitments on the coordination of law and policy in Australia and, conversely, the extent to which arrangements for intra-state coordination might affect relations between international legal regimes.

Traditional Australian legal theory treats international and domestic law as distinct spheres. This essentially dualist position in turn both sustains and is sustained by the constitutional rule that action to commit Australia under international law lies solely with the executive branch. Thus, the negotiation, signing and ratification of treaties fall within the executive power of the Commonwealth, as does any action taken in the international sphere under treaty commitments, in the absence of supervening legislative requirements.[43]

Common law theory as well as, now, the constitutional principle of separation of powers precludes international obligations undertaken by the executive from directly altering Australian law.[44] Where an international obligation requires a domestic legal response, the necessary legislation may be enacted either by the Commonwealth Parliament, relying if necessary on the 'external affairs' power, or by the Parliaments of the States. Australian treaty procedures describe it as 'normal practice' to enact any necessary legislation before Executive Council approval is sought to ratify

[41] See e.g. the exclusion of international agreements from the sale of goods arrangements under the Trans-Tasman Mutual Recognition Arrangement, clause 7.2(d).

[42] E.g. the Trans-Tasman Court Proceedings and Regulatory Enforcement Agreement 2008, implemented for Australia by the Trans-Tasman Proceedings Act 2010 (Cth).

[43] *Barton* v. *Commonwealth* (1974) 131 CLR 477.

[44] *Minister for Immigration and Ethnic Affairs* v. *Teoh* (1995) 183 CLR 273.

the treaty.[45] Nevertheless, in some cases, no legislative change is sought, apparently because a view is taken either that existing Australian law and practice already adequately complies with treaty commitments, or that the treaty obligations in question 'can be implemented progressively and without radical change to existing laws'.[46]

The range and diversity of international law present a particular challenge to the coordination of decisions to enter into and implement international obligations. Functional responsibility for foreign affairs is conferred on a single department, in which it is also linked with trade. The Department of Foreign Affairs and Trade (DFAT) thus has direct responsibility for treaty making and for Australia's participation in certain regimes including the World Trade Organization (WTO). But responsibility for international law generally lies with the Attorney-General's Department and responsibility for compliance with particular international obligations lies with other Commonwealth or, occasionally State departments. By way of example, the Attorney-General's Department deals with human rights; the Department of the Environment, Water, Heritage and the Arts deals with environmental matters, including the Australian Antarctic Territory; and the Department of Broadband, Communications and the Digital Economy handles international obligations relevant to the subject matter of its portfolio. These responsibilities are distributed between ministers by the executive Administrative Arrangements Order, which only occasionally identifies the international obligations associated with many areas of domestic law and government.

The ordinary processes of responsible government provide some mechanisms to coordinate domestic decisions that are or might be linked with international obligations. The stance to be adopted by Australia in international negotiations is sometimes determined in Cabinet or cabinet committees, although it is not clear how often this occurs: the treaty procedures simply provide that: '[d]ecisions about the negotiation of multilateral conventions, including determination of objectives, negotiating positions, the parameters within which the Australian delegation can operate, and the final decision as to whether to sign and ratify are taken at Ministerial level, and in many cases, by Cabinet'.[47] Delegations put together for the purpose of international negotiations include

[45] Australia International Treaty Making Information Kit, July 2000, www.austlii.edu.au/au/other/dfat/reports/infokit.html (viewed 8 July 2011).

[46] Ibid.

[47] Australia International Treaty Making Information Kit, above n. 45. See also *Cabinet Handbook*, above n. 8, para. 78(k).

representatives of 'responsible' departments, who are obliged to consult with other 'relevant' departments. Other 'stakeholders', including representatives of the States, also may be included on delegations of this kind.[48] Decisions to sign or ratify treaties that fall 'outside existing policy guidelines' are sometimes made by Cabinet or through cabinet committees. In other cases, such decisions are taken at ministerial level, with some obligation to consult with other ministers affected. Formal decisions to enter into international commitments on behalf of Australia require Federal Executive Council approval, at the point of both signature and ratification, providing one final point at which coordination may occur. Treaty recommendations are made to the Council by the Minister for Foreign Affairs, with the 'approval … of those Ministers having primary carriage of the subject matter'. According to Executive Council procedures, this process is sufficient '[p]rovided the treaty action proposed is within the scope of existing government policy and the Prime Minister has at least been informed …'[49]

It may be assumed that the Cabinet and Executive Council procedures, collectively, are capable of picking up major discrepancies between new treaty commitments and existing domestic policy, at least at the Commonwealth level. This capability was enhanced to a degree by changes to treaty-making procedures from 1996, although this was not their immediate purpose. The changes were prompted by the election of a new government that had been critical of Australia's international commitments while in opposition; a report of a parliamentary committee; and long-standing concern on the part of the Australian States about the impact of treaty making and implementation on the federal division of power.[50] The new procedures did not alter the formal legal framework for treaty making and implementation but introduced additional informal procedures that have had some impact on coordination within Australia, without necessarily enhancing Australian capacity to affect the relationship between international regimes.

The principal changes were as follows. There is now a requirement for treaties to be tabled in the Commonwealth Parliament at least fifteen sitting days before the executive acts to bring them into force for Australia. The requirement is not legally binding, and 'urgent' or 'sensitive' treaties

[48] Australia International Treaty Making Information Kit, above n. 45.

[49] Federal Executive Council Handbook, above n. 12, 5.5.3.

[50] Senate Legal and Constitutional References Committee, *Trick or Treaty?: Commonwealth Power to Make and Implement Treaties*, November 1995, www.austlii.edu.au/au/other/dfat/reports/tortcon.html (viewed 8 July 2011).

are excepted.[51] Tabled treaties must be accompanied by a National Interest Analysis (NIA), explaining why Australia should become a party. An NIA might deal with, for example, the economic, environmental, social and cultural effects of treaty action; the obligations imposed by the treaty; the direct financial cost of the treaty to Australia; proposals for implementation; the extent of consultation, if any, that has occurred; any relevant view of State governments; and information about whether the treaty provides for withdrawal or denunciation.[52] Thirdly, a parliamentary Joint Standing Committee on Treaties (JSCOT) has been established to report on tabled treaties and the accompanying impact interest analyses. The Committee may hold public hearings; its reports are publicly available; and the executive is expected to respond publicly to its recommendations.[53] An electronic Treaties Library makes information about the current list of treaties to which Australia is a party available to the public at large.[54]

These changes are directed to improved accountability for treaty making within the Commonwealth sphere. The impetus for other changes derives from federalism. These comprise a new set of Principles and Procedures for Commonwealth-State-Territory Consultation on Treaties[55] and the establishment of a Treaties Council, consisting of the heads of Australian Government, to advise on treaties likely to be of particular interest to the States. The Council is supported by a standing committee of officers, which receives a quarterly schedule from the Commonwealth, listing treaties presently under negotiation.[56]

Most of these new procedures take place during the formative stages of an Australian decision to enter into an international arrangement. They thus have little or no effect on coordination either within or outside the state once that decision is made. Nevertheless, there is some evidence that JSCOT and the processes associated with it can pick up

[51] Australia International Treaty Making Information Kit, above n. 45.

[52] National Interest Analyses since 1996 can be found on-line: www.austlii.edu.au/au/other/dfat/nia/ (viewed 8 July 2011).

[53] The Reports of JSCOT are also available on-line: www.austlii.edu.au/au/other/jscot/ (viewed 8 July 2011); see also the Committee's parliamentary home page: www.aph.gov.au/house/committee/jsct/index.htm (viewed 8 July 2011). In a report in 2010 the Committee notes a 'spate of recent requests by the Australian Government for the Committee to expedite its consideration of the treaty', which it attributes to 'poor planning' on the part of the departments concerned: Report 110, March 2010, paras 5.23–5.27.

[54] Available at www.austlii.edu.au/au/other/dfat/treaties/ (viewed 8 July 2011).

[55] Council of Australian Governments' Communiqué, 14 June 1996, reproduced in Australia International Treaty Making Information Kit, above n. 45.

[56] Australia International Treaty Making Information Kit, above n. 45.

discrepancies between proposed treaty action and current policies, which in some instances may also reflect discrepancies between international legal regimes. While the Committee has authority only to make recommendations, the Government has an obligation to respond to its reports. By way of example, in 2008 JSCOT drew attention to the Government's interpretive declaration on ratifying the Convention on the Rights of Persons with Disabilities that its immigration law and practice were in 'full compliance' with the Convention.[57] Rather than handle the problem of avoiding potential discrepancy between immigration policy and the Convention in this way, the Committee recommended a review of the immigration legislation from the perspective of the Convention. In an example of a somewhat different kind, in the same report, JSCOT noted that a proposed Australia-Chile Free Trade Agreement included no reference to International Labour Organization (ILO) and UN labour standards, unlike the Free Trade Agreement between Australia and the United States. On this occasion the Committee received evidence that it was generally contrary to government policy to include such standards in trade agreements and, in the end, it made no 'specific recommendation' beyond referring to the need to 'address these concerns' in the context of future negotiations.[58]

2. *Practice*

(a) Interdependence of domestic and international law

If the distinction between domestic and international law were as sharp in practice as it is in theory, any lack of coordination between international legal regimes would be unlikely to manifest itself directly in the domestic sphere. Given the emphasis on domestic coordination, significant discrepancies between primary international law rules, at least, should be identified and mediated by domestic law in the course of incorporation. Those that remain, which manifest themselves subsequently, should be able to be resolved by domestic courts, using their range of familiar techniques.

The reality is more complex, however, for several interconnected reasons. International law affects domestic law in a variety of ways, whether it is incorporated or not. And sometimes the act of incorporation by legislation draws on international law so indiscriminately that domestic practice has no opportunity to mediate, even if it might otherwise have effectively

[57] JSCOT Report 95, 2008, paras 2.25–2.26, 2.34–2.41.

[58] JSCOT Report 95, 2008, paras 3.49–3.51, 3.60–3.62.

done so. In either case, domestic courts and, occasionally, other institutions are more directly exposed to discrepancies between international legal rules. One response is to draw back from engaging with international law, citing the volume, inconsistency and generality of international law by way of explanation, as well as constitutional principle. To the extent that reluctance to draw on international law is attributable to causes of this kind, the condition of international law inhibits the effect it is given in domestic law and hence its effectiveness overall.

The remainder of this section examines more closely the manner in which international law affects Australian law and a range of judicial responses in recent cases. The following section deals more specifically with the impact of the relationship between special international legal regimes in domestic law, using controversy over whaling as an example.

Many treaties to which Australia is a party are incorporated into Australian law by specific legislation. Some are not, however. In relation to human rights treaties, for example, including the ICCPR, Australia often claims that its law or (sometimes) a combination of its law and practice are already compliant, so that specific incorporation is unnecessary. This claim is contestable and, in any event, is under pressure. Following the national human rights consultation in 2009, the Commonwealth Government announced its support for new statutory procedures whereby proposed new laws would be systematically examined for their compliance with Australian obligations under seven human rights treaties during the pre-enactment phase.[59] If and when these new procedures come into effect, they should have implications for the consistency of Australian and international human rights law. Their potential implications for the interpretive principles applied by the courts will be taken up in that context below.

Legislation to incorporate treaties into domestic law generally is enacted by the Commonwealth Parliament in exercise of its external affairs power in section 51(xxix) of the Constitution where the treaty is outside the bounds of other substantive Commonwealth powers. In this case, the Commonwealth legislation is constitutionally required to adhere relatively faithfully to the terms of the treaty.[60] Treaties may also be incorporated by State Parliaments, however, in accordance with the *Principles*

[59] Australian Government, *Australia's Human Rights Framework* www.ag.gov.au/humanrightsframework (viewed 8 July 2011); see also Human Rights (Parliamentary Scrutiny) Bill 2010.

[60] *Victoria* v. *Commonwealth* (1996) 187 CLR 416 [34]–[38], Brennan CJ, Toohey, Gaudron, McHugh and Gummow JJ.

and Procedures for Commonwealth-State-Territory Consultation on Treaties. This is likely to be considered where, for example, the subject matter of a treaty lies within the field of an existing body of State law. Thus the Convention on Contracts for the International Sale of Goods (CISG) was given effect in Australia through model State legislation, following agreement in the relevant ministerial council, the Standing Committee of Attorneys-General.[61] Legislation incorporating a treaty often refers to the treaty. It is relatively rare for the treaty itself to be scheduled to the legislation, although its terms now are readily available through the Australian Treaties Library.[62]

The increasing significance and volume of international law has been marked by the development of a range of new legislative techniques to give treaties status in Australian law or to draw on international law for instrumental purposes. The following examples are intended merely to illustrate the phenomenon and do not purport to be exhaustive. The first involves the practice whereby five human rights instruments are scheduled to the Australian Human Rights Commission Act 1986 (Cth) as standards for the Commission in carrying out its functions. As these functions in turn are confined to education, inquiry and conciliation of complaints involving Commonwealth action, however, it has been held that the instruments are not thereby incorporated into Australian law, leaving their exact status somewhat unclear.[63]

In an example of another kind, the Spam Act 2003 (Cth) authorises international conventions dealing with commercial electronic messages or address-harvesting software to be given effect by regulation, which may also prescribe penalties for offences.[64] Regulations are a form of delegated legislation and this is a relatively broad use of delegated legislative power by Australian standards, although no action has yet been taken under the sections.

Third, the intergovernmental relations system uses internationally accepted standards and in particular those set under the General Agreement on Tariffs and Trade (GATT) and by the WTO to guide the development of regulation pursuant to intergovernmental schemes by requiring regulatory mechanisms to be 'compatible' with such

[61] See the Sale of Goods (Vienna Convention) Acts 1986, 1987; Fariba Aghili, 'A critical analysis of the CISG as Australian Law' (2008) 21:4 *Commercial Law Quarterly* 15, 17–18.

[62] The CISG is, however, scheduled to the Acts of the respective States and Territories.

[63] *Minister for Immigration and Ethnic Affairs* v. *Teoh* (1995) 183 CLR 273.

[64] Section 45; see also the Do Not Call Register Act 2006 (Cth) s. 44 (international convention dealing with telemarketing calls).

standards.[65] For similar reasons, the mutual recognition arrangements use international standards as the default position, in the absence of agreement between participating jurisdictions. Thus, in cases where mutual recognition is temporarily suspended on health and safety or environmental grounds, the relevant ministerial council is obliged to set a standard to operate during the interim period which 'wherever possible' must be aligned with 'those commonly accepted in international trade'.[66]

Finally and most spectacularly, in at least one instance, Commonwealth legislation has applied international law indiscriminately; on this occasion in providing a framework for broadcasting standards. In the late 1990s, section 160 of the Broadcasting Services Act 1992 (Cth) required the Australian Broadcasting Authority (ABA) to perform its functions in a manner consistent with 'Australia's obligations under any convention to which Australia is a party or any agreement between Australia and a foreign country'. The effect of this provision was raised before the High Court in *Project Blue Sky v ABA*,[67] in the context of a dispute over the validity of a broadcasting standard set by the ABA that was arguably inconsistent with the Closer Economic Relations (CER) Trade Agreement between New Zealand and Australia but that had been made in exercise of a power to set standards relating to 'the Australian content of programs'. The Full Court of the Federal Court treated the 'special provision' dealing with Australian content as overriding the general provision requiring compliance with international obligations and upheld the validity of the standard on that basis. Upholding the appeal, the High Court read the requirement for compliance with international obligations as a qualification of the power to set standards. While the resulting standard was 'unlawful' a majority of the Court held that it was not 'invalid'. In drawing and applying this distinction, it relied on what it argued was the intention of the Parliament that a standard should not be invalid in these circumstances, given the 'indeterminate language' of many international agreements. The majority did not refer to the potential for international

[65] COAG, *Principles and Guidelines for Standard Setting and Regulatory Action by Ministerial Councils and Standard Setting Bodies*. For an analysis of some of the issues raised by this approach in the context of the WTO Agreement on Technical Barriers to Trade (TBT Agreement) see Jan McDonald, 'Domestic Regulation, International Standards and Technical Barriers to Trade' (2005) 4 *World Trade Review* 249.

[66] Trans-Tasman Mutual Recognition Agreement, 6.4 (applying the requirement to standards of both goods and occupations); Mutual Recognition Agreement, 5.4.

[67] (1998) 194 CLR 355.

obligations to also be 'mutually inconsistent', although the minority justice, Brennan CJ, did so.[68] The interpretive approach in *Project Blue Sky* swept away the old distinction between mandatory and directory provisions in a manner that the Court subsequently characterised as having 'changed the landscape'.[69] The legislation itself was changed almost immediately, however, to limit the scope of the international obligations imposed on the ABA to those applicable under the CER Trade in Services Protocol.[70]

Even where international law is not incorporated into Australian law by legislation, there is potential for Australia's international obligations to affect Australian law in other ways. First, at least in theory, it can be used to develop the common law and there are examples where this has occurred including, most famously, in repudiating the characterisation of Australia as 'terra nullius' in *Mabo (No. 2)*.[71] This possibility is used sparingly, however, on separation of powers grounds. Development of the common law by reference to treaties to which the executive has committed Australia once again raises the spectre of executive law-making, while the narrow understanding of the scope of judicial power under the Australian separation of powers doctrine precludes acceptance that a breach of customary international law might constitute an offence under Australian law in the absence of incorporating legislation. The courts are more receptive to reliance on either custom or treaty to interpret legislation. Even here, however, there is evidence of caution.

The question arises in at least two sets of relatively distinct circumstances. The first concerns international rules that have been enacted or 'transposed' as part of the law of Australia, particularly where the rules themselves 'were designed to create a self-contained code … that would not require reference to domestic law'.[72] In such a case, Australian courts recognise the virtue of interpreting the provisions of the treaty and its transposing legislation consistently with a uniform interpretation that

[68] At [29].

[69] *Commissioner of Taxation* v. *Futuris Corporation Ltd* (2008) 237 CLR 146 [70], Gummow, Hayne, Heydon and Crennan JJ.

[70] Broadcasting Services Amendment Act (No 3) 1999 (Cth) Sch. 2.

[71] *Mabo* v. *Queensland (No. 2)* (1992) 175 CLR 1.

[72] *Great China Metal Industries Co Ltd* v. *Malaysian International Shipping Company Berhad* (1998) 196 CLR 161 [19], Gaudron, Gummow and Hayne JJ, citing *Benedict on Admiralty*, 7th edn (rev), vol 2A § 15 at 2–12, in the context of interpreting the Sea Carriage of Goods Act 1924 (Cth), giving domestic effect to the Hague Rules. See also *Povey* v. *Qantas Airways Ltd* (2005) 223 CLR 189, considering the Civil Aviation (Carriers' Liability Act) giving the Warsaw Convention the force of law in Australia.

prevails in other states.[73] They are liable to approach the task of interpretation by reference to the Vienna Convention on the Law of Treaties rather than domestic interpretive rules.[74] The extent to which this approach is followed, however, depends on the nature of the treaty and the terms in which it is incorporated into Australian law. Thus case law on the legislation incorporating the CISG has introduced a range of domestic concepts through the interpretive process, inhibiting its development as an 'autonomous body of law'.[75] The explanation appears to be, at least in part, that the implementing legislation does not clearly displace existing law but is expressed to prevail over it only 'to the extent of any inconsistency'.[76]

The less dependent legislation is on the Convention, moreover, the greater is the likelihood that domestic interpretive techniques will prevail. Thus in *QAAH*, after noting that the Refugee Convention had not been 'enacted as part of the law of Australia' in the Migration Act 1958 (Cth), unlike, for example, the Hague Rules, a majority of the High Court noted that while there were various respects in which 'the Convention may be used in construing the Act, it is the words of the Act which govern'.[77] In a more extreme and less usual example, in *WBM v Commissioner of Police* a justice of the Supreme Court of Victoria expressed caution about reference to international law, including opinions of the Human Rights Committee, in interpreting provisions in the Charter of Human Rights and Responsibilities Act 2006. The rights in the Charter are drawn largely from the ICCPR, and the authority to refer to international law is conferred on Victorian courts by section 32(2) of the Charter itself. In his remarks, Kaye J placed particular emphasis on the separation of judicial power in the Australian constitutional system, which is not necessarily replicated elsewhere and distinguished the position of Australian courts sharply from that of the Human Rights Committee.[78]

As the observation in *QAAH* suggests, even where legislation does not in terms 'transpose' a treaty, the interpretation of domestic legislation may be informed by Australia's international obligations. It is settled law that, in at least some circumstances, an ambiguity in a statute should be

[73] *Great China Metal Industries* [71], McHugh J.

[74] *Povey* [60], McHugh J.

[75] Aghili, above n. 61, citing Michael Bonnell 'Article 7' in C. M. Bianca and M. J. Bonell (eds.), *Commentary on the International Sales Law* (Milan: Giuffrè, 1987) 65, 73.

[76] Sale of Goods (Vienna Convention) Acts ss 5,6.

[77] *Minister for Immigration and Multicultural and Indigenous Affairs* v. *QAAH of 2004* (2006) 231 CLR 1, Gummow ACJ, Callinan, Heydon and Crennan JJ [34].

[78] [2010] VSC 219 [49], Kaye J.

resolved in a manner that is consistent with international law. But there are several variables in this formulation, which make its detailed operation uncertain. These include the extent of the ambiguity that is necessary before the interpretive principle is brought into play; whether the international obligation on the part of Australia must pre-date the legislation; and whether there needs to be a link between the international obligation and the legislation in the sense that the latter is enacted 'pursuant to, or in contemplation of, the assumption of international obligations'.[79] For the moment at least, the more limited formulation seems dominant.

It is possible that, if plans for pre-enactment scrutiny proceed, the interpretive principle will narrow further still in some instances, although it may be enhanced in others. A statement of compatibility of a proposed law with international law by the executive during the pre-enactment phase would not bind the courts.[80] Nevertheless, were legislation to be passed in the face of an acknowledgement by the sponsoring minister that a bill is not consistent with international law it would be more difficult for a court to apply the interpretive principle in the name of the presumed intention of Parliament. As it is, the principle has been attacked as a 'fiction', given the volume of international law. Thus in *Al-Kateb*, McHugh J observed:

> No doubt the rule … had some validity when the rules of international law were few and well-known. Under modern conditions, however, this rule of construction is based on a fiction. Gone are the days when the rules of international law were to be found in the writings of a few well-known jurists … Given the widespread nature of the sources of international law under modern conditions, it is impossible to believe that, when the Parliament now legislates, it has in mind or is even aware of all the rules of international law … [T]he rationale for the rule that a statute contains an implication that it should be construed to conform with international law bears no relationship to the reality of the modern legislative process. Be that as it may, the rule is too well established to be repealed now by judicial decision.[81]

There are at least two other contexts in which attention has been paid to the implications of unincorporated treaties for the meaning and operation of Australian law. One involves the principles of administrative law. In *Teoh* a majority of the Court accepted that Australia's ratification of the

[79] *Plaintiff S157/2002* v. *Commonwealth* (2003) 211 CLR 476 [29], Gleeson CJ; compare *Minister for Immigration and Ethnic Affairs* v. *Teoh* (1995) 183 CLR 273, 287, Mason CJ and Deane J.

[80] Human Rights (Parliamentary Scrutiny) Bill 2010, clause 8(4).

[81] *Al-Kateb* v. *Godwin* (2004) 219 CLR 562 [63], [65], McHugh J.

Convention on the Rights of the Child created a legitimate expectation that the executive would act in compliance with the Convention, which in turn gave rise to procedural obligations if it decided not to do so.[82] *Teoh* was met by a storm of protest, however, and its status now is in doubt, following observations by the High Court in *Lam*.[83] These echo, although less forcefully, the dissent by McHugh J in *Teoh* itself, in which he drew attention to the very large number of treaties to which Australia is a party, 'only a small percentage' of which had been enacted into law, concluding that it was not 'reasonable to expect that public officials will comply with the terms of conventions ... merely because the federal government has ratified them'.[84] The second and final context to consider is whether international law can be used in interpreting ambiguous provisions of the Constitution. For the moment, at least, it is clear that this is disapproved by a large majority of the High Court. In a now famous debate with Justice Michael Kirby in *Al-Kateb v Godwin*, McHugh J argued that international legal rules that came into force in the course of the twentieth century could not throw light on the meaning of a Constitution that commenced operation in 1901.[85]

(b) Impact of regimes

The examples given above are relevant to the interaction between international legal regimes, broadly defined, in several ways. They show that the interpretation of legislation by domestic courts can affect the understanding and operation of some international legal regimes within the state and may, in this way, affect the extent of their practical autonomy. They suggest that any fragmentation may be multi-dimensional, lying not only between regimes in the international sphere but between domestic jurisdictions and the domestic and international spheres. They point to emerging evidence that the volume and lack of coordination of international law discourages or, perhaps, offers an excuse to restrain, its effect in domestic law.

The example in this part deals more specifically with the way in which interaction between special international regimes plays out in a domestic context that may, in some cases, exacerbate the effects of lack of coordination in the international sphere. The particular regimes engaged are

82 *Minister of State for Immigration and Ethnic Affairs* v. *Ah Hin Teoh* (1995) 183 CLR 273.

83 *Re Minister for Immigration and Multicultural Affairs; ex p Lam* (2003) 214 CLR 1.

84 At [38], [39].

85 *Al-Kateb* v. *Godwin* (2004) 219 CLR 562.

the Antarctic Treaty System (ATS), the UN Convention on the Law of the Sea (UNCLOS) and the International Convention for the Regulation of Whaling (ICRW).[86]

The ATS relies on consensus and avoidance of the vexed and disputed question of sovereignty over Antarctica. Australia is accustomed to juggling its claims to the Australian Antarctic Territory with participation in the ATS by enforcing the provisions of other treaty arrangements operating in the area only against Australian nationals.[87] This strategy became compromised, as a matter of policy if not law,[88] when Australia legislated to create the Australian Whale Sanctuary and to prohibit the exploitation of whales with operation in the Exclusive Economic Zone (EEZ) offshore the Australian Antarctic Territory.[89] The rights of a coastal state to an EEZ are recognised by UNCLOS, which also acknowledges that such states may 'regulate the exploitation of marine mammals' in these areas.[90] As a matter of Australian constitutional law, the Environmental Protection and Biodiversity Conservation Act (EPBC) is not necessarily dependent on UNCLOS.[91] The legislation was expressed to be enforceable against non-nationals as well as Australian nationals. Critically, it also allowed any 'interested party' to seek an injunction to restrain unlawful conduct. Nevertheless, under Federal Court Rules, if a respondent is outside Australia, the leave of the Court is required to institute proceedings.

The Commonwealth Director of Public Prosecutions (DPP) took no steps to enforce the legislation against non-nationals, thus facilitating domestic harmonisation of the regimes. But in 2004, the Humane Society International (HSI) initiated proceedings against a Japanese company,

[86] See generally Ruth Davis, 'Enforcing Australian Law in Antarctica: the *HSI* litigation' (2007) 8 *Melbourne Journal of International Law* 142, on which much of the following example draws. I am also grateful to research assistance from Cosima McRae, working under the auspices of the Law Research Service of the Melbourne Law School Law Library.

[87] Tim Stephens, 'Editorial: The Japanese Whaling Case: Implications for Australia and Beyond' (2008) 11 (3–4) *Asia Pacific Journal of Environmental Law* 141.

[88] On the exclusion of whaling from the ATS see Chris McGrath, 'Australia Can Lawfully Stop Whaling within its Antarctic EEZ', EDONSW Seminar, 21 February 2008, www.edo.org.au/edonsw/site/pdf/workshop/whales_chris_mcgrath_paper_080225.pdf (viewed 8 July 2011).

[89] Environment Protection and Biodiversity Conservation Act 1999 (Cth) (EPBC Act).

[90] UNCLOS, art. 65.

[91] Natalie Klein and Nikolas Hughes, 'National Litigation and International Law: Repercussions for Australia's Protection of Marine Resources' (2009) 33 *Melbourne University Law Review* 163, 187, also outlining the constitutional foundations for the legislation.

Kyodo, for whaling activities in the EEZ off the Australian Antarctic Territory. Kyodo had a special research permit issued by Japan pursuant to the International Convention for the Regulation of Whaling. The relevance of this was disputed, because of uncertainty about the meaning of section 7 of the Antarctic Treaty (Environment Protection) Act 1980, giving effect to the ATS 'Madrid' Protocol, which provided that 'notwithstanding any other law … no action … lies against any person … in relation to anything done by that person to the extent that it is authorised by a permit or by a recognised foreign authority'. At first instance, the Federal Court described the resulting problems of construction as reflecting:

> the separate development in public international law of the protection of whales as part of the marine environment and the regulation of whaling. It may also be seen to reflect the development of Australian municipal law in implementing marine and environmental protection in the Antarctic.[92]

The Court stood the initial application over, pending notification to the Attorney-General and submissions from the Commonwealth on 'the proper construction and interpretation of the legislation and treaties involved, in particular in the light of what might be seen to be Australia's national interest, including inter-governmental relations between Australia and Japan'.[93] In due course, these submissions were filed by the Attorney-General as amicus curiae, to the effect that the matter was 'best dealt with by the Executive' and that the Court should not exercise its discretion to allow service out of the jurisdiction (or, if it came to it, to grant relief in the nature of an injunction).[94] The Court duly declined to grant leave to effect service out of the jurisdiction.[95] Summarising his reasons at a subsequent stage, Allsop J said:

> … in light of the international position, including the view of Japan that the assertion of jurisdiction in this matter would be a breach of international law, including, but not limited to, the Whaling Convention, of the place of an international body, the IWC, to deal with the issue of the killing of whales for scientific or other purposes, of the expression of the Executive Government of its (non-justiciable) view of Australia's long-term national interest, of the placing of the Court at the centre of

[92] *Humane Society International Inc* v. *Kyodo Senpaku Kaisha Ltd* (2004) 212 ALR 551 [57].
[93] Ibid., [3].
[94] *Humane Society International Inc* v. *Kyodo Senpaku Kaisha Ltd* (2008) 165 FCR 510 [16] summarising the submissions in the earlier case.
[95] *Humane Society International Inc* v. *Kyodo Senpaku Kaisha Ltd* [2005] FCA 664.

> an international dispute (indeed, helping to promote such a dispute) between Australia and a friendly foreign power, and of the likelihood that any attempt to enforce an injunction against the respondent would be futile (a matter that was never seriously contested by the applicant on the application for leave to serve out of Australia), I was not persuaded that the Court's exercise of discretion to grant leave to serve the respondent outside the jurisdiction was appropriate.[96]

This decision was overturned on appeal to the Full Federal Court, however, and the appellant was given leave to serve the summons on Kyodo. Consistently with domestic public law principle, all three judges agreed that 'political considerations' should not be taken into account so as to avoid adjudication if the issue was otherwise justiciable. Two justices also held that relief should not be refused on the ground of futility; the third justice dissented on this point, in the face of what he described as the 'almost certain futility' of the litigation.[97]

The issue was finally joined in substance before the Federal Court in 2008. Allsop J granted a declaration that Kyodo was in breach of the legislation and issued an injunction to restrain further breach.[98] In doing so he noted that it had not proved possible to serve the respondents through diplomatic channels, so that an order for substituted service had been necessary. He accepted that the respondent had committed the alleged acts, on the balance of probabilities, and that the permit held from the Japanese Government did not alter the situation, thereby resolving the disputed question about the meaning and priority of competing legislative provisions. He held that in the light of the Full Federal Court decision, injunctive relief should not be withheld on the ground of futility.

Nevertheless, the injunction was not enforced. Instead, attempts apparently continued to reach an agreed solution through the International Whaling Commission and in bilateral negotiations. Subsequently, in an apparently unconnected move, the Australian Government announced in May 2010 that it would initiate action in the International Court of Justice, alleging a breach by Japan of its obligations under the International Convention for the Regulation of Whaling.[99]

[96] *Humane Society International Inc* v. *Kyodo Senpaku Kaisha Ltd* (2008) 165 FCR 510 [16].

[97] *Humane Society International Inc* v. *Kyodo Senpaku Kaisha Ltd* (2006) 154 FCR 425 [43].

[98] *Humane Society International Inc* v. *Kyodo Senpaku Kaisha Ltd* (2008) 165 FCR 510. For critique of the outcome from the standpoint of the ATS see Don Anton, 'False Sanctuary: The Australian Antarctic Whale Sanctuary and Long-Term Stability in Antarctica' (2008) *Cornell Law School Berger International Speaker Series* 7.

[99] International Court of Justice, Press Release No. 2010/16, 1 June 2010.

Conclusions

This chapter skims the surface of an important inquiry into how domestic and international law interact in matters of detail, beyond the broad principles that are known to apply. It uses Australia as a case study to illustrate how this may occur, subject to the necessary caveat that patterns of interaction will differ from state to state, depending on such considerations as the domestic status of international law, the design of state institutions, and the degree of commitment of the state to coordination of government action within a framework provided by a single system of state law.

Nevertheless, the chapter provides a basis for the following conclusions.

First, states typically attach a degree of priority to coordination. Of course there are limitations on the extent to which coordination is possible; and states may delude themselves as to the extent to which it occurs. Nor is coordination necessarily as valuable as some may think. Nevertheless, there is a contrast in this regard between the domestic and the international sphere, in relation both to the value attached to coordination and the capacity to achieve it.

Secondly, in some states, of which Australia is an example, the traditional governance procedures are not particularly attuned to the needs of international law and the additional challenges that these may present for coordination. The Australian system of government leaves to the executive the responsibility of undertaking international legal obligations. Tension between international legal regimes will not necessarily be identified at this point. If an international commitment requires domestic legal change, further opportunities for coordination arise through the cabinet and parliamentary processes. These were enhanced in Australia from the 1990s when new treaty-making procedures were introduced. It may be that this reflects a more general trend.

Nevertheless, the significance, proliferation and general characteristics of international law place the assumptions on which coordination takes place within the state under further pressure. Incorporation now occurs in a variety of ways. International law influences domestic law in other ways even when it is not incorporated. There is a degree of resistance to the interpenetration of domestic and international law, despite its inevitability. The fragmentation of international law may be only dimly perceived by domestic decision-makers but contributes to the overall impression that somehow international law does not 'fit' the domestic sphere.

The effect of these developments on international legal regimes varies between regimes. To the extent that a regime is reliant on domestic enforcement or application, domestic action may add to or detract from the 'autonomous' operation of the regime. Exactly what occurs will depend on both domestic and international factors. The more self-contained an international regime, the less significant the effect of domestic procedures is likely to be. Even in such cases, however, the relationship between regimes in the international sphere may complicate coordination within the state.

3

Regime Interaction in Creating, Implementing and Enforcing International Law

MARGARET A. YOUNG

Introduction

International laws and institutions have historically developed to address particular issues and objectives such as trade liberalisation and fisheries exploitation. The disparate results are commonly described as 'regimes', such as the trade regime and the law of the sea. These autonomous and relatively uncoordinated branches of international law have differing mandates, principles and structures, as well as non-identical state membership. Global problems, however, do not fit neatly within single regimes. This gives rise to the potential for conflicting norms between regimes, a preoccupation of much of the current literature addressing international law's fragmentation. It also gives rise to the situation of ongoing institutional diversity and pluralism, and the day-to-day and relatively mundane occurrences of overlapping norms and inter-regime activity. The latter situation is under-explored in the literature. In particular, there is uncertainty about how regimes interact, and how they should interact.

The current chapter addresses this gap by highlighting empirical evidence of regime interaction in the creation, implementation and enforcement of international law relating to fisheries, and building a normative argument for appropriate and accountable regime interaction in international law.[1] Drawing on examples of institutional collaboration and normative overlap between organisations such as the World Trade Organization (WTO), the United Nations Food and Agriculture Organization (FAO), and the Secretariat for the Convention on the International Trade in Endangered Species of Wild Fauna and Flora

[1] Much of the empirical research outlined here is contained in Margaret A. Young, *Trading Fish, Saving Fish: The Interaction Between Regimes in International Law* (Cambridge University Press, 2011).

(CITES),[2] this chapter examines the legal bases for the interaction between international legal regimes. In particular, it seeks to ascertain the theoretical conceptions of legitimacy that underpin such interaction, whether derived from state consent or something else. This leads to an investigation of alternative conceptions of legitimacy, which may depend less on representativeness and more on the deliberative credentials of the participants of regime interaction, including intergovernmental organisations (IGOs) and non-governmental organisations (NGOs). An argument is advanced for a legal framework of regime interaction, where inter-regime scrutiny is constant and continuous, without any hierarchy between regimes.

A. Law-making, implementation and adjudication in fisheries governance

The phenomenon of fragmented fisheries governance provides important insights into the interests and motivation for regime interaction. The normative and institutional pluralism, which is emphasised here using examples from four selected international regimes, give rise to overlapping activities and major challenges during the making and implementation of law and the settlement of disputes, as the current section describes.

1. Selected regimes

In providing a typology of regimes, the introduction to the current volume includes one 'hybrid' definition of regimes as 'sets of norms, decision-making procedures and organisations coalescing around functional issue-areas and dominated by particular modes of behaviour, assumptions and biases'.[3] Applying this definition to the context of fisheries governance points to a number of relevant regimes.

Cooperative efforts to manage fishing across nations, and an increasing awareness of the severity of the global fish crisis,[4] have given rise to multiple international laws.[5] The primary set of norms, decision-making procedures and organisations, which centres on the function and

[2] Convention on the International Trade in Endangered Species of Wild Fauna and Flora, 993 UNTS 243 (in force 1 July 1975).

[3] Young, 'Introduction: The Productive Friction between Regimes' in this volume, p. 9.

[4] The gravity of the over-exploitation of global fisheries stock is depicted in a range of studies, including the FAO's biennial publication, *State of the World Fisheries and Aquaculture* (SOFIA).

[5] A detailed summary is provided in Young, *Trading Fish, Saving Fish*, above n. 1, 32–82.

accompanying vocabulary of sustainable fisheries utilisation, is the law of the sea regime. It seeks to promote sustainable utilisation by dividing the ocean into areas of coastal jurisdiction and high seas with key instruments such as the United Nations Convention on the Law of the Sea (UNCLOS)[6] and the Fish Stocks Agreement.[7] A related regime is the FAO fisheries management regime, which collects and publishes data about the state of the world's fisheries and promotes responsible fishing practices and port-state measures to combat problems in fisheries governance, such as the prevalence of illegal, unreported and unregulated fishing (IUU Fishing).[8] A third regime is the CITES species protection regime, underpinned by CITES and its associated trade-sanctioning mechanisms. Finally, the international trade regime headed by the WTO,[9] which seeks to facilitate trade liberalisation and to discipline certain subsidies that might be distorting trade, has multiple impacts upon, and rules about, the international trade in fish. In particular, the WTO's disciplines on subsidies provide a relevant set of rules that could combat the skewed economics of the fishing sector, which receives massive financial support from states to build more and more boats, even as fish stocks decline.[10]

The list of four regimes outlined above is not an exhaustive one – there are inevitably a number of existing and emerging international, transnational and regional regimes that affect the sustainability of fisheries.[11]

[6] United Nations Convention on the Law of the Sea (1982) 21 ILM 1261 (1982) (in force 16 November 1994).

[7] Agreement for the Implementation of the Provisions of the United Nations Convention on the Law of the Sea of 10 December 1982 relating to the Conservation and Management of Straddling Fish Stocks and Highly Migratory Fish Stocks (1995) 34 ILM 1547 (in force 11 December 2001).

[8] A key instrument is the 1995 Code of Conduct for Responsible Fisheries, which also contains the Agreement to Promote Compliance with International Conservation and Management Measures by Fishing Vessels on the High Seas, adopted in 1993. In 2009, the FAO adopted the Agreement on Port State Measures to Prevent, Deter and Eliminate Illegal, Unreported and Unregulated Fishing, which is yet to enter into force.

[9] See Agreement Establishing the World Trade Organization (signed 15 April 1994) in WTO, *The Legal Texts* (Cambridge University Press, 1999) 3 and associated WTO-covered agreements.

[10] The WTO's Agreement on Subsidies and Countervailing Measures (SCM Agreement) provides disciplines for certain subsidies. See further Margaret A. Young, 'Fragmentation or Interaction: The WTO, Fisheries Subsidies and International Law' (2009) 8 *World Trade Review* 477.

[11] For example, there is an emerging understanding of the potential significance of the climate change regime, headed by the United Nations Framework Convention on Climate Change and its associated instruments such as the Kyoto Protocol, given the causal link between the depletion of fish stocks and global warming. A range of other

Moreover, their short description is offered with all the caveats appropriate to the use of the terminology 'regimes', as set out in the introduction to the current volume.[12] There is, for example, a risk in reducing any of these four regimes to a single set of characteristics that precludes a debate about those characteristics or their evolution – the trade regime, for one, contains many conflicting perspectives and preferences.[13] The danger is especially great if it forecloses the process of regime interaction, or alternatively treats the convergence of legal arrangements as inevitable.[14] Moreover, the study of these regimes must be undertaken in parallel with an understanding of the general principles and overall system of international law.[15] As such, the present chapter highlights the dominant and open-ended characteristics of the selected regimes, with an eye to the perspectives that may be left out when actors within the regimes meet with others in governing fisheries. Indeed, these interactions may be conceived as political wrangling between regimes, or as political contestations about the definitions of regimes themselves.

Four aspects of these four regimes are immediately obvious, which influence how they interact. First, the relevant laws were largely developed at different times. Secondly, they are implemented by different institutions, which have different powers of enforcement and relative strengths.[16] Thirdly, there is not uniform ratification of these laws by all states. They are *mostly* agreed by the same states, of course, but there are differences, and some members meet the membership requirements of some but not all the relevant organisations.[17] Fourthly, as has already been

regimes conceive of illegal fishing behaviour as transnational 'environmental crimes': see United Nations Office of Drugs and Crime, *Transnational Organized Crime in the Fishing Industry* (2011).

12 See Margaret Young, 'Introduction' in this volume, pp. 10–11.

13 See further ibid., p.10 and sources cited therein.

14 For a critique of functionalism, see Roberto Unger, *What Should Legal Analysis Become* (Verso, 1996) 123–126.

15 See further Young, 'Introduction' in this volume at p. 10.

16 The WTO, with its compulsory dispute settlement procedures, represents the strongest regime. The law of the sea's attenuated enforcement procedures rate it higher than both the CITES domestic trade sanctions and the FAO fisheries management regime's soft law instruments.

17 See, e.g. Taiwan enjoys full WTO membership as a customs territory, but without UN status is not able to join the FAO. There are several FAO members that are not WTO Members (from Russia to small African fishing nations such as Seychelles and Sao Tome and Principe).

made clear: these laws aim to fulfill particular sets of preferences within the international legal system, which may not be in harmony.

The potential for collision between preferences (and, therefore, the conflict between the norms of regimes) has led to a range of responses, most obviously in the seminal study by the International Law Commission (ILC). The ILC Study Group concentrated on situations where international norms operated in a relationship of interpretation or conflict, which occur most notoriously when international judicial tribunals are required to resolve conflicting norms.[18] In the regimes selected here, however, it is largely a different set of problems that arise: in responding to the global fisheries crisis, decision-makers are confronted less by conflicting norms and more by constraints and ambiguities in the day-to-day institutional interaction and normative overlap between regimes. The challenges of 'regime interaction' are present not only in disputes between countries, but at other 'stages' of international law-making and implementation.

2. *Interaction across 'stages'*

The most notorious situations of regime interaction occur in disputes. The paradigmatic example is when an international tribunal rules upon norms that span other regimes, such as the WTO Appellate Body's reference to CITES in articulating its concept of 'sustainable development' (and assessing the threats to marine turtles) in the *US-Shrimp* dispute.[19] Even more infamous is the possibility of disputes being heard in parallel forums, as seemed likely by the threatened litigation between the EU and Chile during the *Swordfish* dispute.[20] Such occurrences give rise to the need to resolve conflicting norms (and have recourse to the ILC's toolbox) but also rely on institutional procedures for regime interplay, such as the

[18] ILC Study Group, 'Fragmentation of International Law: Difficulties arising from the Diversification and Expansion of International Law, Conclusions of the Work of the Study Group' (A/CN.4/L.702) (18 July 2006), Conclusion (2), 7–8 (distinguishing between situations where one norm assists in the interpretation of another and where the application of two norms would lead to incompatible decisions). The ILC Study Group's recommendations are briefly summarised in Young, 'Introduction' in this volume, at pp. 2–4.

[19] Appellate Body Report, *United States – Import Prohibition of Certain Shrimp and Shrimp Products*, WT/DS58/AB/R (circulated 12 October 1998) (DSR 1998:VII, 2755).

[20] See Marcos Orellana, 'The Swordfish Dispute between the EU and Chile at the ITLOS and the WTO' (2002) 71 *Nordic Journal of International Law* 55.

filing of *amicus* briefs from environment groups in *US-Shrimp* and the formal consultation between international organisations.[21]

Aside from dispute settlement, regime interaction occurs at other stages of international law. In *law-making* there is uncertainty and ambiguity in how existing institutions interact both in the law's formulation and future application. Efforts to negotiate new disciplines on fisheries subsidies at the WTO, which are hoped to reduce global vessel capacity, are illustrative of the challenges. The inclusion of perspectives on fisheries management and conservation from the law of the sea regime and the FAO fisheries management regime has been essential for the crafting of new rules, especially given allegations in other contexts that the WTO has an 'ecological blindspot'.[22] In the face of formal restrictions on access to the negotiations within the 'Member-driven Organisation' of the WTO, separate processes of knowledge production about fisheries subsidies have emerged, including within IGOs like the United Nations Environment Programme (UNEP) and NGOs like the World Wide Fund for Nature (WWF). Attempts have been made to include the perspectives of 'stakeholders', including trade delegates, fisheries delegates, environmental delegates, secretariat staff, fisheries experts and representatives from NGOs. Significantly, the learning and engagement between a range of actors has led to proposals for innovative institutional and normative arrangements within the rules themselves. As detailed elsewhere,[23] these include the possible use of standards and benchmarks from the Fish Stocks Agreement and FAO soft-law instruments, as well as the involvement of the FAO as a peer-reviewer of WTO member fishing practices. These provisions for ongoing regime interaction have given rise to complaints that the practices of an endogenous set of institutions will alter the rights of WTO members in an illegitimate way.

In addition, in the *implementation of existing obligations*, there are challenges when organisations seek to address similar objectives, such as fisheries conservation, under different principles and structures. Implementation often occurs within lesser-known intergovernmental committees and working parties,[24] and must be particularly attendant to

[21] See further Young, *Trading Fish, Saving Fish*, above n. 1, 189–240. For other WTO-related examples, see James Flett in Ch. 9 of this volume, pp. 272–290.

[22] Oren Perez, *Ecological Sensitivity and Global Legal Pluralism: Rethinking the Trade and Environment Conflict* (Hart Publishing, 2004).

[23] See Young, *Trading Fish, Saving Fish*, above n. 1, 105–133; see also Young, 'Fragmentation or Interaction', above n. 10, 98–508.

[24] Andrew Lang and Joanne Scott, 'The Hidden World of WTO Governance' (2009) 20 *European Journal of International Law* 575.

the possibilities and constraints of regime interaction. Indeed, seemingly innocuous arrangements, like a memorandum of understanding between intergovernmental organisations, can become key tools for entrenching regime hierarchy. This was borne out during efforts to protect endangered marine species, when CITES parties, which had historically concentrated only on land-based species, sought to list endangered marine species such as dolphins, sharks and sea-horses. As part of this process, the CITES Secretariat and the FAO established cooperative arrangements for the sharing of data and technical expertise on marine species. Fishing states, displeased at the effect a CITES listing would have on commercial trade, first argued that CITES had no mandate to deal with fisheries, and then sought to insert a clause that CITES listings of marine species should be 'limited to exceptional cases … when all relevant bodies associated with the management of the species … agree'.[25] The drafting of a memorandum of understanding between the FAO and the CITES Secretariat was thus used by some states to promote 'soft-law' within one regime over harder obligations within another,[26] even when this could amount to an unlawful *inter se* modification of treaty obligations.

These examples demonstrate that regime interaction occurs during the making, implementation and enforcement of international law, and that it involves more than simple technical issues of mandate or coordination. While the literature on fragmentation has so far concentrated mainly on the resolution of conflicting norms, which occurs *after* laws are negotiated or have otherwise become custom, a study into regime interaction must incorporate many stages of legal development and application.[27] To do so involves adopting a perspective on the nature of the law, which requires a sophisticated understanding of state practice, multilateral negotiations, institutional developments and the judicial funtion.[28] A theory of regime interaction that concentrates solely on the paradigmatic case of conflicting norms before a tribunal is underinclusive.

Whenever and wherever regime interaction occurs, it potentially affects the rights and duties of states. My research on global fisheries issues

[25] See further Young, *Trading Fish, Saving Fish*, above n. 1, 134–154.

[26] On the relative strengths of the regimes discussed here, see above n. 16. For examples in other international contexts, see Gregory Shaffer and Mark Pollack, 'Hard Law vs Soft Law: Alternatives, Complements and Antagonists in International Governance' (2010) 94 *Minnesota Law Review* 706.

[27] This point is also made by Jeffrey Dunoff in Ch. 5 of this volume.

[28] See further Young, 'Introduction' in this volume, p. 9.

confirms that a state's conception of its 'sovereignty' is often tested in the meeting of international regimes. For example, a state that has joined the WTO but not the FAO may find itself subject to FAO norms if the FAO has an active role as peer-reviewer of proposed WTO disciplines on fisheries subsidies. If that state is a party to CITES, its rights might be diminished by the application of FAO scientific principles to the listings of marine species on the CITES appendices. On the other hand, a state that is not a party to CITES may nonetheless find that its WTO rights are affected by a listing of species if such a listing is found to be determinative in a WTO dispute to which it is a party.

Given the impact on sovereignty of regime interaction – as highlighted here and elsewhere in this volume – it is important to inquire into its legal basis. If regime interaction is *not* based on the consent of the formal participants of international law – the states themselves – other legal bases for regime interaction must be located, and an assessment made as to their legitimacy, as set out in the next section. Before doing so, the remainder of this section explores the major impediments to regime interaction as encountered in the international fisheries context.

3. *Impediments to regime interaction*

A major impediment to regime interaction is the attempt to limit or reduce the role of one regime vis-à-vis another by carving up international governance into set functional areas. Such attempts occurred in the negotiations on fish subsidies rules and in the drafting of the memorandum of understanding between CITES and the FAO.[29]

The idea that there should be an *a priori* determination of competence for an international organisation to address a particular policy issue accords with some perspectives of international institutional law. In *Use of Nuclear Weapons* the ICJ, by eleven votes to three, rejected a request for an advisory ruling on the legality of nuclear weapons from the World Health Organization (WHO). The majority considered that international organisations, unlike states, do not possess general competence but are governed by the 'principle of speciality'.[30]

Like the dissent of Judge Weeramantry, who considered that the principle of speciality fails to recognise that 'complex problems have

[29] See further Young, *Trading Fish, Saving Fish*, above n. 1, 258–261.

[30] *Use of Nuclear Weapons in Armed Conflict* (1999) (I) ICJ Rep 66.

ramifications in many specialized directions',[31] I conclude that the parcelling out of special and exclusive competences fails to address real complexities. In the fisheries context, classifying and locating policy problems relating to fisheries sustainability within bounded legal structures and institutions is counterproductive. There is no 'right' solution to fisheries sustainability that will be determined when the correct decision-makers are in charge. Addressing perverse incentives is within the realm of the WTO, the FAO and regional and specific organisations such as the Organisation for Economic Co-operation and Development (OECD). Similarly, that the WTO adjudicated the dispute in *US-Shrimp* does not mean that other regimes such as CITES are not relevant to import restrictions on marine species. There is a situation of continuing diversity and imbalance in international law, and emerging problems require different institutional and normative responses.

A further factor that impedes regime interaction is the lack of policy coordination at the domestic level.[32] In consultations for improving general ocean governance, for example, the UN's Under-Secretary-General for Legal Affairs has recognised that national level cooperation and coordination is essential, and that 'coordinated and strategic national government actions and initiatives in different international forums are crucial for the development of the required interlinkages and synergies'.[33] Many states acknowledged the need for national policy coordination during efforts to list endangered marine species on CITES, especially between conservation and fisheries departments.

Although the emphasis on inter-agency collaboration is important, national policy coordination is but one tool for the promotion of regime interaction and should not be overstated. The need for regulation in global fisheries is due to collective problems *between* states. Addressing issues that span national borders requires more than just national decision-making.[34] Similarly, a set of coherent but wrong national policies will not achieve fisheries sustainability. The varying resources of states

[31] Ibid., 151.

[32] See further Young, *Trading Fish, Saving Fish*, above n. 1, 249–253. For descriptions of coordinating efforts within Australia, see Cheryl Saunders in Ch. 2 of this volume.

[33] UN Doc A/55/274, Annex I, para. 15.

[34] For a similar observation in respect of other examples such as global poverty and AIDS, see Andreas Paulus, 'Subsidiarity, Fragmentation and Democracy: Towards the Demise of General International Law' in Tomer Broude and Yuval Shany (eds.), *The Shifting Allocation of Authority in International Law* (Hart Publishing, 2008) 193, 205.

also mitigates against national policy coordination as the sole panacea to problems of regime interaction. The capacity of a least-developed-country member of the WTO to coordinate on domestic policies will be very strained, particularly if it already finds its 'policy space' diminished by the growth of regimes. Morever, enhanced policy coordination cannot remedy the situations when states deliberately argue different positions in different forums.[35]

A further impediment to regime interaction is a lack of transparency and openness within a particular regime. For example, the use of closed 'working groups' within FAO fora, which excluded representatives from the CITES Secretariat, contributed to the delay in the memorandum of understanding between the two organisations. The initial decision by WTO Members to exclude observers to their fisheries subsidies negotiations led to alternative forums for deliberation and information-sharing in external agencies such as UNEP. WTO dispute settlement proceedings remain largely closed to non-parties, although the submission of *amicus* briefs and consultation between panels and IGOs goes some way to allowing for regime interplay. Regime insularity exists during the making, implementation and enforcement of international law, and is maintained because of the concern of states about the legal basis and legitimacy of loosening their control over the relevant forums.

B. Legal bases and legitimacy of regime interaction

A study of regime interaction during the making, implementation and enforcement of international law reveals that there is no single legal basis upon which such interaction occurs. Instead, there are multiple bases, which in the context of fisheries governance fall into three broad categories.[36]

1. *Parallel membership*

The first and strictest conception of a legal basis for regime interaction requires all member states of each regime to have adopted mutual norms

[35] For examples, see Doaa Abdel Motaal, 'The Trade and Environment Policy Formulation Process' in Adil Najam, Mark Halle and Ricardo Meléndez-Ortiz (eds.), *Trade and Environment: A Resource Book* (IISDetal, 2007) 17, 23; see also Stephen Humphreys' observations of the strategic positions put forward by states in Ch. 6 of this volume, pp. 178–182.

[36] Young, *Trading Fish, Saving Fish*, above n. 1, 267–271.

before they can have influence. Otherwise, if a state is not a member of a regime, yet a second regime to which it *is* a member is influenced by that regime, any normative effects of this regime interaction invalidly alter the rights and duties of this state. The idea that regimes must have parallel membership before they interact is true to the positivist commitment to state consent in international law which appears to grant full assurances as to legitimacy.[37] Yet it is a flawed ideal on both practical and theoretical grounds.

In practice, proponents of the idea that 'parallel membership' must be a prerequisite to regime interaction are generally limited to entities that for practical or strategic reasons have not signed up to the relevant regimes (exemplified by a Taiwanese objection to the FAO's proposed role in the WTO subsidies disciplines[38]) or tribunals confronted with the quandary of interpreting conflicting treaties when disputing parties are members of one but not both of the treaties (which bewildered a WTO panel when it interpreted Article 31(3)(c) of the Vienna Convention on the Law of Treaties in the *EU-Biotech* dispute[39]). More commonly, in situations where trade, fisheries and environmental regimes overlap, states that are affected by such overlap ensure that they sign up to the relevant regimes. States that question the mandates of international organisations seem to be doing so *not* because of their lack of consent to norm-setting processes, but because of their perceived lack of *control* over those processes.[40]

At a theoretical level, the idea of 'parallel membership', if applied to the letter, would give non-parties a veto over the evolution of international law. For example, Angola, which is a member of the WTO and the FAO but not CITES, would have a notional veto against the influence of CITES norms on the operation of the WTO and FAO regimes. Uzbekistan, which belongs to CITES and the FAO but not the WTO, would have a notional

[37] For the premise of interstate consensus as a source of legitimacy of law, see, e.g. Andreas Paulus, 'The Legitimacy of International Law and the Role of the State' (2004) 25 *Michigan Journal of International Law* 1047; for critique, see Andreas Fischer-Lescano and Gunther Teubner, 'Consensus as Fiction of Global Law' (2004) 25 *Michigan Journal of International Law* 1095.

[38] As stated above n. 17, Taiwan is a WTO Member but does not have FAO membership; see further Young, 'Fragmentation or Interaction', above n. 10, 503.

[39] Panel Report, *EC – Measures Affecting the Approval and Marketing of Biotech Products Panel Report* WT/DS291/R, WT/DS292/R, WT/DS293/R (circulated 29 September 2006) (DSR 2006:III, 847). See further Margaret A. Young, 'The WTO's use of relevant rules of international law: an analysis of the Biotech case' (2007) 56 *International and Comparative Law Quarterly* 907. For further examples of proponents of the idea, see Young, *Trading Fish, Saving Fish*, above n. 1, 262–266.

[40] See further Young, *Trading Fish, Saving Fish*, above n. 1, 263–264.

veto against the use of trade norms in elaborating the legal activities and influence of CITES and the FAO. Singapore, which is a member of the WTO and CITES but not the FAO, would have a notional veto over the normative influence of the FAO on fisheries issues as they are enforced in the WTO and CITES regimes. The point is not that these countries are actively obstructing the interaction between the regimes – they are mainly on the fringes of regime interplay. Nor do I claim that the views of these states are not important. The point is rather that the model of international law that requires two regimes to have parallel membership before they can influence each other's norms, if applied rigorously, allows a minority of states – even a minority of one – to veto the development of international law.

2. *Mutual agreement*

A less extreme version of the requirement for consent from members of both regimes envisages that states can agree to allow normative and institutional interplay, notwithstanding that not all members have adopted the relevant regimes. This second category of 'mutual agreement' to regime interaction is contained in relevant treaties (such as the provision in CITES that opens its regular conferences to qualified representatives from IGOs and NGOs[41]) as well as standalone agreements (such as the FAO member resolution that provides for ongoing relations with IGOs[42]), and still appears to guarantee legitimacy. The proposed fisheries subsidies rules provide innovative ways in which future interaction between the WTO, FAO and other regimes would assist in disciplining trade-distorting and ecologically harmful subsidies.[43]

Regime interaction through mutual agreement appears at first glance to satisfy legitimacy concerns, given the implicit consent of states parties to resulting normative influence. Yet examples from the WTO's Agreement on Sanitary and Phytosanitary Measures (SPS Agreement)[44] and Agreement on Technical Barriers to Trade (TBT Agreement)[45]

[41] CITES, Art. XI(7).

[42] FAO Guiding Lines Regarding Relationship Agreements Between FAO and IGOs (Resolution of 10th session of FAO Conference).

[43] For further examples, see Young, *Trading Fish, Saving Fish*, above n. 1, 269–270.

[44] Agreement on the Application of Sanitary and Phytosanitary Measures (signed 15 April 1994) in WTO, *The Legal Texts* (Cambridge University Press, 1999) 59.

[45] Agreement on Technical Barriers to Trade (signed 15 April 1994) in WTO, *The Legal Texts* (Cambridge University Press, 1999) 121.

demonstrate that concerns continue to arise. Those agreements draw on standards from exogenous regimes in the following way: in general terms, if members' trade measures conform to international standards, they may be exempted from onerous WTO commitments or presumed necessary for domestic objectives such as the protection of human health. In WTO disputes, parties have argued against this use of standards, especially when the standards were not adopted by consensus within the relevant exogenous regime.[46] Such disagreements place particular pressure on the dispute-settlement bodies involved,[47] but also arise at other 'stages' of law-making and implementation.

3. *Institutional arrangements*

A third basis for regime interaction comes from formal or informal arrangements within and between the international organisations themselves. Formally, such arrangements might be subject to careful control and consent by states parties, as exemplified by the memorandum of understanding between the CITES Secretariat and the FAO regarding marine species. However, such arrangements may also be informal. Arrangements may emerge because in carrying out their functions, IGO secretariats and adjudicating bodies find it necessary to learn, share and adopt norms and information from external sources. For example, even prior to the memorandum of understanding, the FAO was instrumental in updating CITES rules on appendices listings, and the UNEP's fisheries subsidies workshops influenced the WTO negotiations.[48] Such initiatives facilitate mutual learning and play important roles in a kind of post-sovereign, non-hierarchical form of governance.

Divorced from the direct consent or demands of states parties, the possibility that regime interaction through informal institutional arrangements has normative influence gives rise to questions of legitimacy. There is an associated need to ensure that information shared between regimes is sufficiently scrutinised and contested, and that a range of voices are heard (beyond those of scientific or technical experts or the 'managers'

[46] See, e.g. Appellate Body Report, *European Communities Trade Description of Sardines* (WT/DS231/AB/R) (circulated 26 September 2002) (DSR 2002:VIII, 3359).

[47] Joanne Scott, 'International Trade and Environmental Governance: Relating Rules (and Standards) in the EU and the WTO' (2004) 15 *European Journal of International Law* 307.

[48] For further examples, see Young, *Trading Fish, Saving Fish*, above n. 1, 270–271.

of the regimes). I argue in the following section that these questions are answered by a legal framework of regime interaction.

C. Towards a legal framework of regime interaction

If, through its influence on international norms, regime interaction alters the rights of states, it is important to have regard to its legitimacy. Yet locating the source of legitimacy will differ depending on the bases from which regime interaction has emerged, namely parallel membership, mutual agreement or institutional arrangements.[49]

1. Consent and sovereignty

Where regime interaction occurs through parallel membership or mutual agreement, any consequent impact on the rights of affected states appears to be legitimate. As explained above, conceptions of sovereignty emphasise the supreme authority of states, and hold that states should not be subject to specific international laws, or the effects of regime interaction, except by consent. In its most extreme form, most commonly encountered in the context of the WTO, conceptions of sovereignty require regimes to be 'self-contained'. Such conceptions also seek to safeguard coherence by prioritising coordination at the domestic level, which as outlined above is an important corrective to problems of regime interaction on issues of fisheries sustainability.

Regime interaction through institutional arrangements may also conform to traditional conceptions of sovereignty, especially when such arrangements are made according to the express powers of IGOs. Yet the appropriateness of IGO collaboration *without* the direct consent of IGO members rests on other factors. Such factors need to be carefully considered and articulated. As long-emphasised, the theoretical and practical deficiencies of sovereignty do not themselves found radical proposals for change; alternative means must be located and developed first.[50] According to my research into regime interaction, these factors relate to the legal capacities of the particular IGOs, the substance of the

[49] The following ideas are developed from Young, *Trading Fish, Saving Fish*, above n. 1, 267–287.

[50] See e.g. Benedict Kingsbury, 'Sovereignty and Inequality' (1998) 9 *European Journal of International Law* 599.

intersecting norms and the fulfilment of several procedural safeguards for openness and accountability, as I describe below.

2. *Express and implied powers*

The capacity of IGOs to make institutional arrangements with other regimes is sometimes expressed in the relevant constitutive instruments. For example, there is express provision for the WTO to cooperate with the International Monetary Fund (IMF) and the World Bank in its founding instrument,[51] and an express power of the FAO to enter a memorandum of understanding with other IGOs.[52]

By contrast, member states sometimes choose to retain the power to make consultative arrangements with other IGOs and NGOs. WTO members, for example, retain the responsibility for making 'appropriate arrangements' for effective cooperation and consultation with IGOs and NGOs.[53] On this basis, the WTO General Council has entered into agreements with the UN and other IGOs.[54] By corollary, it could be suggested that such provisions deny the ability of IGOs to collaborate independently with external sources.

The legal basis for informal, institution-led collaboration resides, instead, in implicit powers. IGOs such as the WTO may have the implied power to take account of external sources because it is necessary for them to do so as part of their functions. This argument builds on the *UN Reparations* case, in which the ICJ pointed to several necessary UN functions in assessing whether the UN had legal personality and the capacity to bring its claim to the Court.[55]

[51] Marrakesh Agreement Art. III(5).

[52] FAO Constitution, Art. XIII(1); cf. the absence of such power for the CITES Secretariat, notwithstanding the authorisation for the Conference of the Parties to 'make such provision as may be necessary to enable the Secretariat to carry out its duty': CITES Art. XII(2)(a),(b).

[53] Marrakesh Agreement Art. V.

[54] In addition to the UN, the General Council has entered into agreements with the World Intellectual Property Organization (WIPO), the World Bank, the IMF, the World Organisation for Animal Health (OIE) and the International Telecommunications Union. Specialised councils within the WTO, namely the WTO's Services Council and the TRIPS (trade-related aspects of intellectual property rights) Council, had important roles in discussing and adopting the texts of these agreements in the services and intellectual property sector: see Pieter Jan Kuijper, 'Some institutional issues presently before the WTO' in Daniel Kennedy and James Southwick (eds.), *The Political Economy of International Trade Law: Essays in Honour of Robert E Hudec* (Cambridge University Press, 2002) 81, 108.

[55] (1949) ICJ Rep 174.

In assessing the capacity of the UN to bring an international claim, the Court found that its legal personality and rights and duties were different from those possessed by a state.[56] Instead, the rights and duties of an entity like the UN 'must depend upon its purposes and functions as specified or implied in its constituent documents and developed in practice'.[57] In the context of the UN's claims for reparations, the Court found that the UN's functions 'are of such a character that they could not be effectively discharged if they involved the concurrent action, on the international plane, of fifty-eight or more Foreign Offices'.[58] On this basis, the Court concluded that the members of the UN had endowed it with the capacity to bring international claims 'when necessitated by the discharge of its functions'.[59]

The centrality of the test for the UN's capacities was the question of 'necessity'. The Court decided that the UN had the capacity to claim reparations for the injury of one of its agents, both for the damage caused to the UN and to the victim itself.[60] This was found to be necessary to enable the UN to 'entrust its agents with important missions to be performed in disturbed parts of the world'.[61] By contrast, it was not considered necessary by the majority in the advisory opinion on *Use of Nuclear Weapons* for the WHO to have the competence to address the legality of the use of nuclear weapons, 'even in view of their health and environmental effects'.[62] As stated above, the Court found that the principle of implied powers was subject to the principle of speciality of international organisations.

Although sharply limited by the majority approach in *Use of Nuclear Weapons*, the principle of implied powers is highly relevant to the phenomenon of fragmentation in international law. In circumstances where regimes are dependent on other regimes, such as the WTO's proposed reliance on standard-setting and benchmarking functions in the fishery subsidy disciplines, IGOs will have the discretion to learn and apply norms and facts from external sources because such collaboration is necessary for their functions.

In fisheries governance, it is functionally necessary for IGOs to take account of multiple interests and institutions. These interests are variously economic, consumerist, ecological and ecocentric. Where states do

[56] Ibid., 179. [57] Ibid., 180. [58] Ibid.
[59] Ibid. [60] Ibid., 180–181; 184.
[61] Ibid., 193; cf. the dissent by Judge Hackworth that the exercise of the power to make private claims had not been shown to be necessary for the exercise of the UN's powers: ibid., 198.
[62] (1996) ICJ Rep 66, 79.

not represent these interests, it may be functionally necessary for IGOs to collaborate with non-state actors that do, including NGOs and other IGOs. This argument finds support in studies that demonstrate how a lack of awareness of important interests that fall outside traditional structures of representation leads to flawed decision-making. For example, the lack of standing of natural objects such as trees or rivers means that ecological concerns are often not 'matters for judicial cognizance', leading to cases skewed against environmental issues.[63] Ethnographies of domestic and supranational legislative processes have also exposed a need for enhanced representation of non-dominant interests.[64]

An assessment of what is 'functionally necessary' for international organisations to carry out their functions in fisheries governance does not depend solely on issues of representation. Such an assessment also flows from an awareness of the complexity of problems associated with achieving sustainability and the need for open deliberation about these issues. The sustainability of fisheries utilisation and trade is not simply a matter of obtaining cooperation between representative states.[65] There is a range of additional complexities, not least of which are the scientific and technical limitations of predicting stock behaviour in the context of the 'eco-system'. Although the drafters of UNCLOS were conscious 'that the problems of ocean space are closely interrelated and need to be considered as a whole',[66] the problems of ocean space link with problems of land – in short, with the full ambit of human activity. In these terms, the management and conservation of fisheries fulfil conditions of a 'wicked problem'[67] where there can be no definitive formulation or solution.[68] Co-existence of multiple variables makes it impossible to determine whether fisheries sustainability depends on trade policies that target supply and demand,

[63] See Christopher Stone, 'Should Trees Have Standing? Toward Legal Rights for Natural Objects' in Christopher Stone, *Should Trees Have Standing?: and other Essays On Law, Morals, and the Environment* (Oceana Publishing, 1996) 1, 10.

[64] See e.g. Francis Snyder, 'Thinking about "Interests": Legislative Process in the European Community' in June Starr and Jane Collier (eds.), *History and Power in the Study of Law: New Directions in Legal Anthropology* (Cornell University Press, 1989) 168.

[65] The problem of obtaining state cooperation has been centralised in the collective action literature: see e.g. Elinor Ostrom, *Governing the Commons: the Evolution of Institutions for Collective Action* (Cambridge University Press, 1990).

[66] UNCLOS, Preamble.

[67] The term comes from Horst Rittel: see, e.g. Horst Rittel and Melvin Webber, 'Dilemmas in a General Theory of Planning' (1973) 4 *Policy Sciences* 155.

[68] As compared, e.g. to a problem of chess or mathematics: see ibid., 160.

environmental regulation, rights-based approaches or even policies that address a completely different issue like climate change.

As set out above, there is no 'right' solution of fisheries sustainability that will be determined when the correct decision-makers are in charge. Instead, there is need for open cross-forum experimentation seeking to address current and potential fisheries stock failures. Trade policy has been harnessed as a possible tool to ensure the effectiveness of fisheries management strategies, in order to address limitations in enforcement. This has led to the need for IGOs like the WTO and the CITES Secretariat to work with other IGOs and NGOs with expertise and interest in fisheries. To address the sustainability of fisheries, there is a need for learning and peer review within a wide range of international organisations, not just the ones with traditional mandates for fisheries management.

The awareness of the need for diverse and pluralistic solutions accords with literature that downplays the need for representation in governance and explores instead the practical need for diverse perspectives.[69] Even if NGOs do not have representative functions, for example, some commentators call for their participation in WTO decision-making to ensure the inclusion of ideas that are 'overlooked or undervalued by governments'.[70] Enhanced participation can also aid in the practical implementation of the resulting rules, as is demonstrated by studies of international environmental commitments.[71] In the field of systems theory, analysts consider that regularised forms of openness are required in order to counteract the 'closure', or the fixing of processes, caused by the creation of institutions.[72] Apart from these practical imperatives for openness and transparency, the moral content of environmental issues has relevance in demonstrating

[69] See in relation to the setting of product standards, Harm Shepel, *The Constitution of Private Governance: Product Standards in the Regulation of Integrating Markets* (Hart Publishing, 2005) 412–413; and in relation to EU governance, Deirdre Curtin, 'Private Interest Representation or Civil Society Deliberation? A Contemporary Dilemma for European Union Governance' (2003) 12 *Social and Legal Studies* 55.

[70] Steve Charnovitz, 'WTO Cosmopolitics' (2002) 34 *NYU Journal of International Law & Politics* 299, 343.

[71] David Victor, Kal Raustiala and Eugene Skolnikoff, 'Introduction and Overview' in David Victor, Kal Raustiala and Eugene Skolnikoff (eds.), *The Implementation and Effectiveness of International Environmental Commitments: Theory and Practice* (The MIT Press, 1998) 1, 21–24 (noting the role of open participation in implementation).

[72] Philip Selznick, 'Self-Regulation and the Theory of Institutions' in Gunther Teubner, Lindsay Farmer and Declan Murphy (eds.), *Environmental Law and Ecological Responsibility: The Concept and Practice of Ecological Self-Organization* (Wiley, 1994) 395, 398–399.

why it is necessary for IGOs involved in fisheries governance to collaborate with external sources.[73]

The legal framework for regime interaction allows IGOs to take into account external sources in the negotiation, implementation and adjudication of matters relating to fisheries sustainability where they have express or implied capacities to do so. These capacities arise from the necessity of either enhanced representation or deliberation. As such, the capacities of IGOs to collaborate are often dissociated from the consent of the members.

3. *The risk of managerialism*

Suggesting that the powers of IGOs in situations of regime interaction may rely on something other than state consent is a controversial notion, posing as it does a variable notion of the role of the state, and implying that individuals should not just engage with states but with other regime participants in an ongoing quest for change and evolution in international law.[74] Indeed, the independence of IGOs to collaborate with external regimes without reference to the consent of their members may lead to abuse. At its extreme, such independence may signal a 'technicalisation' of international affairs, where managerial procedures and decision-making by unseen experts begins to control global politics.[75] Given the biases of experts within regimes, allowing them greater latitude in regime interplay has significant risks.[76] This issue is particularly visible in fisheries and other environmental matters due to controversies regarding the scientific evidence of harm.

Within adjudicative procedures, adjudicating bodies are relatively restrained by rules of treaty interpretation and consultation that are

[73] See further Young, *Trading Fish, Saving Fish*, above n. 1, 275–276 (detailing moral principles ranging from utilitarianism, human welfare, the capabilities approach, ecocentricism and the theory of 'ecological communication').

[74] Cf. the opposing view that states must be central to overcoming unaccountable and exclusive applications of international law, see Alexandra Khrebtukova, 'A Call to Freedom: Towards a Philosophy of International Law in an Era of Fragmentation' (2008) 4 *Journal of International Law and International Relations* 51.

[75] Martti Koskenniemi, 'International Law: Constitutionalism, Managerialism and the Ethos of Legal Education' (2007) 1 *European Journal of Legal Studies*; see also Martti Koskenniemi, 'The Fate of Public International Law: Between Technique and Politics' (2007) 70 *Modern Law Review* 1; see also Stephen Toope, 'Emerging Patterns of Governance and International Law' in Michael Byers (ed.), *The Role of Law in International Politics* (Oxford University Press, 2000) 91, 106.

[76] Koskenniemi, ibid., 'The Fate of Public International Law', 6–9.

based on the need to interpret treaty texts according to the intentions of the parties. Yet lifting these rules by allowing IGOs to ascertain 'ordinary meaning', for example, can lead to arbitrary decision-making.[77] The need for accountable regime interaction is also apparent in the implementation of existing commitments that traverse regimes. In the development of the memorandum of understanding between the FAO and the CITES Secretariat, for example, there were discrepancies in the access accorded to NGOs, and a clear need to assess the background and credentials of NGOs.[78]

These examples point to a need for IGOs to scrutinise and review the 'sources' of external regimes (the norms themselves, including the degree to which they are supported internationally) and the 'sources of the external sources', including the NGOs that wish to gain access to relevant regimes, in order for regime interaction to be accountable. This need exists for all types of regime interaction, although it is more significant when regime interaction stems from informal institutional arrangements, rather than parallel membership or the mutual agreement of states. As such, the legal framework for regime interaction attempts to address the dangers of managerialism by emphasising accountability. The following section explains these ideas in more detail.

4. *Accountable regime interaction*

The accountability of regime interaction depends upon a number of mechanisms through which IGOs, in extending accessibility to other regimes, also scrutinise the relevant norms and the actors that convey them. Such procedures involve constant and continuous inter-regime scrutiny, without any hierarchy between groupings. This removes impediments to regime interaction, but also ensures that such regime interaction is accountable. Procedural safeguards to ensure openness, transparency and participation are significant amongst these mechanisms.

Such scrutiny and review occurs in some areas of fisheries governance. For example, proposals to list marine species is subject to a vote by the CITES parties. This process opens the collaboration between the FAO and CITES to political scrutiny, at least to some degree. Moreover, where there

[77] As I argue occurred when the *EC-Biotech* panel sought to find the ordinary meaning of terms of the SPS Agreement pursuant to VCLT Art. 31(1): see further Young, 'The WTO's use of relevant rules of international law', above n. 39; see also Nele Matz-Lück in Ch. 7 of this volume, pp. 227–231.

[78] See Young, *Trading Fish, Saving Fish*, above n. 1, 172–174.

has been domestic stakeholder consultation in the development of countries' positions at CITES conferences, there will be an enhanced ability to include and contest a number of scientific, cultural and ecological values. Provisions for information-sharing, observership and periodic reporting, as entrenched in the final version of the memorandum of understanding between the FAO and CITES Secretariat, are positive examples of the potential for mutual learning to be revised and critiqued.[79]

The legal framework for regime interaction posits a kind of gatekeeper role for IGOs to use norms that are exogenous to their own regime. I have demonstrated by reference to the multiple bases of regime interaction above that there is no requirement for parallel membership or mutual agreement of states before norms can exert influence on another regime. However, IGOs must have regard to whether there is a high degree of international consensus to those norms. This may include inquiries into whether the norm has been agreed by a range of developing countries as well as developed countries. Moreover, whether the norm was *itself* developed in an open and accessible way is relevant in a decision to accord it influence in another regime.

Some of these procedures for regime interaction involve peer-level review where experts learn from one another in order to extend their competencies. There is scope in a legal framework for appropriate regime interaction to improve such techniques. In the context of expert evidence presented to legal tribunals like WTO panels, for example, it may be useful to develop adversarial techniques such as 'hot-tubs' that subject experts to cross-examination by their peers rather than relying on effective scrutiny by panellists themselves. Even more promising are procedures that call for wider participation of stakeholders. The UNEP workshops convened outside of the WTO negotiations on fisheries subsidies are an example where both experts and interested stakeholders deliberate together. This concept of stakeholder review is supported by literature in diverse fields. Theories of democratic experimentalism, for example, are based on the

[79] Similarly, standard-setting bodies relevant to the operation of the WTO TBT Agreement are encouraged to operate with open, impartial and transparent procedures: see the 'Decision of the Committee on Principles for the Development of International Standards, Guides and Recommendations with relation to Articles 2, 5 and Annex 3 of the Agreement' (2002): WTO Doc G/TBT/1/Rev.8. For critical assessment, see Robert Howse, 'A New Device for Creating International Normativity: The WTO Technical Barriers to Trade Agreement and "International Standards"' in Christian Joerges and Ernst-Ulrich Petersmann (eds.), *Constitutionalism, Multilevel Trade Governance and Social Regulation* (Hart Publishing, 2006) 383, 392–394.

idea that affected stakeholders are in the best position to review information.[80] Related literature has drawn on scholarship on US civil republicanism to advocate the integration of stakeholders in the WTO.[81]

The framework of accountable regime interaction is also influenced by checks on state authority developed domestically. Noting the link between domestic policy coordination and constitutional values of accountability and democracy is imperative.[82] Principles such as the doctrine of procedural justice in administrative decision-making and the inclusion of stakeholders in legislative rule-making and regulation provide useful sources for study, in addition to the EU open models of governance.[83] These legal developments have emphasised 'process norms' such as transparency and reason-giving to enhance legitimacy in decision-making. They have also highlighted the role of ongoing review and open deliberation to address complex policy issues. As I discussed above, the dynamic and complex nature of fisheries clearly calls for such institutional activity, not only in addressing 'wicked problems', but also in alleviating the so-called 'tragedy of the commons'.[84]

A similar theme is taken up in the work of scholars of 'global administrative law', who seek to locate accountability structures in non-traditional sites of globalised law-making, including by market actors and international committees of IGOs.[85] Such accountability has real and potential effects on global politics as well as law.[86] Although the relationship between international institutions is not a focus of global administrative law, I consider many of the emerging principles of accountability to be relevant to regime interaction. In addition, the general idea of inclusivity in situations of poly-contextuality follows existing literature on transnational governance, especially in arguments that

[80] See e.g. Michael Dorf and Charles Sabel, 'A Constitution of Democratic Experimentalism' (1998) 98 *Columbia Law Review* 267.

[81] G. Richard Shell, 'The Trade Stakeholders Model and Participation by Nonstate Parties in the World Trade Organization' (1996) 17 *University of Pennsylvania Journal of International Economic Law* 359.

[82] See Saunders in Ch. 2 of this volume, p. 55.

[83] See Gráinne de Búrca and Joanne Scott, 'Introduction: New Governance, Law and Constitutionalism' in Gráinne de Búrca and Joanne Scott (eds.), *Law and New Governance in the EU and the US* (Hart Publishing, 2006) 1.

[84] The work of Elinor Ostrom is relevant: see above n. 65.

[85] See Benedict Kingsbury, Nico Krisch and Richard Stewart, 'The Emergence of Global Administrative Law' (2005) 68 *Law and Contemporary Problems* 15.

[86] Joshua Cohen and Charles Sabel, 'Global Democracy?' (2005) 37 *NYU Journal of International Law and Politics* 763.

found an ideal of democratic legitimacy on the involvement of a broad sphere of actors.[87]

As is evident, the legal framework proposed here falls short of a kind of constitutionalism, which has been forcefully argued as the ideal form for situating public power within international society.[88] Although goals of a self-constituting international society are attractive in the context of globalising social and political structures, the trade and environmental quandaries presented in my fisheries examples manifest a strong resistance to hierarchical norms. In the interaction between regimes, arguments for exclusivity within regimes or trumping norms give way to a need to continuously engage and contest social and political solutions and governance structures. As such, the legal framework builds on existing structures and processes to ensure ongoing and open contestation between stakeholders rather than entrenched ideals.[89]

My studies in fisheries governance show that accountability through stakeholder participation in regime interaction requires safeguards of its own.[90] I have argued that both IGOs and NGOs can influence regime interaction through participation in negotiation, implementation and dispute settlement. Most clearly, these stakeholders must be open to scrutiny. Yet the forms of accountability of these stakeholders will be different from traditional forms that focus on legitimate representation, especially when their participation extends from recognition of their deliberative contributions rather than their representative functions.

For IGOs that participate in regime interaction as stakeholders, for example, assessments of their accountability will focus on two main aspects: their functions and on the way they operate. As to the first aspect, the norms for which an IGO is responsible for advancing will be scrutinised. This includes the questions about the level of membership of states,

[87] Patrizia Nanz, 'Democratic Legitimacy and Constitutionalisation of Transnational Trade Governance: A View from Political Theory' in Christian Joerges and Ernst-Ulrich Petersmann (eds.), *Constitutionalism, Multilevel Trade Governance and Social Regulation* (Hart Publishing, 2006) 60, 80; see also Inger-Johanne Sand, 'Polycontextuality as an Alternative to Constitutionalism' in Christian Joerges, Inger-Johanne Sand and Gunther Teubner (eds.), *Transnational Governance and Constitutionalism* (Hart Publishing, 2004) 41, 61–65.

[88] Philip Allott, *The Health of Nations: Society and Law beyond the State* (Cambridge University Press, 2002) 342–379.

[89] Cf. Allott, who sees the notion of governance as 'disintegrat[ing] the integrity of society': ibid., 161–162.

[90] This is especially necessary to respond to the type of critique that may be implied by Allott: ibid.

and the degree to which such membership is spread across developing and developed countries, that I identified above. The OECD, for example, which represents only thirty developed countries, may have less weight in appropriate regime interaction than a body such as the WTO. Moreover, a norm will demonstrate a higher degree of consensus if it has been developed according to principles of openness and transparency. As to the second aspect, the openness, accessibility and transparency of procedures *within* the IGO will be relevant in determining the appropriateness of its participation. For example, if the FAO is to act as a peer-reviewer for the conduct of states in the proposed WTO subsidies disciplines, the WTO should continually assess the FAO's procedures. Such assessments of IGO accountability could fit in with existing procedures.[91]

This form of scrutiny of IGOs will be different from the scrutiny needed to determine whether NGOs can appropriately participate in regime interaction. NGOs differ from both states and IGOs in their functions, constituencies and intended beneficiaries. As such, checks on whether they are credible and accountable need to acknowledge these differences.[92] Forms of accountability will not necessarily depend on the degree of consensus of the norms the NGOs represent. More important will be the issue I identified as the second aspect of IGO accountability: namely, an inquiry into the open, accessible, transparent and participatory way in which the NGO operates.

The challenges of assessing the credibility of NGOs are addressed in varying ways in current international regimes. CITES parties require observers to their conferences to be 'qualified in protection, conservation or management of wild fauna and flora' and to have legal personality and an 'international character, remit and programme of activities'.[93] The UN requires NGOs to reveal the sources of voluntary contributions and explain other sources of funding.[94] The World Intellectual Property Organization (WIPO), in contrast, accredits observers without inquiring into their sources of funding.[95]

[91] For example, the FAO's 'Guiding Lines' mentioned above n. 42 set out criteria according to which an IGO is to be recognised as having intergovernmental character.

[92] See Sasha Courville, 'Understanding NGO-based social and environmental regulatory systems: why we need new models of accountability' in Michael W. Dowdle (ed.), *Public Accountability: Designs, Dilemmas and Experiences* (Cambridge University Press, 2006) 271.

[93] CITES Art. XI(7) elaborated in Resolution Conf. 13.8.

[94] NGO status is based on UN Charter Art. 71 and on ECOSOC Resolution 1996/31 adopted in 1996; see further http://csonet.org/.

[95] See www.wipo.int/members/en/admission/observers.html.

As consistent with the merging of international and transnational law, the work of private bodies is increasingly relevant to this issue. The International Social and Environmental Accreditation and Labelling (ISEAL) Alliance,[96] for example, has developed a voluntary code of good practice for NGOs that set environmental and social standards. The Maritime Stewardship Council, an NGO responsible for labelling standards of fish products, has agreed to this code. Moreover, requiring NGOs to declare their sources of funding should be a first step for all institutional collaboration. The guidelines issued by the WTO Appellate Body Secretariat in the *EC-Asbestos* appeal, which required *amicus* briefs to state the nature of their interest, is a good example of how such ideas can be implemented, notwithstanding that the guidelines engendered criticism amongst WTO Members.[97]

Drawing on these examples, my ideas to improve accountability as part of a legal framework for regime interaction are exploratory and in some instances speculative. Yet they represent an effort to understand the progressive development of international law in the context of fragmentation and an attempt to improve the way fisheries governance adapts to complexity and pluralism. They lead to new conceptions about capacities and duties of IGOs and the scrutiny of NGOs – and can in turn impact upon the norms within regimes and within general principles of international law.

Conclusion

In the global fisheries context, there is an increasing awareness about impending ecological disasters caused by overfishing, vessel overcapacity and other practices governed by diverse regimes. It is right that such awareness guides normative development and general epistemic engagement between international organisations and other groups during the negotiation, implementation and enforcement of laws, notwithstanding that a minority of states have opted out of the relevant regimes. Such regime interaction is assisted by a legal framework that encourages transparency and inclusivity. This legal framework recognises that the full range of 'interests' – of all those affected by fisheries depletion – needs to be incorporated in the meeting of regimes. Whilst clearly a list of all of those

[96] See www.isealalliance.org.

[97] Further examples of situations where regimes quite legitimately block lobbies and other actors seeking to influence regime interaction are detailed in Young, *Trading Fish, Saving Fish*, above n. 1, especially 283–284.

groups would be endless,[98] a general principle of inclusion must inform models of regime interaction in order to respond to the concerns of those wishing to restrict the mandates or activities of particular regimes, and to address the risk of managerialism inherent in the notion of experts determining the modes of regime interplay. The inclusion of such perspectives is not necessarily determinative of issues, but rather serves an important deliberative function, particularly in promoting learning and information-exchange. It may also be required to satisfy the need to accommodate indigenous and artisanal fishing perspectives.[99]

The perspectives of those who are 'affected' by fisheries governance are commonly advanced by states, intergovernmental organisations and non-governmental organisations in the making, implementation and enforcement of law. When the involvement of such actors moves beyond the participation rights granted by states, the legitimacy of regime interaction needs to depend on something other than state sovereignty or consent. Instead, the accountability of actors, and the scrutiny that may be given to competing claims for participation – made within a finite public realm– becomes important. Indeed, procedural safeguards to ensure accountable regime interaction can impact on the relative normativity of intersecting regimes. This argument for a legal framework for regime interaction has major implications for international law's legitimacy and meaning. It is based on the need to address the concerns, not just of states, but of the international community on important global problems such as fisheries depletion.

[98] This relates to the 'boundary problem' confronted by philosophy: see further Robert E. Goodin, 'Enfranchising All Affected Interests, and Its Alternatives' (2007) 35 *Philosophy & Public Affairs* 1, 41.

[99] This is an implication of the conclusions of Gunther Teubner and Peter Korth in Ch. 1 of this volume, at pp. 52–54, which deserve greater study given the cultural and subsistence interests held by many indigenous peoples in fisheries.

PART II

Communities

4

Legal Regimes and Professional Knowledges: The Internal Politics of Regime Definition

ANDREW T. F. LANG

Although the language of 'coordination' and 'coherence' seems to imply otherwise, processes of interaction between international legal regimes involve contested normative choices between competing political projects.[1] Different international legal regimes tend to have different logics which express and embody different normative biases, so that 'coordination' between regimes is therefore always about hierarchising those preferences in particular contexts. Achieving 'coherence' in the international order means achieving a particular *kind* of coherence – 'balancing' the demands of each regime always means achieving a particular *kind* of balance – which inevitably favours some interests and values over others.

This volume is important, therefore, in that it helps to expose regime interaction as a site of international politics, and to investigate the different technical, administrative and discursive processes through which this politics is carried out. At the same time, however, it is important to complement research into the politics of regime *interaction* with research on the internal politics of regime *definition*. I am referring here to work which seeks to explain how particular normative biases and preferences come to be embedded within an international regime at any particular point in its historical trajectory, and explores the processes by which these normative biases are sustained and changed over time. There are at least two important reasons why these need to be central questions for scholarship on regime interaction. The first reason is corrective, at least in a pre-emptive sense. When we focus too exclusively on exposing the political nature of regime interaction, there is a danger that we actually obscure the politics of regime definition. This is because the metaphor of 'interaction' encourages us to reify the international regimes in question – to treat them as 'billiard balls',

[1] Martti Koskenniemi, 'The Politics of International Law – 20 Years Later' (2009) 20 *European Journal of International Law* 7.

to use the typical phrase. We tend to treat each regime and its preferences as given (for the purposes of analysis), and bracket the question of how they came to be the way they are. Furthermore, it encourages us to treat each regime as autonomous or self-contained, in the sense of containing the 'principles of its own dynamic'.[2] For example, we tend to speak of the trade regime as if the logic of its operation derives simply from some abstract conception of its mandate – the trade regime has a free-market bent as a result of its mandate to 'liberalise trade' – rather than being a contingent product of the way that that mandate is understood and constructed and embedded within broader political projects at any particular point in time. To be clear, I am not suggesting that the reification of regimes is a logical precondition of work on regime interaction, but I do think there is a tendency towards such reification in practice. This tendency can be counteracted by more work on the internal processes of regime constitution.

The second reason for investigating the internal politics of regime definition, is that it helps us to understand the politics of regime interaction much more fully. Regime interaction is political not only in the sense that it involves hierarchising and prioritising the competing values and preferences of different regimes. It is also political in the sense that it can – often will – help to reconstitute and reshape the inner logics and dynamics of each regime. Indeed, that is often the point: contemporary interactions between the trade and human rights regime, for example, are to some degree motivated by a desire on the part of human rights actors to change the dynamics of the trade regime to make it more compatible with a particular conception of human rights values – and vice versa. But if we are to understand the impact of regime interaction on the internal politics of regime definition, then we need first to have a detailed understanding of the way those internal political processes work.

This chapter approaches the question of regime interaction from precisely this internal point of view. Taking the trade regime as its case study, it seeks to open one small window on the processes by which the inner 'principles of vision' of the trade regime are constituted and its 'normative biases' are constructed. It does this by focusing on the specific question of how particular governmental actions are constructed over time as barriers or impediments to trade (and others are not). In the first section of the chapter, I introduce the concept of the trade barrier, and explain its constitutive role in shaping the politics of the international trade regime. In the second, I describe in some detail the processes by which the concept

[2] Pierre Bourdieu, 'The Force of Law: Towards a Sociology of the Juridical Field' (1987) 38 *Hastings Law Journal* 805, 816.

of a barrier to trade has been constructed and elaborated in the context of the international legal regime governing trade in services. In the third section, I offer some reflections on the implications of this case study for research into regime interaction, and identify some connections between this chapter and others in the volume.

A. The 'principles of vision' of the trade regime, and the constitution of barriers to trade

It is quite common to view the international trade regime as structurally predisposed towards a kind of free market politics. The trade regime, so the argument goes, is about liberalising trade, and liberalising trade means removing governmental intervention in the market, at least to the extent that such intervention distorts trade flows. At some level the World Trade Organization (WTO) assesses all governmental action in terms of its impact on trade flows, with the effect that within the trade regime many regulatory measures come to be understood as 'non-tariff barriers' to trade. In this way, it can often seem as if the trade regime's function and mandate inevitably lead to a kind of bias within the regime, inculcating a structural preference for the free market, or at least a predisposition to view governmental intervention in the market sceptically, and as presumptively unjustified.

While there is something appealingly commonsensical about this view, in fact it misrepresents the trade regime, and mistakes the nature of projects of economic liberalisation. In reality, to say that the WTO is concerned with the liberalisation of international trade, and therefore with the removal (in principle at least) of distortions of international trade, says almost nothing about the internal logic of the regime, nor anything of its underlying political orientation. As a long line of critical thinkers about international trade law have explained,[3] what counts

[3] See, e.g. John Evans, *The Kennedy Round in American Trade Policy: The Twilight of the GATT?* (Harvard University Press, 1971) 87–88; Daniel K. Tarullo, 'Beyond Normalcy in the Regulation of International Trade' (1987) 100 *Harvard Law Review* 546, 552ff.; Daniel K. Tarullo, 'Logic, Myth and the International Economic Order' (1985) 26 *Harvard International Law Journal* 553; David Kennedy, 'The International Style in Postwar Law and Politics' (1994) 1 *Utah Law Review* 7, 88; David Kennedy, 'The Disciplines of International Law and Policy' (1999) 12(1) *Leiden Journal of International Law* 9; David Kennedy, 'The "Rule of Law", Political Choices and Development Common Sense' in David Trubek and Alvaro Santos (eds.), *The New Law and Development* (Cambridge University Press, 2006) 95; Robert Howse, 'From Politics to Technocracy – and Back Again: The Fate of the Multilateral Trading Regime' (2002) 96(1) *American Journal of International Law* 96.

as a 'trade barrier' or 'trade distortion' is not self-evident, indeed it is highly indeterminate. Virtually every kind of governmental action affects international trade flows in some way, including macroeconomic policy, labour market regulation, environmental regulation, health policy and so on. Conversely, any impediment which a private trading firm encounters in gaining full and effective access to foreign markets will almost always be affected or sustained by, or in some way attributable to, governmental action of some form. A project of trade liberalisation, therefore, does not just involve the removal of distortions of trade, but first of all the construction of some governmental measures *as* distortions of trade – and others not. That is to say, some forms of public action must be foregrounded as 'interventions' on trade, or 'barriers' to market access, and others may be backgrounded as part of the context in which normal trade takes place.

The way in which different forms of governmental action are imagined and described makes a big difference to the way that the international trade regime governs them. Measures understood as distortions of trade are subject to technologies of progressive elimination – exchanges of concessions through multiple negotiating rounds, prohibitive disciplines combined with judicial dispute settlement and so on. Measures understood as providing the necessary regulatory infrastructure to correct market failures, or to support well-functioning markets, are treated differently: here the trade regime has experimented with a range of technologies ranging from harmonisation, proportionality review, technical assistance and mutual recognition, to softer procedural disciplines. Measures which are treated as unrelated to trade – as merely part of the background conditions in which economic activity takes place – tend by and large to be free from scrutiny of any sort within the trade regime. The point is that any particular historically situated project of trade liberalisation takes its character, inner logic and politics in part from the nature of the choices that are made about how to characterise and describe different kinds of governmental measures. Such choices play a crucial role in shaping the governance of trade at an international level, organising the activity of the trade regime, allocating its supervisory resources and technologies to certain issues and not others, directing the attention and energies of professionals working within the field. The politics of the trade regime, then, are not (or not just) in its mandate to liberalise trade, but more importantly in the specific *principles of vision* – the particular implicit frameworks of visibility and invisibility – which the regime deploys to distinguish 'distortions' of trade flows from other kinds of governmental activity.[4] Part of unearthing the internal politics of the trade regime, therefore, must be to explore the processes through which these principles of vision are produced, contested and sustained over time within the field of international trade law and governance.

In stylised terms,[5] it is possible to divide the first fifty years of the history of the trade regime into two periods, divided by the economic turmoil of the 1970s, both of which are associated with very different ways of understanding what did and did not count as a 'trade barrier'. As is well known, for the first twenty or thirty years of its existence, the original GATT (General Agreement on Tariffs and Trade) regime focused almost exclusively on 'border barriers' to trade. The immediate priority for the architects of the post-war trading order was to reduce tariffs, and to remove whatever remained of the more restrictive exotic commercial policy instruments which had been put in place during the inter-war period, including quotas, foreign exchange restrictions, licensing requirements, and so on. Although a range of supportive disciplines were also imposed on 'behind the border' governmental measures – what we might today refer to as 'domestic regulation' – the reality is that these disciplines, despite their very broad formal scope, were only rarely used to challenge measures which would now be understood as 'domestic regulation'.[6] Despite the fact that the styles of economic management which emerged after World War II were highly interventionist, very few forms of intervention were conceived of as 'distortions' of international trade, at least in the sense of being legitimate subjects of discipline and negotiation in the context of the international trade regime.

This limited field of vision was the product of a number of underlying factors. To some extent, the trade regime focused on a limited range of border barriers simply because these were the most prevalent and commercially significant barriers at the time. More importantly, however, this limited focus reflected a shared commitment amongst key states in the GATT regime to highly interventionist forms of domestic economic policy associated with Keynesian economics and the consolidation of the

[4] This is another way of putting the point that the politics of the trade regime is in part in the particular image of 'normal' trade which is implicitly used as an imaginary template against which any particular governmental action is measured for consistency: see Kennedy, above n. 2; Tarullo, 'Beyond Normalcy', above n. 2.

[5] For a significantly expanded version of this story, see Andrew T. F. Lang, *World Trade Law after Neoliberalism: Re-imagining the Global Economic Order* (Oxford University Press, 2011).

[6] See further Lang, ibid., ch. 7.

post-war welfare state. The institutional forms and political purposes of the welfare state provided the background against which trade-affecting measures were implicitly judged as legitimate or illegitimate, with the result that comparatively few stood out as 'trade barriers', or as obvious cases of 'cheating' on international trade commitments. Most domestic measures simply appeared in the trade regime as the normal institutional background of international economic activity, rather than as distortions of international trade. Just as importantly, for the purposes of the present story, the post-war GATT's limited field of vision was sustained and reproduced through the work of the community of professionals given stewardship over the regime during its first decades. As a number of historians of the regime have described, the early GATT was a relatively small and close-knit 'club' of career diplomats, who sought to effect a self-conscious separation of the 'low politics' of international trade from the 'high politics' of other spheres of international life.[7] Part of what was (more or less) shared within this relatively small field of international trade diplomacy was a set of social expectations and norms about what the scope of the GATT provisions was intended to be, and what kinds of regulation could and could not legitimately be challenged under them. Since the GATT's legal regime and dispute settlement system were at the time deeply embedded within this world of trade diplomacy, the operation of GATT law was strongly influenced by these norms and expectations.[8]

As is well known, all of this changed quite radically from around the early 1970s, when the GATT began in earnest to turn its attention to behind-the-border regulatory measures which affected international

[7] Robert O. Keohane and Joseph S. Nye, *The Club Model of Multilateral Cooperation and the World Trade Organization: Problems of Democratic Legitimacy* (John F. Kennedy Sch. of Gov't, Working Paper No. 4 (n.d.)), available at www.hks.harvard.edu/visions/publication/keohane_nye.pdf February 2001; Robert O. Keohane and Joseph S. Nye, 'The Club Model of Multilateral Cooperation and Problems of Legitimacy' in Roger B. Porter et al. (eds.), *Efficiency, Equity and Legitimacy: The Multilateral Trading System at the Millennium* (Brookings Institution Press, 2001); Joseph Weiler, 'The Rule of Lawyers and the Ethos of Diplomats: Reflections on the Internal and External Legitimacy of WTO Dispute Settlement' (2001) 35 *Journal of World Trade* 191; Richard Cooper, 'Trade Policy is Foreign Policy' (1972) 9 *Foreign Policy* 18–36; John Gerard Ruggie, 'International regimes, transactions, and change: embedded liberalism and the postwar economic order' (Spring 1982) 36(2) *International Organization* 379.

[8] Robert E. Hudec, 'The GATT Legal System: A Diplomat's Jurisprudence' (1970) 4 *Journal of World Trade* 615; Arie Reich, 'From Diplomacy to Law: The Juridicization of International Trade Relations' (1996–7) 17 *Northwestern Journal of International Law and Business* 775; Weiler, ibid.

trade. At the most general level, this was the result of the decline of a shared commitment to embedded liberalism, and the rise of a new form of economic liberalism which was much more suspicious of governmental intervention of all sorts, and therefore more inclined to view such intervention as illegitimate 'distortion' of international trade. More immediately, the impetus came from US trade policy elites, which became convinced around this time that foreign markets for US exports were kept closed as a result of the proliferation of hidden and complex 'non-tariff barriers' in foreign countries, most notably Japan. Between the Kennedy and Tokyo Rounds, a great deal of conceptual work was done, as lists of non-tariff barriers were drawn up, and trade professionals learnt to think of new kinds of governmental measures as 'trade barriers'.[9] Then, as has been well chronicled elsewhere, over the next three decades more and more forms of 'domestic regulation' came to be imagined and described by trade professionals as non-tariff barriers to trade, including product standards, food safety regulation, intellectual property standards, environmental measures, currency policy and censorship restrictions, amongst many others.

Increasingly, then, the politics of international trade came to be played out in part as a struggle over which governmental measures could and should be redescribed as distortions of trade, and therefore as legitimate subjects of discipline through international trade law. No longer was it possible simply to refer to shared background understandings amongst a tight-knit community of trade diplomats, about what did and did not constitute a barrier to trade. Thus, the norms and expectations of the original world of trade diplomats ceased to play such a central role in constituting the implicit 'principles of vision' of the trade regime. Instead, trade professionals increasingly began to turn to various forms of technical expertise to justify and objectify their preferred means of distinguishing illegitimate 'distortions' of trade from 'normal' and legitimate governmental measures. More generally, the trade regime began to rely more heavily on experts and their technical knowledge to identify, categorise and assess barriers to international trade, and distinguish them from other kinds of governmental regulation. In the next section, I illustrate this turn to technical expertise, in the context of negotiations over the General Agreement on Trade in Services (GATS) from the Uruguay Round and beyond. The aim is to try to understand – through an

[9] See Gilbert Winham, *International Trade and the Tokyo Round Negotiations* (Princeton University Press, 1987) 86ff.

examination of the 'capillaries'[10] of the international trade regime – precisely how the principles of vision of the contemporary trade regime are constructed, and in particular the role that technical expertise plays in those processes.

B. Barriers in the global services economy

One of the major innovations of the Uruguay Round was the extension of the field of international trade law to the area of services, through the negotiation of the GATS.[11] While it is in some ways a complex agreement, the basic architecture of the GATS is relatively simple to explain. It applies to 'measures affecting trade in services' (Article I:1). 'Services' are only defined tautologically in the text of the agreement (Article I:3(b)), but an exhaustive list of the entire range of all possible services prepared during the Uruguay Round provided practical guidance for negotiators.[12] 'Trade in services' is defined in Article I:2(a) as:

> the supply of a service:
>
> (a) from the territory of one Member into the territory of any other Member;
> (b) in the territory of one Member to the service consumer of any other Member;
> (c) by a service supplier of one Member, through commercial presence in the territory of any other Member;
> (d) by a service supplier of one Member, through presence of natural persons of a Member in the territory of any other Member.

Measures which fall within the scope of the agreement – that is, measures affecting trade in services – are potentially subject to a number of substantive disciplines, of which three are worth mentioning. Article II

[10] David Kennedy, 'Challenging Expert Rule: The Politics of Global Governance' (2005) 27 *Sydney Journal of International Law* 3.

[11] For useful accounts of the services negotiations, see, e.g. Geza Feketekuty, *International Trade in Services: An Overview and Blueprint for Negotiations* (AEI and Ballinger, 1988); Jonathan David Aronson, *Negotiating to Launch Negotiations: Getting Trade in Services onto the GATT Agenda* (Pew Case Studies in International Affairs: Case 125, 1992); William J. Drake and Kalypso Nicolaïdis, 'Ideas, Interests and Institutionalization: "trade in services" and the Uruguay Round' (1992) 46(1) *International Organisation* 37–100; Yi-Chong Xu and Patrick Moray Weller, *The Governance of World Trade: International Civil Servants and the GATT/WTO* (Edward Elgar, 2004), ch. 5 on 'Negotiating Trade in Services'.

[12] Note by the Secretariat, 'Services Sectoral Classification List' (MTN.GNS/W/120) (10 July 1991).

sets out the 'most favoured nation' obligation, prohibiting discrimination between different foreign trading partners. Apart from some relatively minor exceptions, this obligation applies to all measures covered by the GATS. Article XVI singles out six different categories of measure for prohibition – such as limitations on the number of services suppliers operating in a sector, or a limitation on the total value of service transactions, and so on – but this prohibition only applies to measures affecting those sectors which have been specifically inscribed by each WTO Member in its schedule of commitments. If a WTO Member inscribes no sectors in its schedule, then Article XVI cannot be invoked against any measure that it adopts. Article XVII sets out the 'national treatment' obligation, prohibiting discrimination as between foreign and domestic products, but it too applies only to those sectors inscribed in Members' schedules. All of these three disciplines are subject to a variety of exceptions, contained for example in Article XIV and XIV*bis*.

What is important for the purposes of the present argument is that the GATS, as it ultimately emerged from the Uruguay Round, essentially represented a framework agreement – one which contained a range of familiar general disciplines such as non-discrimination and market access, but which provided very little clarity about what those principles might mean in terms of the concrete projects of regulatory reform that they might require in particular service sectors. It was an open-ended agreement, creating many more questions than answers about what its effects were likely to be, and even about what the core concepts on which it was founded actually meant. Is, for example, the online delivery of an electronic book the supply of a service or a good? Does the outsourcing of a manufacturing process turn that process into a service, rather than an aspect of goods production? Are zoning restrictions on the location of hotels properly described as limitations on the supply of tourism services? Might censorship restrictions on the sale of DVDs be understood as a limitation on the supply of entertainment services – and if so, how should one distinguish legitimate from illegitimate censorship restrictions? In order for the GATS to be operationalised, questions such as these had to be answered. Relevant aspects of the world had to be re-described and reclassified in the language of 'barriers to trade in services' – and particular ways of doing so had to be sufficiently commonly accepted amongst the trade community to provide a secure foundation and guide for the process of interpreting and elaborating the GATS.

One interesting illustration of the ways in which such processes of reclassification and redescription were carried out comes from the sectoral negotiations on telecommunications services. By the end of the Uruguay Round the telecommunication negotiations had not reached a conclusion which was satisfactory to the major players. As a result, negotiators agreed to continue the negotiations after the conclusion of the broader round, under the auspices of a newly created Negotiating Group on Basic Telecommunications (NGBT). One of the most significant activities of this group was the drafting between 1994 and 1996 of what came to be known as the 'Reference Paper' – essentially a set of core principles of pro-competitive regulation of the telecommunications sector. While establishing regulatory standards is highly unusual in the context of international trade negotiations, there were at least two reasons why it was thought necessary in the telecommunications context. First, it was generally agreed that the particular structure of the telecommunications sector (where competitors often rely on the incumbent for access to infrastructure) meant that market access commitments in that sector could easily be undermined by the exploitative behaviour of dominant local firms. It therefore seemed clear to negotiators that market access commitments had to be accompanied by some kind of pro-competitive regulatory reform if they were to be meaningful.[13] Second, and just as importantly, it was thought that a document was needed to help negotiators to understand what kinds of regulatory reform might generally be expected to follow from taking market access commitments in the telecommunications sector.[14] This would give some comfort to negotiators offering commitments, and also help to ensure a common set of expectations about what liberalisation commitments in this sector might concretely mean. The process of creating the Reference Paper was therefore understood as 'an opportunity to create a firm set of common understandings' about how the telecommunications sector ought to be governed where market access commitments were undertaken, and how the transition to liberalisation was to be managed.[15]

Negotiators did not have to look far for guidance on regulatory principles, as by the middle of the 1990s there was already a well-established body of specialised technical knowledge on the creation of modern, competitive telecommunications markets, as well as a community seeking

[13] Laura B. Sherman, '"Wildly Enthusiastic" About the First Multilateral Agreement on Trade in Telecommunications Services' (1999) 51 *Federal Communications Law Journal* 61, 71.

[14] Sherman, ibid., 73.

[15] Peter F. Cowhey and Mikhail M. Klimenko, 'The WTO Agreement and Telecommunications Policy Reforms' (2001) World Bank Policy Research Paper No. 2601, 5.

to spread this expertise globally. The experience of telecommunications liberalisation in a handful of industrialised countries during the late 1980s and early 1990s had given rise to what Cowhey and Aronson call an 'international reform coalition' which actively promoted the benefits of competition in telecommunications markets across most industrialised countries.[16] The existing international institution governing telecommunications, the International Telecommunications Union (ITU), had proved resistant to the new ideas coming from this reform coalition. The services negotiations provided an opportunity to bypass the ITU,[17] and as a result some advocates of telecommunications liberalisation were therefore keen to find a home in the GATS for their regulatory expertise. After some 'substantial coaching',[18] major commercial players in the sector also became convinced that the GATT/WTO was the right venue for this effort.

It was, therefore, to this body of specialised knowledge that services negotiators turned for guidance and active input in drafting the Reference Paper. The document was drafted by a select group of delegates called the 'Room A Group', which consisted initially of representatives from those five industrialised countries which had experience in liberalising their own domestic telecommunications markets.[19] In close collaboration with their domestic regulators, this group developed a set of general regulatory principles which they then circulated to all members of the NGBT – merely as a 'tool' to help negotiators understand what regulatory commitments might be on the table for negotiation.[20] This was not an entirely straightforward process, as the regulatory regimes in each of the countries represented were not identical, and delegates were naturally concerned to ensure that their countries would not need to undertake major changes to their existing regulatory structures. But at that time

16 Peter F. Cowhey and Jonathan D. Aronson, *Transforming Global Information and Communication Markets: The Political Economy of Innovation* (MIT Press, 2009) 151. It has also been called an epistemic community: Peter F. Cowhey, 'The International Telecommunications Regime: The Political Roots of Regimes for High Technology' (1990) 44 *International Organization* 169.

17 Cowhey and Aronson, ibid., 151, 154, 169. It should be acknowledged, however, that from about 2000 onwards the ITU embraced this new agenda and there are now strong links between that organisation and the WTO.

18 Cowhey and Aronson, ibid., 307, n. 15.

19 These countries were the United States, Australia, New Zealand, Japan, Korea and the European Union (counted for these purposes as a single negotiating unit): Sherman, above n. 12, 71.

20 WTO, Negotiating Group on Basic Telecommunications, *Report on the Meeting of 26 January 1996* (14 February 1996) S/NGBT/12 para. 6.

there was a sufficiently uniform and coherent body of expertise about how competition in the telecommunication sector ought to be introduced and managed, that these difficulties proved surmountable. Ultimately, then, the Reference Paper was in many respects a codification of the knowledge which had been gained from the first decade of experimentation with liberalisation of telecommunications markets in a handful of developed countries, representing what was at the time considered to be 'best practice'.[21] In the words of one commentator close to the negotiations, the Reference Paper was understood as 'a transfer of know-how to other countries, [a document] that offer[ed] the opportunity to avoid years of trial and error'.[22]

Although the Reference Paper was not originally drafted as a set of binding obligations, in the end it became precisely that. At the formal conclusion of the telecommunications negotiations, 69 countries had scheduled commitments in the telecommunications sector, of which 53 signed on to the Reference Paper as a set of additional commitments they were prepared to accept – a number which has since risen to over 80.[23] However, for the purposes of the present story, the significance is not (just) that the Reference Paper became binding – it is that the process of drafting and negotiating the Reference Paper helped to create within, and disseminate amongst, the relevant community of trade delegates and negotiators a particular body of knowledge about what the liberalisation of trade in telecommunications services would and would not mean. As Cowhey and Aronson have observed, the telecommunications negotiations in the WTO 'changed the … expertise' and 'altered the composition of the expert community' which until then had structured the international governance of international telecommunications.[24] This new expertise not only found a home in the new WTO, it also began to circulate amongst trade professionals themselves, and to become part of the vocabulary of that part of the trade profession with a particular interest in telecommunications services. As telecoms specialists and trade

[21] Lee Tuthill, 'The GATS and New Rules for Regulators' (1997) 21 *Telecommunications Policy* 783, 784.

[22] Daniel Roseman, 'Domestic Regulation and Trade in Telecommunications Services: Experience and Prospects under the GATS' in Aaditya Matoo and Pierre Sauvé (eds.), *Domestic Regulation and Service Trade Liberalization* (World Bank and Oxford University Press, 2003) 83, 90.

[23] Sherman, above n. 12, 63; WTO, 'Services: Sector by Sector, Telecommunications Services', at www.wto.org/english/tratop_e/serv_e/telecom_e/telecom_e.htm (last visited 11 July 2011).

[24] Cowhey and Aronson, above n. 15, 149.

negotiators worked closely together during the Uruguay Round[25] – the close partnership between the US Federal Communications Commission under Reed Hundt and the US Trade Representative (USTR) under Charlene Barshefksy during the Uruguay Round being the paradigmatic example – trade professionals began to look to this regulatory expertise to make the general GATS framework meaningful and commercially significant in the telecommunications sector.

What we have here, then, is one model of the role of technical expertise in the construction of the principles of vision of the trade regime. Negotiations on the elaboration of general GATS principles provided a space and mechanism for the mobilisation of a particular body of regulatory expertise, which in turn circulated within legal discourse and helped to give meaning to general legal principles contained in the GATS. An alliance between indeterminate legal principles and determinate programmes of regulatory reform was created in part through the elaboration of further more detailed legal disciplines (the Reference Paper), but just as importantly through the close relations established between regulatory experts and legal professionals, and the creation of a social system for the ongoing circulation of knowledge between them. Of course, a process like this does not simply happen. In the telecommunications context, it required the directed efforts of the international reform coalition referred to above, who were seeking an international home for their ideas outside the ITU, and were supported by powerful commercial interests. Even then, it required the acquiescence of other countries in the negotiations, and in that respect was aided by the broad sense prevalent at the time that recent revolutions in digital technology meant that 'a profound globalization of the information industry was both inevitable and a driving force for national economic growth'.[26] But whatever the enabling conditions, the point remains that perceptions amongst relevant trade professionals of what constituted legitimate and illegitimate regulation in the telecommunications sector – what constituted a 'barrier to trade in telecommunications services' and what 'trade liberalization' in the telecommunications sector meant – were formed by reference to a particular body of technical expertise, and were partially encoded in legal form.

25 By all accounts, regulators and trade professionals worked closely together in these negotiations: Sherman, above n. 12, 95; Cowhey and Aronson, above n. 15, 166; Jonathan D. Aronson, 'Telecom Agreement Tops Expectations' in Gary Clyde Hufbauer and Erika Wada (eds.), *Unfinished Business: Telecommunications after the Uruguay Round* (Institute for International Economics, Washington, DC, 1997) 17, 19.

26 Cowhey and Klimenko, above n. 14, 3.

Turning now from the telecommunications negotiations, I want to briefly explore a second illustration of the processes by which ideas about the nature of 'trade barriers' in the services context are being formed. Recall from above that prior to the Tokyo Round, there was a concerted effort to gather data on the nature and prevalence of 'non-tariff barriers' to trade in goods, and to teach trade professionals about these barriers, as an important conceptual prelude to the negotiation of new disciplines on domestic regulation affecting trade in goods. In many ways, a similar – though much more decentralised – process has occurred in the context of mapping barriers to trade in services, through the production of catalogues of such barriers in and around trade negotiations themselves.

Some of the earliest work cataloguing and quantifying barriers to services trade was carried out within national trade bodies, or at least closely associated with them. For obvious reasons, a good number of trade ministries have developed practices of collecting information on the trade barriers imposed by other states, either on a routine basis or in the lead-up to a new round of trade negotiations. The inclusion of services on the agenda of the GATT/WTO during the Uruguay Round meant that these national bodies began also to turn their attention to barriers to services trade in their reviews of other countries' trade policies. The office of the USTR, for example, was the first to include information on foreign countries' barriers to trade in services in its National Trade Estimates early in the Uruguay Round. Its European and Japanese counterparts followed suit soon after.[27] Of course these reports are not typically viewed as the most reliable of data sources – for obvious reasons, they reflect the interests of a single country's exporters, and are often based on 'uncollaborated assertions from interested parties'[28] – but for some time at least they were the best that existed. Towards the end of the 1990s, however, as the new round of GATS negotiations approached, a major research project was begun in Australia, involving two major Australian universities in collaboration with the Australian Productivity Commission. This project has produced a good number of studies of barriers to services trade across

[27] See, e.g. USTR, various years, 'National Trade Estimate Report on Foreign Trade Barriers', US Government Printing Office; EC, 1995, *1995 Report on US Barriers to Trade and Investment*, Brussels: European Commission; Japanese Ministry of Economy, Trade and Industry, *Report on the WTO Consistency of Trade Policies by Major Trading Partners* (2003).

[28] See, e.g. Christopher Findlay and Tony Warren, 'Measuring Impediments to Trade in Services', Centre for International Economic Studies, University of Adelaide, CIES Discussion Paper No. 99/19, n. 9.

a variety of different sectors. The bulk of these studies were published in a 2001 collection, which became available, not coincidentally, in time for the early stages of the GATS negotiations.[29] While the body of papers produced in this context focused primarily on sectors of particular interest to Australian service suppliers, it remains tremendously influential – not only as a source of some of the best available information on the sectors addressed, but also as a guide to the different methodologies available to measure and model trade barriers in the services context. Studies since then have virtually uniformly used this Australian body of work as a guide and reference point for their own efforts, and a number of other national trade bodies have also begun to turn their attention to this work since that time.[30]

A number of international organisations have also provided spaces for this kind of work. One of the most influential has been the work of the Trade Committee of the Organisation for Economic Co-operation and Development (OECD), which has had an active and continuing role in the area since 1996, and constitutes a crucial node in the network of knowledge producers working in and around the effort to map barriers to trade in services.[31] One of its most important functions has been its role in creating a network of services experts: since 1999, it has held (almost) annual meetings of services experts – on occasion bringing together trade negotiators with industry experts and economic modellers – to discuss and define core negotiating issues in GATS negotiations, to share information on recent work mapping services barriers and their effects, to discuss difficult conceptual issues standing in the way of this mapping work and so on.[32] The OECD itself has not been prominently involved in the actual

[29] Christopher Findlay and Tony Warren (eds.), *Impediments to Trade in Services: Measurement and Policy Implications* (Routledge, 2000).

[30] For a review of these efforts, in the context of Canadian governmental research in the areas, see Zhiqi Chen and Lawrence Schembri, 'Measuring the Barriers to Trade in Services: Literature and Methodologies' in John Curtis and Dan Ciuriac (eds.), *Trade Policy Research 2002* (Department of Foreign Affairs and International Trade, 2002), at 219–285.

[31] For a useful overview of OECD activities in this area, see OECD Trade and Agriculture Directorate, Trade Committee, 'Towards a Services Trade Restrictiveness Index (STRI): A Proposal for a Road Map for future Trade Committee Work on Services', 27 June 2007, TAD/TC(2007)4, 11–18.

[32] OECD Services Experts Meetings have occurred in June 1999, May 2000, March 2002, November 2003, February 2005 and February 2007, and – in addition to the reports of the meetings themselves – have led to three publications: OECD, *Quantifying the Benefits of Liberalising Trade in Services* (Paris: OECD, 2003); Aaditya Mattoo and Pierre Sauvé, *Domestic Regulation and Services Trade Liberalisation* (Oxford: World Bank and

collection of new data on barriers in its member countries, but it has certainly contributed to the effort by compiling lists of indicative trade barriers on both a universal and sector-specific basis,[33] by evaluating different methodologies for measuring services barriers,[34] by helping to develop a 'trade restrictiveness index' for all countries and all sectors,[35] as well as by modelling the benefits of services liberalisation using the data on existing barriers produced by others.[36]

The United Nations Conference on Trade and Development (UNCTAD) has also emerged as a venue for the production of services expertise, particularly as it relates to development and developing countries. Even before the end of the Uruguay Round, UNCTAD had begun to investigate the possibility of compiling a global searchable database of non-tariff barriers (NTBs) in services, to complement its existing and highly authoritative database on similar measures in the goods context (TRAINS). It has since done exactly that, at least at a preliminary stage, creating its Measures Affecting Trade in Services (MAST) database, which – as sources of data become more sophisticated and comprehensive – is intended to act as a primary statistical and policy tool in the area. In addition, UNCTAD has been working more generally to 'develop methodologies to identify, classify and quantify NTBs', to 'analyse the impact of NTBs on international trade' and to 'build analytical and statistical capacities to assess how NTBs affect developing country exports'.[37] In collaboration with the governments of developing country, it has conducted over thirty assessments of trade in services in particular countries, seeking to identify both the benefits and risks of liberalisation in various service sectors, and to guide the decisions of policy-makers and development experts in this area. It has also produced and commissioned a wide variety of analyses

Oxford University Press, 2003); and OECD, *Trade and Migration: Building Bridges for Global Labour Mobility* (Paris: OECD, 2004). There was also a joint OECD–UNCTAD Workshop on Trade in Services in June 2006 which helped to bring some of this work to WTO Members, particularly developing countries.

[33] E.g. OECD Trade Directorate, Trade Committee, 'Assessing Barriers to Trade in Services: Revised Consolidated List of Cross-Sectoral Barriers', 28 February 2001, TD/TC/WP(99)/FINAL.

[34] E.g. OECD, 'Measuring Barriers to Trade in Services', 1996, TD/TC/WP(96)38.

[35] OECD, n. 30 above.

[36] E.g. OECD, 'Services Trade Liberalisation: Identifying opportunities and gains', 2003, TD/TC/WP(2003)23/FINAL and TD/TC/WP(2003)25/FINAL. The OECD Trade Policy Working Paper Series has also produced a number of papers since 2004 directly relevant to services negotiations.

[37] See www.unctad.org/Templates/Page.asp?intItemID=3848&lang=1 (last visited 11 July 2011).

of the development implications of global services liberalisation and barriers to developing country services exports.[38] This work has been complemented by similar research carried out by key World Bank personnel on the implications for developing countries of services trade.[39] Indeed, the first attempt at a more rigorous and comprehensive mapping of global trade barriers in services was conducted by Bernard Hoekman, a senior economist working at the World Bank, in 1995.[40] In addition, figures on services barriers have been incorporated into the organisation's annual World Trade Indicators publication.[41]

The WTO itself has played an important role in this project. There are a number of activities which the WTO performs which have the effect of producing catalogues of trade barriers – whether deliberately or as a by-product of other activities. The WTO exercises, for example, a rudimentary (but rapidly evolving) surveillance function, through which it seeks to monitor the trade policies of its Members, in part to aid compliance with its agreements. This occurs in part through the Trade Policy Review Mechanism – through which each WTO Member has its trade and economic policies periodically subject to review and criticism by its peers[42] – which provides a valuable, if less than fully reliable, source of data on the trade policies of Members and how they have changed over time. In addition, the Council for Trade in Services itself receives and compiles information on certain trade barriers imposed by WTO Members pursuant to a number of transparency disciplines contained in the GATS. Even the schedules of commitments entered into by each participant in the Uruguay Round negotiations produced a database – albeit an imperfect one – of information about existing barriers to trade in services. Furthermore, the

[38] See, e.g. UNCTAD, *Trade in Services and Development Implications*, 16 January 2006, TD/B/COM.1/77 and 2 February 2007, TD/B/COM.1/85. For a useful review of the literature on services liberalisation and developing countries see John Whalley, 'Assessing the Benefits to Developing Countries of Liberalisation in Services Trade' (2004) 27(8) *The World Economy* 1223.

[39] Both Bernard Hoekman and Aaditya Mattoo, e.g., have been central figures in the development of this literature from within their positions at the World Bank.

[40] Bernard Hoekman, 'Tentative First Steps: An Assessment of the Uruguay Round Agreement on Services', World Bank Policy Research Working Paper No. 1455, May 1995; see also Bernard Hoekman, 'Assessing the General Agreement on Trade in Services' in Will Martin and L. Alan Winters (eds.), *The Uruguay Round and Developing Countries* (Cambridge University Press, 1996) 88.

[41] See, e.g. World Trade Indicators, 2009 available at www.worldbank.org/ (last visited 11 July 2011).

[42] See generally the reports contained on the WTO website: www.wto.org/english/tratop_e/tpr_e/tp_rep_e.htm#chronologically (last visited 11 July 2011).

Secretariat reports produced in the context of an information exchange programme before the GATS 2000 negotiations were early attempts to identify the nature of existing barriers to trade in specific service sectors, and to estimate their incidence and impact worldwide.[43] More specifically, answers to a questionnaire sent out by the Working Party on Professional Services, in respect of domestic regulations in the accountancy sector, produced a rough list of trade restrictions in that sector.[44] Earlier, during the Uruguay Round, the Negotiating Group on Maritime Transport Services distributed a questionnaire requesting information from Members on the different kinds of trade restrictive measures they had in place.[45] While the information produced by the WTO regime through these processes is flawed in many ways,[46] a lot of the scholarly literature and policy analyses on services liberalisation in fact draw heavily on it as one important source of data on existing trade barriers.[47]

What principles of selection have been used to identify the trade barriers catalogued in this work? Unsurprisingly, no clear, codified and uncontested means of identifying trade barriers has emerged. The project is too large, the number of sectors too great, and existing regulatory practices too diverse and too contested for that to occur so rapidly. Sometimes, the compilers draw on survey data, and therefore privilege the perceptions and expectations of the businesses and other organisations surveyed. Sometimes the studies leave the principles of selection implicit, drawing on the author's own expertise, in the sense of his or her familiarity with the typical organisation of public and private power in the sector under study. Sometimes, the compilers of this material have themselves referred to norms of optimal regulation or 'best practice' as the yardstick against which to measure regulation. On this approach, a regulatory trade barrier is a regulation which has an appreciable effect on trade and which varies significantly from 'optimal' regulatory regimes, as codified by

43 See Council for Trade in Services, WTO Documents S/C/M/28–35 (Reports of Meetings from June 1998 to April 1999).

44 See Duc Nguyen-Hong, *Restrictions on Trade in Professional Services*, Productivity Commission Staff Research Paper, AusInfo, Canberra, Australia, August 2000.

45 See Greg McGuire, Michael Schuele and Tina Smith, 'Restrictiveness of International Trade in Maritime Services' in Christopher Findlay and Tony Warren (eds.), *Impediments to Trade in Services: Measurements and Policy Implications* (London: Routledge, 2000) 183, 201.

46 See, e.g. the views expressed in Alexis Hardin and Leanne Holmes, 'Services Trade and Foreign Direct Investment', Staff Research Paper, Industry Commission, Australian Government Printing Service, 1997, 37.

47 See generally, Lang, above n. 4, ch. 9.

expert norms, whether formal or informal. A recent paper published by the OECD, for example, highlights the difficult issue of distinguishing trade barriers from 'regulations that address market imperfections … [or] public policy including distributional objectives',[48] and recommends addressing it in part through a series of 'expert workshops'.[49]

It needs to be acknowledged again that this body of work is still very young, and that so far it has mostly raised questions rather than constructed clear, shared understandings of what does and does not constitute a barrier to trade in the services context. Nevertheless, the processes I have just described are useful illustrations – in an embryonic but still paradigmatic way – of the core function that technical knowledge production can play in defining the terrain of trade politics. I have made the point repeatedly that the question of what constitutes a 'trade barrier' is not amenable to an entirely objective answer, but instead is always a contested matter. The way in which commercial actors draw the line between 'legitimate' and 'distorting' regulation is unlikely to be the same as that of regulators themselves, and the views of consumers, or academic experts, or 'the public', are likely to be different again. The work of data collection I have just described can be understood, therefore, as a way of avoiding or managing the problems caused by these differences of views. More specifically, it is a way of producing one particular view of what constitutes a trade barrier, and transforming that view into an apparently objective description of the world-as-it-is. This objectification is made effective primarily through a logic of repetition, or accretion, the underlying dynamics of which are clear from the material just cited – even if the process is still very far from complete in the specific context of services negotiations described in this chapter. More generally, this kind of work evolves according to an aggregative dynamic, according to which subsequent compilations have tended to draw on, and cumulatively supplement, prior work. At some point – perhaps after a certain period of time, or, perhaps when negotiations move to the more difficult phase of bargaining over what disciplines ought to be applied and what commitments ought to be made – the time for challenging the content and basic assumptions of these documents passes. Documents which are initially produced as purely informative guides for negotiators tend to harden,

[48] OECD, above n. 30, para. 17.

[49] Ibid., para. 16. For a similar approach, see Alessandra Colecchia, 'Measuring Barriers to Market Access for Services: A Pilot Study on Accountancy Services' in Findlay and Warren, above n. 28, 259.

and are treated as if they were more or less authoritative and exhaustive lists of trade barriers in the service sectors under consideration. The 'principles of vision' of the trade regime – that is, the particular framework used to distinguish trade barriers from other kinds of governmental action – therefore seem in this case to be a diffuse effect of technical data collection and description, an emergent product of multiple reports, papers, discussions and catalogues, both produced by and contested within the languages of various forms of expertise.

C. The politics of regime interaction

I have suggested the politics of the trade regime reside in part in its characteristic ways of seeing the world, the 'principles of vision', the schema of classification and analysis which structure the thought and action of trade professionals. Part of these principles of vision – an important part, but only one part – is a set of conceptual tools and habits of thought for classifying different kinds of government in the vocabulary of trade 'barriers', 'distortions', 'impediments' and so on. These conceptual tools and habits of thought change over time, and are of course influenced by broad political currents, change in the practices of government, the realities of international commerce and the priorities and perceptions of international commercial actors.

Using services as a case study, I have argued that the principles of vision which underpin and orient the contemporary trade regime are still under construction, but that they are being constituted and defined by reference to a variety of different forms of expertise: economic expertise; policy or regulatory expertise in particular service sectors; legal expertise in the realm of WTO law itself; commercial expertise in the sense of a 'feel' for the most significant kinds of impediments which businesses face in particular sectors; and what we might call (following Howse[50]) a kind of 'insider' expertise which comes from familiarity with the purposes, limits, modes of operation and range of political possibilities of the trade regime. Of course, these different kinds of expertise may be, and often are, in tension with one another. By using the notion of technical knowledge, I do not mean to evoke an uncontested or apolitical world. On the contrary, the processes of knowledge production I have described are highly contested, with different countries promoting, resisting or reshaping the incorporation of different kinds of regulatory knowledge depending on

[50] Howse, above n. 2.

their perceived interests. The point is simply that, taken together, the interaction of these different forms of knowledge tends to produce over time a set of implicitly shared ideas which become part of the 'professional sensibility'[51] of participants in the trade regime, and produce a characteristic way of categorising the world and orienting their response to it. The politics of the international trade regime, as I have said, reside in part in this sensibility.

Where, then, does this lead us in relation to the theme of 'regime interaction'? Let me limit myself to two brief observations. The first has to do with normative conflicts between regimes and the difficulties of their political resolution. In his chapter in this volume, Dunoff suggestively describes the resolution of conflicts between regimes as requiring a normative choice between competing communities of value without a redemptive narrative in which to ground that choice – 'nomos without narrative' in his evocative phrase. While this lack of a redemptive narrative – the absence, that is, of a shared collective purpose, or a collective political commitment on the basis of which to constitutionalise our fragmented legal order – is in some sense a fact of contemporary international economic governance, the story that I have told raises the possibility that it is in part a product of conditions of our own making. More specifically, it is in part the product of the emergence of a technicalised legal imagination which makes the pursuit of collective projects of global economic governance more difficult to imagine and pursue. The trade regime, I would argue, is best understood not so much as a normative community, but as a 'profession' or 'discipline' in the taxonomy proposed by Haas,[52] or as an 'epistemic community' in the sense of Ruggie's original definition,[53] sharing a common vocabulary, a common set of concepts, causal assumptions, interpretive habits and a professional sensibility. It is a community which does not experience itself as having (which in fact expressly disavows) political commitments, a community which is bound together by a collective purpose but which experiences the implementation of that

[51] See e.g. Kennedy, above n. 9.

[52] Peter M. Haas, 'Introduction: Epistemic Communities and International Policy Coordination' (1992) 46 *International Organization* 1, 16–20. See also Kennedy, 'Disciplines', above n. 2.

[53] 'I have borrowed this term [*episteme*] from Michel Foucault to refer to a dominant way of looking at social reality, a set of shared symbols and references, mutual expectations and a mutual predictability of intention. Epistemic communities may be said to consist of interrelated roles which grow up around an *episteme*; they delimit, for their members, *the* proper construction of social reality'. John Gerard Ruggie, 'International Responses to Technology' (1975) 29 *International Organization* 557, 569–570.

purpose as not requiring political choices, and as compatible with a wide diversity of political preferences. The argument made in this chapter, in other words, raises the possibility that the lack of a redemptive narrative may not just be a condition of the world in which international law works, but also in part the result of an international legal sensibility which disavows and avoids the evocation of explicit political choices, and rejects the deployment of suitably redemptive jurispathic narratives. In this view, international law both demands and helps to create the conditions for the conduct of politics in a technical register.

The second observation has to do with the productive possibilities of regime interaction as a form of contestatory politics. Does a fragmented legal order open up spaces for political contestation even as it reflects and consolidates a move to the technical? Is it possible to conduct a useful sort of politics within the technical registers of contemporary international economic governance? And if so what might this look like? One lesson from the story I have told in this chapter is that, if it is to function in this way, regime interaction must in part be directed towards the destabilisation of the 'principles of vision' characteristic of particular contemporary regimes of international governance. If the politics of the trade regime are in part shaped by the way that 'trade barriers' are made visible, and distinguished from other kinds of governmental intervention, then contestation cannot proceed until existing perceptions of what does and does not constitute a trade barrier lose their self-evidence. In this respect, what needs further emphasis is the radical indeterminacy of economic and other technical bodies of knowledge which are most often used to guide the work of categorisation. We need constant reminding that expert vocabularies are open and indeterminate enough to support different choices.

Another lesson is that, to some degree at least, different forms of expertise can usefully be deployed to contest, just as much to support, existing forms of professional knowledge at work within the international trade regime. Indeed, political contestation in an expert idiom on occasion occurs through the apparently technical forms of 'regime interaction' which are in part the focus of this volume, including forms of peer review, monitoring, information exchange, collaborative dialogue, as well as other strategies oriented towards the facilitation of 'learning'. While some of these mechanisms are closely associated with the process of technicalisation itself, perhaps this should not surprise us, since if these are the mechanisms by which background norms are produced and policed, this is where they must be contested. Now, there are obvious dangers associated with contestation of this kind, and as Young rightly notes (in Chapter 3 of this volume), it is crucial to ensure in such circumstances that 'information shared between regimes is sufficiently scrutinised and contested, and that a range of voices are heard (beyond those of scientific or technical experts or the "managers" of the regimes).'[54] The legal framework she proposes for regime interaction would certainly take us a considerable distance in that direction. But the point remains that part of what is needed in present scholarship on regime interaction is not only to show how the fragmented structure of international governance closes off space for politics, but also to map the spaces and strategies which it leaves open – and to attend closely to the ways in which interactions between regimes can engage those strategies in productive ways.

[54] See Margaret Young in this volume, pp. 97–98.

5

A New Approach to Regime Interaction

JEFFREY L. DUNOFF*

Introduction

Consider the following fact patterns:

> Scenario 1: The World Trade Organization's Appellate Body is asked to determine whether a restriction on trade authorised by an environmental treaty violates international trade rules.
>
> Scenario 2: The International Court of Justice and the International Criminal Tribunal for the former Yugoslavia explicitly disagree over the appropriate legal standard that should be used for questions regarding the attribution of state responsibility.
>
> Scenario 3: An airline pilot requests passengers to turn off laptops and other electronics just before takeoff.

Much international legal scholarship takes fact patterns like the clash between norms from different treaty regimes, and disagreements among diverse international tribunals over legal standards, or the application of those standards to particular facts, as paradigmatic examples of regime interaction. In this chapter, I challenge this conventional wisdom and argue that the scholarly focus on these archetypal fact patterns is, in fact, deeply misguided. Even more surprisingly, I'll suggest that the

* This chapter is a revised and expanded version of a presentation at the conference 'Regime Interaction in International Law: Theoretical and Practical Challenges' at Cambridge University in June 2009, and retains the informality of the presentation. I am grateful to the conference participants, and particularly Georges Abi-Saab, James Crawford, James Fleet and Andrew Lang, for useful comments, and to Margaret Young for the opportunity to participate in this project. I am also grateful to Andre Nollkaemper and other participants at the Vanderbilt Law School Roundtable on Emerging Themes in International Law: Legal Theory, Human Rights, and Financial Regulation, and to Gregory Shaffer and other participants at a seminar on International Law and its Impacts at the University of Minnesota Law School, for useful feedback on this project. Finally, I am indebted to Duncan Hollis and Ilija Penusliski for, in terms used elsewhere in this chapter, an illuminating set of ongoing conceptual interactions regarding the issues discussed in this chapter. This chapter is part of a larger project I am conducting on new approaches to regime interaction, tentatively entitled *Rethinking Regime Interaction*.

third scenario – requesting airline passengers to turn off their electronic devices – can teach us more about regime interactions than the other two fact patterns. To defend this counterintuitive claim, I'll develop several related arguments.

The first is that in addressing regime interaction, legal scholars frequently employ a faulty methodology. Typically, exploration of regime interaction starts – and often stops – with analysis of international court and tribunal decisions. However, for a variety of reasons, relying upon judicial opinions to understand regime overlap and interaction is unlikely to be productive. First, international litigation involves a highly atypical form of regime interaction. Hence, conventional approaches to regime interaction adopt a methodology that obscures the most common – and most important – forms of the phenomena under study. Just as importantly, a focus on courts is of limited utility as international judges lack the jurisprudential tools necessary to resolve the doctrinal tensions that arise when diverse international legal regimes overlap and collide. As a result, analysis of judicial decisions sheds little light on the causal mechanisms through which regimes impact upon and influence each other.

The methodological focus on judicial decisions, in turn, both rests upon and reinforces an inaccurate and incomplete model of regime interaction. By foregrounding international litigations, most analyses implicitly conceptualise regime interaction as a phenomenon arising out of discrete fact patterns that can be localised in time and space. But this 'transactional' model of regime interaction is partial and misleading; in fact, international legal regimes usually interact in ongoing, continuous relationships. These ongoing interactions can take several forms, including regulatory and administrative, operational, and conceptual interactions.

As described more fully below, these 'relational' interactions possess several features that sharply distinguish them from the transactional interactions at issue in most litigations. International litigation is largely about the narrowing of issues for authoritative resolution in one forum – an international tribunal. The relational interactions that I highlight, in contrast, have a highly dynamic character that often expands the range of issues under consideration and involves multiple international fora. In addition, international litigations involving multiple regimes are typically state-centric; states are virtually always parties and often the only parties. The relational interactions described below, in contrast, often involve a more diverse set of actors. In particular, there is frequently significant participation by non-state actors, including a diverse mix of international organisations, non-governmental organisations, regional bodies, and informal networks.

International litigations necessarily have a retrospective focus; they centre upon a discrete event in the past and the determination of whether one party's actions during that event violated international legal norms. Moreover, to the extent they involve conflicting rules found in different legal regimes, international litigations often revolve around efforts to harmonise norms, or to privilege one set of international legal norms and subordinate others. Relational interactions, in contrast, are typically forward looking. Moreover, instead of searching for *the* governing norm, relational interactions explicitly acknowledge that multiple regimes often can and do exercise concurrent authority over actions or events. Hence, relational interactions are often directed towards the articulation of new international norms to prospectively govern behaviour within a particular area of international relations. Thus these interactions are often 'jurisgenerative,' or law-creating.

My goals in identifying and analysing under-studied forms of regime interaction are multiple. First, I wish to critique the dominant court-centred approach to regime interaction by detailing many of its shortcomings. Dislodging this dominant approach will open up the space for consideration of more fruitful lines of inquiry. Second, I wish to redirect scholarly attention to various non-judicial settings where international regimes frequently interact. Doing so will allow us to more fully appreciate relational forms of regime interaction that are largely ignored in current scholarship.

Of course, developing an alternative approach to regime interaction is only worthwhile if it produces new insights and new opportunities for research on significant issues in this area. The approach outlined below does so in several ways. Most importantly, identifying and categorising the hidden forms of regime interaction discussed below is a necessary first step towards building a comprehensive theory of interaction and influence among international legal regimes. Moreover, by foregrounding previously understudied forms of regime interaction, I highlight the ways in which international regimes are purposeful actors in their own right, with independent interests and capabilities. Thus, I offer a view of the power and authority of international regimes that addresses long-standing debates in international relations regarding whether and how regimes matter in international affairs, as well as more recent debates in the legal literature over accountability and control mechanisms for international organisations. Finally, the analysis presented here, although necessarily preliminary, suggests a rich research agenda. For example, future studies might attempt to evaluate the potential benefits of relational regime interactions, including a plurality of regulatory perspectives and a dialogue among different regimes, with their potential costs, such as increased legal complexity. Alternatively, scholars may wish to explore the normative implications of different forms of regime interaction in terms of transparency, accountability and legitimacy, or to examine and identify the interests advanced when regime interaction occurs in one forum rather than another. Thus, this chapter should be understood as an effort to redirect and advance, as opposed to resolve, inquiry into the area of regime interaction.

A. Studying regime interaction: the current landscape

At the risk of over-generalisation, the dominant approaches to regime interaction in legal scholarship are rooted in the study of examples like the first two scenarios that opened this chapter.[1] More specifically, much of the legal scholarship addressing the topic of regime interaction tends to focus on the legal issues that arise out of fact patterns such as:

(i) when norms from two or more international legal regimes are potentially applicable to a situation, such as when human rights and/or international humanitarian law are applicable in specific fact patterns;[2]

(ii) when a court or other body embedded in one legal regime is asked to interpret or apply a norm originating in a different regime, such as

[1] For current purposes, I accept Krasner's now classic description of regimes as the 'implicit or explicit principles, norms, rules and decision-making procedures around which actor expectations converge in a given issue area'; Stephen D. Krasner, 'Structural Causes and Regime Consequences' (1982) 36 *International Organization* 185, 186. Krasner's usage is consistent with other formulations. See, e.g. Robert O. Keohane and Joseph S. Nye, *Power and Interdependence: World Politics in Transition* (Little, Brown, 1977) 19 (regimes are 'sets of governing arrangements' that include 'network of rules, norms, and procedures that regularize behavior and control its effects'). For a strong critique of the idea of regimes as obfuscating and obscuring the interest and power relationships that generate outcomes in international affairs, see Susan Strange, 'Cave! Hic Dragones: A Critique of Regime Analysis' (1982) 36 *International Organization* 479.

[2] For a sampling of the academic debate, see Alexander Orakhelashvilli, 'The Interaction between Human Rights and Humanitarian Law: Fragmentation, Conflict, Parallelism, or Convergence?' (2008) 19 *European Journal of International Law* 125; Philip Alston et al., 'The Competence of the UN Human Rights Council and its Special Procedures in relation to Armed Conflicts: Extrajudicial Executions in the "War on Terror"' (2008) 19 *European Journal of International Law* 183.

when a World Trade Organization (WTO) panel is asked to apply an international environmental norm;[3]

(iii) when the same or related fact pattern comes before multiple courts or institutions, such as the *MOx plant* litigation that came before four different international tribunals;[4] the *Swordfish* dispute that was filed at both the WTO and the International Tribunal for the Law of the Sea (ITLOS);[5] litigations arising out of the Georgia–Russia conflict over Southern Ossetia and Abkhazia, which are currently pending before the International Court of Justice (ICJ) and European Court of Human Rights (ECtHR); cases arising out of armed conflict in the Democratic Republic of the Congo that were filed before the International Court of Justice and the African Commission on Human Peoples' Rights; certain alleged human rights violations;[6] and certain investment disputes;[7] or

(iv) when different international tribunals or courts adopt different approaches to the meaning or application of a legal concept, such as when the ICJ and the International Criminal Tribunal for the former Yugoslavia (ICTY) disagree over the correct legal test for the attribution of conduct by non-state actors to states,[8] and when the ICTY,

[3] See, e.g. European Communities – Measures Affecting the Approval and Marketing of Biotech Products, WT/DS291/R (29 September 2006) (declining to take account of the Convention on Biological Diversity or the Biosafety Protocol); EC – Measures Concerning Meat and Meat Products (Hormones), WT/SD26/AB/R (16 January 1998) (declining to apply precautionary principle). For scholarly discussions of whether and when WTO panels should use non-WTO law, see Petros C. Mavroidis, 'No Outsourcing of Law? WTO Law as Practiced by WTO Courts?' (2008) 102 *American Journal of International Law* 421; Joost Pauwelyn, *Conflict of Norms in Public International Law* (Cambridge University Press, 2003); Jeffrey L. Dunoff, 'The WTO in Transition: Of Constituents, Competence and Coherence' (2001) 33 *George Washington International Law Review* 979; Joel P. Trachtman, 'The Domain of WTO Dispute Resolution' (1999) 40 *Harvard International Law Journal* 333.

[4] See, e.g. Robin Churchill and Joanne Scott, 'The MOx Plant Litigation: The First Half Life' (2004) 53 *International and Comparative Law Quarterly* 643.

[5] See, e.g. Marcos Orellana, 'The Swordfish Dispute between the EU and Chile at the ITLOS and the WTO' (2002) 71 *Nordic Journal of International Law* 55.

[6] Laurence R. Helfer, 'Forum Shopping for Human Rights' (1999) 148 *University of Pennsylvania Law Review* 285.

[7] Steven R. Ratner, 'Regulatory Takings in Institutional Context: Beyond the Fear of Fragmented International Law' (2008) 102 *American Journal of International Law* 475; Susan Franck, 'The Legitimacy Crisis in Investment Treaty Arbitration: Privatizing Public International Law through Inconsistent Decisions' (2005) 73 *Fordham Law Review* 1521.

[8] See, e.g. Richard Goldstone and Rebecca Hamilton, '*Bosnia v. Serbia*: Lessons from the Encounter of the International Court of Justice with the International Criminal Tribunal for the former Yugoslavia' (2008) 21 *Leiden Journal of International Law* 95; Antonio

the International Criminal Tribunal for Rwanda (ICTR) and the International Criminal Court (ICC) adopt different approaches to the permissibility of 'witness-proofing' before trial.[9]

The dominant approach, with its focus upon disputes that give rise to international litigations is well-represented in this volume. Thus, for example, the chapter by James Crawford and Penelope Nevill provides a masterful *tour d'horizon* of the myriad doctrinal and jurisprudential strategies that international tribunals employ when confronting fact patterns that implicate more than one legal regime. Crawford's and Nevill's survey of judicial practice is complemented by James Flett's comprehensive analysis of the ways that dispute organs in one specific regime – the WTO – use legal norms from other bodies of international law in the resolution of particular disputes. Even Gunther Teubner's and Peter Korth's chapter, with its sociologically influenced accounts of 'cultural polycentrism' and the difficulties posed by the 'colliding rationalities' embedded in modern society, is at bottom a plea for courts to adopt and modify conflict of law approaches originally developed in private international law when addressing cases involving regime overlaps.[10]

We should not be surprised that legal analysis of regime interaction typically foregrounds judicial decision-making.[11] The focus on courts

Cassesse, 'The Nicaragua and Tadic Tests Revisited in Light of the ICJ Judgement on Genocide in Bosnia' (2007) 18 *European Journal of International Law* 649.

9 *Prosecutor* v. *Dyilo*, Case No. ICC-01/04–01/06, Decision on Practices of Witness Familiarization and Witness Proofing (8 Nov. 2006); *Prosecutor* v. *Milutinovic*, Case No. IT-05–87-T, Decision on Ojdanic Motion to Prohibit Witness Proofing (ICTY, 12 Dec. 2006); *Prosecutor* v. *Karemara*, Case No. ICTR-98–44-T, Decision Defence Motions to Prevent Witness Proofing (15 Dec. 2006).

10 See the contributions to this volume by Gunther Teubner and Peter Korth (Ch. 1); see also James Crawford and Penelope Nevill (Ch. 8) and James Flett (Ch. 9).

11 To be sure, legal scholarship in the area is not monolithic. As noted below, Margaret Young's detailed description and analysis of the interactions among the World Trade Organization, Food and Agriculture Organization, and the United Nations Convention on the Law of the Sea (UNCLOS) in the context of fisheries is an example of the type of non-judicial regime interaction that I seek to highlight. See, e.g. Margaret Young, *Trading Fish, Saving Fish: The Interaction between Regimes in International Law* (Cambridge University Press, 2011); Margaret Young, 'Fragmentation or Interaction: The WTO, Fisheries Subsidies and International Law' (2009) 8 *World Trade Review* 477. In addition, Andrew Lang's outstanding work on the ways that actors embedded in international regimes create knowledge parallels my own efforts to detail how regime interactions create the conceptual framework by which we come to understand international legal phenomena. See, e.g. Andrew Lang, 'Legal Regimes and Regimes of Knowledge: Governing Global Services Trade' (Working Paper, No. 15, LSE Legal Studies Working Paper Series, 2009).

reflects, in part, substantial developments in international legal practice. The past two decades have witnessed a dramatic increase in the number and scope of international courts and tribunals.[12] A partial list of new adjudicatory fora would include the WTO's dispute settlement system; two ad hoc international criminal tribunals; the ICC; International Tribunal for the Law of the Sea (ITLOS); the World Bank Inspection Panel and its Asian and Inter-American Development Bank counterparts; the dispute systems associated with several trade groupings, including the Andean, Mercosur, NAFTA, ASEAN-China trade agreements and those of other regional trade groupings; ad hoc arbitral tribunals created pursuant to hundreds of bilateral investment treaties; as well as various hybrid and specialised tribunals such as those with jurisdiction over certain events in Lebanon, Sierra Leone, Kosovo, East Timor and Cambodia. In addition, states are increasingly recognising the jurisdiction of these tribunals, and are increasingly bringing these disputes to these new tribunals, as well as to existing courts, such as the ECtHR and European Court of Justice (ECJ).[13] As a result, courts have recently experienced a dramatic increase in their caseload, albeit from an admittedly small baseline. Indeed, by one count, some three-quarters of international tribunal decisions, opinions and rulings have been issued since 1990.[14]

This dramatic upswing in judicial activity has sparked intensive scholarly interest. Indeed, the most recent wave of scholarship on regime interaction was launched by a diplomatic and scholarly debate over the implications of the proliferation of international courts and tribunals,[15]

[12] For purposes of this chapter, I do not distinguish between courts, tribunals and other adjudicative fora.

[13] Laurence R. Helfer and Anne-Marie Slaughter, 'Why States Create International Tribunals: A Response to Professors Posner and Yoo' (2005) 93 *California Law Review* 899, 914.

[14] Karen J. Alter, 'Delegating to International Courts: Self-Binding vs. Other-Binding Delegation' (2008) 71 *Law and Contemporary Problems* 37, 38.

[15] Early statements by ICJ judges highlighted the difficulties raised by the proliferation of international tribunals. See Judge Stephen M. Schwebel, 'Address to the Plenary Session of the General Assembly of the United Nations' (Speech Delivered at the Plenary Session of the General Assembly of the United Nations, 6 November 1999); Judge Gilbert Guillaume, 'The Proliferation of International Judicial Bodies: The Outlook for the International Legal Order' (Speech delivered to the Sixth Committee of the General Assembly of the United Nations, 29 November 2000). Other ICJ judges have taken a more sympathetic view: Rosalyn Higgins, 'A Babel of Judicial Voices? Ruminations from the Bench' (2006) 55 *International and Comparative Law Quarterly* 791. For a sampling of the scholarship, see Thomas Buergenthal, 'Proliferation of International Courts and Tribunals: Is It Good or Bad?' (2001) 14 *Leiden Journal of International Law* 267; Georges Abi-Saab, 'Fragmentation or Unification: Some Concluding Remarks'

and this high-profile exchange sparked a large literature that extended and refined the debate. The influential International Law Commission (ILC) Study Group Report on the fragmentation of international law had a similar court-centric approach, explicitly situating its analysis 'especially by reference to the practice of international courts and tribunals'.[16] In short, the intellectual ferment sparked by the increase in judicial activity noted above has prompted a rapidly growing literature in the disciplines of international law, international relations and comparative politics as well as the launch of a university press series[17] and – astonishingly – a specialised practitioner's journal devoted to law and practice before international tribunals.[18]

Finally, the case-centric methodology reflects much larger trends in legal thought, including the central role of litigated cases in resolving disputes over contested social facts[19] and as the fundamental unit of accretion of judicial authority, not to mention legal scholars' traditional focus on judicial opinions.[20] However, this characteristic form

(1999) 31 *New York University Journal of International Law and Politics* 919; Jonathan I. Charney, 'Is International Law Threatened by Multiple International Tribunals?' (1998) 217 *Recueil Des Cours* 101; Benedict Kingsbury, 'Foreword: Is the Proliferation of International Courts and Tribunals a Systemic Problem?' (1999) 31 *New York University Journal of International Law and Politics* 679; Cesare P. R. Romano, 'The Proliferation of International Judicial Bodies: The Pieces of the Puzzle' (1999) 31 *New York University Journal of International Law and Politics* 709.

[16] ILC, 'Fragmentation of International Law: Difficulties Arising from the Diversification and Expansion of International Law', UN Doc. A/CN.4/L.682 (13 Apr. 2006) (finalised by Martti Koskenniemi).

[17] See Oxford University Press Series on International Courts and Tribunals at http://ukcatalogue.oup.com/category/academic/series/law/icts.do.

[18] See *The Law & Practice of International Courts and Tribunals* (Brill Publishing).

[19] Justice Robert Jackson famously stated that the most important legacy of the Nuremberg trials was the establishment of a historical record. 'Report to the President from Justice Robert H. Jackson', Chief of Counsel for the United States in the Prosecution of Axis War Criminals, 7 June 1945, reprinted in (1999) 39 *American Journal of International Law* (Supp. 1945), at 178. The importance of creating an authoritative historical record has been central to debates over the creation of other international criminal tribunals. For example, Secretary of State Madeline Albright supported international criminal prosecutions on the grounds that they 'will establish the historical record before the guilty can reinvent the truth': Bill Berkeley, *The Graves are Not Yet Full: Race, Tribe and Power in the Heart of Africa* (Basic Books, 2001) 249.

[20] The court-centric nature of legal scholarship – which misleadingly suggests that courts are the only authoritative interpreters of legal materials and overlooks important systemic issues that never become the subject of litigation – has been subject to sustained critique. See, e.g. Tomiko Brown-Nagin, 'Elites, Social Movements, and the Law: The Case of Affirmative Action' (2005) 105 *Columbia Law Review* 1436; J. M. Balkin and

of legal reductionism both oversimplifies the manner in which regime interaction should be understood and narrows the range of potential strategies that can be used in addressing these phenomena. The arguments below represent an attempt to enlarge our understanding of, and potential responses to, international regime interaction.

B. Nomos and narrative

To understand why international tribunals can play only a limited role in resolving the complex challenges raised by regime interactions, I draw on Robert Cover's seminal article entitled 'Nomos and Narrative'.[21] This celebrated article no doubt falls within the category of deservedly classic works that are much better known than read. Since its publication, critics have lamented its dense prose and cryptic arguments. Yet Cover is widely recognised as a highly influential thinker, and 'Nomos and Narrative' is arguably his most important scholarly work.[22] More significantly, the article sets out a highly influential account of how judges grapple with the complexities presented when events or actors are potentially governed by law emanating from multiple sources.

For current purposes, it is not necessary to delve into the article's myriad complexities; rather, a brief summary of Cover's central claims will suffice. Fundamentally, 'Nomos and Narrative' is a challenge to conventional understandings of 'law'. The article suggests that we should understand law not simply as a cluster of rules or even as a mechanism

Sanford Levinson, 'The Canons of Constitutional Law' (1998) 111 *Harvard Law Review* 963, 1003–1004.

21 Robert M. Cover, 'The Supreme Court, 1982 Term – Foreword: Nomos and Narrative' (1983) 97 *Harvard Law Review* 4 (hereinafter, Cover, 'Nomos and Narrative').

22 The article receives extended treatment in, Howard J. Vogel, 'In the Cause of Justice: Reflections on Robert Cover's Turn Toward Narrative' (1989) 7 *Journal of Law and Religion* 173; Perry Dane, 'The Public, the Private, and the Sacred: Variations on a Theme of "Nomos and Narrative"' (1996) 8 *Cardozo Studies in Law and Literature* 15; Symposium, 'Rethinking Robert Cover's Nomos and Narrative' (2005) 17 *Yale Journal of Law and the Humanities* 1; Richard Mullender, 'Two Nomoi and a Clash of Narratives: The Story of the United Kingdom and the European Union' (2006) *Issues in Legal Scholarship*, (available at www.bepress.com/ils/iss8/art3). To date, application of Cover's work to international law is extremely rare. See, e.g. Judith Resnik, 'Law as Affiliation: Foreign Law, Democratic Federalism and the Sovereigntism of the Nation-State' (2008) 6 *International Journal of Constitutional Law* 33; Paul Schiff Berman, 'A Pluralist Approach to International Law' (2007) 32 *Yale Journal of International Law* 301.

for social control, but rather as a *nomos*, or normative universe.[23] Under this approach, law is understood as a holistic mode for assessing good and bad, valid and invalid, right and wrong. For Cover, law is 'not simply a system of rules to be observed, but a world in which we live'.[24]

As a result, law possesses a deeply aspirational character. In 'Nomos and Narrative', Cover claimed that 'Law may be viewed as a system of tension or a bridge linking a concept of a reality to an imagined alternative – that is, as a connective between two states of affairs ...'[25] In a later work, he had condensed his understanding of law: 'Law *is* the bridge – the committed social behavior which constitutes the way a group of people will attempt to get from here to there.'[26]

'Nomos and Narrative' contains another challenge to dominant understandings of law. Specifically, Cover rejected a state-centric understanding of law. 'Although the state is not necessarily the creator of legal meaning, the creative process is collective or social.'[27] He believed that, in addition to the state, many sub-national communities create and maintain normative orders. Paradigmatic examples include minority religious groups – such as the Amish, the Mennonites, the early Mormons and the Pilgrims – that create holistic normative and ethical systems.[28] Only such cohesive communities, 'already self-conscious and lawful by [their] own lights', can generate the 'persistent effort to live a law other than that of the state's officials'.[29] Thus, for Cover, '[i]n th[e] realm of [constitutional] meaning – if not in the domain of social control – the Mennonite community creates law as fully as does the judge.'[30]

In a key move, Cover argues that the normative rules that these groups create gain meaning through narrative: 'No set of legal institutions or prescriptions exists apart from the narratives that locate it and give it meaning. For every constitution there is an epic, for each decalogue a scripture.'[31] As a result, a legal tradition consists not only of a set of norms but also 'a language and a mythos – narratives in which the corpus juris

[23] For the classic discussion of the evolution of the Greek term 'nomos', see Werner Jaeger, 'Praise of Law: The Origin of Legal Philosophy and the Greeks' in Paul Sayre (ed.), *Interpretations of Modern Legal Philosophies: Essays in Honor of Roscoe Pound* (Oxford University Press, 1947) 352–375.

[24] Cover, 'Nomos and Narrative', above n. 21, 5.

[25] Ibid., 9.

[26] Robert M. Cover, 'The Folktales of Justice: Tales of Jurisdiction' (1985) 14 *Capital University Law Review* 179, 181.

[27] Cover, 'Nomos and Narrative', above n. 21, 11.

[28] Ibid., 31. [29] Ibid., 50, n. 137.

[30] Ibid., 28. [31] Ibid., 4–5.

is located by those whose wills act upon it'.[32] Hence, for Cover, 'law and narrative are inseparably related'.

Perhaps the most well-known aspect of 'Nomos and Narrative' is Cover's analysis of judicial behaviour when courts encounter conflicting nomoi that emanate from different groups, or from the state and a specific group. Legal scholars often assume that courts address conflict by clarifying ambiguities, filling gaps in the law, or resolving conflicting interpretations. But to think that courts remove uncertainty by bringing clarity to the law 'seems to presuppose that there is a hermeneutic that is methodologically superior to those employed by the communities that offer their own law'[33] – a position that Cover's non-statist posture explicitly rejects.

When confronted with a clash between nomoi from different law-making communities, courts are expected to impose uniformity. However, in so doing, Cover argues, courts do not *create* law. Rather, in the face of too much law, courts must be 'jurispathic'; that is, they must kill off one of the conflicting norms.[34] In a remarkable passage, Cover claims that:

> Judges are people of violence. Because of the violence they command, judges characteristically do not create law, but kill it. Theirs is the jurispathic office. Confronting the luxuriant growth of a hundred legal traditions, they assert that *this one* is law and destroy or try to destroy the rest.[35]

Cover's characterisation of judicial decision-making as norm destruction begs the question of how courts decide which norm will be destroyed, and which will be privileged. As noted above, Cover rejects as 'too easy' any assumption of the virtue of the courts' interpretative skills, or of the normative superiority of state norms over other norms.[36] Rather, Cover argued, only the invocation of a 'redemptive narrative'[37] has the normative weight to justify killing off a competing nomos.

32 Ibid., 9. 33 Ibid., 42.

34 Ibid., 40. 35 Ibid., 53.

36 Here, Cover takes aim at Owen Fiss's arguments that assume the virtue of the judiciary. See Owen Fiss, 'Objectivity and Interpretation' (1982) 34 *Stanford Law Review* 739.

37 Cover, 'Nomos and Narrative', above n. 21, 34 ('Redemption takes place within an eschatological schema that postulates: (1) the unredeemed character of reality as we know it, (2) the fundamentally different reality that should take its place, and (3) the replacement of the one with the other.'). Following Cover, a number of constitutional theorists have emphasised the (potentially) redemptive nature of US constitutional practice and doctrine. See, e.g. Amy Kapczynski, 'Historicism, Progress and the Redemptive Constitution' (2005) 26 *Cardozo Law Review* 1041; Jack M. Balkin, 'The Declaration and the Promise of a Democratic Culture' (1999) 4 *Widener Law Symposium Journal* 167, 167

Cover used the case of *Bob Jones University* to illustrate these abstract ideas.[38] Bob Jones University was founded by evangelicals and was 'dedicated to the teaching and propagation of its fundamentalist Christian religious beliefs'. To this end, all entering students were 'screened as to their religious beliefs', all teachers were required to be 'devout Christians', and all courses were 'taught according to the Bible'.[39] The University embraced a highly racialised reading of Scripture. As the US Supreme Court gently put it, 'the sponsors of the University genuinely believe that the Bible forbids interracial dating and marriage'. To give effect to this belief, the University refused to admit blacks as students until 1971. Thereafter, for several years, it 'accepted no applications from unmarried Negroes, but did accept applications from Negroes married within their race'. After unrelated litigation prohibited racial exclusion from private schools,[40] the University revised its policy and permitted unmarried Negroes to enrol. However, a University disciplinary rule prohibited interracial dating and marriage, upon pain of expulsion.[41]

Under US tax law, non-profit entities, including universities, enjoy certain tax benefits. Given the University's racially discriminatory policies, in 1978 the Internal Revenue Service (IRS) revoked Bob Jones's tax exemption. The University challenged the Government's action, and the dispute eventually reached the United States Supreme Court.[42] The legal question

('the point of Constitutional government ... is the eventual redemption in history of the principles of our Founding document'); Jack M. Balkin, 'Agreements with Hell and Other Objects of Our Faith' (1997) 65 *Fordham Law Review* 1703 ('the aspirationalist vision [of the constitution] is one of redemption. There can be no redemption without the recognition of sin. Thus, even at the moment when we want to read the Constitution as aspiring to great justice, we much soberly reflect on its evils, both potential and realized.').

[38] *Bob Jones Univ.* v. *United States*, 461 US 574 (1983).

[39] Ibid., at 580.

[40] *McCrary* v. *Runyon*, 515 F.2d 1082 (4th Cir. 1975), *aff'd*, 427 US 160 (1976).

[41] The relevant University disciplinary rule read:
There is to be no interracial dating

1. Students who are partners in an interracial marriage will be expelled.
2. Students who are members of or affiliated with any group or organization which holds as one of its goals or advocates interracial marriage will be expelled.
3. Students who date outside their own race will be expelled.
4. Students who espouse, promote, or encourage others to violate the University's dating rules and regulations will be expelled.

In subsequent years, the University repudiated its history of racism.

[42] The District Court held that the IRS's actions violated the University's first amendment right to free exercise of religion. 486 F. Supp. 890 (DSC 1978). In a divided opinion, the Fourth Circuit reversed. 639 F.2d 147 (4th Cir. 1980).

presented was whether 'private schools that prescribe and enforce racially discriminatory admissions standards on the basis of religious doctrine, qualify as tax exempt organizations' under the US tax laws.[43] The larger jurisprudential and normative issues the case presented involve how the Court should resolve conflicts between a community's deeply held values and conflicting state norms, and how the right to religious freedom interacts with the nation's commitment to racial equality.

The University lost, on the rather bloodless grounds that the IRS's reasonable interpretation of the tax code was entitled to deference. Writing for the Court, Chief Justice Burger upheld the IRS's determination that the University was not a 'charitable organization' for purposes of the tax code because charities provided public benefits that racist educational institutions did not provide.[44] Bob Cover was a fierce advocate for racial justice, but he was sharply critical of the Court's reasoning. He thought the Court's deferential approach to the IRS's interpretation of the statute inappropriately permitted the Court to avoid the fundamental constitutional and normative issues presented.[45] Cover argued that the ruling adopts 'a position that places nothing at risk and from which the Court makes no interpretative gesture at all'. Just as importantly, the Court's technocratic approach paid insufficient respect to Bob Jones as a normative community.

Cover argued that if the Court was going to attempt to override the University's religiously based nomos prohibiting interracial dating, it should have invoked a 'redemptive narrative' such as the historic US commitment to racial equality and the national imperative of overcoming the country's legacy of slavery.[46] For Cover, only the invocation of such a narrative would justify the Court's effort to destroy the sincerely held nomoi of a competing normative community.

[43] *Bob Jones Univ.*, 461 US at 577.

[44] Ibid. at 591–595.

[45] Cover, 'Nomos and Narrative', above n. 21, 599, n. 24. Some scholars believe that the Court's opinion implicitly reaches constitutional conclusions. See, e.g. Mayer G. Freed and Daniel D. Polsby, 'Race, Religion, and Public Policy: Bob Jones University v. United States' (1983) *Supreme Court Review* 1.

[46] Cover, 'Nomos and Narrative', above n. 21, 65. As to whether Cover fairly interpreted the Supreme Court's opinion, see Judith Resnik, 'Living their Legal Commitments: Paideic Communities, Courts and Robert Cover' (2005) 17 *Yale Journal of Law and the Humanities* 17, 43 (characterising the decision as 'a cram-down of a national norm … [that] no private enclave can provide an overtly racist educational environment and obtain the state's assistance').

C. Nomos without narrative

Robert Cover's scholarship is not an obvious source for insights into the international legal issues raised by regime interaction.[47] How does the tax status of a racially discriminatory Christian university bear on the fragmentation of international law? What does the discussion of redemptive narratives have to do with the work of international tribunals? More generally, how can Cover's analysis inform our understanding of the issues raised by interactions among international legal regimes?

I believe that, in at least certain respects, several intriguing analogies – and disanalogies – exist between the conflict of norms situation that Cover addresses and the issues raised when international legal regimes interact. Let us consider whether we can usefully analogise the participants in functionally discrete international legal regimes, such as human rights, trade, or environment, to the cohesive normative communities that Cover identified. Do the actors in these regimes constitute discrete, law-making communities? If so, do the norms that are generated by these communities draw meaning from being embedded within a larger narrative? Finally, how are conflicts among norms emanating from different communities resolved?

It is no longer novel to understand participants in one or another international legal regime as constituting separate and distinct communities. Political scientists have described how 'epistemic communities' have driven international negotiations and the production of international law in various issue areas. Sociologically minded legal scholars, like David Kennedy and Andrew Lang, have described the ways in which 'experts' in particular fields deploy professional vocabularies and expertise in ways that define and drive global governance in various domains.[48] Indeed, it is now conventional wisdom that various specialised international legal regimes are not only organised around their own core legal principles and foundational legal texts, but also that they have 'established [their] separate epistemic communities of lawyers working in the field,

[47] But for the application of Cover's pluralist approach to law to the international legal system; see also Paul Schiff Berman, 'Federalism and International Law Through the Lens of Legal Pluralism' (2008) 73 *Missouri Law Review* 1151 (applying Cover's pluralist approach to law to the international legal system) and Paul Schiff Berman, 'Global Legal Pluralism' 80 *Southern California Law Review* 1155.

[48] See, e.g. David Kennedy, 'Challenging Expert Rule: The Politics of Global Governance' (2005) 27 *Sydney Journal of International Law* 5; David Kennedy, 'The Politics of the Invisible College: International Governance and the Politics of Expertise' (2001) 5 *European Human Rights Law Review* 463.

institutions developing and applying the law, and courts and tribunals enforcing it'.[49]

I wish to advance a related, but distinguishable claim here, namely that we can understand the actors in specific functional international legal regimes as constituting law-making normative communities in the sense that Cover understood sub-national groups in the United States to be law-making normative communities. Consider, for example, the international human rights regime. The professional participants in this regime, including advocates, analysts, NGO employees, international civil servants, and others – commonly referred to as 'the international human rights community' – make up a discrete normative community. That is, by and large the actors in this community, like the communities Cover discussed, share a commitment to a set of relatively well-defined normative principles, bring a shared set of conceptual frameworks and specialised vocabularies to bear on issues of common concern, and self-consciously understand themselves to be participants in a 'movement'. Indeed, the cluster of commitments associated with the human rights movement is often analysed in terms associated with religious belief, i.e. human rights has been characterised as an 'ideology' and criticised as a type of 'fundamentalism'.[50] In addition, like the cohesive communities that Cover studied, the international human rights community is 'jurisgenerative'. That is, through their ongoing efforts the members of this community have created and attempt to implement and enforce an enormous corpus of international human rights law.[51]

Moreover, like the nomoi that Cover analysed, international human rights norms gain meaning through being embedded within larger narratives. Consider the well-known conventional wisdom regarding the birth and rise of the human rights movement. This frequently told tale acknowledges the historical antecedents of human rights,[52] but dates the development of the international human rights regime to the post-World War II period. Under the conventional account of the genesis of human rights law, the victorious Allies shared a common understanding that

49 Bruno Simma, 'Universality of International Law from the Perspective of a Practitioner' (2009) 20 *European Journal of International Law* 265, 275.

50 See, e.g. Makau wa Mutua, 'The Ideology of Human Rights' (1996) 36 *Virginia Journal of International Law* 589; David Kinley, 'Human Rights Fundamentalisms' (2007) 29 *Sydney Law Review* 545.

51 Makauwa Mutua, 'Standing Setting in Human Rights: Critique and Prognosis' (2007) 29 *Human Rights Quarterly* 547.

52 One conventional citation is to John Locke, *Two Treaties of Government* (1690).

Nazi atrocities were rooted in 'a vicious philosophy based on utter disregard for the dignity of human beings'[53] and a common commitment that such atrocities should 'never again' be permitted to occur. As a jurisprudential matter, the revelation of German wartime atrocities prompted the international community to undertake a fundamental reassessment of traditional international law doctrine regarding the juridical status of individuals under international law. To ensure that the war-time horrors would 'never again' occur, the international community pursued a dual track strategy. On the one hand, the Allies pursued prosecutions against individuals responsible for the commission of atrocities. On the other hand, the community of nations, along with numerous civic and religious groups began to create human rights law. In the years that followed, these actors developed a sprawling body of law and an elaborate institutional machinery to promote and protect human rights. Notably, the efforts to promote human dignity through legal protection for individual human rights have been characterised as a 'turning point' in the field of international law[54] and the most 'radical development in the whole history of international law'.[55] Thus, the human rights narrative is grounded in a fundamental commitment to human dignity arising out of the historical experience with Nazism, and a vow that those horrors never again occur.

The trade regime can be described in similar terms. First, like the human rights regime, it is largely the product of a relatively small and relatively closed group of participants. As Robert Keohane and Joseph Nye have noted, from its origins in the post-War era and for many years thereafter, international trade law was constructed by a 'club' of a relatively small number of economists and diplomats from like-minded states.[56] Members of the club quietly made trade policy without significant input from or interaction with officials in other issue areas, such as labour or finance officials – let alone public input or oversight. Over time, members of the GATT club would 'develop close working relationships with their colleagues from other countries, limiting the disruptive force of parochial concerns emanating from domestic politics'.[57] This club

[53] Antonio Cassese, *International Law* (Oxford University Press, 2001) 351.

[54] Ibid.

[55] John P. Humphrey, 'The Revolution in the International Law of Human Rights' (1975) 4 *Human Rights* 205, 208.

[56] Robert O. Keohane and Joseph S. Nye, 'The Club Model of Multilateral Cooperation and Problems of Legitimacy' in Roger Porter et al. (eds.), *Efficiency, Equity and Legitimacy: The Multilateral Trading System at the Millenium* (Brookings Institute, 2001).

[57] Ibid. at 266.

approach to trade persisted for many years because it was successful, in the sense that members of the club oversaw dramatic decreases in tariffs and other trade barriers, and a corresponding increase in global trade and prosperity. To be sure, the club model has fractured in recent years, and the trade regime's closed nature has been subject to a sustained critique. But for current purposes the salient observation is that for many decades members of the international trade community possessed an (accurate) self-understanding of themselves as constituting a discrete and distinctive normative community engaged in a law-making enterprise.

Moreover, like human rights norms, the basic principles associated with international trade law, such as non-discrimination and the reduction of barriers to trade, take meaning from being embedded within a larger narrative about the link between protectionist trade policies and the Great Depression. The standard account starts with the disastrous trade policies of the 1920s and 1930s, when many states pursued mercantilist strategies. In June 1930, President Herbert Hoover signed into law the Smoot-Hawley Tariff Act, which dramatically raised US tariffs on imports to the highest levels in the nation's history.[58] In response, a number of other countries raised their tariffs and imposed quotas or foreign exchange controls. As a result, the volume of international trade plummeted. From 1929 to 1933, imports from Europe to the United States dropped by almost two-thirds, and US exports to Europe fell by half. Overall, between 1929 and 1934, world trade declined by roughly 66 per cent. This spectacular contraction of international commerce, in turn, contributed to the strength and length of the Great Depression.[59]

The post-war trading order was consciously designed to avoid a repeat of this experience. 'The core policy assumption [underlying the GATT] was that liberal trade and other freedoms for economic transactions would best promote the welfare of all in the world, based on well-established economic theories of comparative advantage, gains from trade, and economies of scale.'[60] The theory is that, as nations reduce barriers to trade, each country will specialise in the production and export of goods that it can produce relatively more efficiently than other nations. The resulting increased trade spurs economic growth, productivity gains and job

[58] Smoot-Hawley Tariff Act, § 497, 46 Stat. 590 (1930).

[59] In the 1940s and 1950s, many advanced the additional claim that the turn to protectionism also produced distrust among nations, helping to pave the way for World War II.

[60] John H. Jackson, 'Dolphins and Hormones: GATT and the Legal Environment for International Trade After the Uruguay Round' (1992) 14 *University of Arkansas at Little Rock Law Journal* 429, 441.

creation. In turn, aggregate welfare increases as consumers enjoy lower prices and a greater availability of goods. Thus, trade narrative views the international trade regime as helping the global community avoid the economically and politically destructive experiences of the 1930s and 1940s.

It would not be difficult to draw similar analogies between the normative communities that Cover discussed and the normative communities that generated and populate other international legal regimes, including, for example, international humanitarian law and international environmental law.[61] To be sure, the analogy between the participants in specialised international legal regimes and the cohesive communities Cover discussed is far from perfect. Membership in various insular religious communities is typically mutually exclusive – Orthodox Jews are not, simultaneously, members of Mennonite churches – while the 'members' of various international legal regimes – states – largely overlap. However, to the extent that traditional conceptions of the state as rational, unitary actor are displaced by understandings of the various ways that contemporary states disaggregate the conduct of foreign affairs,[62] and to the extent that we understand that regimes are often created by small groups of actors, including those outside the state apparatus, the analogy between participants in functional international regimes and cohesive normative communities may be considered productive. And even if the participants in various international legal regimes lack the particular quality of religious commitment associated with the groups Cover studied, it is nevertheless true that:

> [t]hrough specialisation – that is to say, through the creation of special regimes of knowledge and expertise in areas such as 'trade law', 'human rights law', 'environmental law', 'security law', 'international criminal law', 'European law', and so on – the world of legal practice is being sliced

[61] For current purposes, it is not necessary to claim that the analogy holds across all international legal regimes.

[62] Although this approach to global governance finds its intellectual roots in the 'transgovernmental relations' approach pioneered by Robert Keohane and Joseph Nye in the 1970s; see, e.g. Keohane and Nye, above n. 1. Anne-Marie Slaughter's writings introduced these ideas to a generation of international legal scholars; see, e.g. Anne-Marie Slaughter, *A New World Order* (Princeton University Press, 2004). More recent contributions that critique or extend this literature include Pierre-Hugues Verdier, 'Transnational Regulatory Networks and Their Limits' (2009) 34 *Yale Journal of International Law* 113; Kal Raustiala, 'The Architecture of International Cooperation: Transgovernmental Networks and the Future of International Law' (2002) 43 *Virginia Journal of International Law* 1; David Zaring, 'International Law by Other Means: The Twilight Existence of International Financial Regulatory Organizations' (1998) 33 *Texas International Law Journal* 281.

> up in institutional projects that cater for special audiences with special interests and special ethos.[63]

Given the competing ethos associated with different regimes, and the divergent narratives that give meaning to the rules from different regimes, what should happen when nomoi from different international legal regimes interact? If, say, a trade norm conflicts with a human rights or environmental norm? 'Nomos and Narrative' suggests that tribunals facing such cases confront the problem of 'too many' norms, and that the solution consists of the destruction of one of the competing norms. 'Nomos and Narrative' also suggests that, to engage in the necessary jurispathic act, courts should invoke an overarching, redemptive narrative.

At this point, the analogy between 'Nomos and Narrative' and regime interaction breaks down. The suggestion that judges should invoke a redemptive narrative when rules from different regimes conflict poses an impossible task upon international tribunals for the simple reason that the international legal system today simply does not possess a redemptive narrative. Hence, the problem that courts face is not simply that international law lacks a 'metarationality,' or overarching principles of authority, as Gunther Teubner and others have argued.[64] And, as Martti Koskenniemi points out in his contribution to this volume, the complexities associated with regime interaction cannot be resolved by technical or managerial responses.[65] At a deeper level, the problem highlighted by litigations involving regime interaction is that at present there is no widely accepted redemptive narrative that sets out a vision of a perfected, or redeemed, international order, and that gives meaning to the norms embedded within that order.

To be clear, the claim that international law lacks a redemptive narrative, an overarching narrative that gives meaning to the different nomoi, is not to suggest that there are no candidates for this role, or that international law could never have a redemptive narrative. Indeed, over time, various international regimes, including human rights and environment,

[63] Martti Koskenniemi, 'The Politics of International Law – 20 Years Later' (2009) 20 *European Journal of International Law* 7, 12–13.

[64] Andreas Fischer-Lescano and Gunther Teubner, 'Regime-Collisions: The Vain Search for Legal Unity in the Fragmentation of International Law' (2004) 25 *Michigan Journal of International Law* 999. See also Martti Koskenniemi, 'The Fate of Public International Law: Between Technique and Politics' (2007) 70 *Modern Law Review* 1.

[65] Martti Koskenniemi, 'Hegemonic Regimes', Ch. 10 of this volume.

have placed redemptive narratives on offer.[66] Moreover, I believe that the emerging literature on international constitutionalism can be understood as, in part, an effort to provide international law with a redemptive narrative.[67] However, to date, none of the contending narratives has achieved a position of predominance; none has been widely accepted by the relevant actors as a redemptive narrative.[68] As a result, the contemporary international legal order has been aptly characterised as a 'global disorder of normative orders'.[69]

Moreover, the descriptive claim that international law lacks a redemptive narrative should not be read to entail a normative claim for the necessity or even desirability of one. The very idea of a redemptive narrative carries religious overtones, and, as Georges Abi-Saab has pointed out, in many ways modern international law represents a turn away from a religiously inspired ordering of the world to a secular ordering of the world. Finally, given the enormously crowded and enormously heterogeneous world that we inhabit, the possibility of finding a redemptive narrative with widespread acceptance in the near future is virtually non-existent. Thus, the arguments above should not be understood as implicitly arguing for the desirability of a redemptive narrative but rather as identifying the implications of a lack of a redemptive narrative.

One need not accept all of Cover's arguments – for example, we might not accept his valorisation of religious groups with racially discriminatory policies – to appreciate his account of the dilemmas judges face when nomoi from different normative communities conflict. In Coverian terms, litigations involving regime interactions often ask courts to privilege one set of norms and to kill off another. But given the absence of a redemptive narrative, this is precisely a task that international tribunals cannot successfully undertake. That is, cases involving regime conflict and collision call upon international courts to use a jurisprudential tool that they simply do not possess. I think that international judges recognise that they

[66] See, e.g. Matua, above n. 51, 595 (noting dominant conceptual approaches to human rights 'share an unequivocal belief in the redemptive power of human rights law').

[67] See, e.g. Jeffrey L. Dunoff and Joel P. Trachtman (eds.), *Ruling the World? Constitutionalism, International Law and Global Governance* (Cambridge University Press, 2009). See also Koskenniemi's contribution to this volume p. 315 (noting how actors in specific regimes may employ a 'universalisation strategy' of offering certain values as if they were universal values or represent preferences of the entire international community).

[68] Jeffrey L. Dunoff, 'International Law in a Time of Perplexity' (2010) 25 *Maryland Journal of International Law* 11.

[69] Neil Walker, 'Beyond Boundary Disputes and Basic Grids: Mapping the Global Disorder of Normative Orders' (2008) 6 *International Journal of Constitutional Law* 373.

lack the conceptual and normative tools to resolve relations among different units of legal, political and moral ordering in the world. This explains why the rare efforts to resolve conflicting jurisprudence among tribunals have, to date, proved unavailing; why inconsistent judgments by various international tribunals remain in an uneasy co-existence; and why international courts in one regime are often reluctant to interpret or apply norms from other regimes.[70] It explains why the various judicial strategies that James Crawford's and Penelope Nevill's chapter identifies can best be understood as exercises in avoidance and temporisation. To be clear, these are not intended as pejorative characterisations.[71] Rather, judicial practice reflects the reality that international courts inhabit a world that is overflowing with international law, a world of multiple nomoi – but cannot be jurispathic. Turning Cover's argument upside down, international courts inhabit a world of nomos without narrative.

D. Toward a new model of regime interaction

International courts and tribunals can play only a limited role in resolving the conflicts presented by cases involving regime interaction, rendering the scholarly focus on judicial opinions of limited utility. But the problem with the dominant approach to studying regime interaction is not simply a function of the fact that, as argued above, international tribunals lack the tools to provide authoritative resolution of the tensions and conflicts among regimes that arise in international litigations. The deeper conceptual problem is that scholarly inquiries that foreground judicial efforts to address regime interaction mislead because they presuppose a partial and hence inaccurate model of regime interaction.

The scholarly focus on the paradigmatic litigations involving the intersection of international legal regimes leads to a conceptualisation of

[70] These efforts are detailed in Jeffrey L. Dunoff, *Nomos without Narrative* (unpublished manuscript, on file with author).

[71] I offer these characterisations as positive rather than normative statements, and have elsewhere argued for a form of judicial minimalism in the face of underlying value conflicts. See, e.g. Jeffrey L. Dunoff, 'The Death of the Trade Regime' (1999) 10 *European Journal of International Law* 733. In offering this defence of judicial minimalism, I draw on a rich domestic law literature. See, e.g. Cass R. Sunstein, *One Case at a Time: Judicial Minimalism on the Supreme Court* (Harvard University Press, 1999); Alexander M. Bickel, *The Supreme Court and the Idea of Progress* (Harper and Row, 1970). For a sense of the debate over the appropriate role of the judge in light of reasonable albeit irreconcilable disagreement, see Neil S. Siegel, 'The Virtue of Judicial Statesmanship' (2008) 86 *Texas Law Review* 959.

regime interaction in terms of discrete transactions or disputes.[72] The analogy is to standard models of private law litigation in domestic courts involving otherwise independent individuals who interact in a discontinuous event. A classic example would be a car crash – a sudden, discrete occurrence, isolated in space and time. To be sure, international regimes can interact around discrete events. A specific armed attack against a particular village might give rise to overlap or potential conflict between norms from the human rights and humanitarian law regimes. One state's imposition of a carbon tax on specific goods from a trading partner might involve an overlap or conflict between norms from international environmental law and international trade law. Discrete fact patterns like these can become the subject of international litigation. However, the focus on litigated cases leads naturally to the conclusion that discrete interactions provide the primary occasion for different regimes to overlap, intersect or conflict. This underlying approach, which I'll label the 'transactional' model of regime interaction, has exercised immense direct and indirect influence on efforts to understand regime interactions. Indeed, this model is so ubiquitous that we seldom recognise its existence or significance.[73]

The transactional model is highly misleading because most regime interactions – and the most important interactions – do not arise out of discrete transactions. Instead, most regime interaction occurs in ongoing relationships among actors and institutions from different regimes that take place outside of international courthouses, including regulatory and administrative,[74] operational, and conceptual interactions, each of which

[72] The analysis in this section has benefitted enormously from Daryl Levinson's thoughtful study of the use of common law and private law transactional frames in constitutional adjudication. Daryl Levinson, 'Framing Transactions in Constitutional Law' (2002) 111 *Yale Law Journal* 1311, 1313 (analysing conceptual difficulties that result from using a common law transactional model in the context of constitutional litigation). I have also been influenced by scholars who have distinguished between transactional and relational interactions in other legal fields. See, e.g. Ian Macneil, *Contracts: Exchange Transactions and Relations* (Foundation Press, 2nd edn, 1978); Ian Macneil, 'Relational Contract: What We Do Know and Do Not Know' (1985) *Wisconsin Law Review* 483.

[73] The few notable exceptions that allude to the transactional nature of ICJ proceedings include Georges Abi-Saab, 'De l'évolution de la Cour internationale: Réflexions sur quelques tendances récentes' (1992) 96 *Revue Générale de Droit International Public* 273, 284. See also Georges Abi-Saab, 'The International Court as a World Court' in Vaughan Lowe and Malgosia Fitzmaurice (eds.), *Fifty Years of the International Court of Justice: Essays in Honour of Sir Robert Jennings* (Cambridge University Press, 1996) 3, 9.

[74] A terminological point: in using this term I do not mean to be invoking the study of administrative law and practices on the international plane that goes under the name of global administrative law. See, e.g. Benedict Kingsbury, Nico Krisch and Richard B.

are discussed in more detail below. The frequency and practical importance of these other forms of regime interactions, which I will label 'relational' interactions, swamp the paradigmatic litigations that we usually discuss. Hence, the first virtue of dislodging the dominant transactional model is that it will open the conceptual and analytic space for the study of various types of relational interactions among regimes that, until now, have been hidden in plain sight. The shift in focus beyond judicial fora will enable us to identify new actors and discover new patterns of regime conflict and cooperation.

Moreover, the shift I recommend suggests a richer understanding of international regimes than that offered by the dominant approach. The transactional model denies regimes any significant measure of autonomy. In this regard, the dominant model follows much mainstream international relations theory, which typically views regimes as arenas or mechanisms through which other actors, primarily states, pursue their own interests.[75] Thus while mainstream theories acknowledge that the existence of regimes can affect outcomes, conventional approaches usually understand regimes to be largely passive vessels. Abandoning the transactional model will permit us to see regimes as more than constellations of rules and institutions.[76] Thus, as demonstrated more fully below, a shift in attention from tribunals to non-judicial fora for regime interaction highlights the ways in which regimes are purposeful actors in their own right with independent interests and capabilities.

1. *Regulatory and administrative interactions*

Much contemporary international law is made through international treaty. However, much of the detail and implementation of treaty

Stewart, 'The Emergence of Global Administrative Law' (2005) 68 *Law and Contemporary Problems* 15.

[75] See, e.g. Robert Keohane, *After Hegemony: Cooperation and Discord in the World Political Economy* (Princeton University Press, 1981).

[76] See generally Michael Barnett and Martha Finnemore, *Rules for the World: International Organizations in Global Politics* (Cornell University Press, 2004) (arguing that regimes can develop dominant frameworks for understanding certain phenomena, as the International Monetary Fund (IMF) did with exchange rate policies; can set the terms of debate, generate schemes of classification and definition, and set norms and standards). Although scholars have focused on the relative autonomy of particular international organisations, such as the World Bank, IMF, UN and European Union, the approach set out in this chapter is the first to examine regimes as autonomous actors in the context of ongoing interactions with other regimes.

norms – including rulemaking, administrative or institutional mediation among competing interests, and other forms of regulatory and administrative decisions and management – occurs outside of highly publicised diplomatic conferences and treaty-making. This activity includes the creation of rules and standards of general applicability by subsidiary bodies, as well as informal decisions made in overseeing and implementing international regulatory regimes. In the aggregate, these decision-making processes regulate and manage vast areas of international relations.

Benedict Kingsbury and his colleagues in the Global Administrative Law (GAL) project have produced an impressive literature that conceptualises much of this activity as a form of global administrative law. The studies in this project have examined international regulatory efforts across an impressive range of subject areas, including international investment, international banking, forestry management, public procurement and the setting of international rules for accounting standards.[77] Notably, the GAL scholarship is regime specific. However, as the arguments set out above suggest, focusing upon regime-specific activity elides the substantial administrative and regulatory activities that take place *across* regimes.

Consider, by way of illustration, the international response to hazardous substances and activities. For many years, efforts to regulate in this area have been marked by collaboration among international organisations that cross regimes. For example, in 1995, several international organisations jointly created the Inter-Organization for the Sound Management of Chemicals (IOMC). Participants include international actors from a diverse set of international bodies, including the World Health Organization (WHO), the Organisation for Economic Co-operation and Development (OECD), the Food and Agriculture Organization (FAO), the International Labour Organization (ILO), the United Nations Environment Programme (UNEP), and the United Nations Industrial Development Organization, with the World Bank and UN Development Programme participating in an observer capacity. IOMC organisations coordinate their activities on chemicals management through an Inter-Organization Coordinating Committee, composed of representatives of the participating organisations, which meets twice a year. Interactions among representatives from the different organisations comprising the IOMC help to identify gaps or overlaps in international efforts, and to

[77] See, e.g. Symposium, 'The Emergence of Global Administrative Law' (2005) 68 *Law and Contemporary Problems* 1–377.

generate recommendations on common policies. The IOMC has engaged in a number of important regulatory undertakings, including the establishment of a globally harmonised system for the classification and labelling of chemicals and efforts to regulate obsolete and unwanted pesticides in Africa. These IOMC initiatives are examples of global regulatory efforts that are the product of interactions among bodies from a variety of international legal regimes.[78]

A more recent effort to address hazardous chemicals provides yet another illustration of the way that international regulatory efforts arise out of iterative collaborations among actors from different regimes. The Stockholm Convention on Persistent Organic Pollutants (POPs Convention), which entered into force in 2004, bans the use of certain pesticides and chemicals that bioaccumulate. During negotiation of the treaty, controversy arose over whether to ban DDT. A broad coalition of environmental groups advocated the elimination of this pesticide. Many developing states and public health advocates opposed this effort on the grounds that DDT was highly effective against malaria, a disease that causes enormous harm in developing countries, and no feasible alternative for malaria control existed. The WHO, which formally participated in the negotiations, argued that a ban would be premature, given the lack of a cost-effective substitute. The WHO position ultimately prevailed, and the POPs Convention restricts, but does not ban, the continued use of DDT.

More important for current purposes, the treaty expressly contemplates a continuing series of interactions between actors from the chemicals regime and the international public health regime. First, the treaty provides that parties may produce and use DDT only in accordance with WHO recommendations and guidelines. Thus, any changes in guidelines

[78] More recently, a new effort to coordinate work on chemical management across international bodies was launched. In February 2006, IOMC, UNEP and the Intergovernmental Forum on Chemical Safety (IFCS) convened the International Conference on Chemicals Management. Three other organisations – the Global Environment Facility, the United Nations Development Programme, and the World Bank – joined the co-convenors in adopting an overarching policy strategy and a Global Plan of Action that together constitute the Strategic Approach to International Chemicals management. An explicit goal of this initiative is to 'strengthen the coherence and the synergies that exist' between existing efforts to manage dangerous chemicals and to address 'existing gaps in the framework of international chemicals policy'. Although thus far this initiative has not produced any legally binding instruments, it is not difficult to envision this collaborative effort, like previous collaborative efforts among international bodies in this area, producing new regulatory instruments in the future.

for DDT use produced within the public health regime automatically produce regulatory changes within the chemicals regime. In addition, states using DDT are required to provide to the POPs secretariat and the WHO information about the amount of DDT used, the conditions under which it is used, and how such use relates to the country's disease management strategy. Most importantly, the POPs Convention expressly provides that every three years the treaty parties will consult with the WHO to determine whether there is still a need to permit the use of DDT for vector control. The clear expectation is that, if and when the WHO determines that there is no longer a need to use DDT for malarial control, the chemicals regime will be changed to ban DDT.[79] Thus, the treaty explicitly structures an ongoing series of interactions between actors in the chemicals regime, namely the POPs secretariat, and actors in the public health regime, namely the WHO, over global efforts to create global regulations for dangerous pesticides.

Examples of regulatory and administrative interactions in other areas of international law abound. In a series of important writings, including her contribution to this volume, Margaret Young has described the interactions over fisheries subsidies among parties to the UN Convention on the Law of the Sea (UNCLOS); the FAO; species-specific and regional fisheries management organisations; environmental treaties, such as the Convention on the International Trade in Endangered Species of Wild Flora and Fauna; and the WTO.[80] Young's work details the continuing and iterative nature of the exchange between and among actors from the

[79] As of June 2009, the WHO position on the use of malaria remains unchanged; it 'still supports the use of DDT for malaria control … provided that WHO guidelines are followed strictly', and the treaty provisions on DDT have not been changed. World Health Organization, 'WHO and DDT for Malaria Control – June 2009' (Global Malaria Program), available at www.who.int/malaria/publications/who_ddt_malaria_control-june.pdf.

[80] See, e.g. Margaret Young, 'Regime Interaction in Creating, Implementing and Enforcing International Law', Ch. 3 of this volume; Young, *Trading Fish, Saving Fish*, above n. 11: Young, 'Fragmentation or Interaction', above n. 11. See also Olav Schram Stokke and Clare Coffey, 'Institutional Interplay and Responsible Fisheries: Combating Subsidies, Developing Precaution' in Sebastian Oberthur and Thomas Gehring (eds.), *Institutional Interaction in Global Environmental Governance* (MIT, 2006) 127.

It is important to stress that not all regime interactions are as productive as those mentioned above. The lengthy and often difficult interactions among the ILO, the International Maritime Organization (IMO) and the Basel Convention (BC) secretariat on the issue of ship scrapping is a prominent example. See, e.g. Joint ILO/IMO/BC Working Group on Ship Scrapping, Report of the Working Group, ILO/IMO/BC WG 1/8 (18 February 2005). In future work, I hope to identify features of interactions that bear on the likelihood of success.

fisheries, environmental and trade regimes. Moreover, she usefully demonstrates how specific WTO negotiating texts on fisheries subsidies have been influenced by a series of ongoing formal and informal interactions with participants from other regimes, and the myriad ways that WTO draft texts expressly incorporate standards from other regimes. Although negotiations in this area continue, and the details of any final legal text are currently unknowable, it is highly likely that eventual WTO disciplines in this area will bear the imprint of the regime interactions Young describes.

Finally, why must airline passengers turn off their laptops and other electronic devices during takeoff? Standards in this area reflect dynamics similar to those identified above, as a large and complex set of regulations to promote safety in civil aviation are the product of an ongoing series of interactions among actors from different international regimes, specifically the International Telecommunications Union (ITU) and the International Civil Aviation Organization (ICAO). The ITU has primary responsibility for ensuring the 'rational, equitable, efficient and economical use of the radio-frequency spectrum' by interested parties. ICAO, a specialised agency of the UN, promulgates standards related to aeronautical radio communication and radio navigation and surveillance systems. Since 1947, the two organisations have actively worked together to address issues of mutual concern.

In recent years, the widespread diffusion of cellular telephones, computers, personal digital assistants (PDAs) and other electronic devices sparked important questions over the potential for interference with essential aeronautical radio-communication and radio-navigation systems.[81] As a result, the ITU decided to address issues involving 'interference as a result of band-sharing between aeronautical and non-aeronautical services' and interference from 'radio communication systems operating in bands outside the aeronautical frequency bands'. In the process of developing these recommendations, the ITU invited the ICAO to 'participate actively' in

[81] See, e.g. ITU, Frequency sharing between mobile-satellite services and other services (6 April 2009) (Question ITU-R 201–1/4); ICAO, Protection of Global Navigation Satellite Systems Operating in the Bank 1559 to 1610 MHz Against Unwanted Emissions From Mobile Earth Stations Operating in the Bank 1610 to 1626.5 MHz (detailing concerns over harmful interference with Global Navigation Satellite System from the mobile satellite service and mobile earth stations); ITU, Frequency sharing between systems in the fixed-satellite service and wireless digital networks around 5 GHz (12 Sept. 2003) (Question ITU-R 248/4).

relevant technical and scientific studies.[82] These invitations, which are common in the ITU's work, will typically spark a series of intensive and ongoing interactions among experts from the two organisations. In particular, the ICAO and ITU engaged in intensive consultations over the intricate technical specifications to ensure that various electronic systems can interoperate without dangerous interference.[83] In these processes, the ICAO becomes, in effect, a partner in the development of technical standards and recommended practices, although in practice the formal documents will issue from the ITU.[84]

Many other examples could be provided, but the general point should be clear. The ongoing dialogue between experts from the chemicals regime with their counterparts from the public health regime over when and how to regulate continued use of DDT; the ongoing interactions between the international civil servants from the UNCLOS regime with their counterparts from the FAO and the WTO over the nature and content of new rules on fisheries subsidies; and the iterative interactions among specialists from the ITU and the ICAO over the allocation of radio frequencies illustrate, by way of example, how international regimes frequently engage in ongoing collaborative interactions in the context of regulatory and administrative law-making. The examples suggest how a pilot's request to turn off laptops before a flight illustrates a frequently productive and often under-appreciated form of regime interaction that is worthy of sustained scholarly attention.

2. *Operational interactions*

As noted above, dislodging attention away from international courts, and considering regimes as independent actors, permits a focus on the many different ways that international legal regimes interact. In addition to the regulatory and administrative fora discussed above, another common site of regime interaction is in the operational activities of international actors. To date, legal scholars have focused on the operational activities of individual international bodies including, for example, peace-keeping

[82] A listing of recent ICAO contributions to ITU processes can be accessed at www.itu.int/md/meetingdoc.asp?lang=en&parent=R07-CPM-C&source=ICAO.

[83] See, e.g. ITU, Interference to the radionavigation-satellite service in the ICAO global navigation satellite system (2009) (Question ITU-R 217–2/4).

[84] See, e.g. ICAO, Interference into Aeronautical Radiocommunication and Radionavigation Systems, AN-Conf/11-WP/16 (23 July 2003).

operations or the United Nations transitional administration in Kosovo and East Timor.[85] But to date few scholars have broadened their focus beyond the operational activities of actors within a single international regime and explored the ways that actors from different regimes interact in the course of performing their operational activities.

Consider, for example, the international response to the HIV/AIDS pandemic. Although international efforts were slow to materialise during the early years of the pandemic, eventually a large number of bodies from a variety of international regimes developed programmes to address different aspects of the HIV/AIDS crisis. The belated upsurge in international efforts was, however, highly decentralised. Over time, many of the international actors undertook activities that addressed the same issue, including, for example, assessment, testing, prevention of mother-to-child transmissions, and AIDS education. This overlap in operational programmes and responsibilities raised concerns about duplicative or wasteful efforts, disorganisation, and unnecessarily high administrative and transaction costs – as well as the opportunity for international actors to enjoy economies of scale and other synergies. As a result, substantial diplomatic efforts were devoted to efforts to streamline, harmonise and strengthen international efforts in this area and to align international efforts with national approaches.[86]

As a result of these diplomatic efforts, international activities are currently centred at the Joint United Nations Programme on HIV/AIDS (UNAIDS). UNAIDS is a joint venture of ten different 'co-sponsors' from a broad spectrum of international legal regimes, including the Office of the High Commissioner for Refugees (UNHCR); United Nations Childrens Fund (UNICEF); World Food Programme (WFP); United Nations Development Programme (UNDP); United Nations Population Fund (UNPF); United Nations Office on Drugs and Crime (UNODC); International Labour Organization (ILO); United Nations Educational, Scientific and Cultural Organization (UNESCO); World Health Organization (WHO); and World Bank. Each of these organisations

[85] See generally Simon Chesterman, *You, The People: The United Nations, Transitional Administration, and State-Building* (Oxford University Press, 2004).

[86] For a sense of the diplomatic undertakings in this area, see, e.g. Monterey, Rome and Paris Declarations, Global Task Team on Improving AIDS Coordination Among Multilateral Institutions and International Donors, Final Report (2005); World Bank, World Development Report 2004: Making Services Work for Poor People (2004); OECD/DAC, 'Survey on Harmonisation and Alignment of Donor Practices (2005).

sponsors extensive AIDS programmes and activities. In an effort to minimise duplication and maximise the rapid, efficient and effective use of international resources, the ten organisations have worked together to develop an agreed-upon 'division of labor'. Thus, following extensive consultation and negotiation, by mutual agreement different entities have been identified as the lead organisation in specific areas of operational activity, such as strategic planning, financial management, prevention, treatment and monitoring. The lead organisation in each area has primary responsibility for coordinating the provision or facilitation of support, establishing global and regional support mechanisms for the delivery of country-level support, and communicating with stakeholders in one or another identified area. This division of labour is designed to exploit the comparative advantage of each of the UNAIDS organisations and to facilitate the delivery of unified and consolidated programming.[87]

To be sure, the brief description barely begins to skim the surface of international efforts to combat HIV/AIDS, but the salient point is that the institutional framework for international efforts to address HIV/AIDS should be understood as an example of a significant but understudied form of regime interaction, which I label operational interaction. Moreover, similar accounts could be given of operational regime interactions across much of international relations. For example, the Collaborative Partnership on Forests (CPF) is a continuing arrangement among fourteen international organisations with substantial programmes on forests.[88] Like UNAIDS, it was started as a way to streamline and harmonise pre-existing international efforts. Each CPF member has been designated as a 'focal agency' for one or more key forest issues for which it has special expertise. CPF members have worked together, inter alia, to launch a joint research platform focusing on integrating livelihoods and biodiversity conservation in tropical forest landscapes, and in coordinating their response to the 2004 Indian Ocean tsunami.

Similarly, a wide range of international bodies, including several regional development banks, the FAO, UNDP, UNEP, UNIDO, the World Bank and other international agencies, work with and through the Global

[87] For a fuller discussion, see, e.g. UNAIDS, UNAIDS Technical Support Division of Labour (2005) (available at http://data.unaids.org/una-docs/JC1146-Division_of_labour.pdf).

[88] Members include the FAO, International Tropical Timber Organization, UNDP, UNEP, and secretariats of the Convention to Combat Desertification, Framework Convention on Climate Change, and UN Forum on Forests. For more on the Partnership, see Collaborative Partnership on Forests Framework 2008 and 2009, E/CN.18/2009/12 (9 February 2009).

Environment Facility (GEF), itself a product of regime interaction among the World Bank, UNEP and UNDP. The Global Alliance for Vaccines and Immunizations (GAVI Alliance) is a partnership involving international organisations such as the WHO, UNICEF and the World Bank, along with developing world and donor governments, vaccine manufacturers, civil society organisations and private sector philanthropists, to increase access to immunisation in poor countries; UNEP, FAO, UNDP, UNECE, UNICEF, UNESCO, UN-Habitat, WHO and other international bodies partner to sponsor and promote World Water Day, an annual event that focuses international attention on the need for sustainable management of freshwater resources.

Many other examples could be adduced. But even this cursory overview illustrates some of the ways that ongoing collaborations among international actors from diverse international regimes – ranging from human rights to international finance to environment – affect the operational activities of international regimes. Notably, the practical results from any one set of interactions – say, over coordinating funding mechanisms in HIV/AIDS prevention – in turn invariably give rise to a new set of issues – say, ensuring integrity in the use of funds. These iterative, sustained and dynamic operational interactions can be understood as an adaptive strategy that arises in response to the fragmented nature of the international legal order, and that permits the international community to address particular problems, such as the HIV/AIDS crisis, in a comprehensive and holistic fashion. Although operational interactions do not attract the same level of scholarly attention as, say, the jurisprudential conundrums raised by high-profile international judicial opinions, operational interactions are more common than the regime interactions that give rise to international litigations. Moreover, as the examples above suggest, robust and dynamic operational interactions can generate impressive substantive initiatives and outcomes in ways that international litigation cannot.

3. *Conceptual interactions*

The two immediately preceding sections highlighted international regimes' regulatory and operational undertakings. But international regimes do more than create regulations and engage in operational activities. Regimes are more than clusters of rules, principles, institutions and practices that regulate behaviour within an issue area. And regimes do not simply produce rules and standards. Legal regimes also create knowledge.

Specifically, the activities of international legal regimes constitute part of 'the processes by which we collectively come to know, describe and imagine the world in which we live'.[89] Indeed, as the discussion of 'Nomos and Narrative' suggests, regimes can be understood as conceptual frameworks for understanding parts of our social world.

Thus, when international actors embedded within an international regime create rules or engage in operational activities, they at the same time engage in the process of creating social knowledge. As Michael Barnett and Martha Finnemore explain, international bodies create social knowledge when they 'define shared international tasks (like "development"), create and define new categories of actors (like "refugee"), create new interests for actors (like "promoting human rights"), and transfer models of organisation around the world (like markets and democracy)'.[90]

International law scholars and academics from cognate fields are starting to explore the various ways that international legal regimes produce and disseminate authoritative ways of understanding and organizing the world. William Drake and Kalypso Nicolaidis and, more recently, Andrew Lang, have provided highly textured accounts of the ways that small groups of well-placed experts, policy-makers and academics at the OECD, UNCTAD and elsewhere engaged in a process that transformed the way that certain international transactions were conceptualised by debating, developing and elaborating the new concept of 'trade in services' – and the relationship between this new conceptualisation and the creation of a legal regime governing trade in services.[91] Similarly, in a series of papers, David Kennedy has explored the ways that the 'vocabularies, expertise and sensibility' of international lawyers working in particular legal orders both represent and reimagine social realities.[92]

Again, however, existing scholarship in this vein has tended to focus on developments in specific regimes, such as international trade or

[89] Andrew Lang, above n. 11; Lang, 'Legal Regimes and Professional Knowledges: The Internal Politics of Regime Definition', Ch. 4 of this volume.

[90] Michael N. Barnett and Martha Finnemore, 'The Politics, Power and Pathologies of International Organizations' (1999) 53 *International Organization* 699. See also Barnett and Finnemore, above n. 76.

[91] William Drake and Kalypso Nicolaides, 'Ideas, Interests and Institutionalization: "Trade in Services" and the Uruguay Round' (1992) 46 *International Organization* 37; Lang, above n. 11.

[92] See, e.g. David Kennedy, *The Dark Side of Virtue: Reassessing International Humanitarianism* (Princeton University Press, 2005); Kennedy, 'Challenging Expert Rule: The Politics of Global Governance', above n. 48.

international humanitarian law. And again the analytic move that I urge is to expand this focus and examine the ways that knowledge production through international regimes results from interactions among, as opposed to within, international legal regimes.

Consider, by way of illustration, controversies over 'trade and' issues and related debates over the scope and limits of the trade regime. These controversies have sparked a series of ongoing relationships between actors from the trade regime, often from the WTO Secretariat, and actors from a number of other international regimes. For example, the relationship between trade and labour standards has given rise to highly charged diplomatic and scholarly debates. In response, the WTO has been engaged in an ongoing set of conceptual interactions with the international labour regime.

Hence, in 2006, members of the WTO and ILO secretariats undertook collaborative research that eventually led to the release, in 2007, of a joint study entitled 'Trade and Employment: Challenges for Policy Research'.[93] The study reviewed different literatures, including scholarship on trade, labour markets, public finance and education. Notably, the study effectively acknowledged that it was an example of a conceptual interaction; it explicitly stated that it was not intended to 'give policy advice' but instead was designed 'to help policymakers think about policy designs and in particular about trade-offs that might be implied'. The conceptual interactions between these two regimes continues; the WTO and ILO recently hosted a workshop of leading international researchers to identify and conceptualise a research agenda on trade and labour issues, including offshoring, trade and inequality, and labour market adjustment to trade reform.

Members of the WTO Secretariat have also engaged in iterative conceptual interactions with the labour regime over the social meaning and significance of globalisation. For example, members of the secretariat attend sessions of the ILO Governing Body as observers and also routinely participate in meetings of the Governing Body's Working Party on the Social Dimension of Globalization. Further collaboration took place in the context of work undertaken between 2002 and 2004 by the World Commission on the Social Dimension of Globalization, an ILO initiative that brought together twenty-six eminent persons to look at different

[93] World Trade Organization Secretariat and the International Labour Office, 'Trade and Employment: Challenges for Policy Research' (Geneva, 2007). Available at www.wto.org/english/res_e/publications_e/wto_ilo_e.htm.

facets of globalisation. The WTO Director-General met with the World Commission, and the WTO Secretariat has continued to participate in follow-up mechanisms to the World Commission, including attendance at meetings of the ILO's Policy Coherence Initiative. In addition, during the last few years, the WTO Secretariat has on several occasions also attended conferences and seminars organised by the ILO, when issues of relevance to the WTO were discussed. All of these interactions are, in effect, an extended dialogue over the most appropriate way to conceptualise and manage complex areas of international affairs. The various reports and studies that result from the interactions between the trade and labour regimes are efforts to shape the processes by which we collectively come to know, describe and imagine the impact of liberalised trade and globalisation on social concerns.

The WTO has engaged in similar conceptual interactions with actors from other international regimes as well. For example, in 2009, the WTO and UNEP jointly published a report addressing the linkages between trade and climate change. Issued at a critical time in the ongoing negotiations over a post-Kyoto climate change treaty, the joint WTO/UNEP report challenges the conventional wisdom that views trade liberalisation as being in tension with efforts to combat climate change. The report argues that trade liberalisation can have a positive effect on greenhouse gas emissions by, inter alia, accelerating the transfer of clean technologies. The report also discusses, at length, two controversial pricing mechanisms that can be used to control greenhouse gas emissions, taxes and emissions trading systems. Like the joint study between the WTO and ILO, the joint WTO–UNEP report does not purport to dispense policy advice. Rather it is designed to introduce new concepts and to shift the debate over the relationship between trade and climate change; in the report's own words, its 'aim is to promote greater understanding of [the interaction between trade and climate change policies] and to assist policy-makers in this complex policy area'.

The WTO/ILO and WTO/UNEP collaborations are examples of conceptual interactions that were focused upon a relatively well-defined set of issues. Other conceptual interactions address a more diffuse set of issues. Consider, for example, the emerging relationship between the climate change and human rights regimes. For nearly two decades, the climate debate has focused on the nature, causes and consequences of climate change. However, in recent years a potentially significant effort has been launched by human rights bodies to change the terms of climate discourse. An important element of this strategy is the instigation of multiple interactions between the climate regime and the human rights regime by human rights bodies.

These efforts began in December 2005 when an alliance of Inuit from Canada and the United States filed a petition with the Inter-American Commission on Human Rights. The petition alleged that global warming caused substantially by the United States has negatively impacted the rights of indigenous peoples of the Arctic. Although the petition attracted some scholarly attention, its practical effect has been rather limited.[94] In a two-paragraph response in November 2006, the Commission dismissed without prejudice the petition, stating that 'the information provided does not enable us to determine whether the alleged facts would tend to characterize a violation of the rights protected by the American Declaration [of the Rights and Duties of Man]'. Although the Commission agreed to hold a hearing on the linkages between human rights and climate change, the case is languishing, and at this point in time this litigation initiative produced few concrete results.

More recently, the human rights community has adopted a different strategy. Specifically, it has sought to provoke a series of regime interactions in non-judicial fora. For example, in 2007, the UN Deputy High Commissioner for Human Rights addressed the Bali Conference and stressed the need to use a human rights perspective when discussing environmental issues. At roughly the same time, a diverse range of international actors, ranging from the UNDP and the Organization of American States (OAS) to Oxfam International and Kofi Anan's Global Humanitarian Forum, began to explore the interface between climate change and human rights. In 2008, the Human Rights Council adopted by consensus a resolution asking the Office of the High Commissioner for Human Rights (OHCHR) to prepare a 'detailed analytical study of the relationship between climate change and human rights'. In undertaking the study, the OHCHR opened up a dialogue with a variety of other UN bodies, international organisations, national human rights institutes, non-governmental organisations, and academic experts. In January 2009, the OHCHR released a study concluding that climate change interferes with a wide range of human rights and that States have an obligation

[94] See, e.g. Hari Osofsky, 'The Inuit Petition as a Bridge? Beyond Dialectics of Climate Change and Indigenous Peoples' Rights' (2006–2007) 31 *American Indian Law Review* 675; Jessie Hohmann, 'Igloo as Icon: A Human Rights Approach to Climate Change for the Inuit?' (2009) 18 *Transnational Law and Contemporary Problems* 295.

under international human rights law to protect those rights from the adverse effects of climate change, including in particular through international cooperation.[95]

As a result of these and other initiatives, actors from the human rights and climate change regimes have engaged in an extended dialogue and exchange of information. More importantly, the dialogue continues. The High Commissioner will present the study at the Copenhagen Climate Conference, and has been active in presenting studies at other recent climate meetings.[96] Moreover, the climate/human rights dialogue is now starting to migrate into other fora. For example, the Special Rapporteur on adequate housing has addressed how climate change challenges the right to housing, and recently visited the Maldives to witness first-hand the effects of climate change, and we should expect to see climate-related initiatives by other special rapporteurs and independent experts within the human rights system.[97]

For current purposes, we should understand these efforts, and particularly the High Commissioner's report, as an effort to initiate a normative dialogue between the human rights and climate regimes. The goal of this effort is nothing less than a reconceputalisation of the climate issue. In the words of a prominent advocate, the effort is intended to transform 'how climate change is perceived'; to date, climate change 'has been viewed as a scientific projection, "a kind of line graph stretching into the future with abstract measurements based on parts per million, degrees centigrade or centimeters …" '.[98] But the introduction of 'human rights thinking' is intended to change this conceptualisation by 'supplying a

[95] Report of the Office of the High Commissioner for Human Rights on the relationship between climate change and human rights, A/HRC/10/61 (15 January 2009).

[96] Formal submissions from OHCHR to the United Nations Framework Convention on Climate Change (UNFCCC) relating to the topic of climate change and human rights, particularly migration and displacement, include: *Forced Displacement in the Context of Climate Change: Challenges for States Under International Law*, Submission by the International Organization for Migration, the United Nations High Commissioner for Refugees and the United Nations University (6 February 2009), available at www.globalmigrationgroup.org/pdf/CL_change_M_Displacement_by_IOM_UNHCR_UNU.pdf.

[97] For a survey of potential initiatives within the human rights regime, see Center for International Environmental Law (CIEL), Practical Approaches to Integrating Human Rights and Climate Change Law and Policy (2009) (unpublished manuscript, on file with author). There are also domestic efforts to address the links between human rights and climate change.

[98] Marc Limon, 'Human Rights and Climate Change: Constructing a Case for Political Action' (2009) 33 *Harvard Environmental Law Review* 439, 451 (citation omitted).

set of internationally agreed values around which policy responses can be negotiated and motivated' and hence 'contribute, qualitatively, to the construction of better policy responses at both the national and international level'.[99] In short, actors in the human rights community are provoking an ongoing set of conceptual interactions intended to change how we come to understand climate change, the problems it poses, and the range of appropriate responses.

These efforts also help to highlight the difference between a focus on 'transactional' and 'relational' regime interactions. The various reports and activities described above are not intended to be one-off interactions. Rather, various actors inside the human rights community are attempting to initiate precisely the type of ongoing, iterative relationship between regimes that falls outside the ambit of the transactional model but is at the heart of the relational model outlined above.

Moreover, the purpose of these relational interactions differs fundamentally from the purposes of transactional interactions. Unlike the litigations at the heart of the transaction model, the interactions between the human rights and climate regimes are not intended to settle jurisdictional boundaries, to identify conflicts of law principles, or to privilege or subordinate one norm or another. There is much more going on here than forum shopping or regime shifting; no one involved in these efforts harbours the illusion that human rights bodies will replace the Intergovernmental Panel on Climate Change (IPCC) and United Nations Framework Convention on Climate Change (UNFCCC) as the locus of climate debates.

Koskenniemi argues that conceptual interactions aimed at creating what he calls 'regime hybrids' are best understood in political terms as struggles for influence.[100] While conceptual interactions between and among regimes are undoubtedly often triggered by political and instrumental motivations, I believe that much more is at stake. The overtures from the human rights regime represent a new way to think about the climate change issue, and a new framework for criticising or justifying international efforts in this area. The human rights advocates are offering new doctrinal and operational approaches to climate change

[99] Ibid. at 451–452.

[100] Koskenniemi's contribution to this volume, pp. 319–320. See also Koskenniemi, The Politics of International Law – 20 Years Later', above n. 63 (noting the 'politics of redefinition' in regime interactions).

that focuses on the vulnerable and marginalised. At a more fundamental level, the human rights regime is seeking a conceptual interaction that is ultimately over the narrative, or the social meaning, of climate change. These types of interactions remind us, as did Bob Cover's analysis of law in 'Nomos and Narrative', of law's central role as a filter through which humans understand and experience the world around them.

Conclusion

This chapter is an effort to unsettle the dominant approach to studying regime interactions. The 'negative' part of the chapter critiques the overemphasis on the treatment of regime interactions in judicial opinions. First, the overemphasis on international litigations is misleading as most interactions occur outside international courthouses. Second, international courts lack the jurisprudential tools to resolve the doctrinal and normative conflicts that occur when regimes overlap and intersect. The 'positive' part of the chapter attempts to map other types of regime interactions, including regulatory, operational and conceptual interactions. In so doing, I provide a more comprehensive account of the various ways that international legal regimes interact, as a necessary step in adequately understanding this phenomenon.

Of course, developing an alternative approach to regime interactions is only worthwhile if it produces significant insights and new opportunities for research into important debates. The approach outlined above contributes new perspectives to several major debates in the field. First, it offers an original perspective on the limits that international courts face when confronted with cases involving regime interactions. It is thus an important corrective to legal scholarship that focuses on interpretative techniques that can supposedly be used to dissolve the doctrinal and normative conflicts that arise when regimes interact. Second, in identifying and classifying important areas of regime interaction, it provides a rich future agenda for research. Future studies can search for patterns in areas of regime interaction that have to date been largely ignored. Third, this chapter provides an empirically grounded basis for treating international regimes as autonomous actors in world politics. It thus provides an important challenge to the state-centric ontology that continues to prevail in both international law and international relations scholarship.

For all the attention that regime interaction has received, we know very little about the phenomena. The arguments above suggest that our ignorance is in large part a product of the research methodology we've employed and the theoretical lens we have applied. This chapter is an effort to recalibrate the research methodology and revamp the theoretical lens, so that we might better understand and manage international regime interactions.

6

Structural Ambiguity: Technology Transfer in Three Regimes

STEPHEN HUMPHREYS

Four terms of art commonly met in international law demonstrate in different ways what I am here calling 'structural ambiguity': technology transfer; self-determination; proportionality; non-discrimination.

These four terms have, I suggest, at least three things in common. First a free-standing definition is not readily available to any of them. Each appears in multiple international law regimes and, in each case, the meaning and utility of the term varies according to the regime. So the principle of proportionality is central to both human rights law and the *jus in bello*, but its application – the manner in which the outcome of an action is judged 'proportionate' to its objective – is applied tantalisingly differently in each.[1] The principle of non-discrimination is fundamental to both human rights and trade law, but with a contrasting signification and different applications in each.[2] 'Technology transfer' appears in (at least) three bodies of

[1] See Françoise Hampson, 'The Relationship between International Humanitarian Law and Human Rights Law From the Perspective of a Human Rights Treaty Body' (2008) 90:871 *International Review of the Red Cross* 549. The very premise of calculating proportionality in *jus in bello* – that the arbitrary killing of civilians ('collateral damage') is sometimes inevitable – appears to violate the same principle under human rights law – that policy objectives must be balanced against the rights of specific individuals. This is a substantive distinction that appears essentially irresolvable and so to require the mutual exclusivity of these two bodies of law on certain issues (as Art. 15 European Convention on Human Rights (ECHR) anticipates). Even as it highlights continuity between these bodies of law, then, the principle of 'proportionality' underlines their discontinuity.

[2] Notably on the central and connected issues of 'national origin' and 'nationality'. Philip Alston, refuting claims by Ernst-Ulrich Petersmann that the principle of 'non-discrimination' 'serve[s] the same "constitutional function"' in the two bodies of law, and shares an identical Kantian root in both, responds that in trade law, 'non-discrimination' is not a 'right … conferred on individuals in the sense of human rights'. It may be, however, that the appearance of this principle in both bodies of law *does* serve a constitutional function of some sort, without it being used identically in each. The resulting tension might itself

international law: environmental, trade, and investment law – but in each regime it carries its own distinctive normative weight, amounting to a term of art that (as we shall see in a moment) cannot simultaneously sustain all of the significations attributed to it. 'Self-determination' crops up in the margins of public international law everywhere, but everywhere without clear definition.[3]

A second commonality is that each term is itself a site of contestation *within* each of the regimes wherein it appears. Everything of course may depend on the determination of what is, or is not, proportionate or discriminatory in human rights law and, respectively, the laws of war and trade. Yet what is proportionate or discriminatory is inescapably subjective (one man's 'proportionate' is another's 'discrimination'); arguably the terms themselves embed a degree of fluidity or indeterminacy that may be vital in permitting the flexibility and organicism of a body of law (general, international) that must accommodate varying interests and interest groups. The meaning of self-determination, too, varies along each of its axes: according both to what we take as a 'self' (ethnic, 'cultural', linguistic group, 'nation', 'country', 'people'), and what it means to 'determine' (holding elections, monopolising violence, achieving autonomy, establishing a parliament, issuing a currency, controlling access to resources, drafting a constitution, interpreting law).

A third element each of these terms shares, in apparent tension with the second, is that everyone apparently agrees that the thing in question is *good*. It is not only lawful, but also right, to act in a manner that is proportionate and non-discriminatory, to 'transfer' technologies, and to 'self-determine' – that is, to be an autonomous, self-governing subject. These all appear to constitute self-evident public goods, and so they are terms around which consensus easily forms.

The reappearance of specific terms in multiple regimes, but with differing meanings and emphases within and between different regimes, points to a certain *systemic* or *structural ambiguity* or *incoherence*. I mean 'incoherence' not only in the sense that the various deployments of these terms – themselves semantically ambiguous – do not align or amount to a

be jurisgenerative, an issue that would bear examination, but that I cannot, unfortunately, pursue here. Philip Alston, 'Resisting the Merger and Acquisition of Human Rights by Trade Law: A Reply to Petersmann' (2002) 13 *European Journal of International Law* 815, 825–826, 836, 838–840.

[3] For a delightful discussion of the shape-shifting nature of this term of art, see Nathaniel Berman, 'Sovereignty in Abeyance: Self-Determination and International Law' (1988) 7 *Wisconsin International Law Journal* 51.

coherent conceptual entity in any given case, but also in that the ambiguities point to a larger lack of coherence between the relevant regimes (the phenomenon referred to as 'fragmentation').[4] So in what follows I will use the first of these problems, that of structural ambiguity, as a way into the second: inter-regime 'fragmentation' (and, so, interaction).

I begin with two intuitions. First, that the reiteration of shared terms in multiple domains acts in part as a thread linking the regimes together: the terms introduce a sense of international legal *familiarity*, and provide one among a number of hooks through which 'systemic integration' can (potentially) be performed: no single regime 'owns' the terms. Second, their iteration in regimes that have different 'objects and purposes', and where they are further subject to competing interpretations and strategic negotiations, tends to militate *against* the terms ever achieving 'closure' – of there ever being a 'final' definition that might apply not only across regimes, but, indeed, within any given one. I emphasise this last point as this is the element of 'regime interaction' with which this chapter is primarily concerned. That is, the reiteration of the same contested term in *multiple regimes* without resolution may have a potentially destabilising effect for its deployment in *any one* regime.

This chapter uses 'technology transfer' as a window onto this set of issues. This is not to say, however, that in what follows 'technology transfer' stands in for the other terms identified above: technology transfer is a special case, showcasing a very particular set of tensions and stakes. So although the inquiry here intends to illustrate a broader phenomenon in international law, the same arguments are unlikely to apply (*mutatis mutandis* so to speak) to each of the terms raised above. The tensions and stakes of technology transfer nevertheless go, as I hope to show, to the heart of a particularly rich and central set of contemporary disagreements underlying (and perhaps concealed by) international law. For that reason, despite its marginal role in international law generally and its stubborn resistance to crisp clarification, 'technology transfer' as a term of art is well placed to offer insights into the set of problems identified above.

The remainder of this chapter has two parts. In the first part I will review three areas of tension or ambiguity in the ILC Report on the fragmentation of international law – its approach to and assumptions about (a) agency, (b) novelty, and (c) authoritative interpretation regarding

[4] UN Doc. A/CN.4/L.682, Fragmentation of International Law: Difficulties Arising from the Diversification and Expansion of International Law, Report of the Study Group of the International Law Commission, Finalised by Martti Koskenniemi (13 April 2006) [hereafter 'ILC Report'], para. 15.

regimes. The discussion aims *inter alia* to render explicit questions of strategy that habitually remain implicit in discussions of fragmentation, including in the Report itself. It further intends, in the same move, to decentre a common narrative of which the ILC Report is perhaps representative that, by remaining silent on strategy, also tends to obscure many of the substantive stakes of inter-regime interaction.

In the second part I turn to 'technology transfer' as a term of art, focusing on three areas of international law where the term appears: climate change, trade, and investment. The discussion aims to show not only that 'technology transfer' is resistant to definition but that this resistance *inheres* in the term as it has developed and that this in turn (bringing together the two threads of the argument) performs a strategic function. The rhetoric of technology transfer promises public intervention in economic affairs. However, no doubt as a result, discussions of technology transfer unfailingly become loci of contestation of the relative roles of public and private, and indeed the term is *also* invoked to *deny* the utility of public intervention. I suggest that this triangular dialectic (if I may be forgiven the solecism) of promise, contestation and denial is played out in each of the three relevant regimes without necessary resolution in any of them – much less *between* them. The result might be thought of as a form of *inoculation* – the injection of concession within the law at a textual and conceptual level, with the effect of pre-empting stronger claims that might otherwise be thought available in other fora.

A. Agency, novelty and interpretive authority in the ILC Report

In the course of its erudite journey, the ILC Report on 'the diversification and expansion of international law' displays a number of areas of ambiguity – complexities about which the authors either have not quite made up their minds, or have decided not to choose between a number of competing explanations for the phenomena they describe, or have, diplomatically perhaps, prioritised narrative consistency over historical accuracy. (It is of course also relevant to the story of fragmentation that the legal and historical professions each have their own structural biases and blindspots, resulting in their own form of inter-regime misunderstanding.)[5] I will look at three areas of ambiguity: agency; novelty; and interpretative authority.

[5] For a discussion of this phenomenon in a different context, see Martti Koskenniemi, 'Between Impunity and Show Trials' in J. A. Frowien and R. Wolfrum (eds.), *Max Planck Yearbook of United Nations Law*, Vol. 6. (2002) 1.

1. *Agency*

A first area of ambiguity/tension concerns the sources/causes of fragmentation. On one hand, the Report leans frequently towards a passive construction of fragmentation – regimes 'develop' in response to 'globalisation' or the 'diversification of international society' or as 'spontaneous reactions to events in the environment'.[6] On the other, there is frequent recognition of the active role played by 'special interests', epistemic 'communities' and 'networks' manoeuvring the international legal machinery in favour of their preferences.[7] The Report tends to reconcile these positions by restricting its recognition of agency to the level of a given regime, and so presupposing that the resulting fracturing *across* regimes is itself incidental or agentless.

And yet, this picture of incidental or accidental fragmentation is not really reflective of the realities of international lawmaking. True, 'special interests' lobby hard both in country and at international negotiations to create and influence law, often with some success, and 'communities of practice' work hard to shape the law and its (subsequent) interpretation – the annual United Nations Framework Convention on Climate Change (UNFCCC) Conference of the Parties (COP) is perhaps an extreme example. But even so – and again the UNFCCC COP process illustrates – insofar as the result is called *law*, it is finally (and necessarily) filtered through the narrow gate of state-level negotiators who, in every case, are (again necessarily) *constrained* to regard each new treaty in strategic relation with its international obligations as a whole. For sure, some states are better equipped than others to perform this duty well. But viewed from the perspective of the better-resourced states – and this distinction between states certainly matters here – international law's 'fragmentation' necessarily takes place within a managed, indeed tightly controlled, environment. The various regimes may not all pull in the same direction, but nor do they exist in chaotic or hermetic isolation from one another. They cannot.

This point is perhaps best illustrated by reference to the statements of states themselves. Here, by way of example, are a series of quotations from the US State Department's 2006 Strategic Plan for the Fiscal Years 2007–2012, co-authored with the Agency for International Development (USAID).[8] I include a lengthy series of citations in order to capture the

[6] See, for examples, ILC Report, paras 493 and 34 respectively.

[7] ILC Report, paras 35, 204, 482, 484.

[8] USAID and US Department of State, *Transformational Diplomacy: Strategic Plan Fiscal Years 2007–2012* (revised 7 May 2007). The examples are taken respectively from pages

richness of synthetic endeavour of this document, reaching far beyond the modest *rapprochement* suggested by such terms as the ILC Report's 'systemic integration'.

> We will provide critical support in negotiating and implementing trade agreements and resolving trade disputes. We will also continue to negotiate civil aviation agreements, develop international communications and information policies, and pursue bilateral investment treaties that open new markets, support job creation in the United States, and provide important protections to U.S. investors. The United States continues to seek successful completion of the WTO Doha Development Round of global trade negotiations. Our trade agenda is also focused on concluding and implementing state-of-the-art free trade agreements (FTA) that open new markets for U.S. agriculture goods, and services and extend strong U.S. investment, transparency, and intellectual property protections abroad. We will continue to support programs linked to our FTAs, including support for labor, environmental, and governance activities, needed to ensure a level playing field for U.S. companies. We will ensure that trade capacity-building programs help developing countries participate in and benefit fully from global, regional, and bilateral trade negotiations.
>
> We will build strong partnerships through robust political-military activities such as defense trade and export control regimes; arms control, nonproliferation, and disarmament agreements and verification protocols; international treaties, alliances, and burden-sharing agreements; security assistance programs; international exercises; and active confidence-building measures.
>
> We will encourage other countries to: deny terrorists access to financial systems and prevent terrorist abuse of charitable institutions; implement the 12 United Nations (UN) counterterrorism instruments that are in force; punish captured terrorists to the full extent of the law; accept return of their nationals who have been detained by the United States for involvement in terrorist activities.
>
> Environmental issues such as climate change, protection of natural resources and forests, and transboundary pollution will continue to play a critical role in our diplomatic and development agendas. We will continue to promote a holistic approach to environmental issues in international fora, integrating our interests in conserving the planet's resources into our economic plans and activities.

27–28, 14, 12, 28. See also USAID, *Foreign Aid in the National Interest: Promoting Freedom, Security and Opportunity* (2002); USAID, *White Paper: U.S. Foreign Aid: Meeting the Challenges of the Twenty-first Century*, Bureau for Policy and Program Coordination (USAID, January 2004); for the UK, DFID, *Eliminating World Poverty: Making Globalisation Work for the Poor. White Paper on International Development* (2000).

The document is of course partially a diplomatic and public relations exercise – it is broad-brush and short on analytic detail. It is nevertheless a statement of official policy, and so at a minimum supplies the language and frame through which a multiplicity of international regimes are viewed and approached at State Department ('State') level. In its rhetorical stance, it is possible to catch a glimpse, at least, of how the fragmentation of international law looks when 'seeing like a state'. And the examples are, of course, explicitly strategic, identifying various international law regimes as worthy of 'promoting' or 'strengthening' in a 'national' interest.[9]

A few summary observations. First, state evidently does not approach 'fragmentation' as a problem *per se*. Not only is there relative equanimity about the existence of various different regimes, there is also a remarkably sanguine tone regarding fragmentation at the sub-regime level too – the co-existence of international, regional and bilateral tools in international trade and investment (the World Trade Organization (WTO), regional and bilateral FTAs, and bilateral investment treaties (BITs)) are unproblematically invoked as various routes to the same set of substantive goals.

Second, while the main international law regimes are covered, some appear in more explicit detail than others – compare the language on terrorism to that on the environment. And there is no inquiry into the regimes themselves, their internal workings or the sources of disputes and resolutions. Rather, it appears as if regime 'objects and purposes' are self-evident, transparent and presumably unambiguous – as though they can be called and relied upon to do certain things and achieve certain ends, and, moreover, as though they all piece together easily: a kind of benevolent jigsaw.

Third, there is an easy movement between law and non-law – between international and bilateral 'treaties' and 'agreements' and 'programs' and 'processes', between obligations and sanctions, on one hand, and 'encouragement' and facilitation, on the other. This relative ease might be interpreted as a mistaken (or, again, strategic) undervaluation of the legal as against the non-legal in international affairs. Or it may also be that from state's perspective, the distinction is *in fact* of minimal consequence. Notably, the obligations in question are not, in this document, those of the United States but those of its allies and partners.

[9] Seven national strategic interests are identified: Achieving Peace and Security, Governing Justly and Democratically, Investing in People, Promoting Economic Growth and Prosperity, Providing Humanitarian Assistance, Promoting International Understanding, Strengthening Consular and Management Capabilities.

In a similar vein, these obligations are not approached from an adversarial or competitive perspective *between* states, as we often think of legal relationships, but rather in terms of their instrumentalisation in the achievement of other, *trans*national, goals that – rather than reflecting the 'community of nations' or 'international society' – explicitly reflect rather the combined public and private interests of particular states. The international is here viewed as a subcomponent of an imperative and structuring transnational. From this perspective the status of a given policy tool as (international) law or non-law is largely a matter of degree. It is perhaps easier to mobilise programmes and 'capacity building' in support of acknowledged legal obligations over (mere) shared economic objectives but the distinction does not appear decisive.

The relative coherence of international law, viewed from the perspective of specific states, hardly figures in the Report, however.[10] This is no doubt because the Report is concerned with '[t]he move from a world fragmented into sovereign states to a world fragmented into specialized "regimes"' (para. 487). The implication appears to be that specialised (presumably private) interests or communities have in some way replaced national (i.e. public) interests. Yet it is also the case that effective pressure groups, like powerful states, do not confine their efforts to a single regime, nor to a single channel in international law; rather they work within and through numerous regimes at once, ensuring their interests are well represented throughout. This involves not just strengthening some regimes and weakening others, but also working across regimes, through 'strategic litigation' and other means, to work specific interpretations through and across regimes, ensuring that some terms are animated while others descend into confusion or desuetude. Beyond this, state and special interests frequently align and may work together to actively reproduce regime fragmentation.[11] In such a world, fragmentation may indeed be produced and reproduced strategically.

[10] Again, however, the view need not be comparable in foreign ministries everywhere; it may also be that the perceived *degree* of fragmentation of international law varies according to which state it is viewed from.

[11] Peter Drahos comments that TRIPS – an exemplary 'industry-driven' instrument – was under negotiation at the same time as *bilateral* intellectual property standards. He quotes the Director for Intellectual Property at the Office of the US Trade Representative: 'What happens if we fail [to obtain TRIPS]? I think there are a number of consequences to failure. First, will be an increase in bilateralism. For those of you who think bilateralism is a bad thing, a bad thing will come about.' Peter Drahos, 'BITs and BIPs: Bilateralism in Intellectual Property' (2001) 4 *Journal of World Intellectual Property* 791 at 791, citing

2. *Novelty*

A second area of ambiguity: is fragmentation 'new' or 'emergent' – as the ILC Report frequently indicates ('[n]ovelty presents itself as "fragmentation" of the old world'[12]) – or is it rather 'endemic' to international law, inherent in its nature as a legal order lacking a single sovereign ('… pluralism should be understood as a constitutive value of the system. Indeed, in a world of plural sovereignties, this has always been so.'),[13] exacerbated, perhaps, as 'international society' has grown 'more complex', but not in itself intrinsically *novel*.[14]

This ambiguity tracks the former to a degree: the more we think of fragmentation as intrinsic to international law – altering with time, certainly, but not in itself *new* – the less it will seem a matter for will or agency. But whereas novelty would seem consonant with agency, such an implication is neither inevitable nor necessary. Indeed, innovation too may inhere in the system. For example, if international law is viewed as a typically *modern* affair – a reflection or channel of the progressive spirit of modernity itself, relentlessly overturning 'tradition' in the name of the newer and better – systemic innovation or renewal would appear 'spontaneously' or 'inevitably' linked to other modernising processes, such as globalisation, social and technological advance. In this case, fragmentation would appear not to be created or directed by strategic actors, but rather a force unto itself, managed, at best, through signposts and incentives.

Yet the Report also comments: 'New rules and legal regimes emerge as responses to new preferences, and sometimes out of conscious effort to deviate from preferences as they existed under old regimes'.[15] The ILC Report thus circles between three positions: fragmentation as intrinsic; or as a systemic response to the inevitability of modernisation or social complexification; or as a willed intervention, that might itself carry or disseminate this familiar modernisation rhetoric.[16] In every case, however – as this last example illustrates – the Report consistently speaks of regimes

Emory Simon, 'Remarks of Mr Emory Simon', Symposium: Trade-Related Aspects of Intellectual Property (1989) 22 *Vanderbilt Journal of Transnational Law*, at 370.

[12] ILC Report, para. 20.

[13] Ibid., paras 486 and 491. See too para. 493: 'The international legal system has never enjoyed the kind of coherence that may have characterized the legal orders of States.'

[14] See e.g. ILC Report, paras 158 and 209.

[15] Ibid., para. 484.

[16] Thus, e.g. at para. 473, fragmentation is described as resulting from 'the need to react to new circumstances and to give effect to interests or needs that for one reason or another have been underrepresented in traditional law'.

as emerging *consecutively*, replacing or marginalising one another: old regimes giving way to new regimes.

Again, however, this account may be queried. To pick four oft-cited regimes – trade, human rights, international criminal law, and environmental law – what is noticeable is that all four emerge more or less simultaneously in the early 1990s: the WTO and the Rio Conventions negotiated in the first years of the decade, entering into force midway through; the International Criminal Tribunal for the former Yugoslavia (ICTY) established in 1993 and the International Criminal Tribunal for Rwanda (ICTR) in 1994. The signing of BITs, too, takes off in these years, and the Vienna Declaration of 1993 supposedly rejuvenates a moribund human rights regime, as does the new High Commissioner's office. Certainly these could all be regarded as novel, or as a response to novelty – but in that case, 'the new' looks like a one-off event – 1989 – rather than some series of adjustments to a particular set of circumstances generated within the 'old regime'.

What is most interesting about this perspective – call it the 'big bang' model of fragmentation – is that it points to fragmentation taking place at the *system* level rather than the regime level. New regimes would not have emerged from the *failure* or *supersession* of old regimes – from *within* the regimes themselves, so to speak – rather, some seismic event at the supra-regime (supra-legal?) level has produced a series of new regimes, whose disconnection from one another might be described as illusory, strategic or competitive, attributable only with difficulty to an existent 'autopoetic' self-containment or self-generation within a given system or discipline, or, if so, not solely. On this vision, the phenomenon of fragmentation would appear more profoundly implicated in a motivated process of post-1989 'globalisation' – rather than merely as reaction, or series of discrete reactions, to it. Different regimes, on this model, would then be the loci of different centres of gravity and of different conceptions of the public good, rather than the discrete spaces of specific and distinct 'special interests'.

One might surmise, then, that each set of negotiations in the immediate post-1989 era provided a site of competition for a broadly opposed set of goals and interests, *each* competing on *each* terrain. The primary distinction between regimes, then, would not hang merely on their *subject matter* – rather the subject matter would provide an occasion for a contest over competing articulations of economic ordering and the public good.[17]

[17] In the words of the Report: 'Different situations may be characterized differently depending on what regulatory purpose one has in mind ... These denominations ["environment",

Regimes would be principally distinguished by the degree to which their final articulation reflects one or another conception of the public good. And, indeed, we find traces of similar or identical competitions *across* regimes in a residue of terms that crop up in multiple regimes, weighted differently in different regimes: terms that are comfortable in one setting, but somewhat alien in the other. So we find talk of creating an 'enabling environment' for investment running through the environmental regime just as we find 'sustainable development' in the trade regime.

3. *Authoritative interpretation*

A third tension in the ILC Report has to do with interpretation. The Report implicitly draws lines between three things: judicial authority, 'structural bias', and 'regime failure'. The tension in this case is familiar from international law more broadly, in its commitment to formal equality in the presence of substantive inequality. Formally, the differing interpretive fora that characterise different regimes ought not – indeed *must* not – be understood as embedding institutional hierarchy *between* regimes. That is to say, *as a matter of principle*, judicial mechanisms can hardly be viewed as intrinsically superior to other compliance mechanisms, given that international law instruments have, *as a matter of fact*, endorsed a variety of mechanisms.[18]

For similar, essentially formal, reasons, the Report's intriguing and brief discussion of 'regime failure' is radically inconclusive on the question as to whether 'failure' to achieve a regime's 'object and purpose' might be attributable to, or at a minimum associated with, the form of compliance mechanism embedded in the regime.[19] Since treaty regimes are said to incarnate the will of states to achieve specific stated purposes, it seems nonsensical to conjecture that the same states may have deliberately embedded elements within some regimes making them more likely to fail than others. Nevertheless, for 'communities' concerned to promote a given regime's 'object and purpose', institution-creation is seen as

"trade", "human rights", "humanitarian", "security"] are not about what rules should apply but how to characterize the relevant features of a state of affairs': ibid., para. 117. On this general issue, see Duncan Kennedy, 'Three Globalizations of Law and Legal Thought, 1850–2000' in David Trubek and Alvaro Santos, *The New Law and Economic Development* (Cambridge University Press, 2006).

18 See e.g. ILC Report, para. 137.

19 'No general criteria can be set up to determine what counts as "regime failure"' (ILC Report, para. 188).

a means of regime-strengthening (witness the push to institute a quasi-judicial forum to monitor the International Covenant on Economic, Social and Cultural Rights (ICESCR), a treaty regime that might justifiably be described as 'failing').

Unsurprising, then – and despite protestations to the contrary – the Report never quite escapes the spectre of inter-regime hierarchy, a murky possibility that is deflected into the vague proposal of an independent non-regime tribunal in cases of regime conflict, to 'guarantee that any settlement is not dictated by organs exclusively linked with one or the other of the conflicting regimes'.[20] The notion touched upon repeatedly in the Report, of an 'impartial third party'[21] to decide in such cases, appears intended expressly to overcome the possibility that (i) regimes appear to embed a degree of structural competition; and (ii) if so, it matters that some regimes seem better equipped to determine the outcome of inter-regime conflicts than others. For 'it might happen' as the Report puts it, 'that the law-applier will be a body or an administrator closely linked to one or another of the (conflicting) regimes. In such case, an open-ended conflict clause will come to support the primacy of the treaty that is part of the law-applier's regime.'[22]

It is in this context that the Report introduces the notion of 'structural bias' (para. 282) as a regime-feature, indeed the salient feature that risks transforming 'fragmentation' from a systemic curiosity into a structural flaw. The problem is not simply that regimes embed different or conflicting objectives. It is rather (albeit always implicitly), that some regimes are apparently better equipped than others to master the inter-regime conflicts that may result. Some have more obviously identifiable 'law-appliers' than others. Were all regimes equal, so to speak, it would be easy to conclude that international law does not elevate judicial interpretation over other forms of conflict resolution. But of course the danger fragmentation poses is precisely that all regimes may not, in practice, prove equal. The

[20] Ibid., para. 493. [21] Ibid., para. 277.

[22] Ibid., para. 280. See also para. 277:

> … it cannot be assumed a priori that a … readiness [to coordinate] exists between parties to treaties across regimes, treaties that seek to achieve physically incompatible solutions, or are inspired by very different (perhaps opposite) objectives in situations experienced as zero-sum games. In such cases … one treaty must be preferred over the other. At that point, focus shifts from coordination to rights and obligations. Even as open-ended or programmatic provisions are easily amenable to accommodation, this cannot be said of provisions laying out (subjective) rights or obligations. For giving effect to them, it remains important that the possibility of recourse to regime-independent dispute-settlement is provided.

key question, then, concerns the authority to interpret: who gets to decide which law is to be applied and how?[23] And here the Report discloses its own structural bias – or perhaps merely affirms (or critiques) an existing systemic bias – in favour of judicial fora.[24]

The paradox in the proffered recourse to such an 'impartial' or 'regime-independent' 'law-applier' or 'dispute settlement' unit is no less intriguing for being obvious. It is, of course, precisely the unavailability of such a body that constitutes the problem of fragmentation and that is distinctive about international law, on the Report's own account. The Report is clear on this point: '*no homogenous, hierarchical meta-system is realistically available to do away with such problems*'.[25] And yet, almost hypnotically, the report returns suggestively to precisely such a meta-system. 'The whole complex of inter-regime relations is presently a legal black hole', it asserts some paragraphs later, so, for the 'settlement of disputes across regimes … there is a particular need to ensure that impartial settlement mechanisms are available'.[26] The Report appears caught on the familiar hook between the realism of fragmentation as the condition of international law and the idealism of interpretive hierarchy as the emblem of law ('properly so called').

An implicit preference for judicial, over other, mechanisms is perhaps a bias attributable to lawyers rather than to law itself.[27] The same bias is apparently substantiated in the observation that *de facto* superiority attaches to those regimes boasting strong judicial organs, which are better equipped, to cite the Report, 'to advance the purposes of the regime'.[28] And yet, in a world of competing regimes, impartiality *per se* seems radically unavailable: there is a 'political obligation on law-appliers to make their decisions cohere with the preferences and expectations of the community whose law they administer'.[29] In short, for its solution to the combined problem of structural bias and the relative *de facto* superiority of some regimes over others, the Report appears to reach, reflexively no doubt, for

[23] '[C]ontrary to what is sometimes suggested, conflict-resolution and interpretation cannot be distinguished from each other' (para. 412).

[24] ILC Report, para. 277: 'it remains important that the possibility of recourse to regime-independent dispute-settlement is provided'.

[25] Ibid., para. 493, italics in the original.

[26] Ibid., para. 493(2)(f)–(g).

[27] The Report authors generally avoid speaking of the judicial function, choosing instead 'conflict resolution', 'dispute settlement' and compliance 'mechanisms'. They nevertheless consistently speak of 'interpretation' – the judicial function *par excellence* – over, say, 'enforcement'.

[28] ILC Report, para. 172.

[29] Ibid., para. 35.

a variation on the very mechanisms that are, under the existing conditions of international law, part of the problem: proliferating tribunals.

To end this section, however, I wish to raise the possibility that its principal implication – that judicialised regimes are likely to be more effective at achieving their purposes – is itself contestable. Intriguingly the ILC Report, in its discussion of regime failure, chooses as an example the Montreal Protocol on Substances that Deplete the Ozone Layer,[30] without remarking that, despite the relative underuse of its (non-judicial) non-compliance complaints mechanism, this is, in fact, a rare example of an environmental treaty generally thought to have largely *succeeded* in its object and purpose.[31] Indeed, in light of the discussion through the three sections above, it is perhaps worth asking whether the existence of judicial mechanisms are a *cause* of the apparent strength of specific regimes, or whether it is not rather the case that judicial-like mechanisms are merely a common *attribute* of strong regimes, the source of whose strength lies elsewhere.

B. Systemic inarticulacy: technology transfer in three regimes

'To die is not the main thing', French philosopher Jean Baudrillard once wrote, 'what matters is to know how to disappear'.[32] I want to turn now to a ghost of international law: technology transfer. I call it a ghost because although technology transfer has existed as a term of art within international law for many decades, it has achieved neither determination nor definition – to all intents and purposes it has died – but yet it has never learned to disappear – if anything, it appears to become more rather than less prominent over time, albeit in a continuingly vague and somewhat ethereal form.

1. *Intra-regime conflict*

The symbolic significance of technology transfer no doubt lies in its origins in the long-fading controversy over the New International Economic

[30] Ibid., para. 190.

[31] For discussion, see Duncan Brack, 'Monitoring the Montreal Protocol' in Trevor Findlay (ed.), *Verification Yearbook 2003* (Vertic, 2003). Parties may complain formally to an Implementation Committee should they have 'reservations regarding [another party's] implementation of its obligations under the Protocol', but they have not done so. Rather the reporting requirements under the Protocol appear to have been the principal means of assessing and encouraging compliance.

[32] Jean Baudrillard, *Cool Memories 1980–1985* (Éditions Galilée, 1987) ['Rien ne sert de mourir, il faut savoir disparaître'].

Order (NIEO) that newly independent post-colonial countries hoped, in the 1970s, to impose on a recalcitrant West, and from which it drew its initial impetus. Its contemporary importance, however, lies in its simultaneous appearance in a variety of regimes: within the still-nascent climate regime (the UNFCCC), the intellectual property regime (the WTO Agreement on Trade-Related Aspects of Intellectual Property or TRIPS), and in international investment law, in a series of BITs. On one hand, the term is found at the centre of what appear to be possible conflicts of norms or obligations *between* regimes. On the other, its contestation extends *into* each regime and so ambiguity infects the term itself wherever it appears.

The UNFCCC requires that 'developed country' Parties 'shall provide financial resources ... for the transfer of technology' (Article 4.3) and 'shall take all practicable steps to promote, facilitate and finance ... the transfer of ... technologies and know-how' to 'developing country' Parties (Article 4.5). It also makes the latter group's commitments under the Convention dependent upon the 'effective implementation' of this commitment by developed country parties (Article 4.7).

TRIPS Article 7 states that 'The protection and enforcement of intellectual property rights should contribute to the promotion of technological innovation and to the transfer and dissemination of technology'. TRIPS Article 66.2 has: 'Developed country Members shall provide incentives to enterprises and institutions in their territories for the purpose of promoting and encouraging technology transfer to least-developed country Members in order to enable them to create a sound and viable technological base.'

Consider the convergence of language in these various clauses. Both treaties invoke a world divided radically into two parts: developed and developing countries. Both have apparently embraced the contentious NIEO language of technology transfer. Both treaties are furthermore, of course, negotiated over the same period of time, by an overlapping, if not quite identical, group of states. And yet, if it is plain that the language is not being used in the same way in both treaties, it is equally plain that the language is not being used *plainly* in *either* treaty. 'Financial resources' in the UNFCCC may sound similar to 'incentives' in TRIPS – but we also know they may be each others' opposites: it is a question of interpretation, of course, but before that it is a question of relevant economic theory or, perhaps, economic faith. Anyway, the obligations are parcelled out differently – between one group of states and another in the UNFCCC, and between rich states and private companies within their jurisdiction, it appears, in TRIPS. There is no coincidence of obligations between these regimes, and moreover, as quickly became clear in subsequent discussion under the UNFCCC, the assertion under TRIPS Article 7 is a source of radical disagreement.

It appears fair to surmise that the term 'technology transfer' starts life in these (contemporaneous) treaties, with an identifiably different normative bearing in each one. In the UNFCCC it retains an overriding overtone of *public intervention* – it is an *aspiration*, it is an *activity*, it signifies inter-state *redistribution*. TRIPS Article 7, by contrast, embeds a quite different conception from the outset: technology transfer describes an existing (rather than aspirational) process by which goods (technologies) circulate or are exchanged across borders. Whether exchange between private actors qualifies as 'technology transfer' is unclear – just as it is not entirely clear what, if anything, the term adds to the simple notion of 'trade' itself. But it is quite clear that *within* the normative context of TRIPS, a series of assumptions familiar from the trade-regime do apply: the role of the state is facilitative and incentivising rather than regulative or proactive. It is emphatically not redistributive.[33] So, the competing significations of 'technology transfer' not only differ from, but may actually oppose, one another.

It likewise seems correct to surmise that these two regimes – the UNFCCC and TRIPS – embody, or at a minimum are receptive to, dramatically different, if not opposed, conceptions of the public good *itself*, and of the economic ordering or framing appropriate to international transactions. Moreover, the differences between the two regimes can be readily located by (among other things) their different approaches to this same term (technology transfer). Technology transfer is thus simultaneously a point of contiguity and of discontinuity between these regimes.

A substantively different normative weighting *between* regimes is not, however, the end of the story. The relevant clauses in both regimes are the subject of continuous and evolving interpretation by various expert bodies and scholars in both regimes. Within the UNFCCC regime, this has been institutionalised within an Expert Group on Technology Transfer

[33] The exception, of course, is intellectual property, which is to be actively regulated. The language of TRIPS Art. 7 reflects continuing uncertainty over the degree to which strong intellectual property protection does, in fact, actually increase cross-border exchange. See Bernard Hoekman, Keith E. Maskus and Kamal Saggi, 'Transfer of Technology to Developing Countries: Unilateral and Multilateral Policy Options', World Bank Policy Research Working Paper No. 3332. 1 June 2004, available at: http://ssrn.com/abstract=610377. I am grateful to Dalindyebo Shabalala for this point.

(EGTT),[34] which has failed to provide a final definition in six years of meetings. Within TRIPS, a national reporting requirement on Article 66.2 has permitted a diversification of interpretation, with no sign of agreement between parties on the term's normative coverage.[35]

Within each of these fora, intriguingly, the same battle over the meaning of the term rages as that identified a moment ago *between* the two. So the EGTT over the years has consistently incorporated a register familiar from the 'rule of law' push of recent decades, passing the burden onto developing countries to create an 'enabling environment' for the absorption of technological investment.[36] At the same time, developing country parties to the TRIPS have expressed dissatisfaction at the lack of progress on implementing Article 66(2) and demanding substantive action on 'technology transfer'.[37] Within both regimes, then, technology transfer, as a term of art, remains stubbornly indeterminate, a locus for disagreement about the appropriate allocation of public and private powers in the public interest.

So inter-regime competition reappears as conflict at the heart of both regimes, both in their initial negotiation and in their continued disputation. It turns out that the conflict is not so much between an 'intellectual property' or 'trade' worldview and an 'environmental' worldview. It is rather that both regimes carry concrete implications for actual economic activities. Indeed, the availability of certain technologies to certain people in certain places where climate change is expected to hit is a matter of life and death – it is precisely this recognition that underpins the UNFCCC provisions on technology.[38] The ghost I am calling technology transfer turns out, on closer inspection, to be the locus of a very live argument – and the nub of the argument turns out to be an age-old dispute over the core organising principles of a modern society: should

[34] The 2009 Conference of the Parties in Copenhagen decided to replace the EGTT with a Technology Executive Committee. See FCCC/AWGLCA/2009/17, Report of the Ad Hoc Working Group on Long-term Cooperative Action under the Convention on its eighth session, held in Copenhagen from 7 to 15 December 2009 (5 February 2010), 26.

[35] See Suerie Moon, 'Does TRIPS Art. 66.2 Encourage Technology Transfer to the LDCs?: An Analysis of Country Submissions to the TRIPS Council (1999–2007)' (unpublished, 2008), available at: www.iprsonline.org/ictsd/Dialogues/2008-06-16/2008-06-16_doc.htm.

[36] See generally Stephen Humphreys, *Theatre of the Rule of Law* (Cambridge University Press, 2010).

[37] See Moon, above n. 35.

[38] See Stephen Humphreys, 'Competing Claims: Human Rights and Climate Harms' in Stephen Humphreys (ed.), *Human Rights and Climate Change* (Cambridge University Press, 2009).

government actively intervene to develop and/or distribute public goods internationally? Or is its proper role to get out of the way and let the market do its magic?[39]

Within both regimes, technology transfer as term of art plays an essentially symbolic function. The very language – the historical associations that accrue to it through the NIEO and the assumption of public action that underlies it – may signal a moment of resistance or at least reluctance within some regimes, or a moment of triumphalism in others. It is like a loose thread within an overarching pattern that, pulled appropriately, might unravel the whole fabric. Its appearance signals the incompleteness of a given regime, the debt each regime carries to external factors and arguments, to a historical and semantic context, and to the reality of ongoing political contest embedded in textual compromise.

And so the 2008 Bali Action Plan, outlining next steps in the UNFCCC process, when it speaks of 'enhanced means for the removal of obstacles to ... the development and transfer of technology to developing country Parties', specifically intends the *removal* of intellectual property (IP) protections.[40] The UNFCCC Parties at Bali further proclaimed a desire, under the heading 'enabling environments for technology transfer' to 'avoid trade and intellectual property rights policies, or lack thereof, restricting transfer of technology' and to seek 'public and/or private partnerships that focus on improving enabling environments for accelerating development and transfer of [technologies]'.[41] Is this contradictory compromise language an example of convergence – a marriage, at last, between the NIEO and the Washington Consensus? Or does it signal a descent into semantic confusion, the release of language (and the law) from any practical contact with its supposed referents?[42]

In short, semantics themselves provide a battleground within and across regimes: the same terms and expressions reappear at the centre

39 See Humphreys, above n. 36, ch. 4.

40 FCCC/CP/2007/6/Add.1, Decision 1/CP.13, Bali Action Plan (14 March 2008), at 4, which speaks of '[e]ffective mechanisms and enhanced means for the removal of obstacles to, and provision of financial and other incentives for, scaling up of the development and transfer of technology to developing country Parties'.

41 FCCC/CP/2007/6/Add.1, Report of the Conference of the Parties on its Thirteenth Session Held in Bali from 3 to 15 December 2007, at 18.

42 Among the options suggested in the Final Document of the Ad Hoc Working Group on Long-Term Cooperation regarding technology transfer, is 'No Reference to Intellectual Property Rights in the text'. FCCC/AWGLCA/2009/17, at 27. This (as well as the other options proffered) suggests that the UNFCCC Conference of the Parties had ceased, by 2009, to be a productive forum for progressing this issue. Still, ghosts have a way of reappearing.

of multiple ongoing contests in a variety of locations. So it is not just that technology transfer is read in one place to require strengthened IP protections and in another to require their loosening – rather there is an endless recycling of a series of competing terms, with each side of the debate continuously attempting to co-opt the other within *each* of the relevant regimes.

2. *Bilateral investment treaties*

Something very different happens in international investment law. In its section on 'performance requirements', the 2004 US Model BIT provides at Article 8:

> Neither Party may, in connection with the establishment, acquisition, expansion, management, conduct, operation, or sale or other disposition of an investment of an investor of a Party or of a non-Party in its territory, impose or enforce any requirement or enforce any commitment or undertaking ... (f) to transfer a particular technology, a production process, or other proprietary knowledge to a person in its territory.[43]

Perhaps the most striking element of this prohibition is its implicit adoption of what we might call the NIEO approach to technology transfer – prioritising *public controls* – rather than its TRIPS counterpart, focusing on *private incentives*. The BIT wording, subsequently adopted in US treaties with Thailand, Rwanda and Morocco, *inter alia*, has a combative quality, aiming not to blur and reshape the language of technology transfer so much as to fix and neutralise it. Being also more amenable to identifiable breach and judicial interpretation, the BIT formula appears almost pre-emptive, the availability of a judicial (or quasi-judicial) forum is now put to the concrete task of exorcising this particular ghost from the international order.

Moreover, as Kevin Davis points out, '[t]he fact that virtually all BITs include most-favored nation clauses ... means that once a state has signed one BIT that limits its ability to impose local content or technology transfer requirements, it is likely precluded from imposing such requirements upon investors from any of the states with which it has concluded BITs.'[44]

[43] 'Treaty Between the Government of the United States of America and the Government of [Country] Concerning the Encouragement and Reciprocal Protection of Investment' [2000 Model BIT].

[44] Kevin Davis, 'Regulation of Technology Transfer to Developing Countries: The Relevance of Institutional Capacity' (2005) 27 *Law and Policy* 6, at 16.

Although BITs rarely refer to other regimes, and arbitral determinations do not carry precedence, these obligations, and the interpretation of the polyvalent term 'technology transfer' instantiated therein, must nevertheless presumably condition the legal battlefield, as it were, extending a normative gravitational force into the general thicket of normative interpretation in various regimes.

Is this, then, a textbook normative conflict, a 'zero-sum game', a case of apparent 'physical incompatibility' between treaties, in which 'one treaty must be preferred over the other'?[45] With so little scope for 'coordination' between an exhortation and a prohibition, and again taking our cue from the ILC Report, it would seem appropriate to ask how this set of issues comports with international law more broadly.[46]

The latter question is referred to in the Report as the 'normative coverage or "thickness" of [a] regime', meaning the extent to which a 'special' regime embeds itself within 'general international law'.[47] One assumption, as the Report frequently notes, is that special regimes aim to disembed themselves, to a degree, from this 'general' context – to create exceptions for special circumstances. This is no doubt the case. But, intended or not, it is surely likely that special regimes have the corollary and implicit effect of *reshaping the general law* with which they must deal, and in particular of providing direction and context on the semantic progress of terms that reappear in several regimes.

It is not merely that no regime is insulated from the general international law context,[48] but also that general international law is not insulated from any particular regime. Functional regimes exert normative influence over specific terms of art as these reappear in other regimes or in the general normative background. The mere existence of the BITs, then, presumably reshapes the interpretations of 'technology transfer' available to the UNFCCC even as negotiations continue on the latter. Indeed, in its section on technology transfer, the 2009 COP produced two optional wordings on intellectual property rights – a first suggesting the issue be passed over in silence, a second couched in a newly combative language of exceptions to other regimes, public interventions and compulsory licensing.[49] Veering between polarisation, then, and contradiction, there is little sign yet of semantic resolution.

[45] ILC Report, para. 277. [46] Ibid.

[47] Ibid., para. 172. [48] See e.g. ibid., para. 480.

[49] FCCC/AWGLCA/2009/17, at 27–28.

C. Systemic integration to come

To conclude, a thought on the implications of the foregoing for the notion of 'systemic integration'. In one of his final publications before his death in 2004, a book called *Rogues*, Jacques Derrida elaborated on a long-standing theme in his work, 'democracy to come' (somewhat richer in French: *la democratie à venir*). By this expression he meant neither, as he put it, a Platonic idea that might constitute the *essence* of democracy but never matched in the real world, nor a regulative idea, in the Kantian sense of an ideal horizon towards which we strive and against which we can measure progress.[50] Rather, by 'democracy to come', Derrida intimates that there is something incomplete in the very idea of democracy, an incompletion that is inescapable due to the term's uniting of a plurality or multiplicity – the *demos* – with a singularity (*kratos*, power, or, as it reaches us, sovereignty). What it is to organise a state *democratically*, Derrida suggests, is a question without a final knowable answer. Thus, 'one will never actually be able to "prove" whether there is *more* democracy in granting or in denying the vote to immigrants ... One electoral law is always and at the same time more and less democratic than another' and '[o]ne could multiply ad infinitum these examples ... and I mean ad infinitum, since they are produced by democracy itself'.[51] Democracy, he says, lacks an ideal: not only do we never know what it actually *is* in the final analysis, it is ultimately in the nature of democracy not to have an 'is' that might be known: there cannot be a 'final' analysis.

The relevance of all this to the idea of 'systemic integration' is, I hope, readily evident. Still, here are two ways in which that relevance might be articulated, one analogical, a second substantive. Analogically, systemic integration appears, like democracy, to be dynamic in this sense: something 'to come', but something that is, on closer inspection, unlikely ever to finally arrive in practice, or at least not to a degree that would presage finality; arguably, any such finality is constitutively unobtainable in international law. The ILC Report appears to acknowledge this. 'Normative conflict', it says at one point, 'is endemic to international law'.[52] 'The world is irreducibly pluralistic' it says at another.[53] 'In conditions of social complexity, it is pointless to insist on formal unity'.[54] Systemic integration, it is intimated, may appear to be a constant work in progress, a constant fix, but in fact it is a condition of international law. It cannot be thought or

[50] Jacques Derrida, *Rogues* (Stanford University Press, 2005).
[51] Ibid., 36–37; 72–73. [52] ILC Report, para. 486.
[53] Ibid., para. 488. [54] Ibid., para. 16.

imagined as an achieved state: international law, if systemic integration were achieved, would no longer be international law.

The substantive point is that the problem of systemic integration of international law is not only *like* democracy – the 'inheritance of a promise', as Derrida calls it – it is in fact the *same* inherited promise – the promise of democracy. That, at least, would appear to be the burden of expressions such as this assertion in the ILC Report: 'Without the principle of "systemic integration" it would be impossible to give expression to and to keep alive, any sense of the common good of humankind, not reducible to the good of any particular institution or "regime".'[55] The difficulty, of course, is establishing that any such thing is in fact the objective of international law. What if we were to conjecture that international law's 'objective', if it has one, is just the reverse? The pluralism of the international order may constitute the other side of the coin of its democratic lack: the absence of a legislative will, the dominance and horse-trading of *interest groups*, be they sovereign states or others. The phenomenon of fragmentation *is*, from this perspective, the lack of international democracy. And it is also this lack that provides the specificity of international law – that makes international law what it curiously is.

As such, fragmentation and systemic integration might better be seen as constituent and mutually dependent drivers of international law in its contemporary form. If that is the case, to imagine *international law as a system* would not be to articulate an existing assumption underlying international law as a whole; it would rather be to pose an unanswerable (if necessary) question or to advert to an irresolvable incompletion. The notion of systemic integrity may be necessary for the conception of coherence despite, or through, fragmentation – but it remains fundamentally notional, a *functional* notion, to be sure, but not a demonstrable one. Thus while it is true that the disputes and debates I have tracked here also appear throughout the domestic context, they are there suborned to an actually existing systemic integrity and are thus continuously resolved even if equally continuously reopened. International law, by comparison, would be marked by its *systemic irresolution* on these points.

D. Conclusion

Systemic ambiguity or *incoherence* is a first inter-regime phenomenon with which the present chapter was concerned; a second was strategy.

[55] Ibid., para. 480.

There is nothing novel about positing a strategic element to the proliferation of international law regimes – indeed, the ILC Report and its precedents frequently assume a strategic function in much regime creation and interaction. In the above, I pursued that notion to inquire into the persistence of ambiguity in key terminology. Questions of strategy pertain to the creation of regimes, of course, but they also pertain to the insertion or arrival of ambiguous terms into, and to their subsequent deployment within, different regimes. Contestation (of positions, of interpretations, of the principles that underlie positions and interpretations) takes place both within and across regimes, with specific terms acting as both the site and the stakes of any given contest.

A number of implications might follow from the hypothesis that the creation of regimes might serve a strategic role. We might expect to find similar substantive issues arising in different guises within different regimes, with a different set of actors expecting to benefit from the differential treatment foreseen within each discrete regime. Indeed, this is a phenomenon highlighted in the ILC Report. We might also expect to find, as corollary, similar formulae or terms of art appearing in different regimes – allowing actors to attempt to shape the meaning of such terms within the regime that better reflects their interests, in the hope or expectation that their preferred meaning will 'stick' and spill over into other areas of international law.

In the present chapter I explored the possibility that regime 'spillover' is to be expected in conditions of fragmentation by reference to one existing term of art, 'technology transfer'. The ghost of technology transfer reminds us that what may appear as inter-regime conflicts are also likely to be *intra*-regime conflicts – that similar battles are being undertaken *within* as between regimes, even if the centres of gravity between the two differ (as between TRIPS and the UNFCCC). It further reminds us that the stakes of these conflicts are waged on multiple fronts. Strategically, for those with a stake in the outcomes, it would presumably make sense to engage on as many fronts as possible. The appearance of fraught terms like technology transfer in multiple contexts, and its contentious and continuous re-articulation and reinterpretation, would appear to indicate that this is indeed happening.

To conclude then, inter-regime and intra-regime disjuncture may be deliberate or purposive, but even if not, it is likely to be durable (if mutable), and to tend to become part of the ordinary landscape of international law. Structural bias is not only an element of relations between regimes, it is also precisely that which is at stake in the construction and interpretation of elements common to multiple regimes. Given that this is the case, legal professionals are likely to be habituated to a degree of flexible and even strategic incoherence within and between regimes and to construct arguments around the expectation of these conditions. Predictable misalignment (and non-alignment) of regimes presumably acquires an implicit function: helping to determine the contextual relevance, predictability and relative superiority of certain kinds of argument and register, and of certain kinds of actor and forum. As such, it is unlikely ever to disappear.

PART III

Control

7

Norm Interpretation across International Regimes: Competences and Legitimacy

NELE MATZ-LÜCK*

A. Approaches to a systemic vision of international law

1. *Introduction*

The issues of specialisation of public international law, the existence and characteristics of an international legal system and its coherence, as well as the role of international courts and tribunals in this context have all been discussed from various perspectives and with decidedly diverse conclusions.[1] International legal writing has been addressing the issue of how and to what extent states can employ interpretation as a tool for the dynamic development of treaties.[2] It has done so, however, primarily in the context of conflict resolution.[3] The issue of fragmentation of international law as formulated by the International Law Commission (ILC) has drawn further attention to the interpretation of treaties as a tool for

* The author is grateful to Freya Baetens, Ingo Venzke and Rüdiger Wolfrum for their valuable comments on previous drafts of this paper.

[1] For different perspectives on the issue see *inter alia* Rosalyn Higgins, 'The ICJ, the ECJ, and the Integrity of International Law' (2003) 52 *International and Comparative Law Quarterly* 1; Karin Oellers-Frahm, 'Multiplication of International Courts and Tribunals and Conflicting Jurisdiction: Problems and Possible Solutions' (2001) 5 *Max Planck Yearbook of United Nations Law* 67; Nele Matz-Lück, 'Promoting the Unity of International Law: Standard-Setting by International Tribunals' in Doris König et al. (eds.), *International Law Today: New Challenges and the Need for Reform?* (Springer, 2008) 99–121; Holger Hestermeyer, 'Where Unity is at Risk: When International Tribunals Proliferate' in König et al. (eds.) at 122.

[2] See, *inter alia*, Nele Matz-Lück, 'Harmonization, Systemic Integration, and "Mutual Supportiveness" as Conflict-Solution Techniques' (2006) XVII *Finnish Yearbook of International Law*, 39.

[3] More generally on normative conflicts see eg the following monographs Jan Klabbers, *Treaty Conflict and the European Union* (Cambridge University Press, 2009); Gunther

harmonisation.[4] In particular, interpretation that takes into account 'any relevant rules of international law applicable in the relations between the parties' as provided by Article 31(3)(c) Vienna Convention on the Law of Treaties (VCLT or Vienna Convention)[5] has been discussed as a means for 'systemic integration'.[6] While this provision had long been neglected in theoretical considerations of treaty interpretation as well as in judicial practice, the work by the ILC on fragmentation and decisions by adjudicatory bodies have brought the clause to the attention of scholars and practitioners alike.[7]

Factual interrelation between different specialised fields of public international law, e.g. a partial overlap of subject matters or common points of reference, and legal interrelation, e.g. rules on interpretation like Article 31(3)(c) VCLT, may lead to the consideration of norms which were created by one regime by the institutions of another. In particular the interpretation of treaties either by the parties or adjudicatory bodies offers the opportunity to specify the meaning of treaty norms by referring to other international rules and regulations, i.e. 'extrinsic norms'. The consideration of such norms as normative guidance in the process of interpretation raises a variety of questions concerning the reasons, the legal foundations and limits, the competent actors, the results, legitimacy, and benefits and disadvantages.

Teubner and Andreas Fischer-Lescano, *Regime-Kollisionen* (Suhrkamp, 2006); Nele Matz, *Wege zur Koordinierung völkerrechtlicher Verträge* (Springer, 2005); Joost Pauwelyn, *Conflict of Norms in Public International Law* (Cambridge University Press, 2003); Seyed Ali Sadat-Akhavi, *Methods of Resolving Conflicts between Treaties* (Martinus Nijhoff Publishers, 2003); Rüdiger Wolfrum and Nele Matz, *Conflicts in International Environmental Law* (Springer, 2003); Jan Neumann, *Die Koordination des WTO-Rechts mit anderen völkerrechtlichen Ordnungen* (Duncker & Humblot, 2002).

4 International Law Commission (ILC), *Report of the International Law Commission*, 58th session, UN Doc. A/61/10 (2006), para. 412 (hereinafter *ILC Report on Fragmentation*).

5 UNTS, Vol. 1155, No.18232.

6 *ILC Report on Fragmentation*, n. 4 above, paras. 413–480. For a thorough analysis see Campbell McLachlan, 'The Principle of Systemic Integration and Article 31(3)(c) of the Vienna Convention' (2005) 54 *International and Comparative Law Quarterly* 279.

7 Among the decisions discussing the scope and interpretation of VCLT Art. 31(3)(c) are the ICJ *Case concerning Oil Platforms (Iran* v. *United States of America)*, 42 ILM (2003), 1334; the *Dispute Concerning Access to Information under Article 9 of the OSPAR Convention (Ireland* v. *UK)* (OSPAR Arbitration), accessible at www.pca-cpa.org; the *EC – Biotech* Case, Panel Report WT/DS291/R, WT/DS292/R, WT/DS293/R; and several cases decided by the European Court of Human Rights e.g. *Al-Adsani* v. *United Kingdom*, Application no. 35763/79, 123 ILR (2001), 24; *Bantovíc* v. *Belgium*, 123 ILR (2001), 94. For further examples see McLachlan, above n. 6, 295.

2. *The proliferation and change of international norms as background to regime interaction*

Increasing global interaction between states, international institutions, private entities and individuals has had a significant impact on political relations but also on the form and content of public international law. This has been reflected by several – partially subsequent, partially parallel – tendencies: variation of subject matter, specialisation, new forms of governance, and decreasing prevalence of formal legal relations. This chapter regards treaties as the most important source of international law and equally relevant in regulating rights and obligations for states and international organisations. At the same time one must acknowledge that the growing relevance and proliferation of non-state actors and international institutions in a broader sense promote the development of non-legal regulation. Moreover, in many instances states deliberately do without the formal conclusion of a treaty, e.g. in the case of the United Nations Food and Agriculture Organization Code of Conduct for Responsible Fisheries and the Proliferation Security Initiative (PSI).

International law today addresses not only a growing variety of different issues – thereby adding to and expanding from the traditional legal regulation of war and peace, boundaries and transnational commerce – but governs these issues through more detailed and specialised norms and institutions. The diversification and specialisation of public international law is a process that gained impetus after World War II and has lasted throughout the second half of the twentieth century when law-making in the form of a multitude of different multilateral treaties was perceived as an effective instrument to regulate international relations in all different fields of political relevance.[8] At that time legal thinking in international law focused on the creation of institutions and their capacity to effectively govern international relations. Attempts to analyse interaction between governance institutions from a legal perspective reflect a relatively modern development that was triggered by different factors, of which new approaches to thinking in networks are but one element.

[8] Prominent examples include international environmental law with its large number of multilateral agreements, the different agreements on the protection of human rights, the law of the sea, and international trade law as reflected by, first, the General Agreement on Tariffs and Trade (GATT) and then, in the form of a specialised multifaceted and institutionalised regime, the World Trade Organization (WTO), and international investment law in the more than 2600 investment agreements.

Today new forms of governance are in competition with treaties as the primary instruments of public international law. In the view of many authors and political theorists new modes of interaction that resemble networks between government officials, non-state actors and other non-formal entities, rather than traditional state-centred relations, have led to a decline of the state as an actor in international relations and, consequently, to a loss in relevance of traditional public international law.[9] If public international law failed to matter as the primary threshold against which the activities of international actors are measured, any discussion of a systemic vision of public international law would be obsolete. Without denying tendencies towards a variation of actors and legal and political instruments, this chapter does not share the views that states have (yet) lost their significance as primary actors and that the law they create has lost its relevance as the supreme normative environment for policy decisions. While the notion of a regime is not a legal term and must not necessarily focus upon international treaties,[10] regimes constituted by international (treaty) norms and institutions, i.e. mainly created by states and for states, likewise remain central elements of international law.

In any case, enhanced need for interaction between different actors involved in policy- and law-making, standard-setting and interpretation corresponds to a decline of formalism in international law. The changes in the international legal landscape mentioned above and the different forms of exchange between specialised normative regimes have, *inter alia*, consequences for traditional notions of treaty interpretation, the relevant competences and legitimacy.

The complexity of economic and political interdependence requires responsive agreements and institutions.[11] Multilateral treaties, however, are in principle static instruments of governance. This refers to the treaty as such in the sense that its further development depends upon the degree of dynamics the parties consent to, e.g. by allowing majority voting for modifications of at least certain parts of an agreement. It also concerns the placement of the instrument in the international legal system, i.e. within the conglomerate of norms established by other treaties and customary international law. Even if based upon treaties, regulatory international

[9] See Anne-Marie Slaughter, *A New World Order* (Princeton University Press, 2004).

[10] On approaches to defining regimes in the context of regime interaction see the introduction to this volume by Margaret Young, pp. 4–11.

[11] Eric J. Pan, 'Authoritative Interpretation of Agreements: Developing More Responsive International Administrative Regimes' (1997) 38 *Harvard International Law Journal* 503, 503.

regimes have in common that they possess a structure that facilitates the regime's potential for flexibility, e.g. by organs and procedures for decision-making and secondary law-making in addition to the primary normative instruments. Interpretation is just one method to enhance this dynamic adaptation and flexibility, e.g. to changes in the contextual environment or political considerations.

3. *Specialisation and coherence: keeping a balance*

The characterisation of the legal system is an essential background, since it sets the stage for different perceptions of a systemic notion and further development in the context of cross-regime interpretation. Diversification and specialisation, including the development of 'branches' of public international law, is a necessary part of a modern and reflective international legal system.[12] The terms relate to the creation of legal instruments and principles in more diverse fields of law and their design to address a specific and apparently confined issue.[13] The alleged proliferation of specialised regimes has raised growing concerns that rules from different branches could conflict. That is particularly so if specialised legal regimes with their divergent preferences are applicable to the same subject of regulation, i.e. the same facts.[14]

Specialisation is not a new phenomenon. In fact positive international law has always consisted of instruments addressing a specific problem or question of political relevance by legal means. With the potential exception of the most fundamental rules of customary international law, there has never been a primary body of definable 'general international law', upon which the subsequent 'special international law' was built. The distinction drawn today between special regimes and 'general international law' often refers to specific 'branches' on the one hand, e.g. human rights, and cross-cutting rules relevant to state behaviour as such, e.g. state

[12] The terms specialisation and fragmentation are often used interchangeably, or the specialisation of public international law and 'the tendency to separate law into compartments' are discussed as examples of a fragmentation of international law. See Ian Brownlie, 'The Rights of Peoples in Modern International Law' in James Crawford (ed.), *The Rights of Peoples* (Oxford University Press, 1988) 1, 15.

[13] In contrast to this, the term fragmentation had originally been used to describe the proliferation of different judicial bodies and the consequences for public international law.

[14] In her contribution to this volume at Ch. 3, Margaret Young gives the example of the overlap of specialised regimes – the Food and Agriculture Organization (FAO), the Convention on International Trade in Endangered Species (CITES) and the WTO – in fisheries sustainability.

responsibility, on the other. Indeed, it is questionable whether the establishment of a defined category of 'general international law' is beneficial, since it seems impossible to identify the content. Moreover it is unclear how such a category should relate to the sources of international law.[15] Still, the term 'general international law' is widely used in contemporary writing.

The discussion on (allegedly) 'self-contained regimes'[16] is slightly different as this notion implies that specialisation has led to specific normative regimes that exist independently from other international law. Although, in theory, all treaties exist 'independently', i.e. in parallel to one another, they are embedded in the existing conglomerate of international norms and interact, e.g. with regard to fundamental definitions or state responsibility. Such interaction would be missing if regimes were 'self-contained'. The development of regimes with a specific body of primary and secondary law, as well as mechanisms to react to breaches,[17] has not led to truly 'self-contained' normative institutions. There are currently no regimes which possess independence from any other international law, whether the latter is characterised as 'general', 'traditional' or 'fundamental' or not.[18] The notion of a 'self-contained regime' in a very narrow sense of the meaning would be appropriate for a subsystem of public international law, which is distinct in all respects and would not tolerate any fall-back

[15] Recently the International Court of Justice (ICJ) seems to have used the term as a synonym for customary international law and adds to a lack of clarity in its usage, see ICJ, *Accordance with International Law of the Unilateral Declaration of Independence in Respect of Kosovo* (Advisory Opinion), para. 74 et seq., available at www.icj-cij.org/docket/files/141/15987.pdf?PHPSESSID=513bf645282438ff95695887b3ba7939.

[16] In the context of this chapter, if the term is used, a 'self-contained regime' is understood in a broad sense, i.e. not restricted to state responsibility. It refers to international regimes that have established special rules and techniques for their administration. On the distinction between different definitions see the *ILC Report on Fragmentation*, n. 4 above, paras 123–129.

[17] This notion includes treaty-specific dispute settlement mechanisms and other treaty organs engaged in compliance control. On the institutional possibilities see Winfried Lang, 'Compliance Control in International Environmental Law: Institutional Necessities' (1996) 56 *Heidelberg Journal of International Law* 685, 687.

[18] The issue of self-contained special regimes created by and under public international law has been discussed extensively. In addition to the *ILC Report on Fragmentation*, above n. 4, paras 123–194, see Bruno Simma and Dirk Pulkowski, 'Of Planets and the Universe: Self-contained Regimes in International Law' (2006) 17 *European Journal of International Law* 483, who focus on the fall-back on the rules on state responsibility; Anja Lindroos and Michael Mehling, 'Dispelling the Chimera of "Self-Contained Regimes" International Law and the WTO' (2005) 16 *European Journal of International Law* 857; Eckart Klein, 'Self Contained Regime' in Rüdiger Wolfrum

on the general rules either in the form of other treaties or customary law.[19] As mentioned none of the different branches of public international law, e.g. 'human rights law', 'WTO law', and 'humanitarian law', meets these characteristics. No matter how specific the regulatory content, *inter alia*, the creation of the instrument, its interpretation and, if appropriate, its modification or termination by the parties follow traditional rules of international treaty-making and allow reference to at least parts of the existing body of public international law. The issue of treaty interpretation is another example for interrelations between specialised regimes and more fundamental functional rules. Regimes, which at least in certain parts consist of treaties, depend upon the customary rules on treaty interpretation for their application and for dispute settlement. Either such a fall-back to the customary rules is tacitly accepted, or regulations like Article 3(2) of the WTO Dispute Settlement Understanding refer to them. As a consequence, even a regime consisting of treaties, institutions and secondary regulations, which is designed to set aside existing law, cannot deny a relationship between itself and other international law.

In addition to reliance upon existing rules of international law in procedural matters, e.g. the law of treaties, and substantive norms, e.g. on the qualification as a subject of public international law, special regimes of international law can also interrelate with each other. Overlap between different regimes, even if only in relation to one very specific question, offers the opportunity for one special regime to profit from the interpretation and experiences of another. It is this context of relationships between regimes that has played a role in several instances of dispute settlement. The reference by WTO dispute settlement institutions to environmental agreements as an aid to interpretation of trade law is an often cited example.[20] Courts, tribunals and other dispute settlement bodies are, however, not the only environment in which regimes may interact in the course of an interpretative decision-making process. Yet decisions by dispute settlement bodies continue to serve as viable examples because they explicitly state the degree to which and the foundations upon which

(ed.), *Max Planck Encyclopedia of Public International Law* (Oxford University Press, 2010) www.mpepil.com.

19 Klein, above n. 18, para. 2.

20 See, e.g. the Panel Report in *US – Shrimp*, WT/DS58/R; Appellate Body Report *US – Shrimp*, WT/DS58/AB/R; *EC – Biotech* Case, Panel Report WT/DS291/R, WT/DS292/R, WT/DS293/R. See also the analysis of the relevant WTO case law in Robert Howse, 'The Use and Abuse of Other "Relevant Rules of International Law" in Treaty Interpretation: Insights from WTO Trade/Environment Litigation', *Institute for International Law and Justice Working Paper* 2007/1 (2007) http://www.iilj.org/publications/2007–1Howse.asp.

norms from different regimes have been taken into account in the process of interpretation.[21] The analysis of the relevant practice, e.g. with a view to use extrinsic norms for interpretation,[22] sparks discussion as to the further development of a more or less systemic vision of public international law as a whole.

In contrast to a perception of public international law that denies a systemic notion but identifies international norms as spontaneous, unrelated and based solely upon political considerations, this chapter argues that, in principle, a certain degree of coherence of the international legal system exists and is beneficial for constructing public international law. Specialisation and systemic coherence are not antagonisms. Several fundamental elements of a coherent international legal system exist despite further specialisation.

Some fundamental elements of law-making in an international legal system are characteristics to describe coherence as well as justifications for attempts to create or uphold procedural and substantive integration. While international law has added significantly to its former focus on peace treaties and the delimitation of boundaries, 'peace through law' continues to be an underlying element of modern specialised regimes as well as 'traditional' law-making on the international level. Although social interests have become more diverse, most fundamental values in international relations have remained unchanged. Ultimately, the creation of legal rules and regulations shall serve the peacefulness of relations between states. Moreover, as already mentioned above, states are still the most important actors, although international organisations and many adjudicatory bodies have achieved an autonomous status. Despite the level of independence international organisations and many adjudicatory bodies have gained, particularly with regard to their capacity to develop international law and set secondary legal standards, in the beginning they were created by states through the conclusion of treaties. The international legal system is closely woven together by states and to

[21] Even if the process and the result are criticised, as was the case in the *EC – Biotech* Case, the approach and legal bases of the consideration of extrinsic norms was made transparent.

[22] See Margaret Young, 'The WTO's Use of Relevant Rules of International Law: An Analysis of the *Biotech* Case' (2007) 56 *International and Comparative Law Quarterly* 907; Freya Baetens, 'Muddling the Waters of Treaty Interpretation? Relevant Rules of International Law in the *MOX Plant* OSPAR Arbitration and *EC – Biotech* Case' (2008) 77 *Nordic Journal of International Law* 197. More generally on the role of courts and tribunals in the context of systemic integration and coherence of international law as a system, see Matz-Lück, n. 1 above, and Hestermeyer, n. 1 above.

some extent also by international organisations as the masters and main addressees of rules and regulations of public international law.

The most significant consistency between normative instruments and, hence, a decisive element of a coherent legal system, however, is about form. The reduction of formalism, like changes in modes of governance and networks of different actors, has not (yet) led to a fundamental transformation of mechanisms. Normative regimes rely on international treaties and international treaties build the largest part of the international legal system. Thus most parts of this system are linked by the rules on the law of treaties. Likewise the need for implementation by actors in a multi-layered legal structure creates interlinks between regimes and actors, thereby establishing an element of coherence of international law.

When discussing mechanisms of normative regime interaction, their potential to provide for enhanced substantive coherence is one – but certainly not the only – characteristic. Coherence of substantive international law is limited due to the nature of public international law and the non-hierarchical design of an international legal system. It shall not mean an overall uniformity of standards. While the crystallisation of legal standards, e.g. due to repetition in different contexts and by different regimes, may assist states and other actors with the consistent implementation of law and enhance effectiveness, uniformity should not be a general objective of international law-making and development. Rather on the contrary: as mentioned the specialisation of international law is an important element of a modern and reflective international legal system. It follows from these considerations that on the one hand standards, norms and procedures specifically designed to address a certain issue shall not be sacrificed in the name of coherence. On the other hand specialisation must not mean that either the wheel has to be reinvented concerning the underlying fundamentals of a transnational legal regime or that interdependence resulting from an overlap of issues, definitions, parties, financial mechanisms and, generally, being part of the same overarching legal system, should be completely neglected.

4. *A systemic vision*

In addition to the consideration of later agreements applicable between the parties as a tool to clarify the meaning of a treaty text, one may consider the utilisation of norms stemming from other regimes as interpretative guidance in a broader sense, i.e. as an idea rather than a clear methodological approach. The notion of a 'systemic vision' of international law as used throughout this chapter describes an approach that envisages an even closer interrelation between norms within the international legal system by different degrees of integration. This includes interpretation in a cross-regime context that goes further than a restrictive understanding of Article 31(3)(c) VCLT and considers extrinsic norms more openly or extensively.

The VCLT provides for stability but also for a degree of inflexibility that may diminish the role of treaties as the primary source of international law and obligation, as it decreases flexibility to adapt to changes and modern requirements of legal governance. A systemic vision of public international law calls for enhanced universality (which does not imply uniformity!) and an effective response to new challenges. The interpretation of treaties in a cross-regime context is one approach to take account of relevant developments in different fields of international law and politics.

A systemic approach should not be confused with a hierarchical order and an interpretation that modifies norms in order not to contradict higher-ranking ones. It must be stressed again that potential conflicts between different international regimes are only one aspect relevant to the interpretation of norms by reference to ones that were established in a different context. Regime interaction is a much broader issue than conflict prevention and resolution. While enhanced coherence of international law as a system is a potential result of cross-regime interaction in the field of interpretation and is, within its limits, considered beneficial, no effort is undertaken to envision different legal norms as being ordered hierarchically or as composing a logical order.[23]

On a hypothetical level regimes may be able to clarify or dynamically develop their member's rights and obligations while saving time and effort due to reliance upon work already undertaken and experiences already gained within the other regime, if and to the extent that they refer to one another and use extrinsic norms for interpretation. At the same time regimes must safeguard that the 'specialty' of its instruments is left intact to effectively address the issue for which they were established.[24] If

[23] On the 'German approach' to public international law and its systemic vision in the sense of a hierarchy of norms and a coherent, logical order, see Eyal Benvenisti, 'The Conception of International Law as a Legal System' (2007) 50 *German Yearbook of International Law* 393, 393.

[24] Martti Koskenniemi, 'Hegemonic Regimes', Ch. 10 of this volume, argues that from the perspective of regimes' natural desire to be hegemonic any interaction must be examined to calculate whether a regime would gain by dominating other fields of policy with its

overarching elements become apparent, legal standards may crystallise by repetition and enhance systemic coherence.[25] However, the benefits may come at the price of leaving the traditional path of treaty interpretation and state consent and may thus be rejected as unpredictable, arbitrary and illegitimate. These attributes seem to contradict the notion of a systemic approach, and the resulting paradox is difficult to address. Can a more systemic vision of international law in the context of regime interaction by interpretation require reconsidering or abolishing elements of the system that have been praised as providing for procedural coherence and stability and, hence, a fundamental element of international law's systemic nature?

B. Cross-regime interpretation as a systemic element: competences and potential

1. Interpretation in the context of regime interaction

When discussing regime interaction through cross-regime interpretation, this chapter assumes that states, treaty organs and dispute settlement bodies interpret treaty norms of one regime by taking into consideration other primary or secondary extrinsic norms. Hence, the rules on treaty interpretation of the VCLT or under customary international law are, in principle, applicable to such a process. While not all provisions of the VCLT can be considered to reflect customary international law, the rules on treaty interpretation are accepted as such.

Cross-regime interpretation is not restricted to questions of interpretation in dispute settlement. Many regimes interact by an exchange of information, observance and different means of cooperation.[26] A survey of practice on explicit reference to cross-regime interpretation in processes other than dispute settlement, however, is not conclusive. While states parties or treaty organs could take advantage of existing definitions

own methods and goals or whether it would end up losing dominance by subordination under another regime's policies.

[25] Again, the arguments raised by Koskenniemi, ibid., imply that there is no objective evaluation of 'the best' legal standards and that the idea of coherence is to some extent biased by an underlying preference for a specific regime.

[26] One example for cross-regime cooperation in international environmental governance is the Joint Liason Group, which was established in 2001. This informal body consists of institutional representatives of the three Rio Conventions and works on proposals for mutually supportive activities.

developed in other regimes to clarify treaty terms, rights and obligations, there is hardly explicit evidence of such practice.[27] Hence, in practice, the issue of interpreting one agreement by referring to another mainly arises in dispute settlement procedures.[28] This explains the focus on dispute settlement in general as well as the focus on specific decisions when the issue of cross-regime interpretation is discussed in legal writing.[29] Yet, a systemic vision would profit from cross-regime interpretation which is not restricted to dispute settlement.

Different situations for cross-regime interpretation can be distinguished. First of all the individual party to a treaty is responsible for its interpretation and may also take into account rights and obligations stemming from other regimes in the process. The principal distinction is based upon collective efforts of states parties and dispute settlement bodies to interpret a treaty in the light of extrinsic norms. Collective interpretation by, e.g. the plenary body of a treaty has been labelled 'authentic' or 'authoritative' interpretation.

Interpretation across international regimes, whether by treaty organs or in dispute settlement, raises, *inter alia*, the question of who has the competence to interpret an international treaty by taking into consideration norms which were agreed in a different context and setting and, potentially, by different parties. If parties differ, the notion of consent-based treaty-making leads to necessary considerations of legitimacy when extrinsic norms are considered as a means for interpretation.

Article 31(3)(c) VCLT is the central norm for the interpretation of treaties with a systemic notion. It has gained particular attention in the realm of the current debate on fragmentation[30] and in the course of several dispute settlement proceedings.[31] Yet, the provision has raised questions in regard to the understanding of the meaning of applicable law between

[27] An example for reference by one treaty to others is the text of the Energy Charter Treaty, which contains a clause in its Art. 29 that the treaty shall be adapted to the outcome of the Uruguay Trade Round. While the Energy Charter Treaty does not incorporate definitions from the agreements covered by the WTO, it is evident that any conflicts between the instruments will be avoided by amendments to the Energy Charter Treaty. From this it follows that the interpretation of WTO agreements is likewise relevant to the Energy Charter Treaty.

[28] See Jeffrey Dunoff, 'A New Approach to Regime Interaction', in Ch. 5 of this volume, for a critique as to why a focus on judicial decisions sheds only little light on regime interaction.

[29] See, e.g. Young, n. 22 above; Baetens, n. 22 above; Howse, n. 20 above.

[30] See the legal analysis in the *ILC Report on Fragmentation*, n. 4 above, paras 424–480.

[31] See Howse, n. 20 above.

'the parties'. The interpretation of Article 31(3)(c) VCLT is decisive for the degree of 'openness' of a treaty for the consideration of extrinsic norms in the process of interpretation.[32] McLachlan has considered four different options:

(1) all parties to the treaty under interpretation must also be parties to the extrinsic one;
(2) at least the parties to a judicial dispute must be parties to the treaty relied upon in the interpretative process;
(3) if there is disparity of parties to the two treaties, the treaty rule in question must have the status of customary international law to be applicable;
(4) when there is no complete identity of parties, the extrinsic rule must be implicitly accepted or tolerated.[33]

These options range from a very narrow reading of Article 31(3)(c) VCLT to a broader systemic vision.

When interpretation is performed by treaty organs Article 31(3)(a) VCLT can play a role as well. This norm lacks the systemic element of Article 31(3)(c) VCLT but provides an instrument for the dynamic development of treaties within one regime. Still, it could gain relevance if states parties authoritatively interpret an agreement in the light of norms which are part of another regime.

2. *Individual interpretation by regime members*

Interpretation of treaty provisions is a natural part of the implementation of international rights and obligations into the domestic sphere of member states. As far as a treaty is concerned each member to the instrument necessarily interprets its provisions in the process of national implementation and application. In this respect, interpretation of norms is, in domestic as well as in international law, an individual and unilateral undertaking. The attachment of unilateral declarations of interpretation to a treaty by the parties is an expression of this conception.[34] Unless the parties decide collectively on the interpretation of a provision by

[32] On the construction and drafting history see McLachlan, n. 6 above, 290–293.

[33] Ibid., 314.

[34] On theory and practice of declarations of interpretations see Iain Cameron, 'Treaties, Declarations of Interpretation' in Rüdiger Wolfrum (ed.), *Max Planck Encyclopedia of*

authoritative interpretation,[35] there is hardly any clear guidance on the understanding of a norm.

If states interpret treaties in order to define their rights and obligations they are bound by the rules on treaty interpretation as laid down in the VCLT or in customary international law, if the VCLT is not applicable. The wording, the object and purpose of the treaty, the preamble, the context, subsequent agreements or, as a subsidiary means, the *travaux préparatoires* of a treaty are part of the exercise of understanding a norm.[36] The content of the norm as determined by interpretation is crucial for the establishment of the parties' rights or obligations. Yet often the different elements of interpretation allow for a wide array of conclusions concerning a norm's meaning and content. A drafting practice that keeps treaty language deliberately vague in politically contested fields gives considerable room to the individual party in the interpretation process.[37] This circumstance could also open the interpretation to the consideration of extrinsic norms.

An interaction of different international regimes in the process of national implementation occurs if states are parties to different international regimes and link them in the implementation process. A party to the Cartagena Protocol on Biosafety to the Convention on Biological Diversity (Biosafety Protocol)[38] may hence be inclined to interpret its obligations under the WTO Agreement on the Application of Sanitary and Phytosanitary Measures (SPS Agreement)[39] differently than a non-party to the Biosafety Protocol. Different perceptions have, *inter alia*, become apparent in the WTO *EC – Biotech* case.[40] Only if such an understanding and subsequent practice are challenged in dispute settlement might a state be bound to change its interpretation and national practice.

Public International Law (Oxford University Press, 2010), online edition, www.mpepil.com.

35 See below pp. 218–224. 36 Arts 31, 32 VCLT.

37 The evaluation as 'deliberately vague' concerns a large number of treaties ranging from the Framework Convention on Tobacco Control to the EU Treaty of Lisbon. Whether the vague wording should be qualified as a drafting technique or regarded as compromise owed to political reality is a purely theoretical issue. In any case interpretation is the central tool for establishing the relevant norms' content.

38 39 ILM (2000), 1027 et seq.

39 Agreement on the Application of Sanitary and Phytosanitary Measures (signed 15 April 1994) in WTO, *The Legal Texts* (Cambridge University Press, 1999) 59.

40 See reasoning in the WTO *EC – Biotech* case, n. 20 above.

The German decision to set aside a decision by the Conference of the Parties (COP) to the Convention on Biological Diversity (CBD)[41] on a moratorium on the fertilisation of the oceans[42] is an example of a national process of decision-making in a cross-regime context.[43] The issue of ocean fertilisation not only has relevance as a potential means to combat climate change[44] but also under the Convention on the Prevention of Marine Pollution by Dumping of Wastes and Other Matter (London Dumping Convention)[45] and under the CBD. The cross-regime aspects became apparent when Germany conducted a scientific experiment in cooperation with India, in the course of which dissolved iron sulfate was introduced into the water to monitor the growth of algae and subsequent activities by other organisms. The CBD by its COP decision IX/16 only allows exceptions from the moratorium on ocean fertilisation for small-scale experiments in coastal waters. If implemented, the German/Indian research experiment, which took place on the High Seas, would not have been permissible. In contrast to the decision in the realm of the CBD, the parties to the London Dumping Convention agreed that generally large-scale projects would be defined as dumping, but that exceptions are made for scientific research.[46] Possible implications from the application of the CBD in maritime areas under national jurisdiction were not considered.

[41] 31 ILM (1992), 818 et seq.

[42] Decision IX/16, Doc. UNEP/CBD/COP/DEC/IX/16, 7 requests a moratorium on ocean fertilisation and exempts only 'small scale scientific research studies within coastal waters'.

[43] The experiment was highly debated on the domestic level due to contradictory opinions as to legality by the Federal Ministry for Education and Research on the one hand and the Federal Ministry for the Environment, Nature Conservation and Nuclear Safety on the other. The German permission to undertake the experiment has also been discussed in the context of the CBD.

[44] The introduction of iron into the water serves as a fertiliser and leads to algae bloom. The sunlit layer of the seawater surface, in which the algae bloom, is in equilibrium with the atmosphere. Hence, absorption of carbon dioxide from this layer of water causes a deficit that is compensated from the air. In essence, carbon dioxide would be removed from the atmosphere, strengthening the oceans' capacities as sinks and reservoirs of greenhouse gases. See www.lohafex.de. While the aim of the experiment was to explore ocean fertilisation as, *inter alia*, a means to combat climate change, expectations to that extent were not fully met. Although algae bloomed as a result of the fertilisation with iron and absorbed dissolved carbon dioxide from the seawater, living organisms fed on the algae and apparently prevented a long-lasting effect.

[45] 11 ILM (1972), 1291 et seq.

[46] Germany is a party to both conventions. India is a party to the CBD but not to the London Dumping Convention. In the case of Germany it must be presumed that the different

The parties only took note of the decision on the moratorium in the preambular language of the resolution not in the operative part.

Ultimately, despite protests from the German Federal Ministry for the Environment and after having attained several expert opinions on the legal situation, the experiment was licensed by the German Government and undertaken.[47] Cross-regime interpretation could have led to a different result. Under the London Dumping Convention the experiment was not forbidden, if qualified as legitimate scientific research in accordance with Resolution LC-LP.1(2008) On the Regulation of Ocean Fertilization.[48] If 'legitimate scientific research' was interpreted as referring to the rules under the United Nations Convention on the Law of the Sea (UNCLOS),[49] this would not result in a prohibition or significant restriction, since the experiment was to take place on the High Seas and standards on the protection of the marine environment are not set by UNCLOS itself but by other institutions such as the International Maritime Organization (IMO). Hence, standards would refer back to the London Dumping Convention. Had 'legitimate scientific research' been interpreted while taking into account the CBD-COP decision IX/16, the understanding of permissible projects could have been reduced to small-scale experiments in coastal waters. However, while taking note of the moratorium under the CBD, the parties to the London Dumping Convention refrained from any interpretative references. Instead in Resolution LC-LP.1(2008) they defined 'legitimate scientific research' as 'those proposals that have been assessed and found acceptable under the assessment framework'.[50]

When evaluating the interrelation between both conventions and the relevance of the two decisions, much depends upon their legal nature[51] as well as on the question which agreement enjoys supremacy. This,

decisions, a moratorium on the one hand and a general exception for research on the other, depend upon which ministries send delegates to attend the meetings. While the Federal Ministry for Education and Research actively promotes the role of scientific research in international conferences the Federal Ministry for the Environment, Nature Conservation and Nuclear Safety generally expresses a more restrictive approach.

47 The internal governmental dispute as to the legality and desirability of the project led to the peculiar situation that the German Federal Ministry for the Environment protested against the promotion of the project by the German Ministry of Education and Research.

48 IMO Doc. LC 30/16 of 9 December 2008, Annex 6.

49 21 ILM (1982), 261 et seq.

50 Resolution LC-LP.1(2008), n. 48 above.

51 It has been argued that neither of the decisions, neither that by the CBD-COP nor that by the Contracting Parties to the London Dumping Convention, was legally binding.

again, depends upon interpretation: if Article 22(2) CBD is interpreted as granting supremacy to UNCLOS and related instruments concerning the law of the sea, there is no obligation to interpret the London Dumping Convention in the light of a (non-binding) CBD decision. There is a difference, however, between not being obliged to do something (while nevertheless being allowed to do it) and actively being impeded from doing so. In the former case there is room for systemic integration. Had Germany come to a different conclusion – as did its Federal Ministry for the Environment – most likely the result would not have been questioned. Indeed interpretative practice to include the CBD in the interpretation of the decision of the Contracting Parties to the London Dumping Convention could have developed, although not required by law.

On the level of national interpretation of international norms, states only – if at all – have to take into consideration those norms stemming from treaties to which they are a party. It has to be noted that, theoretically, states could also adopt or consider other standards or norms to which they have not formally consented in international fora as an expression of (changed) national policy. Since many treaties come as package deals, the decision not to consent to an agreement does not exclude approval of certain definitions or standards.

In the *Dispute Concerning Access to Information under Article 9 of the OSPAR Convention (Ireland* v. *UK)* (OSPAR Arbitration)[52] the arbitrators had to deal with the question of whether the Convention on Access to Information, Public Participation in Decision-making and Access to Justice in Environmental Matters (Aarhus Convention)[53] is applicable law between the parties. If so, it would have had an influence in interpreting the Convention for the Protection of the Marine Environment of the North-East Atlantic (OSPAR Convention) in accordance with Article 31(3)(c) VCLT. Griffith in his dissenting opinion agrees that the Aarhus Convention was not binding international law because none of the parties to the dispute had ratified it. However, he draws the attention to the fact that the UK had not only signed the Aarhus Convention but had maintained the intention to be bound by and to implement it.[54] This also implies an influence of the Aarhus Convention on the UK's interpretation of other agreements, namely the OSPAR Convention. Accordingly, Griffith, against the majority opinion, argues that the Aarhus Convention

[52] See n. 7 above. [53] 2161 UNTS 447.

[54] Dissenting Opinion of Gavan Griffith, OSPAR Arbitration, n. 7 above, para. 17.

should have been considered as falling within the definition of applicable law and Article 31(3)(c) VCLT.[55]

3. *Authoritative interpretation by regime-organs*

The issues relevant in the context of individual interpretation become more complicated if a plenary organ or a dispute settlement body is faced with extrinsic norms because their acceptance as normative guidance is deemed to depend upon consistency in membership to both or all relevant agreements. A dialogue between regimes with a view to create mutually supportive norms for effective governance of all different branches of international law would be an option that could simultaneously respect the needs for specific regulation on the one hand and overarching coherence of the legal system on the other. Many treaties have recognised the need for mutually supportive actions and refer to interpretation in a mutually supportive way but the interaction is focused upon authoritative interpretation by either treaty in light of the other.

From the perspective of systemic approaches to interpret treaties as interrelated parts of the international legal system, authoritative interpretations of international agreements by the plenary organs seem viable. As authoritative interpretation is a collective process involving all parties, decisions by adjudicatory bodies settling disputes between two or more (but not all) parties are not relevant in this context. In a cross-regime situation, treaty organs can react to new developments of international law: they can create synergies and facilitate implementation of their own regime by accepting normative guidance from outside. In terms of a systemic vision of public international law, interrelations between regimes could easily be established by accepting and incorporating extrinsic definitions. The choice concerning which norms of another instrument are useful for the understanding and implementation of the regime would in principle lie with the competent plenary organ. Hence, it depends upon the parties if and to what extent they refer to extrinsic norms in the process of interpretation.

Under the rules on the law of treaties the method of determining – or at least influencing – a specific interpretation by all parties corresponds to Article 31(3)(a) VCLT. Later agreement between the parties is

[55] Ibid., para. 19. Young, n. 22 above at 917–918, discusses the example as an approach to 'implicit' agreement of treaty terms.

only one tool for the interpretation of a text. Yet, if the decision on the authentic interpretation of a treaty is binding as a result of the relevant organ's law-making competence and the internal rules on decision-making, interpretation in the light of Article 31(3)(a) VCLT gains particular weight. One objective for seeking collective agreement on the interpretation of a treaty is to overcome the uncertainties owed to political preferences and interests if parties interpret (and apply) a treaty individually.

In principle, authentic interpretation can be the result of an informal process by silent agreement on a certain understanding of a treaty provision.[56] In this case, unless the understanding is verifiable by state practice,[57] the legal consequence is uncertain as such a process would not be considered binding upon the parties. Indeed this consideration is largely theoretical as a silent process, which is not reflected by practice, is not demonstrable and, thus, one must ask whether such a tacit agreement exists at all.[58] It is not excluded that collective state practice concerning the interpretation of one regime could serve as normative guidance for another regime. The relevant link consists of states that are parties to both regimes. Yet difficulties in relation to verification make silent authentic interpretation seem less relevant in a cross-regime context.

The alternative is an authentic interpretation agreed upon by formal procedure, e.g. by a decision specifying the common interpretation,[59] by

[56] Such a process has been named 'quasi-authentic interpretation' by Serge Sur, *L'Interprétation de Droit International Public* (Librairie générale de droit et de jurisprudence, 1974) 361.

[57] If accompanied by state practice a modified interpretation due to silent – or rather informal – agreement would most likely be qualified as falling under Art. 31(3)(b) VCLT.

[58] Anthony Aust, *Modern Treaty Law and Practice* (Cambridge University Press, 2nd edn, 2007) 243. Aust states in the context of 'subsequent practice' that '[i]t is not necessary to show that each party has engaged in practice, only that all have accepted it, albeit tacitly.' Such silent acceptance could be concluded from acquiescence by all remaining parties in the light of some existing state practice by other members.

[59] An example of an agreement on a common understanding of obligations by the members of an organisation is the Understanding on the Interpretation of Article XXIV of the General Agreement on Tariffs and Trade 1994 (signed 15 April 1994, as part of WTO Uruguay Round) in WTO, *The Legal Texts* (Cambridge University Press, 1999) 26, accessible at www.wto.org/english/docs_e/legal_e/10-24_e.htm. Likewise the parties to the UNCLOS agreed upon a different understanding of the ten-year timeframe for making claims for an extended continental shelf in Art. 4 of Annex II; see Doc. SPLOS/72 of 29 May 2001, accessible at www.un.org/Depts/los/clcs_new/issues_ten_years.htm. For more examples see Aust, n. 58 above, 239–241.

interpretative declaration[60] or even by a protocol[61] or a supplementary treaty.[62] Article 31(3)(a) VCLT does not specify the relevant form and thus leaves room for interpretation that takes into account 'any subsequent agreement between the parties'. In the case of a legally binding supplementary instrument like a protocol or another treaty, however, the potential benefits of authoritative interpretation, e.g. the consistent understanding of a norm without the need for ratification by all parties, would be lost.

The general competence of the states parties to a treaty to agree upon an authoritative interpretation is deduced from the power to agree on a modification of the instrument.[63] Whether, more specifically, a treaty organ possesses the competence to decide upon an authoritative interpretation in accordance with the rules on procedure of the instrument is a distinct question. Competence for authentic interpretation, if not explicitly stated in the treaty text, may be construed by reference to the general or subsidiary competence to address all relevant matters, e.g. a provision like Article 23(4)(i) CBD.[64]

One might also take recourse to the doctrine of implied powers. Although this doctrine stems from the law of international organisations, it could be transferred by way of analogy to the plenary organs of normative regimes in international law. Plenary organs of regulatory regimes consisting of primary treaty law and secondary norms are to a large degree comparable to international organisations. The main distinction between

[60] As a recent example shows, collective interpretative declarations are also used in the context of non-binding standards. The European Commission for Democracy through Law (Venice Commission), which was established under the auspices of the Council of Europe but is open to non-European states, adopted an Interpretative Declaration on the Stability of the Electoral Law in 2005, Doc. CDL-AD(2005)043 (accessible at www.venice.coe.int/docs/2005/CDL-AD(2005)043-e.asp). This declaration serves to clarify a provision of the Code of Good Practice in Electoral Matters, Doc. CDL-AD (2002) 23 rev (accessible at www.venice.coe.int/docs/2002/CDL-AD(2002)023rev-e.asp). This soft-law instrument was adopted in 2002.

[61] The question of the legal implications of an interpretative protocol already played a role in the Advisory Opinion by the Permanent Court of International Justice concerning the Jurisdiction of the European Commission of the Danube in 1927, *Publications of the Permanent Court of International Justice*, Series B, Opinion No. 14 (1927), 12.

[62] On more examples concerning the form see Richard Gardiner, 'Treaties and Treaty Materials: Role, Relevance and Accessibility' (1997) 46 *International and Comparative Law Quarterly* 643, 648–649.

[63] Aust, n. 58 above, 239.

[64] Art. 23(4)(i) CBD: 'The Conference of the Parties shall keep under review the implementation of this Convention, and, for this purpose, shall: ... Consider and undertake any additional action that may be required for the achievement of the purposes of this Convention in the light of experience gained in its operation.'

the two is that plenary treaty organs such as the conference of the parties lack independence from the governments of participating states. This, however, is an argument for accepting competence for authentic interpretation. The states parties as the masters of the treaty decide upon issues crucial for the implementation, application and further development of the law. The reason for institutionalising modern treaty regimes and allowing decisions concerning the implementation of the treaty is to overcome the disadvantages of traditionally static agreements. Treaty organs have demonstrated an active practice of filling the frameworks of their primary legal instruments. Interpretative competences are one element that may assist with a common understanding of norms and more effective implementation.

An authoritative interpretation is the result of a collective process by states parties to a treaty and, generally, an expression of agreement by all.[65] In this context some sort of 'bindingness' of the agreed outcome would be preferable. The VCLT refers to subsequent agreement as one of several methods of interpretation. It is silent, however, on the legal effect of such a subsequent agreement as binding or non-binding. While non-binding interpretations will carry some weight, they are not definitive.[66] Whether the agreement on the interpretation by decision of the plenary body of a regime has legally binding effect for the parties depends upon the regime's general rules of procedure as agreed upon in the treaty or subsidiary legal instruments. If there is generally no competence to adopt binding decisions, a binding nature of authentic interpretation cannot be construed. Some plenary organs have explicitly been provided with the relevant power, while for others law-making and law-development competences depend upon an interpretation of the organ's function and more specific tasks.[67] Article 1131(2) North American Free Trade Agreement (NAFTA) contains a specific clause that explicitly states that interpretations by the NAFTA Free Trade Commission (FTC) of a NAFTA provision is binding on a Tribunal established under chapter 11, section B, i.e. for disputes between a party and the investor of another party.[68]

[65] Knut Ipsen and Wolff Heintschel von Heinegg, *Völkerrecht* (Verlag C.H. Beck, 5th edn, 2004) § 11, para. 2.

[66] For an example of the non-binding authoritative interpretation of the United Nations Convention Relating to the Status of Refugees see Aust, n. 58 above, 240.

[67] The Conference of the Parties to the Montreal Protocol on Substances that Deplete the Ozone Layer, for example, has competence to decide upon binding measures. In contrast thereto, the COP to the CBD has not been provided with such competence.

[68] One of the functions of the NAFTA Free Trade Commission is to 'resolve disputes that may arise regarding [the] interpretation or application of NAFTA' (Art. 2001(2)(c)).

Often treaty texts make no explicit reference to the legal effect of decisions made by its organs. The Rules of Procedure for the Meeting of States Parties of the UNCLOS,[69] for example, distinguishes different modes of decision-making: by general agreement (rule 52(1)), by qualified majority vote on questions of substance (rule 53) or by simple majority of the parties present and voting for decisions on procedural matters (rule 55(1)). While decision-making by voting implies a legally binding effect on all members, such a conclusion is not expressly provided for in the Rules of Procedure and is subject to debate among the parties.

The Antarctic Treaty Consultative Meeting (ATCM) as another example from a regulatory regime makes recommendations to the consultative governments in the form of measures, decisions and resolutions. These categories differ in regard to the legal nature. On the matter of legally binding force Rule 24 of the ATCM Rules of Procedure refers to Decision 1 (1995). This decision, which was adopted by ATCM XIX in 1995, clarifies that a text that shall be legally binding upon approval by all parties is expressed as a measure.[70] All other decisions, resolutions or recommendations become effective upon adoption.[71] 'Effectiveness', however, is not equivalent to a legally binding nature. Provided that the ATCM is competent to decide upon an authentic interpretation of the treaty – and one must presume that it is because the decision on the distinction between measures and other decisions is qualified as such[72] – it could do so only as a legally binding measure. In ATCM practice, the majority of measures concern the designation of protected sites and the establishment and revision of management plans. Yet, as the amendment of the Environmental Protocol by ATCM Measure 16 (2009) shows, further development of the relevant legal instruments in legally binding form is possible.

In the decision-making process concerning the interpretation of their agreement, the states parties are, unless they agreed otherwise, bound by the rules on the interpretation of treaties. Authoritative interpretation has been discussed as a means of changing an instrument without using the cumbersome method of formally amending a treaty and without the

[69] Doc. SPLOS/2/Rev.4 of 24 January 2005.

[70] Decision 1 (1995) is accessible at www.ats.aq/devAS/info_measures_list.aspx.

[71] The aim was to separate substantive questions under Article IX, para. 1 of the Antarctic Treaty from procedural matters. Since legally binding measures require approval by all parties, they sometimes became effective years after adoption.

[72] Aust, n. 58, 240–241.

need for ratification of modifications by the parties.[73] If one accepts such a function, however, one moves away from the original reason for the interpretation of treaties, i.e. the clarification of an unclear meaning of a treaty provision. While this blurs the distinction between interpretation and modification, an agreement to modify primary treaty norms through an 'interpretation', which goes beyond Article 31 VCLT is unlikely to be questioned, if the parties so agree. At least, this is true for the parties themselves. If adjudicatory bodies are involved, that are responsible for guarding application of the treaty, modifications by an interpretation may be rejected as illegal if a treaty organ is competent for interpretations but not amendments.

An example of relevant difficulties is given by the statements of interpretation by the NAFTA's FTC and their acceptance or rejection by tribunals under chapter 11, section B NAFTA. As mentioned above, the interpretation of a NAFTA provision by the FTC is binding upon the tribunal in accordance with Article 1131(2) NAFTA. Here the question is one of distinguishing binding interpretations from *ultra vires* amendments by the FTC. In contrast to Article 1131, Article 2202 NAFTA allows only for amendments by the parties (and not by the FTC) and refers to the relevant national procedure, e.g. ratification, for the modifications to become binding. This should be done by reference to the customary rules on treaty interpretation and the primary objective of interpretation: the clarification of an unclear text. Accordingly, the binding effect of the FTC's interpretation statements could have been rejected if an 'interpretation' was considered a disguised amendment and if the tribunal was competent to decide on the *ultra vires* question.[74] In the case of *Mondev International Ltd.* v. *USA* (*Mondev*) the tribunal considered the NAFTA states parties' conduct when the FTC issued an interpretation of an article which played a major role in the pending case. Moreover, the FTC's interpretation contradicted the findings of several previous tribunal awards in regard to Article 1105 NAFTA. In the end, the tribunal in *Mondev* did not have to decide on its competence to disregard *ultra vires* amendments

[73] Jan Klabbers, 'Treaties, Amendment and Revision' in Rüdiger Wolfrum (ed.), *Max Planck Encyclopedia of Public International Law* (Oxford University Press, 2010), online edition, www.mpepil.com; Pan, n. 11 above, 509–510.

[74] Canada argued in the case of *Pope & Talbot* that the tribunal had no jurisdiction to decide whether a statement that was presented as a binding interpretation under Art. 1131(2) NAFTA was outside the powers of the FTC. The tribunal, however, did not find this argument persuasive; *Pope & Talbot Inc.* v. *Canada*, Award in Respect of Damages, 31 May 2002, www.naftaclaims.com/Disputes/Canada/Pope/PopeAwardOnDamages.pdf, paras 22–24.

because, in contrast to *Talbot & Pope*,[75] it argued that the FTC's interpretative statement was in fact an act of interpretation.[76]

Yet, even if, strictly speaking, in specific cases authentic interpretation may not be interpretation according to the relevant rules under the law of treaties, parties are relatively free to decide upon the understanding of their agreement. This also applies to the incorporation of extrinsic norms by a systemic interpretative approach. Since the development of a regime despite all formalism depends to the largest extent upon the will of the parties, consensual authentic cross-regime interpretation is possible, even if the rules on the interpretation of treaties are not complied with.

4. *Cross-regime interpretation in adjudicatory proceedings: competence*

Adjudicatory bodies, no matter whether they are engaged in arbitration, binding judicial settlement of disputes between (states) parties or handle individual complaints against states as in human rights proceedings or an investment dispute between the investor and a state, have to define the law applicable to the dispute in question. Already this general question can involve cross-regime references, e.g. when the question is raised if human rights law and international humanitarian law are simultaneously applicable, or whether and to what extent the applicability of the latter restricts the other.[77] While not directly concerned with the interpretation of one treaty in the light of another, the consideration of different treaties which are or might be applicable by an adjudicatory body shows the close linkage of treaties in the international legal system and points to the issue of competence.

[75] On the relevance of Art. 31(3)(c) VCLT in the context of *Pope & Talbot* see the analysis by McLachlan, n. 6 above, 296–299.

[76] Award, 11 October 2002, www.state.gov/documents/organization/14442.pdf, paras 120–125.

[77] Many cases before the Inter-American Commission of Human Rights and the Inter-American Court of Human Rights concern this question, e.g. *Juan Carlos Abella* v. *Argentina*, Case 11.137, Report no. 55/97, Inter-Am C.H.R., OEA/Ser.L/V/II.95 Doc. 7 rev. at 271 (1997), para. 148. In the *Mox Plant Case (Ireland* v. *United Kingdom)*, Order of 3 December 2001, accessible at www.itlos.org, para. 50, the International Tribunal for the Law of the Sea (ITLOS) referred to the OSPAR Convention, the Treaty Establishing the European Community (EC Treaty) and the Treaty Establishing the European Atomic Energy Community (Euratom Treaty) and concluded that even if they 'contain[ed] rights or obligations similar to or identical with the rights or obligations set out in the Convention, the rights and obligations under those agreements have a separate existence from those under the Convention' in order to establish parallel jurisdiction.

If parties disagree on the interpretation of an international legal norm relevant in the relationship between them, they may enter into negotiation or mediation or formal dispute settlement.[78] Some specialised regimes provide for their own dispute resolution institutions and procedure. The WTO dispute settlement system is a particularly prominent example, *inter alia*, due to the significant number of decisions. Other regimes either refer more generally to arbitration or the International Court of Justice or establish these options in addition to a specific institution and procedure. An example for a choice of procedure is provided by Article 287 UNCLOS. If disputes concerning the interpretation and application of UNCLOS are not settled by other means, e.g. conciliation, parties can choose between the International Tribunal for the Law of the Sea (ITLOS), the International Court of Justice (ICJ) or different forms of arbitration as procedures entailing binding decisions.

The competence of a dispute settlement body to decide upon the interpretation of a treaty and the relevant procedure are, hence, agreed upon by the parties to the treaty regime. A general reference to dispute settlement before an existing court or tribunal also implies agreement with regard to the relevant rules of procedure, and generally requires consent by the parties to the dispute either by the general declaration of acceptance of jurisdiction or on a case-by-case basis.

If not specifically addressed in the rules of procedure, the degree to which norms from 'outside' the agreement can be referred to in the process of interpretation follows from the rules on treaty interpretation as laid down in the VCLT and customary international law.[79] Since Article 31(3)(c) VCLT as an expression of customary international law allows for 'systemic integration' of other law applicable between the parties, dispute settlement bodies that rely upon the rules on treaty interpretation are competent to take into account such norms. Examples for the consideration of extrinsic treaty norms in a cross-regime context involve, *inter alia*, reference to Article 38(1)(c) of the Statue of the International Court of Justice to establish whether Article 6 of the European Convention on Human Rights and Fundamental Freedoms (ECHR)[80] guaranteed

[78] On solutions to colliding regimes in dispute resolution see James Crawford and Penelope Nevill, 'Relations between International Courts and Tribunals: The "Regime Problem"', in Ch. 8 of this volume.

[79] Art. 3(2) of the WTO Dispute Settlement Understanding refers to the 'customary rules of interpretation of public international law'.

[80] 213 UNTS 222.

access to civil courts;[81] the consideration of the applicability of the Aarhus Convention to interpret Article 9(3)(d) OSPAR Convention;[82] and the reference to the Convention on International Trade in Endangered Species of Fauna and Flora (CITES)[83] to establish whether sea turtles are 'exhaustible' resources in accordance with Article XX(g) GATT.[84] The given examples have been limited to situations where adjudicatory bodies have considered other treaty law as tools for interpretation.[85] Although it depends upon the definition of a regime whether customary international law could qualify as such, the issues of competence and legitimacy in the context of regime interaction upon which this paper focuses are less relevant if rules of customary law are applied as extrinsic norms in the context of treaty interpretation.

The relevant adjudicatory bodies first of all interpret the agreement under which the dispute was referred to dispute settlement. Reference to other legal rules of the international legal system, even if developed in the context of a different setting, is part of this process.[86] Interpretation of the agreement by reference to the accepted methods of interpretation is not only within the dispute settlement body's competence, it is the essence of its existence and practice, if there are no obstacles to jurisdiction.

Still, competence for interpretation may be questioned from the perspective of an informal or implicit interpretation of the norm from another regime. The application of legal rules, e.g. as normative guidance for another regime, cannot be separated from an interpretative act. Part of the 'trade and environment' debate concerns the question whether a WTO Panel would be competent to interpret an environmental agreement, e.g. in the context of Article XX GATT, from a trade-centred perspective and without guidance from, e.g. this treaty's organs. When one

[81] *Golder* v. *United Kingdom* 57 ILR 200, 213.

[82] OSPAR Arbitration, n. 7 above.

[83] 12 ILM (1973), 1088.

[84] WTO, *United States: Import Prohibition of certain Shrimp and Shrimp Products – Report of the Appellate Body*, 12 October 1998, WT/DS58/AB/R, 38 *ILM* (1999), 118.

[85] Many examples from adjudicatory practice that explicitly deal with the application of Art. 31(3)(c) VCLT in substance concern customary rules of international law, e.g. the question whether 'generally recognized rules of public international law on State immunity' can restrict the right to access to court in accordance with Art. 6(1) ECHR, see *Al-Adsani* v. *United Kingdom*, n. 7 above, paras 55–56.

[86] Howse, n. 20 above, 38, in footnote 38 correctly distinguishes between the application of extrinsic norms and their use as an aid to interpretation of another norm. Judge Buergenthal in his Separate Opinion in the ICJ *Oil Platforms* Case, n. 7 above, however, indicates a lack of jurisdiction to consider extrinsic norms, i.e., in the context of the case the law on the use of force.

norm is considered as a tool to interpret another norm, the former is necessarily also interpreted as specifying its content, relevance and influence in the interpretative process. This act is more implicit but nevertheless existent. Thus, the dispute settlement body, like any other institution that interprets norms in a cross-regime context, performs two interpretative acts. The process of implicitly interpreting the rules stemming from another regime may raise the issue of legal competence and the question of participation and guidance by the extrinsic regime. The rules on treaty interpretation and the relevant rules of procedure, however, do not distinguish between different regimes. If a treaty is to be interpreted in the light of another applicable treaty between the parties, competence to consider and interpret this agreement as part of the process is granted. From the perspective of reciprocal interaction consultation of the other regime as to the interpretation of relevant terms would seem desirable.

Competence to refer to extrinsic norms in dispute settlement has the potential to set standards concerning the understanding of the relevant norms of both regimes. Generally, decisions in dispute settlement procedures only have legally binding force for the parties to the dispute (*inter partes* rule). In fact, however, decisions concerning a treaty's interpretation by the competent dispute settlement organ have relevance for the interpretation of the agreement as such and may also have an effect on the interpretation of an extrinsic agreement.

If the organs of an extrinsic regime have doubts concerning the interpretation of, e.g. an environmental norm in the context of trade, they could attempt to formulate an authentic interpretation of the relevant norms. Such an authoritative interpretation, while not formally binding upon the dispute settlement body of another regime, must be assumed to give normative guidance in a further cross-regime interpretation context. At least it could stop or reverse interpretative practice not previously agreed upon and not currently agreeable by the parties.

C. The question of legitimacy

Competence and legitimacy are interrelated. Lack of competence implies a lack of legitimacy. The mere fact that the competent institution acted, however, may not necessarily lead to legitimate results. Depending upon the substance of the decision and procedure, competent institutions can make decisions lacking legitimacy. In the context of interpretation across international regimes this means that the decision of a formally competent institution, e.g. a regime's adjudicatory body, may be questioned with regard to legitimacy if extrinsic norms have been considered to which not all parties to the treaty in question consented. The main relevant factors are prior state consent concerning the norms taken into consideration in the interpretative process and the legal nature of the decision, e.g. as binding or non-binding. With regard to individual interpretation by parties to an agreement a distinction between competences on the one hand and legitimacy on the other is less relevant. It is largely a national policy choice to include extrinsic norms into an interpretative process, even if the state is not a party to the relevant regime.

Doubts concerning legitimacy of cross-regime interpretation of norms come almost as a reflex when one imagines institutions interpreting treaties adopted outside their institutional setting. This issue, as seen above, can be addressed from the perspective of competence as well as legitimacy. An implied lack of legitimacy arises in particular if specialised dispute settlement institutions, e.g. WTO panels, interpret treaties other than the ones for which they were established. The crucial question concerns the consideration of treaties as an aid to interpretation when the parties to both treaties do not coincide or, more precisely, when not all parties to the treaty that is being interpreted have also consented to the extrinsic norm.[87] The interpretation of Article 31(3)(c) VCLT is subject to debate as to whether applicable law between 'the parties' refers to the parties in a specific judicial dispute or to all parties to the treaty subject to interpretation by an adjudicatory body. While the ICJ in the *Oil Platforms* case has adopted a broad approach, the WTO *EC – Biotech* case is an example of an (overly) restrictive interpretation. A narrow interpretation leads to the result that only if all parties to an agreement have also consented to the extrinsic treaty can the latter be referred to in the process of interpretation. This is particularly problematic if the treaty that is being interpreted is of a global nature. In this case identity of parties with regard to another treaty is very unlikely and reference to law outside the regime impossible, even if a large number or parties have ratified both or all instruments.[88]

Consent is perceived as the central element of the law of treaties and, due to the ever-present notion of sovereignty, of current public international law as a whole. It is also considered the key to legitimacy of treaty law-making. This fundamental concept extends to the interpretation of a treaty if the relevant decision is legally binding. If a dispute settlement

[87] On this issue see Young, n. 22 above, and Baetens, n. 22 above.
[88] See also McLachlan, n. 6 above, 314.

body for interpretation purposes takes into account norms which not all parties to the dispute have consented to, this reference is problematic.[89] If Article 31(3)(c) VCLT is construed narrowly, not only is the consent of the parties to the judicial dispute relevant but all parties to the treaty under interpretation must also be parties to the treaty relied upon.

The attempt by the WTO Panel in *EC – Biotech* to distinguish between applicable law and 'informative law' allows for an opening of the trade law regime to guidance from outside the regime, but it does so through doubtful means. The argument that an extrinsic norm, in principle, can assist the establishment of an understanding of a treaty, even if not all parties have consented to it,[90] is a valid consideration. However, it is questionable whether Article 31(1) VCLT, which stipulates that treaties must be interpreted in accordance with the ordinary meaning of the terms, the context and the object and purpose, can be used to overcome the limitations of Article 31(3)(c) VCLT. Rather, a broader understanding of Article 31(3)(c) VCLT or the acceptance that the provision is not exhaustive would have been preferable.

From a systemic perspective one must ask whether potentially the lack of consent of one state or a few states could prevent effective and transparent cross-regime interpretation and enhanced coherence of the international legal order. Howse has undertaken an attempt to replace consent as the only relevant indicator of legitimacy by different concepts, such as appropriate cross-contextuality, the values of democracy and self-determination, the analysis if 'the norms to be applied in interpretation reflect recognized universal values', and the publicness of the process.[91] While these elements reflect viable considerations and should be taken into account, it is doubtful whether they will ever substitute the close linkage between consent and legitimacy. Replacing formal state consent with a broader notion of international consensus with regard to extrinsic norms might lead to different results.[92] However, an interpretative system based

[89] On the need for parallel membership in the context of inter-state consensus and legitimacy see Young, n. 14 above, 94–96.

[90] *EC – Biotech*, n. 20 above, para. 7.94.

[91] Howse, n. 20 above, 41–42.

[92] The term consensus is usually tied to a specific form of procedure in international decision-making, see Rüdiger Wolfrum and Jakob Pichon, 'Consensus' in Rüdiger Wolfrum (ed.), *Max Planck Encyclopedia of Public International Law* (Heidelberg and Oxford University Press, 2010), online edition, www.mpepil.com, para. 1. As opposed to the notion of positive state consent, this chapter uses the term consensus to indicate the absence of objections in a broader sense, i.e., not restricted to voting procedure.

upon a notion of a consensual legal system has yet to be defined. Its position in the current rules on interpretation would be difficult to establish,[93] if one argued for a general opening of the process to consideration of all sorts of norms as long as they are part of the international legal system.

It needs to be noted that many instances of cross-reference seem rarely problematic from the perspective of legitimacy. If, for example, treaty organs refer to an instrument to clarify terms and provisions of their relevant instrument, lack of legitimacy to do so is hard to construct, even if not all of the treaty's parties are a member of the other. In the context of authentic interpretation by treaty organs, the issue would only arise when a decision would consider norms from another regime, be legally binding and rely upon majority voting. Only in this case could an extrinsic norm influence a treaty in a legally binding manner against the will of parties that are non-members of the extrinsic regime. If a plenary treaty organ interpreting the agreement by reference to another decides unanimously, consent by all parties extends to the specific normative guidance by the other regime. This is even the case if all or some states are not parties to the regime as such.

Even if the decision is made by voting and has binding force concerning the minority, legitimacy could be construed by consent to the decision-making procedure in general. One can even construe that under the current international law on interpretation states have consented to the inclusion of treaty norms to which they are not a party, if they consented to competence and procedure for authentic interpretation and to the inclusion of other law applicable between the parties in the process of interpretation.

Lack of participation of other actors may likewise be discussed under the heading of legitimacy. Currently, neither authoritative interpretation nor dispute settlement regulation provide for procedural rules on the inclusion of extrinsic norms. Participation by institutions, e.g. the organs of the other regime from which the norms originate, could give interpretative guidance on the understanding of the norm before it is used to interpret other norms in turn. This could enable the interpreters to make a more informed decision on the relevance of the extrinsic norm in the process and its influence on the interpretation of their instrument. In *EC – Biotech* the WTO used consultation with international organisa-

[93] See the discussion by Young, n. 22 above, 929–930; see also Young in Ch. 3 in this volume, pp. 98–109.

tions, scientific and technical experts and those interested parties filing *amicus curiae* briefs.[94]

Although a valid consideration from the perspective of a systemic vision, the current legal structure knows no obligations for inclusion of other actors. This may be due to a lack of legal effect of the interpretative process upon other institutions. Neither in dispute settlement nor in authoritative interpretation would the decision have general binding effect, i.e. it would not formally be relevant for other parties or the extrinsic regime. However, the persuasive force of such decisions taken together with a substantive overlap of parties of multilateral treaties should not be underestimated. If a collective organ decides upon authoritative interpretation based upon consensus this decision will have a factual effect on the regime from which the norms stem depending upon the power of the relevant regime and political preferences as well as state practice.

D. Towards a more systemic vision?

The acknowledgement of extrinsic norms by the institutions of a regime takes valuable account of the interrelations between norms within the legal system of public international law. From the perspective of a systemic vision an underlying perception is that interpretation as a method is construed too narrowly. Interpretation as a tool for dynamic development and cross-regime action has limited relevance if one reads narrowly the VCLT. The fundamental rule to establish the 'ordinary meaning' is only of limited relevance when it comes to cross-regime interpretation of norms in order to gain some insight or even guidance from the normative approaches by other institutions.[95] Although the objectives of the rules of treaty interpretation are important, a more systemic vision may make it necessary to leave the traditional track or complement it by accepting implicit agreement, i.e. silent acceptance or at least a lack of objections, as an entrance condition for extrinsic norms in the interpretative process.[96]

The issue of state consent sets further limits to the consideration of a variety of legal rules existing as part of the legal system. Even if Article 31(3)(c) VCLT is understood more broadly than in *EC – Biotech*, consent

[94] For an analysis of these consultations in the light of the Panel's use of extrinsic sources see Young, n. 22 above, 925–928.

[95] This is, if the WTO Panel approach in *EC – Biotech* to use the ordinary meaning as opening the interpretative process to any kind of extrinsic norms is rejected.

[96] This corresponds to McLachlan's fourth option when defining 'the parties' in Art. 31(3)(c) VCLT, n. 6 above, 314.

is crucial. There is *de lege lata* no positive rule allowing for the inclusion of any norm in the interpretative context, if reference extends beyond the principle of systemic integration under Article 31(3)(c) VCLT.

The interpretation of treaty norms by reference to other instruments of international law, regardless of an overlap of parties to both, would have the following consequences: a systemic vision of public international law would be promoted by the open approach to take into account all relevant instruments. At the same time the interpreting institutions would be flexible to choose which instruments they find the most helpful in order to reach effective solutions for the understanding and further development of their regime.[97] This bears potential for cross-fertilisation and the evolution of certain standards through interpretive practice by different regimes while leaving the contextual choice to the institutions. Either specific standards will crystallise because different regimes use the same approach to interpretation or it may show that specialisation requires a diversity of approaches and that the interpretation of similar provisions in different treaties must not necessarily lead to the same results.[98] This would uphold the benefits resulting from specialisation within a system of international law because special regimes would keep their status and cater for their specific needs. It cannot be generalised whether a term used by different legal instruments should have a different meaning and application in different treaties or whether it should be understood in a consistent manner across several regimes. Ultimately, a consensus and practice-based system of standards could find a balance between unity and necessary diversity. If attempting to overcome the focus on the notion of state sovereignty, an element of enhanced transparency would be crucial. It is essential that institutions make the process of decision-making in a cross-regime context transparent. This is most relevant for the development of a practice on cross-fertilisation.

A flexible use of extrinsic norms regardless of whether the parties of the two relevant regimes coincide has, however, some serious

[97] The relevant institutions include adjudicatory bodies, international organisations and treaty organs. The discussion whether an institution should be established that would be responsible for answering preliminary questions, comparable to the relevant procedure on the EU level, is outside the scope of this paper, although such an institution could in principle contribute to a more coherent interpretation of international law across different regimes.

[98] This has also been noted by the ITLOS in the *Mox Plant Case*, n. 77 above, para. 51.

pitfalls: the established rules on treaty interpretation would to some extent be set aside and the resulting pick-and-choose approach, despite transparency, may be seen as unpredictable and arbitrary. A process so qualified could be taken as evidence for a further dissolution of traditional international law-making and law-application. Despite all shortcomings, the rules on treaty interpretation are fundamental to the structure of the international legal system, although they are not preemptory norms of international law. Parties to a treaty could provide for changed standards of interpretation, if they explicitly decide to do so. Overcoming state consent in favour of a broad notion of a consensual system could lead to reluctance to engage in further international law-making. Moreover standards for a 'consensus-based' interpretive environment are difficult to set.

Certainty and reliability are categories which are praised as the benefits of treaty-law. In the context of the interpretation of treaties, by freely choosing from the body of norms from other regimes, one expects the standards of certainty and reliability to be reduced. However, it is questionable whether this is the case and, if so, whether this amounts to a deficit. Usually the parties interpret agreements in the course of implementation and application within the sphere of domestic law. This process, particularly if states attempt to reconcile obligations under different international instruments with national policy choices and preferences, is by no means predictable, certain or reliable. Likewise, even if following the established rules of treaty interpretation, the outcome of dispute settlement procedures can hardly be predicted. The interpretation of Article 31(3)(c) VCLT concerning the meaning of 'the parties' may serve as an example of differences of approach which also influence the result of the interpretation process of the treaty norm.

The need for predictability is potentially less relevant than it appears on first sight. States as the quasi-legislative instance on the international level can easily turn political decisions into legal guidance, if they so desire. There is thus a distinction between the individual in a domestic context who needs to rely upon predictability to make informed personal decisions. In the context of regime interaction other than dispute settlement, states first set the rules for secondary decisions and are also involved in the process of substantive decision-making. At least this appears so, if approached from a strictly legal perspective. The role of individuals in the process and the impact of a principal-agent-dilemma must not be underestimated. On the level of dispute settlement states have consented to accept the decision and in many instances maintain influence upon the rules governing the process,[99] although adjudicatory bodies have gained considerable autonomy.

Many issues in the context of a more systemic vision of public international law are still to be further elaborated upon. Whether currently enhanced coherence of the international legal system can be used as a justification to set aside state consent and to open treaty interpretation for all norms of the international legal system, regardless of coincidence of consenting parties, is, however, most unlikely. First of all, due to a lack of empirical evidence, it is not clear if cross-regime interpretation in fact leads to more coherence. If, as this paper does, one argues in favour of a more open process to take into consideration various norms, more coherent standard-setting may arise but is not evident. Hence, the hypothesis that an open process of consideration of extrinsic norms leads to more coherence and effectiveness, while preserving specialisation, remains unproven and should be subject to future research.

[99] An example of considerable influence is the role of the NAFTA FTC. As mentioned above, the states parties, via the FTC, can give binding guidance for tribunals established under Chapter 11. In other instances, the possibility of influencing the rules for dispute settlement seems to remain merely theoretical. To modify or amend the WTO Dispute Settlement Understanding, for example, since it lacks specific provisions and not all WTO parties are parties to the VCLT, the customary rules on treaty amendment are applicable. Due to the need of ratification such procedure is cumbersome and agreement of all parties to an almost universal treaty unlikely.

8

Relations between International Courts and Tribunals: The 'Regime Problem'

JAMES CRAWFORD AND PENELOPE NEVILL

Introduction

There are no codified rules of international law which tell courts and tribunals what to do when a conflict arises as a result of what is referred to in this volume as 'regime interaction'.[1] Nor is there an agreed constitution or defining 'redemptive narrative'[2] from which a hierarchy of courts or regimes can be inferred, still less deduced.[3] Nonetheless, we continue to ask judges and arbitrators to resolve the conflicts which arise from regime interaction and we expect that, applying standard interpretative methods, they will manage to do so. Indeed, within the confines of the task before them, they generally do so. How they do so is the focus of the first part of this chapter. The cases discussed below, not all of which involve regime interaction in the strict sense, present a number of ways of resolving conflicts in the absence of conflict rules or a determining constitutional structure.

Any description of legal practice invites reflection on both the extent to which it contributes to our understanding of the concept of law, and the legitimacy of using decided cases for this purpose. The second part of

[1] But cf. Vienna Convention on the Law of Treaties, 22 May 1969, 1155 UNTS 331.

[2] See Jeffrey Dunoff's contribution to this volume, p. 154.

[3] The nearest approaches to hierarchy in international law are (a) in treaty law, Art. 103 of the Charter; and (b) in customary international law, the notion of peremptory norms. Neither has yet been employed to give any priority to the judicial function even of the International Court of Justice (ICJ), whose Statute is part of the Charter. See as to (a), *Case Concerning Questions of Interpretation and Application of the 1971 Montreal Convention Arising from the Aerial Incident at Lockerbie (Libyan Arab Jamahiriya* v. *United States of America)*, Preliminary Objections, Judgment, [1998] ICJ Rep 115; as to (b), *Case Concerning East Timor (Portugal* v. *Australia)*, Judgment, [1995] ICJ Rep 90; *Armed Activities on the Territory of the Congo (New Application: 2002) (Democratic Republic of the Congo* v. *Rwanda)*, Jurisdiction and Admissibility, Judgment, [2006] ICJ Rep 6.

this chapter touches on the contribution, if any, of the decisions concerning regime and rule conflict – we could call this their 'normative value' – beyond the parties to which, legally, their binding authority is confined. More specifically, do these decisions tell us something about rules governing regime interaction in international law or does their value lie merely in illustrating the problems? And what light do they shed on our tendency as lawyers to view, understand and reason about conflicts in international law through the perspective of our own legal system? In the third part of this chapter we come back to the theme of regime interaction, suggesting that perhaps problems of regime interaction are as much ones of definition as of law.

A. Judicial techniques for resolving norm and regime conflict

What does international law say about regime and rule conflict? Unlike a fully constitutionalised legal system, international law does not exclude rule conflict. One might say that it is a characteristic of a national system of law that there cannot ultimately be a conflict for the individual subject between being required to do A and being required not to do it. International law contains no such rule, even for states. Nor does it preclude states from assuming conflicting obligations to different states (or, apparently, even presume against their having done so[4]). International law allows that there will be conflicting norms for states, just as it allows that there will be conflicting breaches by them. But that is not to say that international law has no role in trying to moderate or regulate that conflict. The International Law Commission (ILC) study on fragmentation could have been labelled a study on ways of addressing norm conflict.[5] Fragmentation is the terminology of the discourse and so we use the term fragmentation, but the techniques the ILC invokes are techniques of general international law. They are mostly interpretative techniques in the broad sense, not limited to the interpretative techniques referred to in Articles 31 to 33 of the Vienna Convention on the Law of Treaties. The reason they are interpretative techniques rather than conflict rules strictly speaking is that international law does not ultimately say that there

[4] Such a presumption may exist as between the same states. But a third state, not bound by the prior obligation, is not presumed not to seek a conflicting one. *Pacta tertiis non nocent*, even as to matters of interpretation.

[5] Fragmentation of International Law: Difficulties Arising from the Diversification and Expansion of International Law, Report of the Study Group of the International Law Commission, ILC 58th Session, A/CN.4/L.682, 13 April 2006.

cannot be irreconcilable conflicts between two norms. But it does say that we may interpret our way out of conflict. When we cannot, the rather frail way we resolve conflict is to remit it to the black box of state responsibility: in effect, conflict becomes a matter of remedies or reconciliation of 'competing breaches' through circumstances precluding wrongfulness or through the vagaries of availability of remedies.

We give here nine techniques to deal with regime and rule conflict in adjudication under international law. The techniques are based on actual cases and are listed in no particular order. The list is not closed.

1. *'The principle of the exclusive mandate'*

The first possibility is that of two cases involving the same underlying dispute before two forums, each asserting an exclusive mandate. State A brings its case in forum A and state B brings its case in forum B, each of them preferring their respective forums because they think they will give them the answer they want. The cases operate in parallel but never meet, requiring resolution of the dispute extra-judicially. This is an apt description of the 'Swordfish Dispute' between Chile and the European Union (EU). After 10 years of dispute, the EU brought an action against Chile in the World Trade Organization (WTO) in respect of Chile's refusal to allow access to Chilean ports by EU vessels transshipping or landing catches of swordfish that did not comply with Chile's fisheries legislation. Although the EU acknowledged Chile's serious concerns about depletion of swordfish stocks, it wanted commercial access into Chilean ports for Spanish vessels and catches because this enabled access to Chilean and US markets.[6] Chile sought resolution of the dispute under the United Nations Convention on the Law of the Sea (UNCLOS) because it wanted the EU to comply with its national measures concerning sustainable exploitation and conservation of trans-migratory fisheries.[7]

Parallel tracks may appear to converge in the distance, but this is only a trick of perspective: they appear to converge in the distance because it

[6] Case WT/DS193, commenced in April 2000. A panel was established in December 2000.

[7] See *Case Concerning the Conservation and Sustainable Exploitation of Swordfish Stocks in the South-Eastern Pacific Ocean (Chile/European Community)*, Order of 20 December 2000, ITLOS, (2001) 40 ILM 475. The parties thereafter agreed to suspend proceedings on a periodic basis pending the outcome of negotiations: see the history of the UNCLOS proceedings recorded in the Order of 16 December 2009 and *Chile – Measures Affecting the Transit and Importing of Swordfish, (European Communitites* v. *Chile)*, WT/DS193/2, *Request for the Establishment of a Panel by the European Communities*, 7 November 2000 (WTO proceedings).

is a long way away. If you actually get to the horizon the tracks are not converging. The starting point for analysis for each claim in each forum is fundamentally different: in the WTO, trade rights subject to the limited exceptions in the General Agreement on Tariffs and Trade (GATT), Article XX; under UNCLOS, states' sovereign rights to pass fisheries conservation measures in their exclusive economic zones (EEZs). Neither forum has jurisdiction to interpret and apply the other treaty. You therefore resolve by non-judicial means. Indeed, a final resolution of the swordfish dispute by negotiation and agreement has nearly been concluded.[8]

A sub-mode of this first situation occurs where each treaty excludes a defence based within the realm of the other; this is an extreme form of conflict but it is possible. In the *Mexico Soft Drinks* dispute it was held by the WTO Appellate Body that the law of the WTO precluded countermeasures taken by one state party to enforce another's obligations under non-WTO treaties.[9] Mexico had a plausible claim that the measures challenged by the US in the WTO (the imposition of tax measures concerning products using corn rather than cane sugar sweeteners) were lawful countermeasures designed to force the US to comply with its North American Free Trade Agreement (NAFTA) obligations in the matter of sugar imports. The Appellate Body held that measures allegedly undertaken to enforce international obligations (i.e. the US's NAFTA obligations) did not fall within the GATT Article XX(d) exception for measures 'necessary to secure compliance with laws or regulations which are not inconsistent with the provisions of this Agreement'. The reference to 'laws and regulations' was to domestic not international laws such as NAFTA.[10] Further, WTO law did not recognise as lawful actions by way

[8] See, e.g. 'EU and Chile settle WTO/ITLOS swordfish dispute', dated 24 January 2001, available at www.europa-eu-un.org/articles/en/article_2230_en.htm (last accessed 21 July 2011). But proceedings in both WTO and the International Tribunal for the Law of the Sea (ITLOS) were kept open. The parties entered into a provisional arrangement on 25 January 2001 (the ITLOS proceedings were commenced on 18 December 2000 and submitted by agreement between the parties), and agreed to suspend the ITLOS proceedings on a periodic basis pending the outcome of negotiations: see the history of the UNCLOS proceedings recorded in the Order of 16 December 2009. A 2008 Understanding Concerning the Conservation of Swordfish Stock in the South Eastern Pacific Ocean has been agreed between the parties and is currently in the process of being ratified. The ITLOS proceedings have been discontinued by Order dated 16 December 2009.

[9] *Mexico – Tax Measures on Soft Drinks and Other Beverages*, AB-2005-10, WT/DS308/AB/R, adopted 6 March 2006.

[10] Ibid., para. 79.

of countermeasures taken in breach of WTO law, other than the countermeasures provided in the Dispute Settlement Understanding.[11] Therefore Mexico's tax law was WTO-inconsistent and had to be repealed as a matter of WTO law. This outcome shows the importance that remedies play in this situation.[12] A panel established under NAFTA Chapter 11 also held that Mexico could not rely on the law of countermeasures in a case brought by an investor challenging the same tax measures. This time the reason was that Mexico could not raise as a defence to the breach of the investor's equal treatment rights under NAFTA a countermeasure directed at the investor's state of nationality.[13]

The underlying facts of the matter were that (on Mexico's view) the US was in violation of its NAFTA obligations, including its obligation to cooperate on the formation of a tribunal under NAFTA Chapter 20 to hear Mexico's claim concerning US barriers to imports of Mexican cane sugar. Yet all relevant judicial forums excluded the possibility of considering Mexico's substantive claim and countermeasures defence, except the one which the United States refused to activate.[14] This is a graphic illustration of the point that international law does not exclude rule conflict.

2. *The principle of 'devil take the hindermost': two tribunals racing to judgment in the same matter*

The second possibility is that of two tribunals racing to judgment in the same dispute. This is what happened in the two sets of bilateral investment treaty (BIT) proceedings brought respectively against the Czech Republic by Mr Lauder under the US–Czech BIT and his company CME

[11] Ibid., para. 77.

[12] The Appellate Body (AB) also upheld the Panel's refusal to dismiss the US claim on the grounds of inadmissibility. Mexico had argued that, even though the WTO Panel had jurisdiction, it should refuse to exercise that jurisdiction pending the outcome of the NAFTA Chapter 20 proceedings initiated by Mexico against the US, and that only a NAFTA panel could resolve the dispute as a whole: ibid., paras 44–57. It also considered that if WTO law allowed breaches of its rules as countermeasures taken to enforce states' parties non-WTO obligations, it would require WTO panels and the AB to become adjudicators of non-WTO disputes. This, said the AB, it had no jurisdiction to do: ibid., paras 56 and 78.

[13] *Corn Products International Inc* v. *Mexico (Decision on Responsibility)*, ICSID Case No. ARB(AF)/04/01, 15 January 2008.

[14] The US was impeding dispute settlement under NAFTA Chapter 20 by refusing to appoint tribunal members.

Czech (through which he owned his interests in the investment) under the Netherlands–Czech BIT.[15] Both proceedings concerned the same underlying investment in a Czech television company, both concerned the same facts concerning damage to the investment and both sought recovery of the same loss. Nevertheless, both tribunals rejected a *lis pendens* argument against jurisdiction on the grounds that the parties and causes of action were different in each case.[16]

The two tribunals arrived at conflicting results. The *Lauder* tribunal concluded in an award of 3 September 2001 that the actions which caused Mr Lauder's losses were not those of the Czech Republic but of his commercial associate, Mr Železný, and that the Czech Media Council's actions were based on objective grounds to ensure compliance with the state media law and were not unlawful.[17] By contrast, the *CME Czech Republic BV* tribunal in an award ten days later (13 September 2001), considering the same actions of the Media Council, held they were a 'silent and coerced vitiation of CME's basis for its investment' in breach of the BIT and that the Council actively supported Mr Železný's destruction of its investment.[18] In fairness it has to be said that the Czech Republic refused the suggestion that the cases be consolidated,[19] and there is no compulsory mode of consolidation between proceedings under different BITs (as there is under NAFTA[20]).

3. *Using a treaty as a 'gateway' to general international law: the presumption of general jurisdiction*

Another, perhaps egregious, example is the following: you go through the relatively narrow framework of a dispute under a particular treaty and you are confronted with the sea of international law, and you are free to swim in the sea at large. Thus the Annex VII UNCLOS Tribunal in *Guyana v Surinam*, charged with delimiting a maritime boundary, held itself free

[15] *Lauder* v. *Czech Republic (Final Award)*, 3 September 2001, 9 ICSID Reports 66 (proceedings commenced 19 August 1999); *CME Czech Republic BV (The Netherlands)* v. *Czech Republic (Partial Award)*, 13 September 2001, 9 ICSID Reports 121 (proceedings commenced 22 February 2000).

[16] *Lauder*, paras 161–166, 171–175; *CME Czech Republic BV*, paras 409–412, 419.

[17] *Lauder*, paras 260–274.

[18] *CME Czech Republic BV*, paras 533, 558. A good summary of the cases can be found in Z. Douglas, *The International Law of Investment Claims* (Cambridge University Press, 2009) 59–69 (para. 114).

[19] *Lauder*, para. 178. [20] See Art. 1126 NAFTA.

by virtue of its applicable law provision[21] to apply the UN Charter rules in relation to the use of force.[22] However, the presumption of general jurisdiction is not applicable to special jurisdictions such as UNCLOS arbitral tribunals.[23]

4. *A restrictive interpretation of 'dispute' for the purposes of a treaty*

The fourth possibility for resolving norm or regime conflict is at the other end of the spectrum to technique (3): it involves a very restrictive interpretation of what it is for a dispute to arise under a particular convention. A good example of technique (4) is the arbitral tribunal's attribution of a very narrow scope to the material subject matter of the Convention for the Protection of the Marine Environment of the North-East Atlantic Coast (OSPAR) in the *Dispute Concerning Access to Information Under Article 9 of the OSPAR Convention.*[24] Ireland had raised complaints about the discharge of radioactive wastes and other consequences of the commissioning and operation of the new MOX Plant nuclear facilities at Sellafield on the UK's Cumbrian coast facing the Irish Sea. The facts in dispute as pleaded potentially fell within the jurisdiction of three treaties: UNCLOS, the EURATOM Treaty and OSPAR. Ireland initially pursued proceedings simultaneously under both UNCLOS and OSPAR.

Before the OSPAR tribunal Ireland sought access under OSPAR Article 9 to information redacted from reports supplied to it by the UK. The reports had been prepared by the UK as part of the approval processes for the MOX Plant required by Article 37 of the EURATOM Treaty, secondary EU legislation and national law. The tribunal found that none

[21] Art. 293 UNCLOS provides that 'A court or tribunal having jurisdiction under this section shall apply this Convention and other rules of international law not incompatible with this Convention.'

[22] *Guyana* v. *Suriname (Award of the Arbitral Tribunal)*, 17 September 2007. The Annex VII tribunal found that the Surinamese navy had breached its obligations under Art. 2(4) of the UN Charter and international law when it threatened to use force against the rig and drill ship of a company licensed by Guyana to undertake exploratory activities in its claimed maritime area: paras 439, 445.

[23] On this view, decisions of the ICJ do not provide any support for the admissibility of a dispute concerning the use of force by a specialist Annex VII tribunal charged with delimiting a boundary: cf. paras 423–424 of the Award.

[24] *Dispute Concerning Access to Information Under Article 9 of the OSPAR Convention, (Ireland* v. *United Kingdom)*, Permanent Court of Arbitration, Final Award of 2 July 2003, 126 ILR 334.

of the fourteen pieces of redacted information sought by Ireland related to the state of the maritime area, activities or measures adversely affecting or likely to affect it, or activities or measures introduced under OSPAR, as required by Article 9(2). Rather, the redacted information concerned only economic justification.[25] Of course, the tribunal could have treated the dispute as concerning whether the UK had met the Article 9 information disclosure requirement by reference to the reports *as a whole*, which may have led to the conclusion that the reports – rather than the redactions – concerned activities adversely affecting the maritime area and therefore the whole documents ought to have been disclosed.[26] On the other hand, this finding was probably justified in relation to the claim that was made.

5. *The principle of special jurisdictional deference*

The fifth technique, at play in the UNCLOS *MOX Plant* proceedings, is special jurisdictional deference.[27] As noted, Ireland pursued proceedings under both OSPAR and UNCLOS. The UNCLOS Annex VII Tribunal found that the priority between the dispute settlement provisions of the various treaties was determined by their terms.[28] Under Article 292 of the EC Treaty (now Article 344 of the Treaty on the Functioning of the European Union (TFEU)[29]), member states undertake not to submit a dispute concerning the interpretation and application of the EU treaties

[25] Ibid., para. 181. Nor, pointed out the tribunal, had Ireland made any submissions as to the adverse nature of the activities, a precondition of the disclosure requirement.

[26] As pointed out in the Dissenting Opinion of Gavan Griffith: see the summary at p. 431. The UK would then have had to defend the redactions under the exceptions to disclosure (such as confidentiality) listed in Art. 9(3).

[27] The decisions of various tribunals in the *MOX Plant* dispute are: *The MOX Plant Case (Ireland* v. *United Kingdom), (Request for Provisional Measures)*, International Tribunal for the Law of the Sea, Order of 2 December 2001, 126 ILR 260; *The MOX Plant Case (Ireland* v. *United Kingdom), Order No 3 (Suspension of Proceedings on Jurisdiction and Merits, and Request for Provisional Measures and Orders Nos 3 and 4)*, UNCLOS Annex VII Tribunal, sitting in the Permanent Court of Arbitration, 24 June 2003 and 14 November 2003, 126 ILR 310.

[28] *Order No. 3*, ibid.

[29] Under the provisions of the Lisbon Treaty, which came into force on 1 December 2009, the EC Treaty has been amended and renamed the Treaty on the Functioning of the European Union (TFEU). The European Community (EC) and the European Union (EU) are now one entity, the EU. Accordingly we refer generally to 'EU law' or the 'EU Treaties' unless more specific reference to the old EC or EC Treaty is called for. The EURATOM Treaty is still in force between EU Member States.

to any method of settlement other than those in the EU treaties. As the European Court of Justice (ECJ) has exclusive jurisdiction over the interpretation and application – i.e. the scope – of the EU treaties, the question of whether the claims made by Ireland fell within the scope of EU law was a question for the ECJ alone.[30] If the ECJ decided they were, then, for the purposes of UNCLOS Article 282, it had jurisdiction to resolve the dispute and this displaced the UNCLOS dispute settlement mechanisms under Part XV.[31] And any decision on the merits by the ECJ would be final and binding on the parties for the purposes of Article 296 of UNCLOS Part XV and Article 11 of Annex VII,[32] thereby excluding the jurisdiction of the *MOX Plant* Annex VII Tribunal. The Annex VII Tribunal held that it had *prima facie* jurisdiction over the subject matter of the dispute but, it continued, while it might have concluded that certain UNCLOS provisions did not fall within the scope of the EU treaties, the ECJ alone had exclusive jurisdiction to make that determination.[33] The Tribunal demurred to the ECJ accordingly:

> In the circumstances, and bearing in mind considerations of mutual respect and comity which should prevail between judicial institutions both of which may be called upon to determine rights and obligations as between two States, the Tribunal considers that it would be inappropriate for it to proceed further ...[34]

The resulting Order deferred the UNCLOS proceedings to allow the ECJ to decide on the scope of its substantive jurisdiction.[35]

This is an example of deference of one international tribunal to another in the context of a general principle of cooperation between international jurisdictions – obviously a meta-principle. Those who are in favour of order in the international system will praise it; those who are in favour of deference to a particular jurisdictional mandate will be opposed.

[30] Art. 267 TFEU, ex-Art. 234 EC Treaty.

[31] 'If the States Parties which are parties to the dispute concerning the interpretation or application of [UNCLOS] have agreed, through a general, regional or bilateral agreement or otherwise, that such dispute shall, at the request of any party to the dispute be submitted to a procedure that entails a binding decision, that procedure shall apply in lieu of the procedures provided for in [Part XV], unless the parties to the dispute agree otherwise.'

[32] Art. 296 provides that any decision by a court or tribunal having jurisdiction under Part XV is final and binding on the parties to the dispute.

[33] *MOX Plant, Order No. 3*, paras 22–26.

[34] Ibid., para. 28. [35] Ibid., para. 29.

6. *Exclusive jurisdiction clauses prevail over general jurisdictional clauses as lex specialis: the principle of the specially chosen forum*

A sixth principle is that exclusive jurisdiction clauses prevail over general jurisdictional clauses as *lex specialis*. If you agree that a particular tribunal has exclusive jurisdiction over a particular matter, other courts, though they may have general jurisdiction over it, must defer to the court with special jurisdiction even if that court has not yet been convened. This further meta-principle of order was articulated by the majority in the *SGS v Philippines* case.[36] The tribunal held that the contract provision between the parties conferring exclusive jurisdiction over contract claims on the Philippine courts rendered inadmissible a claim under the general provisions of the BIT conferring jurisdiction over contract claims (the 'umbrella' provision). This followed from the maxim *generalia specialibus non derogant* and the presumed intention of the BIT drafters to supplement rather than override actual negotiated investment arrangements.[37] It was subsequently taken to its logical conclusion in another BIT case.[38]

7. *The priority of the court first seised: the principle of priority in time*

Seventh, and somewhat outside the field of general international law, we have the technique established by the EU Brussels Regulation in the context of private international arbitration. This can be characterised as 'the priority of the national court first seised trumps the principle of respect for arbitration clauses', at least on one reading of the *West Tankers* judgment.[39] Here the applicants, insurers of a charterparty relying on their right of subrogation, issued tort proceedings in the Italian courts in July 2003 against West Tankers for insurance cover paid by them for damage caused to a jetty in Italy when the vessel owned by West Tankers collided with it. However, arbitration proceedings to recover the damages incurred over the insurance cover limit had already been commenced under the charterparty in London.

[36] *SGS Société Générale de Surveillance SA* v. *Philippines (Decisions on Objections to Jurisdiction)*, ICSID Case No. ARB/02/6, 29 January 2004, 129 ILR 445.

[37] Ibid., para. 141.

[38] *Bureau Veritas, Inspection, Valuation, Assessment and Control, BIVAC BV* v. *Republic of Paraguay* (ICSID Arb. 07/09), Decision of the Tribunal on Objections to Jurisdiction, 29 May 2009.

[39] Case C-185/07 *Allianz SpA & Or* v. *West Tankers Inc*, Judgment of the Grand Chamber, 10 February 2009, [2009] ECR-I 663.

West Tankers issued proceedings against the applicants in the UK courts in September 2004 seeking a declaration and anti-suit injunction. The grounds were that the jurisdiction of the Italian courts was excluded by the dispute settlement clause of the charterparty, which provided for arbitration in London and the application of English law. The applicants responded that the issuance of an anti-suit injunction by the UK courts was contrary to their obligations under the Brussels Regulation, Council Regulation (EC) No 44/2001 'on jurisdiction and the recognition and enforcement of judgments in civil and commercial matters'.[40] On a preliminary ruling reference made by the English court, the ECJ agreed that, by virtue of Article 1(2)(d) of the Brussels Regulation, arbitration was excluded from the scope of application of the Regulation. However, verification of the validity of an arbitration clause as a preliminary issue in a damages claim *did* fall within the scope of the Regulation. Indeed, West Tankers had made this argument before the Italian court.[41] It was, said the ECJ, for the Italian court first seised of the matter to determine its own jurisdiction. The UK would therefore be in breach of the Regulation if the English court issued the injunction in favour of West Tankers because it would undermine the effectiveness of the Regulation.[42] By virtue of this decision, UK courts are now precluded from issuing anti-suit injunctions against individuals who, contrary to their contractual undertaking in an arbitration clause not to do so, initiate substantive claims in domestic courts of other EU member states.

8. *Later in time jurisdictional mandates prevail: the principle of lex posterior*

Eighth, there is the principle that later in time jurisdictional mandates prevail, as preferred by one arbitrator in the *SGS v Philippines* case.[43] Not for the first time the *lex specialis* principle conflicted with the *lex posterior* principle. Indeed, what is *lex posterior* when it comes to treaties is a very difficult question. The parties to the treaties may be different, the date of entry into force of the treaty negotiated and concluded earlier in time might be later than the date for entry into force of the treaty negotiated

[40] OJ L 012, 16/01/2001, 1–23. [41] [2009] ECR-I 663, para. 27.
[42] Ibid., para. 24.
[43] Professor Crivellaro, Declaration, 508, paras 9–10. Cf. the majority's view of the *lex posterior* argument at paras 142–148.

and concluded later in time, or the subject matter may overlap, but not be coextensive.

The difficulties of application in practice of what appears on first sight to be a straightforward principle arose in our next example, the *Southern Bluefin Tuna* case (*SBT* case).[44] Here the treaty which entered into force earlier in time (in 1994) concerning southern bluefin tuna (the Convention for the Conservation of Southern Bluefin Tuna (CCSBT)) was concluded after UNCLOS and referred to it.[45] However, UNCLOS did not enter into force for the parties to the CCSBT until 1996. UNCLOS also contains substantive provisions which would cover conservation of southern bluefin tuna but were not precisely the same as those in the CCSBT.

9. *A mandate not to have jurisdiction prevails over a mandate to have jurisdiction: the principle of opt-out*

The technique adopted by the Tribunal in the *SBT* case – technique (9) – to resolve the relationship between UNCLOS and the CCSBT was essentially that a mandate by the parties not to have jurisdiction prevails over a mandate to have jurisdiction. The dispute settlement provisions of the CCSBT, unlike UNCLOS, provided for adjudicated settlement by agreement only. On the failure to reach agreement on an increase in commercial fishing quota and an experimental fishing programme, Japan unilaterally announced and implemented an experimental fishing programme that increased its overall catch by 25 per cent. Despite protests by Australia and New Zealand and extended negotiations between the parties, the dispute remained unresolved. Nor was agreement reached under the CCSBT dispute settlement provision for reference of the dispute to an arbitral tribunal or the International Court of Justice (ICJ). Given that UNCLOS also contains substantive provisions concerning the conservation and management of migratory fish stocks such as SBT, New Zealand and Australia sought to bring the dispute under the UNCLOS compulsory dispute settlement provisions.

Australia and New Zealand successfully secured provisional measures orders from the International Tribunal for the Law of the Sea (ITLOS)

[44] *Southern Bluefin Tuna Case (Australia and New Zealand* v. *Japan)*, Award of 4 August 2000, 119 ILR 508 (Arbitral Tribunal established under UNCLOS Annex VII).

[45] Convention for the Conservation of Southern Bluefin Tuna, 10 May 1993, 1819 UNTS 360, Preamble, para. 4 and Art. 4.

on the basis of *prima facie* UNCLOS jurisdiction. But when it came to the merits, the Annex VII Arbitral Tribunal held that Article 16 of the CCSBT excluded the UNCLOS dispute settlement provisions, and Articles 281 and 297 to 299 of UNCLOS anticipated that its states parties could exclude compulsory jurisdiction in such an instance by agreeing to resolve disputes by peaceful means of their own choice. It therefore had no jurisdiction.[46] Essentially, Japan could opt out of the compulsory, or apparently compulsory, jurisdiction clauses of UNCLOS by a specific provision not to have jurisdiction in a fisheries agreement.

Thus there is an array of techniques or principles from which international law draws to choose how to deal with conflicts between regimes and/or rules. Some of the examples given are not interactions between regimes but are interactions between fields of law, or interactions between different treaties. We do not suggest that all nine techniques are of equal value, nor that one technique cannot produce the opposite outcome to another.[47] It is a rather motley, incoherent collection. The next section of this chapter considers whether, nevertheless, we can make any claim of normative value for the collection.

B. Normative value or a mere set of techniques?

It may be observed that what is offered is a simple list of nine techniques to sift and resolve disputes, without ranking them or commenting on the order in which one would use them. A related observation is that the various judicial strategies identified are essentially exercises in avoidance and temporising.[48] Both observations suggest description without thesis. This is true. There is no thesis in the sense of constitutional international order capable of resolving conflicts.[49] If you say 'what's the point of having these techniques without a thesis?' the answer is that there is every point in having them: we can use one or another depending on the interest of the client.

46 *SBT Case*, paras 57–65. Sir Kenneth Keith dissented on this point.

47 *Viz.* the outcome in *Guyana* v. *Suriname* (technique (3)) as compared with those in the *Mexico Soft Drinks* dispute (technique (1)).

48 See Dunoff's contribution to this volume, p. 156. He stresses that this is not intended as 'pejorative characterization', emphasising the value of judicial minimalism in the face of underlying conflicts.

49 Cf. Dunoff, ibid., p. 154: 'the problem highlighted by litigations involving regime interaction is that at present there is no widely accepted redemptive narrative that sets out a vision of a perfected, or redeemed, international order, and that gives meaning to the norms embedded within that order'.

The first part of this chapter focused on litigation and adjudication and judges' or arbitrators' solutions to rule conflicts. It was not a discussion of the 'commercial' or transactional[50] side of international legal practice, an important area of empirical study and critique examined by others in this volume.[51] However, two related points should be made. First, the practice of law entails two basic aspects: advising clients as to how to make things work to achieve an objective or avoid a problem (the 'transactional/commercial element'); and advising on and carrying out dispute resolution when problems arise and/or objectives are not met (the litigation and adjudication element). Criticism of the law from realist, liberal, critical and other perspectives may inform what we do as lawyers, and emphasises the importance of a legal education that teaches law as a political, philosophical and sociological discipline. But law is nevertheless also, and above all, a professional and technical practice.

The second point goes to the relationship between the commercial aspect of law and the adjudication aspect. When we advise clients what to do and how to do it, the decisions of courts and tribunals together with rules and principles give us important information about how to problem solve in the specific situation before us. In terms of strategic advice, the possibility of litigation is an important factor to be taken into account in determining the level of risk that the client wishes to assume on undertaking a given course of action, whether it be on the terms they wish to promote in any treaty regime negotiations, or the court or tribunal in which to commence proceedings or the arguments formulated in response to any proceedings. Predicting and explaining the merits of various dispute settlement provisions within a treaty (the ICJ, a specialist tribunal or silence), or the likely outcome of a piece of litigation, or the benefits and disadvantages of one court over another, is an important part of the practice of law. Lawyers thus mediate between the conceptual and institutional structures of the law and what their clients do in fact. The fact that clients seek us out to do this suggests at least some level of external buy-in to an enterprise called international law, whether or not it can also be critically described as the product of a self-instituting society, or a self-creating

50 What Dunoff terms a 'relational' aspect of regime interaction, ibid., p. 158. That is, what goes on in terms of negotiating interaction between existing law and regimes when states and other actors decide to establish a new regime or what happens when actors from separate regimes interact in the everyday operation of regimes.

51 See the empirical and theoretical contributions to this volume by Dunoff (Ch. 5), Andrew Lang (Ch. 4) and Margaret Young (Ch. 3).

community of lawyers,[52] and whether or not it has gaps. Similarly, the specific problems which judges and adjudicators have to decide are before them because, one way or another, the parties have 'chosen' to seek resolution from that particular tribunal or court.

When considering the difficulties of, and solutions to, 'regime interaction' and international law in general, we must always bear in mind the limitations that law as trade and profession imposes: it informs how we read individual decisions and limits how much we can read into them; and it limits how much responsibility we might place on a tribunal or court for failing to satisfactorily resolve metaphysical and constitutional questions. Further, there are the limitations of understanding imposed by our legal backgrounds. We look at the jurisdiction and practices of international courts and tribunals very much through our national spectacles. No one, or almost no one, has their primary allegiance to international law amongst legal systems. This feature of international law is not frequently noted, but is highlighted by conflicts between rules and regimes. Those in the common law tradition were brought up with its underlying concept of a court of general jurisdiction. Specialised courts are subordinate to courts of general jurisdiction, and courts of general jurisdiction have an inherent power, including power to control inferior courts. But we are not in that situation at all when we talk about international tribunals, where the notion of a court of general jurisdiction is an inapt analogy. The International Court comes closest. The Court developed concepts of jurisdiction based on the provisions of its Statute. It took a very broad view, because of its applicable law clause, of the notion of a dispute arising under a treaty.[53] For the purposes of the Court, this approach did not give

[52] Martti Koskenniemi, *From Apology to Utopia: The Structure of International Legal Argument* (Cambridge University Press, rev. edn, 2005).

[53] Art. 38 of the Statute of the ICJ:

1. The Court, whose function is to decide in accordance with international law such disputes as are submitted to it, shall apply:
   a. international conventions, whether general or particular, establishing rules expressly recognized by the contesting states;
   b. international custom, as evidence of a general practice accepted as law;
   c. the general principles of law recognized by civilized nations;
   d. subject to the provisions of Article 59, judicial decisions and the teachings of the most highly qualified publicists of the various nations, as subsidiary means for the determination of rules of law.
2. This provision shall not prejudice the power of the Court to decide a case *ex aequo et bono*, if the parties agree thereto.

See e.g. *Oil Platforms, (Islamic Republic of Iran* v. *United States of America)*, Preliminary Objection, Judgment [1996] ICJ Rep 803, 811–812 (para. 21) and 816 (para. 35).

rise to many difficulties: the Court, having been let into the arena of putative general jurisdiction via a particular treaty, could then range across the international law terrain, something the judges like to do, if only in an impressionistic mode. Thus decisions of the ICJ on the same treaty are not necessarily going to be the same as decisions of the specialist bodies, because the Court still regards itself as having a potentially general jurisdiction and as dealing with one treaty, say the Genocide Convention, very much alongside another, say the Convention on the Elimination of All Forms of Traffic Accidents. But the Court is limited in its reach. When it was created in 1922 (based upon an American model of 1907) and reformulated in 1945, the reason it could be given general jurisdiction *ratione materiae* is that it was given no jurisdiction *ratione personae* at all (other than incidental jurisdiction).

The first thing that you have to do when you analyse regime and rule interaction from the perspective of the tribunals is to survey the landscape. What emerges is that there is a spectrum of cases brought before international tribunals, those where the tribunal has a very high degree of proprietorship of its law, of which the ECJ is an example, to an assertion of the generality of the law, of which the ICJ is an example, with a variety of intermediate positions. As observed above, practitioners – as distinct from scholars – need to know the forum in which they are trying to operate. Moreover, appreciation of different forums may have informed any choice to establish or submit to the jurisdiction of a particular tribunal, especially on the part of the applicant, and will inform the conduct of the proceedings.

The position of a judge or an arbitrator is different again. Their allegiance (they are almost always plural) is to the mandate that they are fulfilling. This position entails what can be described as a 'meta-position' of seeking coordination rather than competition between norms and treaty regimes. But this meta-position of seeking coordination rather than competition is not directed by the texts themselves. Most of the texts judges deal with, for example in the investment arbitration field or in an *ad hoc* inter-state arbitration, do not provide answers to conflicts. The answers to conflicts are certainly not there in the poorly drafted provisions of UNCLOS. So the judge is seeking, hopefully, to exercise legal imagination so as to impose some order on that situation.

No doubt the statement that the judge's position '*entails* a meta-position seeking coordination' can be criticised as a bare assertion of an 'oughtness' without seeking to explain why this is so. Indeed, the preference for order and coordination between tribunals under separate treaties (shown by the tribunals, e.g. in the *MOX Plant* and *SGS v Philippines* cases) received criticism from those who say that the function of the law of the sea system is not to defer to the EU and the ECJ, and the function of the BIT arbitration is to protect investment and not to coordinate with other investment institutions, still less with non-investment institutions in the fields of human rights or the environment. It does not follow that judges ought to seek order and coherence just because some exercise the power to do so.[54] Are we suggesting that an exercise of 'legal imagination' is an exercise of unconstrained and ungrounded discretion? Indeed, to attempt to cast the techniques as 'principles' itself implies a claim to universal application associated with the 'rule of law'.[55] How is this consistent with our no-thesis thesis?

We have said there is no thesis to be derived from the collection of techniques. But we have not said there is no possibility of thesis. The limited thesis put forward here is that we still learn quite a lot about international law *qua* law by reflecting on the practice of lawyers and what tribunals and courts actually do, even if it does not lead us to theoretical closure. To have no thesis in this sense is of course to have a thesis. The excessive scholarly focus on adjudication, as both the point of interaction between regimes within international law and as a symbol of disaster or hope in the study of its fragmentation, has been criticised.[56] This is valid, insofar as empirical and sociological work on law and legal systems can advance understanding and help us make decisions and rules about what we ought to do (or not to do). But it is still worth asking ourselves why adjudication, judgments and awards do take such a prominent position in studies of the problem of fragmentation in Western jurisprudence. One possibility is that what judges do in the penumbral case – of which decisions concerning regime and rule conflict in international law would seem to be paradigm examples – may tell us something about the idea of international law.[57]

[54] One answer to this is to adopt the law as process thesis. This holds that law is authoritative decision-making by authorised decision-makers that, as such, does not consider as relevant whether we purport to apply law as it is or law as it ought to be because 'there are always tools for authoritative decision-making on the problem … notwithstanding the absence of a precise rule which must be applied': Rosalyn Higgins, *Problems & Process: International Law and How We Use It* (Clarendon Press, Oxford, 1995) 10.

[55] Cf. Tom Bingham, *The Rule of Law* (Allen Lane, London, 2010); for the rule of law at the international level see ch. 10.

[56] See Dunoff in this volume, Ch. 5.

[57] The authors here draw on Nigel Simmonds' discussion of Hart's exposition of the penumbral case, in *Law as a Moral Idea* (Oxford University Press, 2007) ch. 6, 14–21.

We instead propose to approach regime interaction in international law through the decisions made by judges, engaged in the purposive activity of judging according to their mandate, in the absence of a clear rule (still less the instantiation of the rule of law). In this respect, we incline to the approach of scholars in recent common law jurisprudence who stress the value of enquiry into law and its normative basis based on a reflection on practice and the controversies arising from practice, even if we cannot articulate, or even assume, any ideal or redemption narrative.[58] We do not believe there is a meta-system of international law (or, for that matter, of non-international law) which finally resolves regime and rule conflict, at least not one currently available. However, the possibility of law is allowed in the process of judgment, even if in a nanosecond between apology and utopia.[59] In this context, calls for more explicit reasoning by judges when they determine what law is relevant to a dispute,[60] or openness and transparency as to the reasons for adopting one solution over another,[61] are pleas that we make ourselves easier for ourselves to understand.[62]

C. The problem with problems

Fuller explorations into the philosophy of international law drawing on general jurisprudence are available elsewhere.[63] Our argument here is more limited. It amounts to no more than an endorsement of the view that answers based on reflection on practice and our philosophical traditions are possible, and a few suggestions as to what we might reflect on. What

[58] Simmonds, *Law as a Moral Idea*, ch. 6, esp. 176–182 ('structures of meaning that are inhabited before we come to examine them reflectively' (at 180); Andrew Halpin, 'The Methodology of Jurisprudence: Thirty Years Off the Point' (2006) 19 CANJLUR 67, esp. 90–92. Perhaps this is what the tribunal in *SGS* v. *Philippines* referred to as 'development of a common legal opinion or *jurisprudence constante*, to resolve difficult legal questions' (para. 97).

[59] Here we draw on Martti Koskenniemi (n. 52 above), except that the process of judgment takes a bit longer: let's call it a moment of law.

[60] James Flett's contribution to this volume, p. 304.

[61] Andreas Paulus, 'International Adjudication' in Samantha Besson and John Tasioulas (eds.), *The Philosophy of International Law* (Oxford University Press, 2010) 221. He advocates such transparency in international adjudication when it is impossible for judges to achieve balance between state and individual rights and thus a choice must be made in the absence of a rule.

[62] See e.g. Lon Fuller, 'The forms and limits of adjudication' in S. A. Scheingold, *Legality and Democracy: Contested Affinities* (Ashgate Publishing, London and Burlington, VT, 2006) 17.

[63] See e.g. the essays in Samantha Besson and John Tasioulas (eds.), *The Philosophy of International Law* (Oxford University Press, 2010).

would we identify as the 'moment of law' in the cases from which we have derived the nine techniques? The moment of law resides in the avoidance by tribunals of both conflict *and* zero-sum outcomes that would either deny or disregard the regimes or rules in conflict or fail to achieve the purpose of litigation, that of resolving disputes peacefully.

The parties as participants in the process also assume a role. For example, in the *MOX Plant* case before the Annex VII Tribunal, the UK and Ireland agreed with the analysis of the relationship between UNCLOS and the EU treaties, whereby if the dispute fell within the scope of the EU treaties, the ECJ had jurisdiction. They also agreed that under the terms of UNCLOS itself this would exclude UNCLOS dispute settlement mechanisms. The Tribunal for its part emphasised that any procedure which could result in two conflicting decisions on the same issue would serve no purpose, and would be unhelpful to the resolution of the dispute.[64] This could be viewed as one manifestation of three of Fuller's eight desiderata: that the law be clear, not contradictory and not require the impossible. But to have eschewed jurisdiction altogether on this basis would possibly have resulted in removing a means of resolving the dispute, undermining the efficacy of the law and running counter to the specifically consent-based international law under UNCLOS. The Annex VII Tribunal thus retained 'provisional' jurisdiction until the ECJ had determined the matter of its jurisdiction.[65] Further, it awarded provisional measures in similar terms to those awarded by ITLOS before it, imposing more detailed cooperation obligations on the UK in respect of its MOX Plant operations. Both parties were obliged not to do anything which would aggravate the dispute, to expedite the ECJ proceedings, and to submit six monthly reports on compliance and developments.[66]

The ECJ subsequently held that the dispute did fall within its jurisdiction.[67] Before regarding this as a usurpation of power or an abnegation of UNCLOS, it should be noted that the approval process for construction of the MOX Plant had been carried out under, and in accordance with, detailed provisions of EU law. This had entailed the involvement of the EU

[64] *MOX Plant Case, Order No. 3 of 24 June 2003*, para. 28.

[65] The UNCLOS proceedings were only finally terminated by *Order No. 6 (Termination of Proceedings)*, 6 June 2008.

[66] *MOX Plant Case, Order No. 3*, 331 (para. 68). The obligation to submit reports on compliance was only suspended on 22 January 2007: *Order No. 5 (Suspension of Periodic Reports by the Parties)*.

[67] *Commission* v. *Ireland* [2006] ECR-I 4635.

Commission which approved the plans. It was not, therefore, as if the ECJ had come along and asserted its right to sit in place of ITLOS or an Annex VII Tribunal on a matter solely concerning the international law of the sea. Further, the EU is a party to UNCLOS in its own right and UNCLOS is a mixed agreement, meaning that member states and the community share competence to act and legislate to implement its provisions. Where the EU has acted, member states' competence to that extent is displaced. The fulfilment by the EU of its UNCLOS obligations is via the member states. Insofar as UNCLOS is part of EU law, the ECJ has exclusive competence over it. The convention now forms an integral part of the EU legal order, binding on the EU institutions, and member states have conferred exclusive competence on the EU to act and legislate in certain areas covered by the law of the sea. Indeed, Ireland's statement of claim had asked the Annex VII Tribunal to take EU secondary legislation and laws into account.

The SBT Arbitral Tribunal for its part found that in principle a dispute could be covered by more than one treaty, that the dispute fell under the provisions of both the CCSBT and UNCLOS, and that it would not exclude the possibility of jurisdiction being established by virtue of UNCLOS Article 300 in spite of CCSBT Article 16.[68] However, no argument was made that Japan was independently responsible for a breach of the obligation of good faith which would have triggered that provision.[69] Moreover, although the finding of a lack of jurisdiction meant that the provisional measures terminated, the Tribunal held that the parties were not entitled to disregard their effects.[70] It recorded and emphasised the significant progress that had been made between the parties over the course of the UNCLOS proceedings to reach agreement on the substance of the dispute, and Japan's offer of binding arbitration under CCSBT Article 16.[71] It also noted that when the 1995 UN Convention Relating to Straddling Fish Stocks and Migratory Species came into effect, it would address both the substantive and procedural issues between the parties.[72] This might (perhaps charitably) be characterised as a moment of law, in particular in its purposive emphasis and affirmation of continuing legal obligations and the existence of a forum for binding judicial settlement.

[68] *SBT Case*, paras 52, 64.

[69] Ibid., para. 64. In fact unequivocal evidence of bad faith on the part of Japanese fisheries authorities was not available at the time (there had been systematic undisclosed over-quota fishing, later paid back). The episode shows the insecurity, not to say irregularity, of jurisdictional exclusions predicated upon 'good faith' of states.

[70] Ibid., para. 67. [71] Ibid., paras 68–69. [72] Ibid., para. 71.

The moment of law in the *Swordfish* dispute between Chile and the EU occurred outside the parallel WTO and ITLOS proceedings but was contingent on those proceedings and resulted in their suspension. That is, the law-making by the parties took the form of concluding a treaty on management of swordfish stocks and access of EU vessels to Chilean ports.

While on one reading the ECJ's *West Tankers* judgment represents the loss of autonomy for international arbitration, another reading is more positive. The ECJ's reasoning turned on the view that it was for the Italian court first seised to determine the preliminary or ancillary matter of the exclusive arbitration provision, without being stripped of its power to do so by an anti-suit injunction issued by the UK courts.[73] The principle in play in the judgment is the principle of trust between member states integral to the principle of free movement, itself a key example of 'regime interaction' between the national legal systems of the EU member states. Issuing an anti-suit injunction against the proceedings in an Italian court undermined that principle.[74] Nor did the ECJ dismiss the international context and the operation of the New York Convention: it sought to reconcile the two. It considered that its holding on the relationship between the English and Italian courts was consistent with Article II(3) of the New York Convention, which requires the courts of contracting parties to refer the matter to arbitration at the request of one of the parties unless it finds the arbitration agreement is null and void, inoperative or incapable of being performed.[75] The response to *West Tankers* by the 'clients' of the private international arbitration industry has been muted. The loss of the anti-suit injunction within the UK court system in certain cases simply alters their course of action and options: it does not nullify the arbitration clause. Further, like the *SBT* and *Swordfish* disputes, the case has resulted in further law-making. The European Commission commenced a review of the operation of the Brussels Regulation and has suggested amendments with a view to better regulating ancillary court proceedings in arbitration cases, such as *West Tankers*.[76] The reasoning in the House of Lords preliminary reference ruling for upholding anti-suit injunctions turned

[73] *Allianz SpA, Generali Assicurazioni SpA* v. *West Tankers Inc*, Judgment of the Grand Chamber, Case C-185/07, 10 February 2009, para. 28.

[74] It 'runs counter to the trust which the Member States accord to one another's legal systems and judicial institutions and on which the system of jurisdiction under Regulation No 44/2001 is based': ibid., para. 30.

[75] Ibid., para. 33.

[76] Green Paper on the Review of Council Regulation (EC) No 44/2001 on Jurisdiction and the Recognition and Enforcement of Judgments in Civil and Commercial Matters,

on the practical realities of commerce and litigation.[77] Cogent as these are, they are nevertheless only values to be weighed alongside others, in this case, the importance of national regime interaction within the EU.

Some conflicts cases are nonetheless embarrassing. The conflicting outcomes in *Lauder/CME* not only run counter to the requirements of the possibility of compliance with the law, clarity and predictability but also bring the law into disrepute. On the upside, the possibility of double recovery by Lauder directly through the *Lauder* proceedings and indirectly as shareholder of CME through the *CME* proceedings was avoided by the inconsistent findings of fact. In any event, both tribunals suggested that the possibility of conflict could be addressed, in this instance, through remedies and damage quantification.[78]

These examples show that the resolution of regime and rule conflicts by international tribunals rarely results in a zero-sum outcome for either the parties involved or the law. The irony is that as international law becomes more law-like in the sense of a greater possibility of peaceful dispute settlement by independent judicial bodies, the possibility is exposed of its being less law-like in another respect, as clarity, order and coherence are diluted in particular domains – an example is the 'regime' interaction between state immunities and human rights. However, the success or failure of international tribunals in exacerbating or reducing fragmentation very much turns on one's perspective. Indeed, as Andrew Lang suggests in Chapter 4 of this volume, our perception of 'regime' and 'conflict' creates our understanding of whether we consider ourselves actors in an international legal system or systems. Regimes have been reified by the use of terminology.

Conflict which occurs between regimes is often without reference to the content of the rules but instead concerns the arena within which a particular conflict is to be addressed. The regimes' rules may actually not be in conflict if there was a tribunal with jurisdiction over both sets of rules. Or the rules may appear to be inconsistent but could be made consistent by interpretation. While many regimes rely on reciprocity or political persuasion to maintain themselves,[79] and occasionally there are

COM(2009) 175 final. See also www.globalarbitrationreview.com/news/article/28592/report-suggests-reversing-west-tankers (last accessed 21 July 2011).

[77] *West Tankers Inc* v. *RAS Riunione Adriatica di Sicurta SpA and Ors* [2007] UKHL 4, per Lord Hoffman, paras 15–16, 21.

[78] See *CME*, paras 212–215; *Lauder*, para. 172.

[79] E.g. the non-proliferation regime under the Treaty on the Non-Proliferation of Nuclear Weapons, 1 July 1968, 729 UNTS 161 (NPT) and related agreements.

regimes which depend for their continued existence on the *non*-resolution of disputes,[80] compulsory dispute settlement provisions remove the conflict to courts and tribunals with exclusive jurisdiction over 'their' regime. The feature of a regime is that it says 'my rule governs'. Unlike the ICJ, a tribunal that only has jurisdiction under a particular treaty regards that treaty as specifically and especially 'its own'. The conflict moves beyond resolution at the level of negotiation and agreement between state officials who can find a way to reconcile or make inconsistent rules consistent – a potentially law-creating transaction – and becomes defined as a particular type of conflict in the moment of being handed over to the particular specialist tribunal.

This occurs in part because specialist courts and tribunals facilitate regime 'stickiness'. 'Stickiness' is a very non-legal term, but one might apply it to systems which tend to arrogate to themselves power beyond the parties to the relevant treaty. A feature of self-described regimes is that they tend to make assertions *erga omnes* even if they are arrangements *inter partes*. The stickiness can arise to the state of complete *grandeur*, as it does with the ECJ in *Kadi*,[81] or at least to a rather condescending attitude to the rest of international law like that of the WTO dispute settlement body.[82] This stickiness is also there in a number of courts and tribunals which naturally regard themselves as having a special mandate to do that particular thing which they are asked to do, for example the human rights courts.[83]

A second problem is that the notion of the term 'regime' promotes an exclusivity and comprehensiveness that obscures and excludes the general law. The progressive looseness of discourse in international law around the

[80] E.g., Article XI (agreement to consult over and if no resolution is reached, all Parties are to refer the dispute to the ICJ) of the Antarctic Treaty, 1 December 1959, 402 UNTS 71, integrally linked to Article IV, the famous agreement to disagree. See James Crawford, 'The Antarctic Treaty after 50 Years' in Duncan French, Matthew Saul and Nigel D. White (eds.), *International Law and Dispute Settlement. New Problems and Techniques* (Hart Publishing, Oxford, 2010) 271.

[81] E.g. the development of fundamental rights law from the 1970s (a well-canvassed area of EU law, but for one description see Paul Craig and Gráinne de Búrca, *EU Law: Text, Cases and Materials* (Oxford University Press, 4th edn, 2008), ch. 11), and the treaty as constitution prevailing over the terms of the treaty itself in *Yassin Abdullah Kadi* v. *Council of the European Union*, Joined Cases C-402/05 P and C-415/05 P, Judgment of Grand Chamber, 3 September 2008 (paras 281–290).

[82] See, e.g., *European Communities – Measures Affecting the Approval and Marketing of Biotech Products* (*EC-Biotech Case*) WT/DS291/R, 29 September 2006.

[83] For an example from another context, see *Lauder*, para. 177.

notion of regime has not helped. The use of the term 'regime' dates back to the nineteenth century where it had a particular legal connotation. A regime was a legal framework which governed and controlled a particular area of conduct, usually concerning an area of territory. Regimes had distinctive features: first, they involved institutions; second, they tended to involve some form of management of territory outside the framework of regular sovereignty arrangements; and, third, they claimed to be *the way* of doing the particular thing that was being done. A good example is the agreement by the Danube riparian states establishing the European Commission of the Danube and the rules governing their management and use of the Danube as well as its use by third states.[84] If you wanted to navigate on the Danube you had to opt into the Danube regime. The Danube regime had customs collectors: if you wanted to navigate you had to pay the money, so it had a system of raising money directly and it had a budget.[85]

The notion that the term 'regime' had a broader field of application and applied to areas of international law established by treaties and institutions was the result of various factors: it was partly a leakage from the things that one could reasonably describe as regimes in that they had a set of rules governing a specific activity and an administrating body, such as the Danube regime; partly a result of loose language; and partly a result of international relations scholars who started to be interested in norms but could not really buy into international law as a norm-narrative for itself because that would have been a confession of failure by the discipline invented by Hans Morgenthau. Instead international relations scholars had regimes, which were a way of having normativity in a confined space. You could have a regime that you could accept was normative in itself, but unconnected systematically to anything else. Therefore you did not have to accept anything about the international legal system *qua* legal system or international law *qua* law.

The use of the term regime and the now enormous international relations scholarship on regimes obscures the generality of law.[86] The law of the sea has been described as a regime, but it is odd to use this term to describe the way we regulate the oceans. If it is a regime, what about the

[84] The authors thank Georges Abi-Saab for this example and his discussion of the meaning of 'regime' at the conference that led to this volume.

[85] See Convention Regarding the Regime of Navigation on the Danube, Belgrade, 18 August 1948, 33 UNTS 181, Arts 1, 30 and 35.

[86] The fact is that regimes turn on the existence of the whole; otherwise they could not claim exclusivity of anything.

law of the land? General international law and its various component areas (airspace, outer space, the oceans) cannot usefully be described as a regime, anymore than tort, contract and unjust enrichment can be described as 'regimes' of domestic law. To take another example, the institutions of diplomatic relations cannot be usefully described as a regime. It is no doubt a way of doing things: if you want to have diplomatic relations with another state in the normal mode, international law tells you how to do it. It is a facilitative system. Unfortunately the ICJ in the *Tehran Hostages* case used the word 'regime' when referring to diplomatic relations.[87] This was an unnecessary step. The Court was seeking to make the point that diplomatic relations is a self-contained system insofar as the arrangement for sanctions or taking measures against diplomats is set out in diplomatic law rather than any other part of general international law. But the specific rules sit within general international law, to which we resort alongside and in the absence of specific subject-matter rules. The Court was not suggesting that the law of diplomatic relations is somehow cut off from general international law. It would be better if the word regime is used in a more discriminating way, and in particular was not used to describe branches of general international law.[88]

Conclusion

The field of regime and rule conflict in international law highlights the point that international law has to do quite a lot – including resolving conflicts between rules and tribunals' overlapping jurisdictions – with not very much in terms of an informing meta-principle from which answers can be deduced by the application of reason, or a shared allegiance to the system of law amongst the actors who deal with it. Again in Dunoff's words, there is no redemptive narrative.[89] International law started not with a bang but with a whimper – the whimper of what was left when natural law expired. But there is always some kind of aspiration to increase the level of order in the world so as to allow human survival.

[87] *Case Concerning United States Diplomatic and Consular Staff in Iran (United States* v. *Iran)* [1980] ICJ Rep 3 (para. 86).

[88] We would define a regime, then, as a more or less institutionalised system of dealing with a particular field of behaviour, often associated with the governance of territory, which claims a substantial measure of comprehensiveness and exclusivity.

[89] See Dunoff, Ch. 5 in this volume, p. 154.

Human survival seems something that is worth a redemption story.[90] If that is so, we have either not got the story yet or have not understood it.

But the fact that we cannot locate, agree upon or articulate a redemption story does not mean that we should stop acting until we do. Conflicts will arise with no clear conflicts rules to resolve them. The cases offer nine examples of principles or techniques to address potential conflicts. We offer no guide as to selection between them; suggest no order of application in a given case. They are not necessarily consistent, or free from doubt or criticism. We could say that the listing of conflict principles is mere formalism or (which seems more forgivable these days) legal pragmatism.[91] But that understates their importance. The reasoning invoked by the judges and arbitrators in those cases, and law-making that occurs contingently on litigation, contributes to our understanding of international law's character, purpose and potential. Moreover, the existence of different techniques of conflict resolution offers possibilities for enhanced understanding of a kind of regulatory competition, with its attendant dialogue.

[90] Cf. Lon Fuller's engagement with H. L. A. Hart on the 'one central indisputable element' of natural law in *The Morality of Law* (Yale University Press, 2nd rev. edn, 1964) 184–186, citing H. L. A. Hart, *The Concept of Law* (Clarendon Press, Oxford, 1961) 198–195 (now 191–200 of the 2nd edn, 1994).

[91] Martti Koskenniemi, 'What is international law for?' in Malcolm Evans (ed.), *International Law* (Oxford University Press, 3rd edn, 2010) 32, 42–46.

9

Importing Other International Regimes into World Trade Organization Litigation

JAMES FLETT*

Introduction

The International Law Commission (ILC) Study Group's conclusions on the fragmentation of international law[1] state that international law is a system of norms whose interrelationships, whether harmonious or conflicting, are to be worked out by applying certain rules. The Study Group recognises that, subject to general principles, specific law, including special regimes (such as World Trade Organization (WTO) law), rather than general law, may be determinative. This volume focuses less on the question of whether international law is relatively integrated or fragmented, and more on the question of how special regimes within international law interact. This chapter focuses particularly on how WTO law interacts with other international regimes. Being focused on such interaction, this chapter does not focus on delimiting precisely what constitutes WTO law as distinct from other international law.[2] Nor does it focus on what precisely constitutes international law: the discussion extends to

* Any views expressed are personal and do not represent the views of the Commission, its Legal Service or the European Communities. I am grateful for the comments from many other speakers and participants at the conference upon which this volume is based, although any errors remain, of course, my own.

[1] ILC, *Fragmentation of International Law: Difficulties Arising from the Diversification and Expansion of International Law*, 58th sess., UN Docs A/CN.4/L.682 and Corr.1 and Add.1 (13 April 2006). The UN General Assembly took note of the conclusions and study on 4 December 2006: *Report of the International Law Commission on the Work of Its Fifty-Eighth Session*, GA Res 61/34, UN GAOR, 61st sess., 64th plen. mtg, Agenda Item 78, UN Doc. A/RES/61/34 (4 December 2006).

[2] For a discussion of what constitutes WTO law (as opposed to other international law) see, e.g. Petros C. Mavroidis, 'No Outsourcing of Law? WTO Law as Practiced by WTO Courts' (2008) 102 *American Journal of International Law* 421; Joost Pauwelyn, *Conflict of Norms in Public International Law: How WTO Law Relates to Other Rules of International Law* (Cambridge University Press, 2003) 40–52.

certain documents regardless of whether or not they fall within the scope of Article 38(1) of the Statute of the International Court of Justice (ICJ Statute).[3] Similarly, this chapter does not focus on the question of whether WTO law is correctly described as a 'regime' (rather assuming WTO law to be the quintessential example of a 'regime');[4] nor whether the other referenced material should be described as part of a 'regime' or part of international law in general.[5] Finally, this chapter does not address the relationship between two municipal laws (whether or not characterised as a 'socially embedded legal system of an indigenous society'), or the relationship between an international regime and one or more municipal laws.[6]

This chapter's basic proposition is that, if one looks beyond the questions of applicable law and rules of interpretation, to what is actually happening in WTO litigation,[7] one finds that, in fact, a great deal of international law is finding its way into WTO law – and indeed, on a moment's reflection, it is difficult to see how matters could be otherwise.[8] Thus, this chapter approaches the matter from a more pragmatic and less theoretical perspective – without first positing a formal view about

[3] International conventions, whether general or particular; international custom or general practice; general principles of law recognised by civilised nations; judicial decisions and academic publications. For a discussion of the sources of international law, see e.g. Hugh Thirlway, 'The Sources of International Law' in Malcolm D. Evans (ed.), *International Law* (Oxford University Press, 2nd edn, 2006) 115–140.

[4] See Margaret Young, 'Introduction: The Productive Friction between Regimes', in this volume, pp. 4–11; James Crawford and Penelope Nevill, 'Relations between International Courts and Tribunals: The "Regime Problem"', Ch.8 of this volume, pp. 257–259.

[5] See Nele Matz-Lück, 'Norm Interpretation across International Regimes: Competences and Legitimacy', Ch. 7 of this volume, pp. 205–207; Crawford and Nevill, ibid.

[6] Gunther Teubner and Peter Korth, 'Two Kinds of Legal Pluralism: Collision of Transnational Regimes in the Double Fragmentation of World Society', Ch. 1 of this volume. Contrary to what is suggested in that chapter, I am not certain that the collisions identified are entirely novel from a legal point of view: the former would tend to be regulated by any applicable international treaty law and/or municipal private international law conflict rules; and the latter by rules in the international regime and/or the municipal laws.

[7] This chapter does not focus on interaction at the law-making stage, but rather interaction between the different laws, once made – and specifically interaction in the arena of adjudication as opposed to implementation (Cf. Margaret Young, 'Regime Interaction in Creating, Implementing and Enforcing International Law' Ch. 3 of this volume, pp. 89–92).

[8] See the discussion in Young, ibid., pp. 97–98; and the references to 'a decline in formalism' and the need for responsiveness and flexibility in Nele Matz-Lück, Ch. 7 of this volume, pp. 204–205.

international law as a whole,[9] or the relationship between WTO law and other international law.

As has often been observed, the WTO is different from the General Agreement on Tariffs and Trade (GATT) that preceded it particularly because of the introduction of mandatory and binding dispute settlement, potentially leading to compensation or suspension of concessions and possibly more.[10] This is a significant event not only in the context of international trade law, but also in the context of public international law in general. It makes the question of the relationship between WTO law and other international law of particular interest. For example, if such other international law can be referenced in WTO dispute settlement then, in effect, such other international law might also become, at least in some degree, subject to the same mandatory and binding dispute settlement mechanism.[11]

As the WTO Appellate Body observed in its first report, WTO law is not to be read in 'clinical isolation' from other public international law.[12] The language of the WTO preambles is ambitious[13] and the scope of the WTO

[9] As similarly indicated by Crawford and Nevill in Ch. 8 of this volume, p. 247.

[10] Through the doctrines of direct effect or interpretation in conformity, one of which is arguably required by Article XVI:4 of the WTO Agreement ('Each Member shall ensure the conformity of its laws, regulations and administrative procedures with its obligations as provided in the annexed Agreements'), at least when read in conjunction with other provisions.

[11] For recent contributions to this discussion, see, e.g. Tomer Broude, 'Principles of Normative Integration and the Allocation of International Authority: The WTO, the Vienna Convention on the Law of the Treaties, and the Rio Declaration' (2008) 6 *Loyola University Chicago International Law Review* 173; Anja Lindroos and Michael Mehling, 'Dispelling the Chimera of "Self-Contained" Regimes in International Law and the WTO' (2006) 16 *European Journal of International Law* 857; Stephen Humphreys, 'Structural Ambiguity: Technology Transfer in Three Regimes', Ch. 6 of this volume, pp. 186–188.

[12] Appellate Body Report, *US – Gasoline*, 17. The short form case citations in this chapter are taken from the table published by the WTO at: www.wto.org.

[13] Marrakesh Declaration of 15 April 1994: 'Determined to build upon the success of the Uruguay Round through the participation of their economies in the world trading system'; an 'historic achievement' destined to 'strengthen the world economy and lead to more trade, investment, employment and income growth throughout the world'; 'a new era of global economic cooperation, reflecting the widespread desire to operate in a fairer and more open multilateral trading system for the benefit and welfare of their peoples'; 'greater global coherence of policies in the fields of trade, money and finance, including cooperation between the WTO, the IMF and the World Bank'; an 'historic step towards a more balanced and integrated global trade partnership' with developing countries; 'significant measures of economic reform and autonomous trade liberalisation in many ... formerly centrally planned economies'.

agreements broader than the GATT.[14] The WTO has relations with many other international bodies,[15] and the WTO agreements contain several references to documents emanating from other international regimes.[16] This reflects the fact that trade is a nascent form of community and is inextricably linked to many other issues with which nation state governments have traditionally been concerned, and which other concerns are therefore also reflected in other international agreements they have authored. The situation is reminiscent of EU law. Economics and trade are driving the process, and law and broader political issues are thereby inevitably engaged. In fact, in many respects, far from having 'tunnel

[14] Referring, e.g., to: the covered agreements (goods, agriculture, sanitary and phytosanitary measures, textiles and clothing, technical barriers to trade, trade-related investment measures, anti-dumping, customs valuation, pre-shipment inspection, rules of origin, import licensing, subsidies, safeguard measures, services, intellectual property, civil aircraft, government procurement); the decisions and declarations (global economic policy making, International Monetary Fund (IMF), standards, environment, movement of natural persons, financial services, maritime transport, telecommunications, professional services); the GATT 1994 (non-discrimination, tariffs, internal taxation and regulation, films, transit, quantitative restrictions, balance of payments, currency exchange, state trading enterprises, development policy); and its exemptions (public morals, gold or silver, enforcement, prison labour, national treasures, exhaustible natural resources, commodity agreements, essential domestic materials, local short supply, security, regionalisation).

[15] The International Trade Centre UNCTAD/WTO is a joint subsidiary organ of the WTO and United Nations Conference on Trade and Development (UNCTAD). The WTO has agreements with the IMF and World Bank. The following have permanent or *ad hoc* observer status in various WTO bodies: FAO, IMF, ITC, OECD, UN, UNCTAD, World Bank, WIPO, EBRD, EFTA, ITCB, WCO, ITU, UPU, ICAO, WHO, WTO-OMT, UPOV, ACP, IGC, WFP, IPPC, Codex, ISO, OIE, IICA, SELA, OIRSA, OAS, ALADI, ANEAN Community, CARICOM, CAEMC, Commonwealth Secretariat, GCC, IADB, SIECA, SADC, UNDP, ECA, ECE, ECLAC, ESCAP, UNIDO, AU, AMU, CFC, ECOWAS, ECO, IAIGC, IsDB, OIC, Pacific Islands Forum, UNEP, WAEMU, CBD, CITES, ICCAT, IPGRI, CSD, UNFCCC, UNIDO, SEAFDEC, IEC, OILM, UNCITRAL, ICAO, UNWTO, Basel Convention, Montreal Protocol, Rotterdam Convention, Stockholm Convention. See www.wto.org (also for full names).

[16] Notably: the Havana Charter (GATT 1994, Article XXIX and Ad note to Article II:4); UN Charter (GATT 1994, Article XXI); OECD Arrangement (SCM Agreement, Annex I, item (k), second paragraph) (by implication); the Codex Alimentarius Commission, the International Office of Epizootics (now known as the World Organisation for Animal Health) and the International Plant Protection Convention (SPS Agreement); and the agreements referenced in the TRIPs Agreement (the Paris Convention for the Protection of Industrial Property; the Berne Convention for the Protection of Literary and Artistic Works; the International Convention for the Protection of Performers, Producers of Phonograms and Broadcasting Organisations, adopted at Rome on 26 October 1961; the Treaty on Intellectual Property in Respect of Integrated Circuits (IPIC Treaty); and the World Intellectual Property Organization (WIPO)). Article 3.2 of the Dispute Settlement Understanding (DSU) also refers (by implication) to the Vienna Convention.

vision', WTO law is dealing *internally* with 'collisions between different social functional systems and the legal norms coupled to them',[17] and also for that reason WTO law is moving 'from the fringes of international law to the very forefront of it'.[18]

Much of the discussion has focused on applicable law, the jurisdiction of panels, the rules of interpretation, and general principles of international law.[19] Aside from some general observations, this chapter does not focus on applicable law. Nor does this chapter focus particularly on issues of legal interpretation – although I do comment on relevant provisions of the Vienna Convention on the Law of Treaties.[20] Rather, based on the author's experience and impression that there are many ways in which other international law may influence the outcome of WTO litigation in perhaps more subtle ways, this chapter selects a number of specific areas for further comment:

- the fact that the 'dead' Havana Charter continues to be frequently referenced in litigation, and on occasion appears to carry significant weight in the outcome; and this without it always being clear if it is referenced as preparatory work, context or even applicable law;
- the frequent and varied references to the International Court of Justice (ICJ) (or for that matter other international courts), particularly in the more general context of the United Nations Charter (UN Charter);[21]

[17] The phrase is from Teubner and Korth, Ch. 1 of this volume, p. 27 (in other words, WTO law *is* the called-for 'legal norm' combining elements of the municipal laws of its Members and its predecessor (the GATT 1947) – it has *already* been created and is *already* being applied, and would likely have something to say about whether the actions of the US and Korean judiciaries (which are imputable to those states) are WTO consistent. See also the discussion of 'intra-regime' conflict in Humphreys, Ch. 6 of this volume, pp. 188–193.

[18] Pauwelyn, *Conflict of Norms in Public International Law*, n. 2 above, 29–35.

[19] See e.g.ibid.; Joost Pauwelyn, 'The Role of Public International Law in the WTO: How Far Can We Go?' (2001) 95 *American Journal of International Law* 535; Joel Trachtman, 'Jurisdiction in WTO Dispute Settlement' and Georges Abi-Saab, 'The WTO Dispute Settlement and General International Law' in Rufus Yerxa and Bruce Wilson (eds.), *Key Issues in WTO Dispute Settlement: The First Ten Years* (Cambridge University Press, 2005); Mavroidis, above n. 2; Andrew D. Mitchell, *Legal Principles in WTO Disputes* (Cambridge University Press, 2008); James Cameron and Kevin R. Gray, 'Principles of International Law in the WTO Dispute Settlement Body' (2001) 50 *International and Comparative Law Quarterly* 248; Michael Lennard, 'Navigating by the Stars: Interpreting the WTO Agreements' (2002) 5 *Journal of International Economic Law* 17.

[20] Vienna Convention on the Law of the Treaties, opened for signature 23 May 1969, 1155 UNTS 331 (entered into force 27 January 1980).

[21] The Charter of the United Nations of 26 June 1945 (Text: UNCIO XV, 335).

- the way in which non-binding documents, such as the OECD Arrangement on Officially Supported Export Credits or private international accounting standards, may be transformed into binding WTO law, and, once integrated in the assessment, spill over into other areas;
- the possibility of documents from other international regimes being taken into consideration as evidence of fact, or evidence of meaning;
- the way in which advice or opinions emanating from other international regimes can influence the outcome of disputes (such as the *Hormones* case); and
- the way in which documents emanating from other international law regimes can alter the burden of proof (as occurred in the *Sardines* case).

This chapter does not, however, address all possible channels through which international law could become relevant in WTO disputes.[22]

The chapter explores how, even if the WTO legal regime is separate from international law, it is immersed in international law, and is constantly under pressure to interact with international law through complex, subtle and not always apparent processes, feeding upon it and growing in stature and authority. A certain tension is thus apparent. On the one hand, because of the substantial economic and other interests that underpin it, and particularly because of its binding and enforceable rules-based approach, WTO law has the potential, through such interaction, to catalyse an acceleration or step-change in the evolution and effectiveness of international law. On the other hand, the authority of the WTO system as objective as opposed to result-oriented, particularly with respect to the trade objective, must to some extent depend upon the doctrinal rigour with which such interaction is managed in legal terms. If the challenge for the WTO is to mature within the system of international law in a manner that is both relevant, and, at the same time, commands respect, then the key to achieving that objective may lie in successfully developing

[22] It does not consider, for example: the waiver provisions of Article IX:3 of the WTO Agreement (as occurred in *EC – Bananas III* with reference to the Lomé Convention); incorporation through schedules (Appellate Body Report, *EC – Poultry*, para. 79 and GATT 1994, Article II:7); the enforcement provisions of Article XX(d) (rejected in *Mexico – Soft Drinks* with respect to NAFTA); mutually agreed solutions; free-trade agreements under Article XXIV of the GATT 1994; *amicus curiae* briefs; the ILC Articles on State Responsibility; international agreements between the WTO and the IMF and World Bank; intergovernmental commodity agreements referenced in Article XX(h) of the GATT 1994; etc.

and managing the extent and manner of interaction between the different systems.

A. Applicable law: not just for the defendant

I begin, then, with the question of applicable law – not in order to cover the ground others have already covered, but rather to comment on one specific aspect of that debate – the proposition that only defending parties, but not complaining parties, can invoke other international law in the WTO.[23] In my view that proposition may be based on a false distinction between provisions imposing obligations and provisions granting rights. The observation that WTO law constitutes a balance of rights and obligations[24] may be true,[25] but it is equally banal. The same is true of any contract, agreement or treaty, and even of any legislation or rule, that is, of any law. Thus, it is not particularly illuminating to characterise Article III:4 of the GATT 1994, for example, as imposing an *obligation* on WTO Members to treat imported and domestic goods alike when adopting regulatory measures, whilst characterising Article XX(b) as granting a *right* to adopt measures necessary to protect human health. Rather, each of these provisions, viewed independently, encapsulates both obligations and rights. Thus, pursuant to Article III:4, the importing Member has the *obligation* to provide national treatment and the exporting Member has the *right* to receive it. And pursuant to Article XX(b) the importing Member has the *right* to adopt an SPS measure[26] and the exporting Member the *obligation* to accept and comply with it. *Together*, Articles III:4 and XX(b) create a rule or demarcation line that Members are *obliged* not to transgress, and within which they have the *right* to act freely. Embedded within this single (if complex) legal rule is a policy conflict between the trade interest protected by Article III:4 and the regulatory interest with respect

[23] Pauwelyn, *Conflict of Norms in Public International Law*, above n. 2, 472–473: 'other rules of international law … cannot form the legal basis of a WTO complaint'; 'defending parties [are] allowed to invoke other rules of international law'.

[24] DSU, Article 3.2: 'The Members recognize that [the dispute settlement system] serves to preserve the rights and obligations of Members under the covered agreements'; DSU, Article 3.4: 'Recommendations or rulings made by the DSB shall be aimed at achieving a satisfactory settlement of the matter in accordance with the rights and obligations under this Understanding and under the covered agreements.'

[25] Chios Carmody, 'A Theory of WTO Law' (2008) 11 *Journal of International Economic Law* 527.

[26] For further detailed discussion on the Agreement on the Application of Sanitary and Phytosanitary Measures (SPS Agreement), see below, pp. 297–301.

to human health protected by Articles III:4 and XX(b). Poor or subjective legal interpretation might shift the balance between these conflicting policy objectives; but objective legal interpretation can never completely eliminate the policy conflict, because it is so entrenched in the structure and language of these provisions. Thus, the real game, in terms of the outcome of litigation, is played out in the *application* of this law to the particular *facts* of a case. It is in deciding whether or not a particular factual instance fits within one or other abstract legal category, and, in weighing the probity, value and relevance of the evidence, that a first instance judge really judges.[27] And when the abstract legal categories are not just nouns, but include other word classes; when they are expressed not just in words, but also in phrases, clauses and sentences connected in complex or conflicting ways; and when the relevant facts and evidence are voluminous and conflicting, the scope for judging is considerable.[28]

These observations have considerable implications for the proposition that the applicable law in a WTO court can and should extend to non-WTO treaties, but only for the *defending* party, not the *complaining* party. Assuming that both the WTO rule and the other rule of international law encapsulate both rights and obligations (as all rules do), it is not clear why only part of the other international law rule should come into play; or even if the whole rule comes into play, why only one party should be able to invoke it. In many instances the characterisation of one party as the complainant and the other as the defendant is purely procedural, it being unclear, if one looks at the substance of the matter, how to characterise the parties, other than observing that they are in disagreement.[29] In fact, there may often be rather more to a case than simply claim and defence. A defence may trigger counterarguments that refer to other provisions of the other international law document, which the defendant might have attempted to leave on one side if unfavourable to its case – and this might trigger further arguments from the defendant. Thus, leaving aside the

[27] By construing mixed questions of law and fact as susceptible to appeal; and through the application of Article 11 of the DSU, which requires an objective assessment also of the facts, the Appellate Body often finds itself, in effect, re-considering the same or similar types of questions – a trend that may however diminish with the passage of time, the novelty of the jurisdiction, and the increase in frequency and volume of litigation.

[28] That is why consent to be bound, whether by means of physical or economic force, by a judge interpreting and applying the law, in relation to specific matters, is a seismic political event that must be at once protected and not abused if the system is to retain the political support upon which all legal systems ultimately rely.

[29] Consider, e.g., the *US – Continued Suspension* and *Canada – Continued Suspension* cases, and their implications for the further conduct of compliance panels.

question of whether or not, in practice, it may tend to be defendants who have, until now, sought to rely on such documents, if they can be relied upon, I think that both parties should be entitled to refer to them.

B. Rules of interpretation: *other* provisions of the Vienna Convention

I turn now to the rules of interpretation. As is well known, WTO law is to be interpreted in accordance with customary rules of interpretation of public international law.[30] These include (but are not limited to) Articles 31 and 32 of the Vienna Convention.[31] Reference has also been made to Article 33 of the Vienna Convention concerning the interpretation of treaties authenticated in two or more languages.[32] As indicated above, a full description of the way these provisions have been referenced in WTO disputes is not the main focus of this chapter. They clearly provide an opportunity for other international law to interact with WTO law. This is notably the case with respect to Article 31(3)(c), depending upon whether the term 'parties' is taken to refer to all WTO Members,[33] or only the Members engaged in a particular dispute.[34]

One point that is interesting to note is that other provisions of the Vienna Convention have also been referenced in the litigation. For example, the Appellate Body has held that 'the interpretation principle' codified in Article 28 of the Vienna Convention concerning the non-retroactivity of treaties[35] is relevant to the interpretation of the covered agreements.[36] However, there must be some doubt about whether

[30] DSU, Article 3.2: 'The dispute settlement system of the WTO is a central element in providing security and predictability to the multilateral trading system. The Members recognize that it serves to preserve the rights and obligations of Members under the covered agreements, and to clarify the existing provisions of those agreements in accordance with customary rules of interpretation of public international law. Recommendations and rulings of the DSB cannot add to or diminish the rights and obligations provided in the covered agreements.'

[31] Appellate Body Report, *US – Gasoline*, p. 17.

[32] Appellate Body Report, *EC – Asbestos*, para. 91; Appellate Body Report, *US – Stainless Steel (Mexico)*, n. 200. The WTO Agreements are authentic in English, French and Spanish (WTO Agreement, Article XVI:6).

[33] As the Panel in *EC – Biotech* thought.

[34] See Young, Ch. 3 of this volume, particularly pp. 95–96.

[35] Article 28 of the Vienna Convention provides: 'Unless a different intention appears from the treaty or is otherwise established, its provisions do not bind a party in relation to any act or fact which took place or any situation which ceased to exist before the date of the entry into force of the treaty with respect to that party.'

[36] Appellate Body Report, *EC – Sardines*, para. 200 and the other cases there cited.

or not Article 28 of the Vienna Convention is correctly described as a rule of interpretation. It is not contained in Part III, Section 3 of the Vienna Convention (which is titled 'Interpretation of Treaties' and consists of Articles 31, 32 and 33) but rather in Part III, Section 2 (which is titled 'Application of Treaties'). Furthermore, whilst it is true that Article 28 does direct the reader to consider whether a 'different intention appears from the treaty', the remainder of the provision is rather in the nature of a substantive default rule. Thus, if this is a rule of interpretation, it is rather in the nature of a rule interpreting silence, where that silence is not circumscribed by other treaty provisions, but simply reflects an omission on the part of the drafters to address the question of the treaty's temporal application.[37] Whether or not Article 28 of the Vienna Convention is a customary rule of interpretation of public international law within the meaning of Article 3.2 of the Dispute Settlement Understanding (DSU) is not a trivial matter. If it is, it will be likely to determine the temporal application of all the covered agreements, and this may have very significant substantive consequences. For example, in the *EC – Airbus* case, the US challenges many alleged subsidies that pre-date the entry into force of the GATT 1994 and the Agreement on Subsidies and Countervailing Measures (SCM Agreement), and one of the provisions invoked by the EC in its defence is Article 28 of the Vienna Convention.[38]

If provisions of the Vienna Convention other than those referenced in Part III, Section 3 are relevant in WTO dispute settlement, that raises the question of what other provisions could be invoked. Reference has been made in the case law to several other provisions of the Vienna Convention, such as, for example: Article 2 (Use of terms, particularly 'treaty' and 'party');[39] Article 7 (Full powers);[40] Article 16 (Exchange or deposit of instruments of ratification, acceptance, approval or accession) (by the

[37] Article 28 is itself laconic, insofar as it does not state expressly how to deal with an act or fact occurring before entry into force, which creates a situation continuing after entry into force. The text suggests that the new treaty should not apply, although it may also be relevant to consider the preparatory work ('Report of the International Law Commission on the Work of Its Eighteenth Session (4 May–19 July)' [1966] II *Yearbook of the International Law Commission* 172, 212). Even if the new treaty would apply, all the indications are that an appropriate transitional period would have to be granted, pursuant to Article 21.3 of the DSU or otherwise.

[38] The EC publishes its submissions to the WTO at: www.ec.europa.eu/trade/.

[39] Panel Report, *Argentina – Footwear (EC)*, para. 368 ('treaty'); Panel Report, *EC – Biotech*, para. 7.68 ('party').

[40] Panel Report, *US – 1916 Act (EC)*, n. 340.

EC);[41] Article 18 (Obligation not to defeat the object and purpose of a treaty prior to its entry into force);[42] Article 26 (*Pacta sunt servanda*);[43] Article 27 (Internal law and observance of treaties);[44] Article 30 (Application of successive treaties relating to the same subject matter);[45] Article 34 (General rule regarding third states) (by the EC);[46] Article 44 (Separability of treaty provisions);[47] Article 45 (Loss of right to invoke ground for invalidating, terminating, withdrawing from or suspending the operation of a treaty) (by the EC);[48] Article 48 (Error);[49] Article 58 (Suspension of the operation of a treaty under its provisions or by consent of the parties) (by the US);[50] Article 59 (Termination or suspension of the operation of a treaty implied by conclusion of a later treaty) (by Brazil and the EC);[51] Article 60 (Termination of suspension of the operation of a treaty as a consequence of its breach);[52] Article 65 (Procedures to be followed with respect to invalidity, termination, withdrawal from or suspension of the operation

[41] Panel Report, *EC – Export Subsidies on Sugar (Thailand)*, para. 7.118; Panel Report, *EC – Export Subsidies on Sugar (Brazil)*, para. 7.118; Panel Report, *EC – Export Subsidies on Sugar (Australia)*, para. 7.118.

[42] Panel Report, *EC – Biotech*, para. 7.53 and n. 251; Panel Report, *Argentina – Poultry Anti-Dumping Duties*, n. 49; Panel Report, *US – Offset Act (Byrd Amendment)*, para. 7.64 and n. 314; Panel Report, *US – Shrimp*, para. 7.41.

[43] Appellate Body Report, *Canada – Continued Suspension*, para. 314; Appellate Body Report, *US – Continued Suspension*, para. 314; Panel Report, *Canada – Continued Suspension*, paras 7.316 and 7.356 and n. 481; Panel Report, *US – Continued Suspension*, paras 7.316 and 7.358 and n. 488; Appellate Body Report, *US – Corrosion-Resistant Steel Sunset Review*, para. 296; Appellate Body Report, *EC – Sardines*, para. 278; Panel Report, *US – Countervailing Measures on Certain EC Products*, n. 377; Appellate Body Report, *US – Line Pipe*, n. 117; Panel Report, *US – Shrimp*, n. 175; Panel Report, *Korea – Government Procurement*, para. 7.93; Panel Report, *India – Patents (EC)*, n. 135; Panel Report, *Argentina – Textiles and Apparel*, n. 167.

[44] Panel Report, *Mexico – Telecoms*, para. 7.244; Panel Report, *US – Countervailing Measures on Certain EC Products*, n. 139; Panel Report, *Brazil – Aircraft (Article 21.5 – Canada)*, n. 23; Panel Report, *Australia – Salmon (Article 21.5 – Canada)*, n. 146; Panel Report, *US – Section 301 Trade Act*, nn. 652 and 664; Panel Report, *Canada – Dairy*, n. 424.

[45] Panel Report, *Japan – Film*, para. 10.65 (although not applicable in that case); Panel Report, *EC – Poultry*, paras 205–206.

[46] Panel Report, *Brazil – Retreaded Tyres*, nn. 1442 and 1448.

[47] Panel Report, *Korea – Government Procurement*, n. 769.

[48] GATT Panel Report, *EEC (Member States) – Bananas I* (unadopted), para. 141.

[49] Panel Report, *Korea – Government Procurement*, para. 7.124.

[50] GATT Panel Report, *US – Softwood Lumber II*, adopted 27 October 1993, para. 41.

[51] Panel Report, *EC – Poultry*, para. 205; Appellate Body Report, *EC – Poultry*, paras 52 and 54.

[52] Panel Report, *US – Certain EC Products*, para. 6.133; Panel Report, *EC – Commercial Vessels*, n. 396.

of a treaty);[53] Article 66 (Procedures for judicial settlement, arbitration and conciliation);[54] and Article 70 (Consequences of the termination of a treaty).[55]

Whilst in some instances these references are associated with a discussion of whether or not the provision in question reflects a general principle of international law, that is not always the case. Obviously, given the range of provisions in the Vienna Convention, and the concepts or principles that some of those provisions express, if they are to be admitted as generally relevant in WTO disputes, that could constitute a significant addition to the role of public international law within the WTO.

C. Examples of 'imports' from other regimes

1. *Havana Charter*

I would like to turn now to a discussion of the Havana Charter. Whilst at first sight this might appear to be largely of historical interest, there are certain aspects of its position and role in the WTO that are worthy of note, and of interest in the context of this chapter.

To recall, following the Second World War, negotiations took place to create three institutions for international economic cooperation: the World Bank, the International Monetary Fund (IMF) and the International Trade Organization (ITO). The Havana Charter for an International Trade Organization (Havana Charter) of 24 March 1948[56] was negotiated between 1946 and 1948 in London, Geneva and Havana. Ultimately, it was not accepted by the United States, and has never entered into force. In parallel, the GATT of 30 October 1947, which had a narrower scope than the Havana Charter, was negotiated and agreed between 1946 and 1947 by countries (including countries involved in the negotiation of the Havana Charter) that wished to move more rapidly to reduce tariffs. Many of its provisions were identical or similar to provisions in the Havana Charter. Provisional application of the GATT 1947 began on 1 January 1948. Parties to the GATT 1947 undertook to observe to the fullest extent of their executive authority the general principles of

[53] Panel Report, *Korea – Government Procurement*, n. 769.

[54] Panel Report, *EC – Biotech*, n. 241.

[55] Appellate Body Report, *Brazil – Dessicated Coconut*, p. 20.

[56] Havana Charter for an International Trade Organization, UN Doc. E/Conf. 2/78 (24 March 1948).

Chapters I to VI and Chapter IX of the Havana Charter[57] pending their acceptance of the Havana Charter in accordance with their constitutional procedures.[58] With the entry into force of the Havana Charter, Part II of the GATT 1947 was to be suspended; and Members of the ITO were to be precluded from invoking any provision of the GATT 1947 so as to prevent the operation of any provision of the Havana Charter.[59] During and after the Havana Conference various amendments to the GATT of 30 October 1947 were agreed, bringing the text closer to that of the Havana Charter and to that extent making the preparatory work of the Havana Charter also the preparatory work of the GATT 1947, as amended.[60] With the conclusion of the WTO agreements, the GATT 1947, as amended, was re-cast as the GATT 1994.[61] The WTO agreements provide that in case of conflict between the GATT 1994 and another Annex 1A agreement, the latter prevails to the extent of the conflict.[62]

Thus, the Havana Charter never entered into force, and it has a particular relationship with the WTO because the preparatory work for the GATT 1947 and the preparatory work for the Havana Charter are closely related and even intertwined or overlapping. Furthermore, the express references in the GATT 1947 to the Havana Charter[63] reflect and are coloured by this historical context, and in this sense are different from other express references in the WTO agreements to other international law.

The WTO website opines that the Havana Charter and the ITO are 'effectively dead',[64] and the view has been expressed that Article XXIX of the GATT 1994 has, through practice, fallen into desuetude and become

[57] Chapter I (Purpose and Objectives); Chapter II (Employment and Economic Activity); Chapter III (Economic Development and Reconstruction); Chapter IV (Commercial Policy); Chapter V (Restrictive Business Practices); Chapter VI (Inter-Governmental Commodity Agreements); and Chapter IX (General Provisions). Ad Article XXIX of the GATT 1947 states that Chapters VII and VIII of the Havana Charter are excluded from paragraph 1 because they generally deal with the organisation, functions and procedures of the ITO.

[58] GATT 1947, Article XXIX:1. This provision addresses the *obligations* rather than the *rights* in the Havana Charter; and more specifically the principles. See: GATT Panel Report, *Canada – Administration of the Foreign Investment Review Act*, adopted 7 February 1984, paras 3.9 and 5.12.

[59] GATT 1947, Article XXIX:2 and XXIX:6.

[60] For a more detailed explanation, see World Trade Organization, *Guide to GATT Law and Practice: Analytical Index* (World Trade Organization, 6th edn, 1995) Vol. I, 3–8.

[61] GATT 1994, Article 1(a).

[62] WTO Agreement, *General Interpretative Note to Annex 1A*.

[63] GATT 1947, Article XXIX, ad Note to Article XXIX:1 and ad Note to Article II:4.

[64] www.wto.org.

legally inoperative, at least from the perspective of applicable law.[65] On the other hand, there are some 62 instances of references to the Havana Charter in the case law: 30 out of 101 GATT panel reports and 21 out of 130 WTO reports (including three Appellate Body reports). After a slow start, from the late 1980s, there are several references per year, with less frequent but nevertheless regular references in the WTO reports, most recently on 27 April 2009.[66] Some issues, come back repeatedly;[67] but the range of issues is also wide.[68] In many cases the argument appears marginal; but in others the Havana Charter appears to weigh relatively heavily in determining the outcome.[69] All of the major protagonists in dispute settlement have been willing to reference the Havana Charter when it suits them;[70] and in several cases the references appear to have been initiated by a panel or by the Appellate Body.[71] There are also some references to parts of the Havana Charter that have never been directly transposed into the text of the GATT 1994.[72] It is particularly striking that, whilst the predominant judicial technique is to refer to the preparatory work (although with little discipline as to treating it as a supplementary means of interpretation in

65 Mavroidis, above n. 2, 421.

66 Panel Report, *Colombia – Ports of Entry*, para. 7.395. The Panel appears to have treated Article 33 of the Havana Charter as 'preparatory work' (with the meaning of Article 32 of the Vienna Convention) to Article V of the GATT 1994, but concluded that differences in the texts shed no light on the interpretation of Article V.

67 Notably the interpretation of various provisions of the GATT 1994, Articles II and III.

68 Including references to GATT 1994, Articles I, II, III, XI, XII, XIII, XVI, XVIII, XIX, XX, XXI, XXIII, XXIV, XXV, and XXIX.

69 E.g. in *EC – Poultry*, para. 92, the Appellate Body referred to the preparatory work of the Havana Conference to confirm its interpretation of the term 'global annual tariff quota' as referring to a tariff quota administered on a non-discriminatory basis pursuant to Article XIII of the GATT 1994.

70 Including the US, EC, Japan, Canada, Australia, Chile, New Zealand, Mexico, India, Turkey, China and several others.

71 For example, in *Japan – Taxes on Alcoholic Beverages*, n. 52, the Appellate Body referred to the preparatory work of the Havana Conference to support its conclusion regarding the legal status of the ad Note to Article III:2. In *Canada – Periodicals*, p. 34 and n. 73 the Appellate Body referred to the preparatory work of the Havana Charter to support its conclusion that Article II:8(b) of the GATT 1994 does not exclude from the disciplines of Article III a measure that taxes (or charges) imports but not like domestic products. In *US – Line Pipe*, n. 171, the Appellate Body referred extensively to the preparatory work of the Havana Conference, but concluded that it did not provide guidance on the question of whether or not Article XIX of the GATT 1994 and the Agreement on Safeguards requires a discrete determination of serious injury or threat of serious injury.

72 E.g. in *Mexico – Telecoms*, para. 7.236, the Panel referred to Article 46 of the Havana Charter as 'informing' the meaning of the phrase 'anti-competitive practices' contained in Mexico's GATS schedule (that is, apparently as context).

accordance with the limitations in Article 32 of the Vienna Convention), there are also some references (at least in the arguments) to context, and even applicable law, and in many instances the basis for the reference is simply not specified. It is also striking that in no instance have a party's arguments been dismissed as simply irrelevant as a matter of principle. Havana arguments always appear to be treated with respect, whether they coincide with the outcome of the litigation or not.

I think it is striking to see how the Havana Charter continues to make an appearance in the case law, despite the tenuous legal basis for such references, and the lack of clarity about the judicial technique being used. One has the impression that it is just treated as an established part of the landscape – its relevance being rarely if ever questioned. It seems to come into its own when it is necessary to settle a particularly obscure interpretation, and one senses a certain sense of pride when esoteric documents that it may be difficult for the public to access are winkled out to provide a basis for or confirm the solution. However, recourse to the Havana Charter does tend to look non-systematic and therefore somewhat arbitrary, and reference to the preparatory work can always be two-edged – does one argue that an earlier document confirms the mooted interpretation, or that its rejection disproves it? Nevertheless, one cannot help feeling that if the Havana Charter can soldier on, then there must be hope for pretty much any other international law document, with a bit of imagination on the part of litigants.

2. *The UN Charter and the International Court of Justice*

The next area I would like to take a look at is references in WTO litigation to the ICJ, because I am particularly struck by the range and what appears to be the increasing frequency of such references.

Before doing that, however, I would like to put the matter in the context of the UN Charter, of which the ICJ Statute is a part, and which is expressly referred to in the GATT 1994. Thus, Article XXI of the GATT 1994 is titled 'security exceptions' and Article XXI(c) of the GATT 1994 provides that nothing in the GATT 1994 shall be construed to prevent any WTO Member from taking action in pursuance of its obligations under the UN Charter for the maintenance of international peace and security.[73] This provision may be seen as a recognition of, and complement to, Article 103 of the UN Charter, which itself provides that, in the event of a

[73] An analogous provision is contained in Article XIVbis of the GATS.

conflict between the Charter and any other international agreement, the Charter shall prevail. This raises the question of precisely which UN obligations are referenced in Article XXI(c) of the GATT 1994.

Chapter VII, and particularly Article 41 of the Charter provides that the UN Security Council may call upon Members to apply measures providing for the complete or partial interruption of economic relations.[74] UN sanctions have been imposed in a number of cases, also involving WTO Members,[75] but perhaps not surprisingly have never been directly at issue in DSU proceedings. However, the maintenance of international peace and security might be considered to be part of the overall objectives of the UN Charter;[76] and several Chapters or provisions of the UN Charter refer expressly to peace and security.[77] Further, according to Article 92 of the UN Charter, the ICJ is the principal organ of the United Nations. In addition, Article 31(3)(c) of the Vienna Convention requires that there be taken into account, together with the context, any relevant rules of international law applicable in the relations between the parties. Leaving aside the technical position with respect to certain customs territories, such as the EC, all 153 members of the WTO are members of the United Nations, whose 192 members account for almost all states.

There are several examples of the provisions of Chapter I of the UN Charter (Purposes and Principles) being referenced in WTO litigation.

[74] Panel Report, *Mexico – Taxes on Soft Drinks*, para. 8.178. In interpreting the phrase 'secure compliance' in Article XX(d) of the GATT 1994 as referring to the domestic rather than the international level, the panel referred in passing to Article XXI(c) of the GATT 1994 and Chapter VII of the UN Charter, apparently by way of contrasting context.

[75] Afghanistan (WTO observer); Angola (terminated 9 December 2002) (WTO Member since 23 November 1996); Congo (WTO Member since 27 March 1997); Côte d'Ivoire (WTO Member since 1 January 1995); Ethiopia and Eritrea (terminated 15 May 2001) (WTO observer); Federal Republic of Yugoslavia/Kosovo (terminated 10 September 2001); Haiti (terminated 29 September 1994) (WTO Member since 30 January 1996); Iraq (terminated 22 May 2003) (WTO observer); Iran (WTO observer); Lebanon (WTO observer); Liberia (terminated 22 December 2003) (WTO observer); Rwanda (terminated 10 July 2008) (WTO Member since 22 May 1996); Sierra Leone (WTO Member since 23 July 1995); Somalia; South Africa (terminated 26 May 1994) (WTO Member since 1 January 1995); Southern Rhodesia (terminated 21 December 1979); Sudan (WTO observer); and former Yugoslavia (terminated 1 October 1996). WTO observers must start accession negotiations within five years of becoming observers. See www.un.org and www.wto.org.

[76] UN Charter, preamble and Article 1.1.

[77] Chapter I (Purposes and Principles); Chapter V (The Security Council); Chapter VI (Pacific Settlement of Disputes); Chapter VII (Action with Respect to the Peace, Breaches of the Peace, and Acts of Aggression); Chapter VII (Regional Arrangements); Chapter XI (Declaration regarding Non-Self-Governing Territories).

Thus, it has been (successfully) argued that 'self-help' in the context of the WTO (that is, unilateral retaliation) is inconsistent with Article 23.1 of the DSU (which requires WTO Members to have recourse to and abide by the DSU when they seek redress of any violation), and that this is underpinned by the principle of the peaceful settlement of disputes in accordance with international law enshrined in Article 1.1 of the UN Charter.[78] In *US – Tuna (Mexico)* New Zealand argued that the US measure effectively imposed US environmental standards on other countries, inconsistently with the principle, expressed in Article 2.7 of the UN Charter, of non-intervention in the domestic jurisdiction of states.[79] Similarly, in *US – Shrimp* India, Pakistan and Thailand argued that, pursuant to Article 31(c) of the Vienna Convention, Articles 1.2, 2.1 and 2.7 of the UN Charter were applicable law between the parties, and recognised the sovereign equality of states and the principle of non-interference in the internal affairs of another state, supporting the view that the US measure should not be considered covered by the exceptions in Article XX(b) or XX(g) of the GATT 1994.[80] In *India – Quantitative Restrictions* India referred to the UN Charter when contending that a general principle of institutional balance was relevant to interpreting and applying the WTO agreements.[81] In *US – Continued Suspension* the Panel referred to Article 2.2 of the UN Charter in support of the proposition that good faith is a general principle of international law.[82]

There are also instances in which other UN documents have been adduced in dispute settlement. For example, in *EC – Tariff Preferences* the EC, within its system of generalised preferences for developing and least-developed countries, provided for differentiation in favour of certain countries as an incentive to combat drug trafficking. This was found inconsistent with Article I of the GATT 1994 and the instruments establishing the Generalised System of Preferences (GSP) system. The EC

[78] Panel Report, *US – Section 301 Trade Act*, paras 5.230–1. The Panel ultimately found against the US. The Panel Report in *EC – Commercial Vessels* also found that the EC had acted inconsistently with Article 23.1 DSU (paras 7.208–7.222). Similar sentiments might support the case law confirming that no specific action against dumping or subsidies is permitted, other than as provided for in the Anti-Dumping Agreement and the SCM Agreement.

[79] GATT Panel Report, *US – Tuna (Mexico)*, unadopted, para. 4.38.

[80] Panel Report, *US – Shrimp*, paras 3.104, 3.157, 3.161, 3.163, 3.167, 3.170 and 3.204.

[81] Appellate Body Report, *India – Quantitative Restrictions*, para. 9.

[82] Panel Report, *US – Continued Suspension*, n. 468; Panel Report, *Canada – Continued Suspension*, n. 468.

attempted to justify the measure under Article XX(b) of the GATT 1994 as necessary to protect human health. In doing so the EC referred to certain UN documents to support the argument that market access and alternative development is one component of the comprehensive strategy of the UN to combat drugs. The Panel carefully examined these documents, but ultimately concluded that the EC measure was not justified by Article XX(b).[83] One may also find other passing references to Article XXI(c) of the GATT 1994 or the UN Charter in the case law.[84] Notably, in *Canada – Aircraft* Canada referred to the express provisions in the ICJ Statute providing for discovery – in support of its argument that there was no discovery rule in WTO law.[85]

Thus, in my view, it is important for any WTO litigator to be aware of the content of the UN Charter. Whilst the relevant provisions may as a rule be expressed in general terms, and are unlikely in themselves to win cases, nevertheless they can be brought to bear in various ways in the context of litigation, adding weight to or colouring a case one way or another. As any litigator knows, cases do not generally reach the dispute stage unless there are different ways of looking at the matter, each of which appears reasonable at least from a non-legal perspective. Against that background, every little argument can help – and cases may be won simply through accumulating arguments in a manner that is more meticulous and imaginative than one's opponent.

Turning to the ICJ itself, there are numerous WTO cases referring to ICJ case law, for example:[86] in connection with the principle of *jura novit curia* (the court knows the law), according to which burden of proof relates to facts, not legal interpretations;[87] in support of the proposition

[83] Panel Report, *EC – Tariff Preferences*, paras 7.203–7.207.

[84] GATT Panel Report, *US – Tuna (Mexico)*, unadopted, para. 4.10; Panel Report, *Brazil – Aircraft (Article 21.5 – Canada II)*, Annex B-3, para. 52; Panel Report, *Mexico – Taxes on Soft Drinks*, p. C-41.

[85] Panel Report, *Canada – Aircraft*, n. 68.

[86] Or the Permanent Court of International Justice (PCIJ), which preceded it. We include here references by panels and the Appellate Body in WTO litigation. There are many further instances in which the parties or third parties have referred to the ICJ or PCIJ, and several GATT panel reports that also contain similar references.

[87] Appellate Body Report, *EC – Tariff Preferences*, para. 105 and n. 220; Panel Report, *EC – Export Subsidies on Sugar (Australia)*, n. 437; Panel Report, *EC – Export Subsidies on Sugar (Brazil)*, n. 437; Panel Report, *EC – Export Subsidies on Sugar (Thailand)*, n. 437; Panel Report, *US – Zeroing (Japan) (Article 21.5 – Japan)*, para. 7.7, referring to: *Military and Paramilitary Activities in and against Nicaragua (Nicaragua* v. *United States of America)*

that newspaper articles should be afforded little if any weight;[88] in support of the proposition that WTO rights cannot be considered relinquished unless that intention appears clearly from the document in question;[89] with respect to the interpretation of treaties authenticated in more than one language;[90] with respect to the value of precedent;[91] with respect to the interpretation of the term 'deliberations' in the context of open hearings;[92] with respect to the proposition that the burden of proof is on the party asserting the affirmative;[93] in declining to rule on the question of whether or not the 'precautionary principle' is a general principle of international law;[94] in support of the proposition that a state may not be bound to recognise a grant of nationality if it does not represent a genuine connection between the natural person and the state granting the nationality;[95] in dismissing a US claim that a panel had issued an 'advisory opinion';[96] in considering the possible relevance of the principle of *res judicata* (the matter is

(*Merits*) [1986] ICJ Rep 14, para. 29 (quoting *Fisheries Jurisdiction Case (United Kingdom of Great Britain and Northern Ireland* v. *Iceland) (Merits)* [1974] ICJ Rep 9 (para. 17)).

88 Panel Report, *China – Intellectual Property Rights*, n. 607.

89 Appellate Body Report, *EC – Bananas III (Article 21.5 – Ecuador II)/EC – Bananas III (Article 21.5 – US)*, n. 276, referring to *Temple of Preah Vihear (Cambodia* v. *Thailand) (Preliminary Objections)* [1961] ICJ Rep 32.

90 Appellate Body Report, *US – Softwood Lumber IV*, para. 59 and n. 50; Panel Report, *China – Auto Parts*, n. 357, referring to *Elettronica Sicula S.p.A. (ELSI) (United States* v. *Italy) (Merits)* [1989] ICJ Rep 15 (para. 132).

91 Panel Report, *Argentina – Textiles and Apparel*, n. 175; Panel Report, *India – Patents (EC)*, n. 106; Appellate Body Report, *US – FSC*, n. 120; Appellate Body Report, *Japan – Alcoholic Beverages II*, pp. 12–15; Panel Report, *US – Upland Cotton*, n. 1141; Appellate Body Report, *US – Stainless Steel (Mexico)*, n. 308, referring to Article 59 of the ICJ Statute.

92 Panel Report, *US – Continued Suspension*, n. 350; Panel Report, *Canada – Continued Suspension*, n. 343, referring to Article 49 of the ICJ Statute.

93 Appellate Body Report, *US – Wool Shirts and Blouses*, p. 14; Appellate Body Report, *Japan – Agricultural Products II*, para. 121; Panel Report, *US – Certain EC Products*, n. 154; Appellate Body Report, *Canada – Dairy (Article 21.5 – New Zealand and US II)*, para. 64; Appellate Body Report, *Japan – Apples*, para. 154; Panel Report, *US – Gambling*, para. 6.12; Panel Report, *US – Shrimp (Ecuador)*, n. 22; Panel Report, *Turkey – Rice*, para. 7.3; Panel Report, *US – Continued Suspension*, para. 7.382; Panel Report, *Canada – Continued Suspension*, para. 7.379.

94 Appellate Body Report, *EC – Hormones*, paras 123–124; Panel Report, *EC – Biotech*, n. 261, referring to *Gabčíkovo-Nagymaros Project (Hungary* v. *Slovakia)* [1997] ICJ Rep 7 (paras 140, 111–114).

95 Panel Report, *EC – Trademarks and Geographical Indications (Australia)*, n. 217; Panel Report, *EC – Trademarks and Geographical Indications (US)*, n. 180 referring to *Nottenbohm Case (Liechtenstein* v. *Guatemala) (Second Phase)* [1955] ICJ Rep 4.

96 Appellate Body Report, *US – Offset Act (Byrd Amendment)*, n. 135, referring to the ICJ Statute.

decided) in WTO dispute settlement;[97] in support of the proposition that a treaty be interpreted so as to give meaning and effect to all its provisions;[98] in support of the proposition that ordinary meaning is to be determined in the context of the treaty as a whole;[99] in a discussion of the assessment of 'circumstantial evidence';[100] in considering the principle of *estoppel*;[101] in finding that panels may and must consider jurisdictional issues at any time;[102] in considering that the question of the interpretation of municipal law is ultimately a matter for WTO judges;[103] in recognising and applying the concept of error in the conclusion of a treaty;[104] in considering that panels have the authority to draw adverse inferences from a refusal to provide information;[105] in considering that a panel had no authority to

[97] Panel Report, *India – Autos*, para. 7.62 and nn. 336 and 337, referring to: Articles 59 and 60 of the ICJ Statute and the *Haya de la Torre* case ([1951] ICJ Rep 77).

[98] Panel Report, *Korea – Dairy*, para. 7.37 and n. 421; Panel Report, *Canada – Patent Term*, para. 6.49 and n. 30; Panel Report, *US – Section 211 Appropriations Act*, footnote 122, referring to: *Corfu Channel* Case [1949] ICJ Rep 24; and *Territorial Dispute* Case (*Libyan Arab Jamahiriya* v. *Chad*) [1994] ICJ Rep 23.

[99] Appellate Body Report, *Japan – Alcoholic Beverages II*, n. 19; Appellate Body Report, *Korea – Dairy*, para. 81 and n. 44; Panel Report, *US – Cotton Yarn*, para. 7.46 and n. 220, referring to: *Ambatielos Case* [1953] ICJ Rep 10; *Reservations to the Convention on the Prevention and Punishment of the Crime of Genocide* [1951] ICJ Rep 15; and *Rights of Nationals of the United States of America in Morocco* [1952] ICJ Rep 176, 196–199.

[100] Panel Report, *Argentina – Hides and Leather*, para. 11.28 and n. 340, referring to: the judgment of the ICJ in the *Corfu Channel Case* (Merits), Judgment of 9 April 1949, [1949] ICJ Rep 18.

[101] Panel Report, *EC – Asbestos*, para. 8.60 and n. 45, referring to: the decision by the ICJ in the *North Sea Continental Shelf Cases* [1969] ICJ Rep 3, 26 (para. 30).

[102] Appellate Body Report, *US – 1916 Act*, para. 54 and n. 30, referring to: *Case Concerning the Administration of the Prince von Pless (Preliminary Objection)* (1933) PCIJ Series A/B, No. 52, p. 15; Individual Opinion of President Sir A. McNair, *Anglo-Iranian Oil Co. Case (Preliminary Objection)* [1952] ICJ Rep 116; Separate Opinion of Judge Sir H. Lauterpacht in *Case of Certain Norwegian Loans* [1957] ICJ Rep 9, p. 43; and Dissenting Opinion of Judge Sir H. Lauterpacht in the *Interhandel Case (Preliminary Objections)* [1959] ICJ Rep 6, 43.

[103] Panel Report, *US – Section 301 Trade Act*, n. 635; Panel Report, *US – 1916 Act (EC)*, para. 6.53 and nn. 328 and 329; Panel Report, *US – 1916 Act (Japan)*, para. 652 and nn. 455 and 456, referring to: *Case Concerning Elettronica Sicula S.p.A. (ELSI)* (*United States of America* v. *Italy*) [1989] ICJ Rep 15, 47 (para. 62); and *Brazilian Loans*, PCIJ, Series A, Nos. 20/21, p. 124.

[104] Panel Report, *Korea – Procurement*, para. 7.123 and nn. 764 and 765, referring to: *Legal Status of Eastern Greenland* (1933) PCIJ, Series A/B, No. 53, p. 22, at p. 71 and dissenting opinion of Judge Anzilotti, at pp. 91–92; and *Case concerning the Temple of Preah Vihear* [1962] ICJ Rep 6, 26–27.

[105] Appellate Body Report, *Canada – Aircraft*, para. 202 and n. 128, referring to: *The Corfu Channel Case* [1949] ICJ Rep 4, 18; *Case Concerning Military and Paramilitary Activities In and Against Nicaragua* [1986] ICJ Rep 14, 82–86, paras 152, 154–156; and *Case*

direct the EC to participate as a party or third party in a dispute between India and Turkey regarding a Turkish measure implementing a bilateral agreement between the EC and Turkey;[106] in support of the proposition that the term 'natural resources' in Article XX(g) of the GATT 1994 is by definition evolutionary, and that a treaty must be interpreted and applied within the framework of the entire legal system prevailing at the time of interpretation;[107] in support of the proposition that good faith and *pacta sunt servanda* (agreements must be kept) are general principles of international law;[108] in referring to the principle of *in dubio mitius*, according to which, if a treaty term is ambiguous, the interpretation that is less onerous to the party undertaking the obligation is to be preferred;[109] in considering whether or not litigants must have a legal interest in bringing a case;[110] and in support of the proposition that the general rule of interpretation in Article 31 of the Vienna Convention has attained the status of a customary rule of interpretation of public international law.[111] There are

Concerning The Barcelona Traction, Light and Power Company, Limited [1970] ICJ Rep 3, 215 (para. 97).

[106] Panel Report, *Turkey Textiles*, para. 9.5 and n. 243, referring to: the practice of the ICJ in the *Military and Paramilitary Activities in and Against Nicaragua* case [1984] ICJ Rep 392, 430–431; and the *Phosphate Lands in Nauru* case [1992] ICJ Rep 240, 259–262 (preliminary objections).

[107] Appellate Body Report, *US – Shrimp*, para. 130 and n. 109, referring to: *Namibia (Legal Consequences) Advisory Opinion* [1971] ICJ Rep 31; and *Aegean Sea Continental Shelf Case* [1978] ICJ Rep 3.

[108] Panel Report, *US – Shrimp*, para. 7.41 and n. 644, referring to: judgment of the ICJ of 27 August 1952 in the *Rights of Nationals of the United States of America in Morocco* [1952] ICJ Rep 176, 212.

[109] Appellate Body Report, *EC – Hormones*, para. 165 and n. 154, referring to *Nuclear Tests Case (Australia* v. *France)* [1974] ICJ Rep 267; *Access of Polish War Vessels to the Port of Danzig* (1931) PCIJ, Series A/B, No. 43, p. 142; *USA – France Air Transport Services Arbitration* (1963) 38 ILR 243 (Arbitral Tribunal); and *De Pascale Claim* (1961) 40 ILR 250 (Italian – United States Conciliation Commission). In my view, this proposition, which may conflict with the proposition that all treaty terms should normally be given effectiveness, is particularly ill-suited to a multilateral treaty constituting a complex balance of rights and obligations, such as the WTO.

[110] Appellate Body Report, *EC – Bananas III*, para. 133 and n. 66, referring to: the ICJ and PCIJ Judgments in: the *South West Africa Cases* (Second Phase) [1966] ICJ Rep 4; the *Case Concerning the Barcelona Traction, Light and Power Company, Limited* (Second Phase) [1970] ICJ Rep 4; the *Mavrommatis Palestine Concessions Case*, PCIJ (1925) Series A, No. 2, p. 1; the *S.S. 'Wimbledon'* case, PCIJ (1923) Series A, No. 1, p. 1; the *Case Concerning the Northern Cameroons* [1963] ICJ Rep 4.

[111] Appellate Body Report, *US – Gasoline*, p. 17 and n. 34, referring to: *Territorial Dispute Case (Libyan Arab Jamahiriya* v. *Chad)* [1994] ICJ Rep 6.

also a number of references to other international courts.[112] Further, there are many references to academic publications.[113]

It is particularly interesting to see how this material is surfacing in WTO litigation without there necessarily being a systematic discussion of the legal basis on which it is being cited. Certainly some, but not all, of these cases might be taken to reflect general principles of international law – but even that observation does not provide a complete explanation for their inclusion. Again, one has the impression that difficult doctrinal discussions about applicable law and the rules of interpretation might be overlooking the fact that, in the background, international law is steadily trickling into the WTO *acquis*, apparently without any of the WTO Members taking particular exception.[114]

[112] See, e.g. Panel Report, *US – Continued Suspension*, n. 350 and Panel Report, *Canada – Continued Suspension*, n. 343 (ITLOS and the International Criminal Tribunal for the Former Yugoslavia); Panel Report, *US – Stainless Steel (Mexico)* (by the EC) (the European Court of Human Rights (ECtHR), the ICJ, ITLOS, the International Criminal Tribunal for the Former Yugoslavia (ICTY), the International Criminal Tribunal for Rwanda (ICTR), the International Criminal Court (ICC) and the International Centre for Settlement of Investment Disputes (ICSID)); Panel Report, *EC – Biotech*, n. 262 (ITLOS); Appellate Body Report, *US – Stainless Steel (Mexico)*, n. 313 (ICTY, ICC and ICSID); Appellate Body Report, *US – Gasoline*, n. 34 (ECtHR).

[113] See, e.g. Panel Report, *US – Section 110(5) Copyright Act*, n. 114 (panel takes into account 'teachings of the most highly qualified publicists' within the meaning of Article 38(d) of the ICJ Statute as a 'subsidiary source for the determination of law'); Panel Report, *EC – Trademarks and Geographical Indications (Australia)*, paras 7.196–7.197 (genuine connection between person and state for grant of nationality); Panel Report, *India – Autos*, para. 7.62 and n. 336 (*res judicata*); Panel Report, *Canada – Patent Term*, para. 6.49 and n. 30 and Panel Report, *US – Section 211 Appropriations Act*, n. 122 (effective interpretation of treaties); Appellate Body Report, *Korea – Dairy*, para. 81 and n. 44; Panel Report, *US – Cotton Yarn*, para. 7.46 and n. 220 (ordinary meaning to be determined in context of whole treaty); Panel Report, *EC – Asbestos*, para. 8.60 and n. 45 (estoppel); Appellate Body Report, *US – 1916 Act*, para. 54 and n. 30 (panel must consider jurisdictional issues at any time); Appellate Body Report, *Canada – Aircraft*, para. 202 and n. 128 (panel authority to draw adverse inference from refusal to provide information); Panel Report, *Australia – Automotive Leather*, n. 210 (press reports as evidence); Appellate Body Report, *US – Shrimp*, para. 130 and n. 109 (evolutionary nature of term 'natural resources'); Panel Report, *Indonesia – Autos*, para. 14.28 and n. 649 (conflicts between treaties in public international law – GATT 1994 and the SCM Agreement); Appellate Body Report, *EC – Hormones*, para. 165 and n. 154 (*in dubio mitius*).

[114] But see, e.g. TN/DS/W/82 (24 October 2005), Negotiations on Improvements and Clarifications of the Dispute Settlement Understanding, Communication from the United States (seeking to limit the role of other international law in WTO dispute settlement).

3. *The OECD Arrangement on Officially Supported Export Credits*

The next document I would like to discuss is the OECD Arrangement on Officially Supported Export Credits (OECD Arrangement).[115] I find this document, and its treatment in WTO law, of particular interest for a number of reasons. First, it conceives of itself as a non-binding document, and yet the WTO has effectively transformed it into a binding treaty – a fascinating precedent for much other international soft-law that is out there and potentially relevant in WTO disputes. Second, I am struck by the way in which the content of the document, once it has accessed the WTO regime, seems to have spilled over and become relevant for the interpretation of other WTO provisions, including the core disciplines of the SCM Agreement. Third, I find it interesting to see how, through the process of interpretation, the WTO has effectively taken from this document what the WTO apparently approves of, and rejected what it apparently finds unacceptable.

To recall, the SCM Agreement prohibits export subsidies,[116] but not an export credit practice that is in conformity with the interest rate provisions of an international undertaking on official export credits to which at least twelve original Members to 'this Agreement' are parties as of 1 January 1979 (or a successor undertaking which has been adopted by those original Members).[117] This provision has been found to refer to the OECD Arrangement.[118]

[115] The OECD Arrangement (also originally referred to as the OECD Consensus) emerged gradually in the margins of annual IMF and World Bank meetings, and was brought into the ambit of the OECD in the late 1970s. It has been frequently modified (see, for recent examples, OECD documents: TD/PG(2004)12/REV, 27 January 2005; TD/PG(2005)38/FINAL, 5 December 2005; TAD/PG(2007)18, 17 August 2007; TAD/PG(2007)28/FINAL, 21 December 2007). The most recent version is the Arrangement on Officially Supported Export Credits, OECD, TAD/PG(2009)6, 16 February 2009. Annexed to the OECD Arrangement are Sector Understandings on ships, nuclear power plants, civil aircraft, and renewable energies and water projects. The development of the OECD Arrangement is described in detail in *The Export Credit Arrangement, Achievements and Challenges 1978–1998* (OECD, 1988) and in Janet West, *OECD, The Export Credits Arrangement 1978–2008 – Achievements and Challenges Continued* (OECD, 2008), see www.oecd.org/dataoecd/17/24/40594872.pdf.

[116] SCM Agreement, Article 3.1(a): 'Except as provided in the Agreement on Agriculture, the following subsidies, within the meaning of Article 1, shall be prohibited: (a) subsidies contingent, in law or in fact, whether solely or as one of several other conditions, upon export performance, including those illustrated in Annex I ...' (footnotes omitted).

[117] SCM Agreement, Annex I, item (k), second paragraph (the so-called 'safe haven').

[118] Appellate Body Report, *Brazil – Aircraft*, para. 180.

The main purpose of the OECD Arrangement is to provide a framework for the orderly use of officially supported export credits[119] – it has been described, at least in its inception, as a creditors' cartel for developed countries. It seeks to eliminate competition between Participants in the provision of official support for export credits; and thus encourage competition between exporters on the basis of the quality and price of the exported goods. It applies to officially supported export credits with repayment terms of two years or more; and also regulates trade-related tied aid and partially untied aid. Military equipment and agricultural commodities are excluded. The OECD Arrangement limits the terms and conditions of export credits that benefit from official support (maximum repayment terms, minimum interest rates, minimum premium rates (MPRs), etc.).[120]

The term 'this Agreement' in item (k) refers to the SCM Agreement,[121] notwithstanding the fact that this language has been carried over directly from the plurilateral Tokyo Round Subsidies Code.[122] The twelve original Participants in the OECD Arrangement (that is, 'parties as of 1 January 1979')[123] all acceded to the SCM Agreement on 1 January 1995. The Sector Understandings have to date been assumed to be integral to the OECD Arrangement or to be 'successor undertakings' within the meaning of item (k).[124] Any WTO Member that conforms 'in practice' to the OECD Arrangement can benefit from the safe haven provided by item (k), whether or not they are Participants in the OECD Arrangement. However, the parameters of that safe haven are effectively determined

[119] OECD Arrangement (TAD/PG(2009)6), Article 1(a).

[120] The minimum interest rates are based on Commercial Interest Reference Rates (CIRRs). There is a CIRR for the currency of each Participant, based on long-term bond yields for that Participant plus a fixed margin.

[121] The 'original Members' in this sense are those acceding to the WTO Agreements on 1 January 1995. The list of WTO Members on the WTO website indicates the dates of accession (www.wto.org).

[122] Tokyo Round Subsidies Code, Annex, item (k), second paragraph. The original signatories of the Tokyo Round Subsidies Code are listed in GATT, *Analytical Index: Guide to GATT Law and Practice* (updated 6th edn, 1995), Vol. 2, App. VII, Acceptances of Tokyo Round Agreements.

[123] Australia, Canada, EC, Finland, Greece, Japan, Norway, Portugal, Spain, Sweden, Switzerland and the US (Janet West, *OECD, The Export Credits Arrangement 1978–2008*).

[124] See: Panel Report, *Canada – Aircraft (Article 21.5 – Brazil)*, n. 69; Panel Report, *Brazil – Aircraft (Article 21.5 – Canada)*, n. 51). The Sector Understanding on Export Credits for Civil Aircraft (in which Brazil, a non-OECD Member, is a Participant since 2007) provides expressly that it is an 'integral part' of the OECD Arrangement and that it succeeds the preceding Understanding.

by the limited number of WTO Members that are OECD *Arrangement* Participants.

The OECD Arrangement describes itself as a 'Gentlemen's Agreement among the Participants'[125] and 'not an OECD Act'.[126] It is not signed by the Participants; there is no provision for ratification; no dispute settlement; no procedures designed to ensure its proper application; and its interpretation is managed by the Participants acting unanimously. This ambiguous 'soft law' status of the OECD Arrangement appears to have been preferred by the Participants in pursuit of the objectives of flexibility and pragmatism.[127] However, through the cross-reference in the SCM Agreement, the OECD Arrangement has been considered to determine rights and obligations of WTO Members and has been interpreted and applied in the context of WTO dispute settlement, including disputes involving WTO Members that are not Participants in the OECD Arrangement.[128] Aside from that direct legal incorporation by reference, there are other significant channels of interaction.[129] Thus, the WTO has observer status in the OECD Working Party on Export Credits and Credit Guarantees,[130] which is a subsidiary body of the OECD Trade Committee, and which provides a forum for technical discussion of issues in advance of negotiations between the Participants of the OECD Arrangement.[131] The OECD has observer status in numerous WTO bodies and committees.[132]

[125] The current nine Participants in the OECD Arrangement itself are: Australia, Canada, the European Community, Japan, Korea, New Zealand, Norway, Switzerland and the United States, although other OECD Members may be invited to become Participants (OECD Arrangement 16 February 2009 (TAD/PG(2009)6), paragraph 3). Of the current 30 OECD Members, leaving aside countries that are EU Members, only Iceland, Mexico and Turkey are OECD Members but not Participants in the OECD Arrangement (www.oecd.org). OECD countries account for 78% of world gross national income and 68% of world trade (OECD Annual Report 2008). Only six of the nine are Participants in the *Sector Understanding on Export Credits for Ships*; and since 2007 Brazil (a non-OECD Member) is a Participant in the *Sector Understanding on Export Credits for Civil Aircraft*.

[126] OECD Arrangement 16 February 2009 (TAD/PG(2009)6), [2].

[127] John Ray, 'The Arrangement from the Inside' in OECD, *The Export Credit Arrangement: Achievements and Challenges 1978–1998* (1988) 33.

[128] Panel Report, *Canada – Aircraft (Article 21.5 – Brazil)*, [5.79] and n. 67. The fact that item (k) speaks of 'undertaking', 'parties' and 'adopted', whilst the OECD Arrangement speaks of 'Arrangement' or 'Gentlemen's Agreement', 'Participants' and does not speak of 'adoption', has not been considered a bar to this interpretation.

[129] See Margaret A. Young, 'Fragmentation or Interaction: The WTO, Fisheries Subsidies and International Law' (2009) 8 *World Trade Review* 477, 502–506.

[130] Originally the OECD Group on Export Credits and Credit Guarantees.

[131] www.oecd.org. [132] www.wto.org.

The OECD Arrangement has featured prominently in a number of disputes under the SCM Agreement, notably the aircraft disputes between Canada and Brazil,[133] the *Korea – Commercial Vessels* case and the *US – Upland Cotton* cases.

In the *Brazil – Aircraft* case the Panel rejected Brazil's argument that the term 'material advantage' in the first paragraph of item (k) should be extensively interpreted in light of the assertion that the item (k) OECD safe-haven was designed by and for developed countries, and was too expensive for developing countries – so that there should be no material advantage if the terms of Brazil's measure were equivalent to the terms of potentially competing offers (in this case from Canada). The Panel considered that a developing country Member could under the second paragraph of item (k) provide interest rate support to reduce the interest rates on export credits to the levels allowed by the OECD Arrangement if it considered that direct financing at those rates was too expensive.[134] On appeal, the Appellate Body considered that the appropriate comparison to be made in determining whether a payment is used to 'secure a material advantage' within the meaning of paragraph 1 of item (k) is between the actual net interest rate and a market benchmark, one possible example being the rates set out in the OECD Arrangement.[135] Thus, the OECD Arrangement was considered relevant not only to the interpretation of the second paragraph of item (k) (where the implicit reference is found) but also the first paragraph of item (k), and thus, by further implication, Article 1 (definition of subsidy) and Article 14 (calculation of the amount of a subsidy in terms of benefit to the recipient) of the SCM Agreement; the equivalent provisions of the Agreement on Agriculture;[136] and Article 22 of the DSU, relating to the calculation of compensation or suspension of concessions equivalent to the level of nullification or impairment suffered.[137]

In *Canada – Aircraft (Article 21.5 – Brazil)* Canada argued that it had adopted Policy Guidelines ensuring that any future finance measures

[133] Since those disputes, Brazil, which is not a Member of the OECD, has become a Participant in the Sector Understanding on Export Credits for Civil Aircraft.

[134] Panel Report, *Brazil – Aircraft*, paras 7.29–37.

[135] See further above n. 120 and surrounding text.

[136] Agreement on Agriculture, Article 21(1): 'The provisions of GATT 1994 and of other Multilateral Trade Agreements in Annex 1A to the WTO Agreement shall apply subject to the provisions of this Agreement.'

[137] Whilst noting that the OECD Arrangement permits 'matching', the Appellate Body left open the question of whether or not this would be permitted by item (k): Appellate Body Report, *Brazil – Aircraft*, paras 180–187.

would conform to the OECD Arrangement. The Panel confirmed that eligibility for item (k)'s safe haven is defined entirely in terms of the OECD Arrangement and that it was necessary for the Panel to interpret certain provisions of the OECD Arrangement.[138] The Panel proceeded to interpret the term 'export credit practices' in item (k) broadly; to identify which provisions of the OECD Arrangement are 'interest rates provisions' within the meaning of item (k);[139] to reason that the item (k) safe haven was potentially only available to direct credits/financing, refinancing and interest rate support at fixed interest rates with repayment terms of two years or more; and that conformity would have to be judged by reference to the rules of the OECD Arrangement that support or reinforce the minimum interest rate.[140] The Panel's conclusion was that the safe haven is considerably narrower than argued by Canada, whose interpretation would be inconsistent with the overarching principles and purposes of the WTO Agreement and the SCM Agreement, introducing an imbalance to the detriment of developing countries.[141]

In the parallel *Brazil – Aircraft (Article 21.5 – Canada)* case Brazil repeated and the Panel again rejected Brazil's argument concerning 'material advantage',[142] findings that were confirmed on appeal.[143] In *Brazil – Aircraft (Article 21.5 – Canada II)* the Panel confirmed the analysis previously given in *Canada – Aircraft (Article 21.5 – Brazil)*.[144] The Panel also confirmed that the reference in item (k) is a dynamic reference, that is, to the most recent version of the OECD Arrangement.[145] The Panel found Brazil's revised measure to be in conformity with the SCM Agreement.

In *Korea – Commercial Vessels*, the Panel, confirming earlier case law with respect to item (k), declined to interpret items (k) and (j)[146] of Annex

[138] Panel Report, *Canada – Aircraft (Article 21.5 – Brazil)*, para. 5.79 and n. 67.

[139] The Panel conceived of these provisions much more narrowly than Canada – excluding in particular various exceptions or derogations, notably with respect to 'matching').

[140] Ibid., paras 5.80–5.127. [141] Ibid., para. 5.1401.

[142] In an extensive discussion of the Appellate Body Report in the original case, the Panel entertained the possibility that a below CIRR rate might not confer a material advantage (or benefit) if at a market rate, but concluded that Brazil had failed to demonstrate that: Panel Report, *Brazil – Aircraft (Article 21.5 – Canada)*, paras 6.74–6.106.

[143] Appellate Body Report, *Brazil – Aircraft (Article 21.5 – Canada)*, paras 59–77.

[144] Panel Report, *Brazil – Aircraft (Article 21.5 – Canada II)*, paras 5.92–5.118.

[145] Ibid., paras 5.72–5.91.

[146] Item (j), which is part of the illustrative list of export subsidies, reads as follows: 'The provision by governments (or special institutions controlled by governments) of export credit guarantee or insurance programmes, of insurance or guarantee programmes against increases in the cost of exported products or of exchange risk programmes, at

I of the SCM Agreement *a contrario* (that is, in the case of item (j), as also indicating that programmes that covered long-term costs are not export subsidies or not subsidies).[147] Item (j) has also been a key provision in the *US – Upland Cotton* litigation, and context for the interpretation of similar provisions in the Agreement on Agriculture.[148] In particular, the minimum premium rates (MPRs) in the OECD Arrangement have been considered relevant 'evidence' in the assessment under item (j).[149]

There are a number of comments one can make, by way of summary, about these legal provisions and the case law, which are of interest for the subject matter of this chapter. First, through the mandatory language of the second paragraph of item (k) and footnote 5 of the SCM Agreement, the OECD Arrangement existing on 1 January 1979 (which is not identified expressly, but which in fact is the only document capable of fulfilling the criteria set out in item (k)) and any successor undertakings have been considered applicable WTO law. This is so notwithstanding the fact that the second paragraph item (k) speaks of 'undertaking', 'parties' and 'adopted', whilst the OECD Arrangement speaks of 'Arrangement' or 'Gentlemen's Agreement', 'Participants' and does not speak of 'adoption'. Second, the reference to 'successor undertakings' in item (k) has been interpreted as dynamic, and to-date it has been assumed that this captures all modifications of the OECD Arrangement, including substantial changes to its provisions, scope and participants, as well as the Sector Understandings annexed to the OECD Arrangement. Third, the scope of the safe haven in the second paragraph of item (k) may be determined, within the parameters of that provision, by the current Participants in the OECD Arrangement. Fourth, a potential for 'conflict' clearly arises, not least since the OECD Arrangement may be interpreted and applied both by WTO panels and the Appellate Body, as well as by the Participants. Fifth, the Participant's response to this situation is ambivalent: whilst they appear to continue to value the flexibility inherent in the 'soft law' nature of the OECD Arrangement, at the same time they appear to welcome interaction with the WTO. Sixth, the WTO response has been to

premium rates which are inadequate to cover the long-term operating costs and losses of the programmes.'

147 Panel Report, *Korea – Commercial Vessels*, paras 7.207 and 7.310–7.313.

148 Panel Report, *US – Upland Cotton*, paras 7.800–7.869; Appellate Body Report, *US – Upland Cotton*, paras 658–674; Panel Report, *US – Upland Cotton (Article 21.5 – Brazil)*, paras 14.54–14.134 and 14.151–14.157; Appellate Body Report, *US – Upland Cotton (Article 21.5 – Brazil)*, paras 255–323.

149 Appellate Body Report, *US – Upland Cotton (Article 21.5 – Brazil)*, paras 303–306.

interpret the SCM Agreement and the OECD Arrangement in such a way as to integrate what is viewed positively[150] whilst at the same time rejecting what is viewed negatively.[151] Seventh, the implied reference to the OECD Arrangement in the second paragraph of item (k) has spilled over into other provisions of the SCM Agreement, such as the 'material advantage' language of the first paragraph of item (k) and item (j). This has in turn implied further spill-over to the core rules of the SCM Agreement relating to benefit (Article 1) and amount of benefit (Article 14) and thus the provisions of the DSU that relate to compensation and suspension of concessions (Article 22), as well as the similar provisions in the Agreement on Agriculture.

4. *International accounting standards*

The OECD Arrangement is 'soft' public international law, but it is interesting to note that it is not excluded that non-public international norms also find their way into the WTO legal system.[152] One example is the role of international accounting standards in the Anti-Dumping Agreement. The Anti-Dumping Agreement permits the imposition of an anti-dumping duty to offset injurious dumping, that is, the export of a product at a price below 'normal value' (the domestic price in the country of manufacture). If domestic prices are unreliable, normal value may be established on the basis of costs of production. Costs of production must normally be calculated on the basis of the records kept by the exporter, provided that such records are in accordance with the generally accepted accounting principles of the exporting country.[153] Typically, these refer to or are based upon international accounting standards (IAS) emanating from a body such as the International Accounting Standards Board (IASB).[154] In a number

150 I.e., CIRRs and disciplines on MPRs.

151 I.e., matching, whether in the context of the first or second paragraph of item (k), as inimical to the basic objectives of the SCM Agreement.

152 The legal assessment of private international norms within the WTO is, however, outside the scope of this chapter. For a recent discussion, see Steven Bernstein and Erin Hannah, 'Non-State Global Standard Setting and the WTO: Legitimacy and the Need for Regulatory Space' (2008) 11 *Journal of International Economic Law* 575.

153 Anti-Dumping Agreement, Article 2.2.1.1.

154 The International Accounting Standards Committee (IASC) Foundation is a not-for-profit, private sector body that raises funds to support the operations of the IASB as an independent accounting standard-setter. It is funded by a wide range of market participants from across the world's capital markets (www.ifrs.org/The+organisation/IASB+meetings.htm).

of WTO disputes, argument has been exchanged as to how to interpret such standards, and on the question of whether or not an investigating authority has been correct in concluding that relevant records were not in accordance with such standards.[155] Such standards have also arisen in other cases outside the field of anti-dumping.[156]

D. Further examples

1. *International law as fact or evidence of fact*

Another possibility for other international law to make an appearance in the WTO is when it appears as fact or evidence of fact.[157] Like other international law jurisdictions, the WTO is familiar with the proposition that, for the WTO, municipal law is fact.[158] Given that the boundaries between municipal law and international law are not always clear,[159] it is immediately apparent that the same must be true for other international law. More specifically, what can happen is that in WTO litigation a party adduces a non-WTO international law document (be it a treaty, secondary law, a court judgment, or some other type of document) as evidence of an asserted fact. There is no basis upon which a panel or the Appellate Body can lawfully ignore such a document when presented as evidence of an asserted fact. Panels must make an objective assessment of the matter before them, including an objective

155 Panel Report, *Egypt – Steel Rebar*, paras 7.229–7.230; Panel Report, *EC – Bed Linen (Article 21.5 – India)*, para. 183; Panel Report, *EC – Salmon (Norway)*, para. 4.178 and n. 636.

156 Panel Report, *Canada – Dairy (Article 21.5 – New Zealand and US II)*, para. 343 and n. 54; Panel Report, *Japan – DRAMs (Korea)*, nn. 86 and 164.

157 Trachtman, above n. 19, 140: 'general international law can affect WTO dispute settlement ... where it constitutes facts that are relevant under WTO law'.

158 See, e.g. Appellate Body Report, *US – Section 211 Appropriations Act*, paras 105–106. To be clear on a point that does not always emerge with clarity from subsequent case law, the *meaning* of municipal law is not fact. It makes little sense to speak of meaning as fact, since facts are sensed, whilst meaning is deduced. There may be evidence of meaning, other than the text of the municipal law itself, such as a judgment or administrative decision or academic article interpreting municipal law in a particular way. In such a case, the WTO fact is not 'municipal law means X', but rather that 'municipal court Y has interpreted municipal law as meaning X'. In deciding whether or not the measure at issue is WTO consistent a WTO judge must take such evidence into account, but it never determines the outcome of the assessment of conformity, which remains a question of the legal characterisation of the facts, and thus ultimately a matter for the WTO judge, both at first instance and on appeal.

159 An obvious example being EU law, and recalling that both the European Communities and its Member States are WTO Members.

assessment of the facts, which necessarily includes an objective assessment of the evidence.[160] A panel may question the probity of the document, or the extent to which it demonstrates the asserted fact, or the relevance of the asserted fact to the litigated matter, or the applicability of the obligation, but it must deliver an objective assessment, setting out the findings of fact, the applicability of the relevant provisions and the basic rationale behind any findings and recommendations that it may make.[161] The only other way that a panel can avoid referencing such document is if, on some other valid basis, it finds in favour of the party adducing the international law document. In such a case, it may happen that the other international law document in fact weighs significantly in persuading the panel, even if, in order to see how the outcome of the case chimes with such other international law document, one has to look beyond the panel's assessment, and beyond even the summary of the parties' arguments, to the parties' submissions themselves, if they have been made public.

To fully appreciate the potential of this type of submission, it is worth recalling that inconsistency with any WTO obligation can be demonstrated 'in law' or 'in fact'. Some WTO obligations, unnecessarily, spell this out. For example, the SCM Agreement prohibits subsidies contingent, in law or in fact, on export.[162] The Appellate Body has correctly observed that this constitutes a single legal standard, the question of whether the claim is framed in law or in fact being merely a question of different evidence.[163] The Appellate Body has also correctly observed that the same approach applies in the context of subsidies contingent on the use of domestic products, even though the relevant provision does not expressly refer to 'in law' or 'in fact'.[164] Other examples in the SCM Agreement include the rules on specificity, which provide that, notwithstanding the appearance of generality, a subsidy may 'in fact' be specific;[165] and the basis on which entrustment or direction (or more generally public involvement) may be demonstrated on the basis of all the facts[166] (particularly given that it can be very difficult for complaining Members to obtain information about subsidisation and its

160 DSU, Article 11.

161 Ibid., Articles 11 and 12.7.

162 SCM Agreement, Article 3.1(a) and n. 4.

163 Appellate Body Report, *Canada – Aircraft*, para. 167; Appellate Body Report, *Canada – Autos*, paras 99 and 107; Appellate Body Report, *Canada – Aircraft (Article 21.5 – Brazil)*, n. 46; Panel Report, *US – FSC*, para. 8.54.

164 Appellate Body Report, *Canada – Autos*, paras 140–142; Appellate Body Report, *EC – Bananas III*, para. 233 and n. 146.

165 SCM Agreement, Article 2.1(c).

166 See, e.g. Appellate Body Report, *US – DRAMs*, para. 158.

effects).[167] The same is true of any WTO claim: it can be couched in 'in law' terms or in 'in fact' terms, or both. To be clear, an 'in fact' inconsistency will not necessarily derive from the so-called 'head count' approach alone.[168] Rather, it is a question of adducing sufficient evidence of a set of facts that permit some other fact, of which there is no direct evidence, to be inferred.

Further, it is also worth recalling that there is a general obligation in WTO law to produce documents, particularly when requested,[169] failing which inferences may be drawn on the basis of the facts and evidence that are before the adjudicating body.[170]

These observations raise the question of what kind of relevant facts might be evidenced by documents emanating from other international law. This could include, for example, the potentially critical issues of both the existence and content of the measures at issue.[171] It might also include, for example, any fact that is relevant to the justification for the impugned measure, potentially bringing into play not only the general exceptions in Article XX of the GATT 1994,[172] but any other exception, or any agreement based in whole or in part on such exception (such as the SPS Agreement and the TBT Agreement),[173] or indeed, based on what I have said above about rights and obligations, potentially any provision in the covered agreements. It could also be relevant to questions of object and purpose (for example, *a contrario*, where the issue is the scope of WTO law, and there is another international agreement regulating the matter). It could also include issues regarding the knowledge of the opposing Member, which in turn can go to questions of good faith or estoppel.[174]

[167] See also the procedures in Annex V of the SCM Agreement for developing information concerning serious prejudice.

[168] Appellate Body Report, *Dominican Republic – Import and Sale of Cigarettes*, para. 96, reversing the panel's finding of inconsistency with Article III:4 of the GATT 1994 (imported products treated less favourably than domestic products), which was based only on the fact that sales of domestic cigarettes were greater than sales of imported cigarettes.

[169] Notably pursuant to Article 13 of the DSU, which provides a panel with the authority to seek information and technical advice from any individual or body it deems appropriate.

[170] Appellate Body Report, *Canada – Aircraft*, para. 202.

[171] E.g., the outcome in the *EC – Biotech* case depends entirely on the finding (erroneous in my view) that a 'moratorium' existed – a device that permitted the panel to avoid any detailed consideration of the science – and this finding is in turn based largely on declarations by certain groups of EC Member States that are neither part of the municipal laws of the EC Member States nor part of EC law.

[172] See, e.g. the discussion of *US – Shrimp* further below.

[173] The Agreement on Technical Barriers to Trade (TBT Agreement) is discussed in further detail at pp. 301–302 below.

[174] See further below the discussion of the 1992 Agreement in the *EC – Airbus* case.

Further, the distinction between fact and law is itself problematic.[175] We all have some sense of what a fact is (essentially, something that belongs to the realm of the senses and is susceptible to being demonstrated with evidence) and how it is distinct from a pure question of legal interpretation (which involves reconciling, through a balanced and exhaustive process of systematic and logical deduction, potentially conflicting treaty provisions, to arrive at an harmonious reading that gives meaning to all the relevant treaty terms). However, because of the categorical nature of all language, which is used both to reference facts and set out law, it can be difficult to distinguish a fact from a legal characterisation of a fact; and equally difficult to distinguish a legal characterisation of a fact from a legal interpretation. Fortunately, this tricky issue can usually be avoided, because the great majority of WTO treaty provisions do not call for a sharp distinction between fact and law. One notable exception is the rule, also common in other tiered judicial structures, that appeals may only be lodged on a point of law.[176] However, as is also equally common in other tiered judicial structures, especially where the appellate organ apparently wishes to take jurisdiction, the line between what might or might not be appealed can easily become blurred or even extinguished altogether, either through the device of treating legal characterisations of the facts as questions of law, or by allowing appeals in cases of gross error in the statement or assessment of the facts.[177] There does appear to be a trend in the propensity of the Appellate Body to engage in factual issues, consistent with a relatively young organ, with available resources, looking to take jurisdiction. Some of the recent Appellate Reports are particularly striking both for their length and the factual detail they address, also by way of 'completing the analysis'. If this line can be blurred in the context of appellate proceedings, it might also be blurred, albeit in a slightly different manner, in the context of international law being adduced in DSU proceedings. Thus, the proposed or effective status of the adduced international law might remain unclear: is it fact, or evidence, or could it be preparatory work, or context, or even applicable law – or could it perhaps be none of these?

An example of the various possibilities that arise is illustrated by the question of how the so-called 1992 Agreement will be dealt with in the *EC – Airbus* case. To recall, the WTO Agreement itself includes four

[175] See, e.g. Ronald J. Allen and Michael S. Pardo, 'The Myth of the Law – Fact Distinction' (2003) 97 *Northwestern University Law Review* 1769.

[176] DSU, Article 17.6. [177] Ibid., Article 11.

plurilateral agreements, two of which are still in force[178] and which constitute part of the single WTO Agreement, and which are also covered agreements.[179] It remains an open legal question whether a plurilateral signatory could invoke the provisions of one of these agreements as a defence in a DSU dispute initiated by a non-signatory, although that is probably not the case,[180] and in any event it is not easy to envisage such a scenario. Nevertheless, it is interesting to recall that the WTO agreements themselves are no stranger to the idea of agreements not concluded by all WTO Members being applicable law between parties to them in WTO dispute settlement.

One of the plurilateral agreements is the Agreement on Trade in Civil Aircraft (the 1979 Agreement).[181] In application of the 1979 Agreement the US and the EC concluded a bilateral agreement, the 1992 Agreement.[182] In the 1992 Agreement, the US and the EC agreed to accept certain government measures taken by the other party in this sector. Thus, the EC accepted certain US measures with respect to Boeing, and the US accepted certain royalty-based financing[183] of Airbus by EC Member States. On 6 October 2004 the US purported to terminate the 1992 Agreement and subsequently commenced litigation against the EC under the SCM Agreement, also with respect to measures adopted by the EC pursuant to the 1992 Agreement. As part of its defence, the EC invokes the 1992 Agreement both as context for the interpretation of the SCM Agreement, but also as fact. Specifically, the EC argues that, in assessing the US claim that royalty-based financing is a prohibited export subsidy 'in fact', the panel must take into consideration all the relevant facts, which include the 1992 Agreement. The EC asserts that the plausibility of the US assertions regarding the interpretation and application of footnote 4 of the SCM Agreement must be considered in the light of the fact that for some ten years the US concluded an agreement with the EC specifically providing

[178] The Agreement on Trade in Civil Aircraft and the Agreement on Public Procurement.

[179] WTO Agreement, Annex 4; *DSU*, Article 1.1 and Appendix 1. See Panel Report, *Korea – Government Procurement* (the only dispute concerning the Agreement on Government Procurement).

[180] WTO Agreement, Article II:3.

[181] The Agreement on Trade in Civil Aircraft, done at Geneva on 12 April 1979 (BISD 26S/162), as subsequently modified, rectified or amended.

[182] Agreement between the European Economic Community and the Government of the United States of America concerning the application of the GATT Agreement on Trade in Civil Aircraft on trade in large civil aircraft, OJ L 301/32 of 17 October 1992.

[183] In royalty-based financing a loan is extended to finance the development of a new aircraft, the loan being repaid in increments as the aircraft are subsequently sold.

for the adoption of such measures. It remains to be seen how the panel and eventually the Appellate Body may deal with this issue.

2. *International law as evidence of meaning*

A slightly different approach is the proposition that international law can be taken into account as 'evidence' of meaning. In the *EC – Biotech* case the EC invited the panel to interpret the WTO law at issue consistently with specific provisions of the 1992 Convention on Biological Diversity and the 2000 Cartagena Protocol on Biosafety to the Convention on Biological Diversity, as well as the 'precautionary principle' as a general principle of international law. The panel refrained from considering the 'precautionary principle' a general principle of international law.[184] Furthermore, the panel considered that the term 'parties' in Article 31(3)(c) of the Vienna Convention referred to all the parties to the WTO Agreements, rather than the parties to the dispute, and observed that in any event not all parties to the dispute were parties to those other international agreements. Significantly, I think, the panel was (understandably) unable to ascertain how the specific provisions referenced by the EC would affect the interpretation of the relevant provisions of the SPS Agreement, or otherwise contribute to resolving the dispute. The SPS Agreement itself adequately set the legal framework for addressing the disagreement between the parties. However, the panel stated that, pursuant to Article 31(1) of the Vienna Convention, it would take into consideration other international agreements, including the Convention on Biological Diversity, as 'evidence' of the 'ordinary meaning' of terms used in the SPS Agreement.[185] The Panel considered that this was consistent with the Appellate Body Report in *US – Shrimp*.[186] The panel then proceeded to what was, in my

[184] I agree with that view, and see 'precaution' not as a balanced legal principle allowing one to determine the outcome of finely balanced cases, but rather as a one-sided slogan consistently invoked by the risk averse. (But see the recent reference to the 'precautionary principle' in Appellate Body Report, *US – Continued Suspension*, para. 680.)

[185] Which is what the panel did with respect to the information obtained from Codex, FAO, the IPPC Secretariat, WHO, OIE, the CBD Secretariat and UNEP. See: Panel Report, *EC – Biotech*, paras 7.64–7.96.

[186] In *US – Shrimp* (paras 127–134 the Appellate Body famously considered sea turtles to be 'exhaustible natural resources' within the meaning of Article XX(g) of the GATT 1994, notably referring, in doing so, to documents emanating from the World Commission on Environment and Development, UNCLOS, the Convention on Biological Diversity and the Convention on the Conservation of Migratory Species of Wild Animals.

view, an obviously over-extensive interpretation of the scope of the SPS Agreement, pursuant to which genetically modified organisms (GMOs) were capable of being 'pests', 'diseases', 'additives', 'contaminants' or 'toxins'; and any concern related to them would be capable of being 'other damage'[187] – although at the end of the day even if the panel had addressed some of the issues under the TBT Agreement the outcome of the dispute is likely to have been the same, notwithstanding the lesser role of science under the TBT Agreement.

The panel's proposition that other international law could be evidence of ordinary meaning is problematic. The Appellate Body has correctly observed that burden of proof relates to facts (and evidence is adduced to support facts), not the law (thus, including issues of legal interpretation, such as ordinary meaning).[188] Furthermore, dictionaries, particularly the *Oxford English Dictionary*, by reference to which the panel reasoned by extension, do not contain definitions, only examples of how words have been used, including shades of meaning, some ordinary, some special, amongst which the treaty interpreter will probably have to choose – and the same is likely to be true of documents emanating from other international regimes. The concepts of 'ordinary' and 'special' meaning are juxtaposed in the Vienna Convention,[189] and suggest the idea of a framework (or context) within which one can determine whether a particular meaning is normal or exceptional, begging the question of what the framework should be.[190] Significantly, if the advocated meaning turns out to be 'special' (an outcome that is a function of the context), the party advocating that meaning may have the burden of demonstrating that all the parties intended it – and if 'the parties' here means all the Members of the WTO, and the meaning is not apparent from the text, that may prove an exceptionally difficult task.

187 For a more detailed discussion, see Margaret Young, 'The WTO's Use of Relevant Rules of International Law: An Analysis of the *Biotech Case*' (2007) 56 *International and Comparative Law Quarterly* 907.

188 Appellate Body Report, *EC – Tariff Preferences*, para. 105 and n. 220; Panel Report, *EC – Export Subsidies on Sugar (Australia)*, n. 437; Panel Report, *EC – Export Subsidies on Sugar (Brazil)*, n. 437; Panel Report, *EC – Export Subsidies on Sugar (Thailand)*, n. 437; Panel Report, *US – Zeroing (Japan) (Article 21.5 – Japan)*, para. 7.7.

189 Vienna Convention, Article 31(1) ('A treaty shall be interpreted in good faith in accordance with the ordinary meaning to be given to the terms of the treaty in their context and in the light of its object and purpose') and Article 31(4) ('A special meaning shall be given to a term if it is established that the parties so intended').

190 To take a trivial example, and recalling the description of the UK and the US as two nations divided by a common language, the ordinary meaning of the term 'pants' is different depending on whether one is in London or New York.

As to what constitutes the context, sometimes the case law uses such language as 'the four corners of the agreement', and it is often observed that all of the single WTO Agreement is potential context, albeit relatively immediate or relatively remote. Thus, the proposition that one can look to another international agreement as 'evidence' of 'ordinary meaning' is hardly different from saying that such other document is relevant context, and even immediate context. Clearly, this could change the ordinary meaning; and could even result in a 'special meaning' being assimilated to an ordinary meaning. Furthermore, if the other international law document could be 'evidence' of 'ordinary meaning', then presumably it could also be 'evidence' of 'context', 'object and purpose', 'special meaning' or for that matter 'preparatory work' or 'good faith'.

In short, recalling that the title of Article 31 of the Vienna Convention refers to a single rule of interpretation, in which considerations relating to good faith, ordinary meaning, context, object and purpose and even the preparatory work are eventually to be assimilated, admitting other international law as 'evidence' of ordinary meaning may have the effect of admitting it more generally to the interpretative process, and even, indirectly, to the category of applicable law. It is not certain that such a process could be systematically managed in a way that would ensure the avoidance of arbitrary decisions. Nevertheless, following the *EC – Biotech* panel approach, the opportunity for litigants to pursue this line is there, at least until such time as the matter comes before the Appellate Body.

3. International law and expert advice: the SPS Agreement and the Hormones case

I would like to turn in further detail to the SPS Agreement. This is of interest for two particular reasons: first, its 'open' list of references to other relevant international agreements; and second, the role of international expert advice in litigation.

To recall,[191] unlike, for example, the SPS system within the EU, the WTO SPS Agreement does not require full international harmonisation: Members remain free to set their own appropriate level of protection

[191] For more detailed discussion of these issues, see, e.g. Alberto Alemanno, *Trade in Food: Regulatory and Judicial Approaches in the EC and the WTO* (Cameron May, 2007); George A. Bermann and Petros C. Mavroidis (eds.), *Trade and Human Health and Safety* (Cambridge University Press, 2006).

(acceptable level of risk), which may be zero.[192] How to reconcile the fact that the importing Member sets its own appropriate level of protection with the proportionality disciplines of Article 5.6 is the puzzle at the heart of the SPS Agreement. The legal rules simply frame a policy conflict which, requiring as it does a choice between incomparable imponderables, is eminently political, and thus essentially amenable to legislative but not judicial resolution. The judge can still address procedural issues, but addressing the substance of the matter in legal terms is very difficult. This is a problem that the EU has itself experienced within its own single market, when the European Court of Justice (ECJ) has been called upon to rule on similar questions as yet unregulated by Community legislation. All of the SPS disputes to date[193] have avoided this problem by focusing – excessively – on the science requirements of the risk assessment under Article 5.1 – an approach that generates a different set of problems about how judges deal, or can deal, with science. This imbalance has recently been corrected by the Appellate Body in principle.[194] It remains to be seen whether or not the next cases processed by the system faithfully reflect this correction.[195]

Against this backdrop, one may observe that other international bodies have an important role to play in the SPS Agreement. The Agreement recognises the important contribution that international standards, guidelines and recommendations can make to achieving its objectives, including (but not only) the Codex Alimentarius Commission, the International Office of Epizootics and the International Plant Protection Convention, and aims to further their use. SPS measures that conform to international standards are deemed necessary, and presumed consistent with the relevant provisions of the SPS Agreement and the

[192] SPS Agreement, sixth recital, Articles 3.3, 5.6 and Annex A, para. 5; Appellate Body Report, *US – Continued Suspension*, para. 523; Appellate Body Report, *Canada – Continued Suspension*, paras 523, 534 and 685; Appellate Body Report, *Australia – Salmon*, para. 125. Naturally, the scientifically identified risk cannot be zero or purely theoretical (Appellate Body Report, *EC – Hormones*, para. 186).

[193] *EC – Hormones, Australia – Salmon, Japan – Agricultural Products, Japan – Apples, EC – Biotech.*

[194] Appellate Body Report, *US – Continued Suspension*; Appellate Body Report, *Canada – Continued Suspension.*

[195] For the time being, the EC and the US have concluded a provisional agreement in the *Hormones* dispute; the *Australia – Apples* dispute is pending; the US have requested consultations with the EC in *EC – Poultry*; China has requested a panel in *US – Poultry*; and there is some discussion about how cloning techniques being developed particularly in the US will be received in the EC.

GATT 1994. Risk assessments must take into account risk assessment techniques developed by such international organisations; and provisional measures are to be adopted on the basis of, *inter alia*, available pertinent information from the relevant international organisations. Members maintaining SPS measures not based on relevant international standards must provide an explanation for the measure. In disputes, expert advice may be obtained and the relevant international organisation consulted. WTO Members must play a full part, within the limits of their resources, to promote within such organisations the development and periodic review of such standards, guidelines and recommendations. The WTO SPS Committee monitors and coordinates such efforts; encourages the use of such standards, guidelines and recommendations; aims to increase international coordination and integration; maintains close contact with the relevant international organisations; and establishes a list of such standards, guidelines and recommendations.[196]

Thus, there is here as elsewhere in the covered agreements, essentially an incorporation by reference (albeit less apparent), making what is incorporated applicable law. This is especially so because Article 3.2 deems 'necessary' SPS measures that comply with international standards, thus arguably insulating them from further scrutiny under Article 5.6. Further, the Article 3.2 presumption of conformity with other provisions of the SPS Agreement would be likely to prove almost impossible to rebut. These are the incentives for Members to comply with international standards: they create a safe haven not unlike the one I have discussed in item (k) of Annex I to the SCM Agreement concerning the OECD Arrangement. In this respect, it is particularly striking to note that the list of international

[196] SPS Agreement, fourth and fifth recitals, Articles 3.2, 3.4, 3.5, 5.1, 5.7, 5.8, 11.2 and 12 and Annex A, paragraph 3. Another provision of the SPS Agreement that is of interest in the context of this chapter is Article 4, which provides for mutual recognition of the equivalence of SPS measures, and specifically Article 4.2, which requires Members upon request to enter into consultations with the aim of achieving bilateral and multilateral agreements in this area. This raises the question of how such bilateral or multilateral (but not WTO-wide) agreements might be relevant in a subsequent WTO dispute. The provision being directed towards recognition by the *importing* Member of the *exporting* Member's measure, one could envisage a situation in which such an agreement would be concluded, but not honoured by the importing Member (that is, the importing Member would continue to require the exporting Member to comply with the importing Member's measure). It would appear that such an agreement, and the failure to comply with it, might then become relevant, in fact if not in law, in proceedings directed against the importing Member's measure.

organisations is open, and extends to any international organisation open for membership to all WTO Members.[197]

It is also interesting to note how applicable law can here easily shade into context, or the preparatory work of the other referenced documents; and how fact or evidence or 'information' can easily shade into 'advice' and interpretation of such other documents. As the trade-oriented litigation has tended to focus on the 'soft-target' of finding something to disagree with in the way the science has been assessed (not such a difficult task), so the role of the science, and particularly the role of the scientists in providing advice, has become particularly important. Expert scientific advice has been sought in all the SPS cases. This systematically raises the difficult question of the role of the scientists in the litigation. Sometimes one is struck by how un-useful the advice can be.[198] On other occasions, in expressing general views about whether one or other measure might or might not be justified, scientists (we sometimes refer to them as 'political scientists') sometimes appear not to appreciate the point at which their role as scientists ends, and the role of the risk manager begins; or appear to welcome the opportunity to step into the unfamiliar arena of a court room and express their personal views. Thus, it is not easy to keep the advice being given to panels strictly within the confines of elucidating and rendering more accessible for the panel the scientific materials that have been submitted. And it is all too easy for a panel to be selective as to the advice it subsequently refers to.[199] This difficult aspect of dispute settlement has now spilled into the process by which the scientific advisors themselves are selected, as well-illustrated by the fact that, in *US – Continued Suspension* and *Canada – Continued Suspension*, the Appellate Body faulted the Panel for relying too heavily on 'advice' from experts who had themselves framed the international standard in question. In this respect, it is difficult to see what the future might hold. Perhaps panels will refer to a group of scientists, rather than individuals, or merely contact international organisations; or dispense with scientific

[197] SPS Agreement, Annex A, paragraph 3(d). Compare the interpretation of Article 31(3)(c) of the Vienna Convention in *EC – Biotech* as requiring all WTO Members to be parties to the other international agreement (Panel Report, *EC – Biotech*, paras 7.49–7.96). In *EC – Biotech* the panel sought information from CBD, Codex, FAO, IPPC, OIE, UNEP and WHO (Panel Report, *EC – Biotech*, para. 7.31).

[198] E.g. a statement such as 'the available evidence does not demonstrate a risk greater than the risk with respect to any other product' is both remarkably common and quite useless for a risk manager. It is the SPS equivalent of a 'local showers' weather forecast – whatever subsequently transpires, the advice cannot be faulted.

[199] As well illustrated by the Panel Report in *EC – Biotech*.

advice altogether, focusing instead on the legal issues in the litigation before them.

4. *International law and altering the burden of proof: the TBT Agreement and the Sardines case*

Finally, I would like to comment on alterations in the burden of proof, drawing upon examples from the TBT Agreement. What is true for the SPS Agreement is also often true for the TBT Agreement, which is structured in a broadly similar way, but with less emphasis on science, taking more account of the fact that harmonisation or standardisation processes may be considered, by definition, to some extent arbitrary.

Thus, the TBT Agreement recognises the important contribution that international standards can make to its objectives, and aims to encourage their development. Terms shall normally have the meaning given to them by definitions adopted within the UN system and by international standardising bodies. Members must use existing international standards unless ineffective or inappropriate for achieving the desired objective. Measures complying with international standards are rebuttably presumed not to create unnecessary obstacles to international trade. Members must play a full part, within the limit of their resources, in international standardising bodies. They must explain any departure from international standards. Similar considerations apply with respect to conformity assessment procedures.[200] The TBT Agreement also makes extensive reference to the 'ISO/IEC Guide 2',[201] which provides general terms and definitions regarding standardisation and related activities. Thus, like the SPS Agreement, the TBT Agreement creates a safe if not storm-proof harbour for measures that comply with other international agreements. And documents from other international regimes can be adduced as fact or evidence in disputes under the TBT Agreement.

Not surprisingly, other international materials have played a significant role in both of the main disputes under the TBT Agreement, albeit it in slightly different ways. Thus, in *EC – Asbestos*, considerable emphasis was placed on the evidence and advice emanating from other international

[200] TBT Agreement, third, fourth and eighth recitals and Articles 1.1, 2.4, 2.5, 2.9.3, 5.4, 5.5, 5.6, 6.11, 9.

[201] International Organization for Standardization, International Electrotechnical Commission. See TBT Agreement, Annex 1 (Terms and their Definitions for the Purposes of this Agreement) and Annex 3 (Code of Good Practice for the Preparation, Adoption and Application of Standards).

institutions.[202] In *EC – Sardines* Peru objected to an EC measure according to which only *Sardina pilchardus* (a fish common in European waters) could be marketed in the EC as 'sardines' and *Sardnops sagax* (a fish common in Pacific waters) could not be marketed as, for example, 'Peruvian sardines'. An international standard (Codex Stan 94) was found to be a 'relevant international standard' within the meaning of the TBT Agreement, notwithstanding the fact that it was not adopted by consensus. Based on a careful interpretation of that international standard the EC measure was found not to be 'based on' the international standard. Further, absent evidence that consumers in the EC associated the name 'sardines' with *Sardina pilchardus*, the Codex Stan 94 standard was found not 'ineffective or inappropriate' to fulfil the legitimate objectives of the EC measure, which was accordingly considered inconsistent with Article 2.4 of the TBT Agreement.[203]

This case is particularly interesting because in the end it was the EC that was placed in the position of having to adduce evidence to justify its measure. To recall, the relationship between both the SPS Agreement and TBT Agreement and the GATT 1994, and particularly its Articles III (discrimination between domestic production and imports) and Article XI (quantitative restrictions on imports) is controversial. On one view the SPS Agreement and TBT Agreement implement Article XX(b) of the GATT 1994, so a breach of GATT 1994 (such as Articles III or XI) must precede any discussion of these agreements. On another view (preferred by the panel in *EC – Hormones* and not for the time being appealed), these agreements are in effect 'stand alone', so it is not necessary to demonstrate any breach of GATT 1994 before considering the obligations under these agreements. The consequences are highly significant, given that, notably under Article III of the GATT 1994, a defending Member is not generally obliged to justify internal regulatory measures, provided that they apply equally to domestic production and to imports. However, if one proceeds directly to the TBT Agreement, then the consequence of the reference to international standards, with which EC was considered not to have complied, was to impose on the EC the obligation of proving consumer concerns about the correct use of the designation 'sardines'. In this subtle way, international law effectively determined the outcome of the case.

[202] Appellate Body Report, *EC – Asbestos*, paras 17, 29, 47, 114, 135, 151 and 162 (particularly the International Agency for Research on Cancer and the World Health Organization).

[203] Appellate Body Report, *EC – Sardines*, paras 217–291.

Conclusion

As a litigator moving continuously from one case to the next, under constant pressure to find arguments prejudicial in fact to the other side, without necessarily addressing in the written briefs 'deep theory' about the relationship between WTO law and other international law, one has the distinct impression that the WTO is, in fact, relatively open to interaction with other international law regimes. One also has the impression that, for those actually working on these cases in Geneva, the potential relevance of other international law is not something that is necessarily surprising or even problematic. This impression is comforted by the observation that there are established channels for interaction between the WTO and other international organisations capable of influencing the development of both WTO law and other international law regimes.

Against this background, perhaps it is not surprising that a sharp distinction is not always made in the case law between applicable law or sources of WTO law, various interpretative rules (context, preparatory work), and other international law as fact or evidence or altering the burden of proof.

In fact, there are numerous references from WTO law to other international law regimes, including soft-law and non-public norms, not all of which are express or evident. Furthermore, through such references, the role of the other international regime may become enhanced or may spill over to other areas. In addition, the proposition that other international law can be presented as fact or evidence is potentially relevant to any WTO provision. And there are several other examples of potential channels for international law to be received into WTO law, which are mentioned at the start of this chapter, but not further analysed.

These specific and essentially empirical, if incomplete, observations appear to coincide with and confirm – at least with respect to the WTO – the more general or theoretical statements by a number of other contributors to this book about recent or future developments, as well as the manner in which they consider that international law *should* evolve. That is, I do not present a thesis without examples; nor examples without a thesis[204] – but perhaps this material, together with the other examples I have referenced but not analysed, would be sufficient to support some general propositions about what has been happening in the past in the WTO and what is likely to continue happening in the future.

[204] Cf. Crawford and Nevill, Ch. 8 of this volume, p. 247.

Within the WTO, there would appear to be a range of legal mechanisms available to manage this process of interaction with other international law, reasonably capable of striking an appropriate balance between legal certainty and flexibility. Because of the mandatory jurisdiction and binding nature of WTO dispute settlement this process can contribute to the effectiveness of international law in general. But it can also make agreement in other international bodies more difficult. In my view, in the interests of security and predictability, WTO law, whilst remaining relatively open to other international law, should exercise particular rigour in determining whether or not such other international law is relevant to a particular WTO dispute, and, in this respect, WTO judges should pay very close attention to explaining the reasons for the approach they adopt in any particular case.

10

Hegemonic Regimes

MARTTI KOSKENNIEMI

'Regime interaction' – the expression is part of a managerial vocabulary that foregrounds the technical nature of social problems, connoting efficiency as the overriding value of the relevant complexes of norms and institutions ('regimes') and their nature as instruments of problem-solution.[1] A well-known problem with managerialism is its obsessive concentration on the outcome produced by the single institution (state, company, organisation, treaty-system, any other type of regime) and its lack of concern for the effects on the surrounding world, including other regimes. Talk about 'regime interaction' highlights awareness of this problem but suggests that it can be overcome by coordinating and adjusting the operation of single regimes so as to ensure the smooth functioning of the whole.

Coordination requires evaluation and hierarchy – the assessment of the value of individual regimes and their ultimate organisation in some order of priority. It cannot therefore be taken for granted that everybody would always immediately agree. The viewpoint from which a coordinating proposition is presented may not appear to come 'from nowhere' but may seem to embody a bias failing to give adequate consideration to some of the conflicting preferences. How to deal with disagreement? How to ensure that the coordinating proposal has *authority* vis-à-vis competing suggestions? To begin to discuss 'regime interaction', it is useful to take

[1] 'Managerialism' is an ideology under which the strategic leadership of an institution (or regime) is separated from its assumed beneficiaries in the belief that when a specialised elite of managerial experts carries out strategic choices, then the outcomes for the beneficiaries will be optimal. Under this view the regular staff of the institution is responsible only to the managerial leadership and its performance is assessed by criteria set down by it – criteria only looking for the optimal result. The application of managerialism in global governance, understood as 'administration' of particular territories (and populations) has been very usefully discussed in Anne Orford, 'Book Review Article: International Territorial Administration and the Management of Decolonization' (2010) 59 *International and Comparative Law Quarterly* 227.

a brief glance at the way law and political science have discussed interaction between those most familiar of regimes – 'states' – in the past.

A. Common good and individual goods

One way to deal with this would be to assume that the coordinating proposal embodies the 'common good' that also embodies the real or well-understood interests of each individual regime. This way of thinking captures the assumption that international relations experts have termed the 'harmony of interests' under which every conflict between states appeared as a superficial coordination problem, while at some more basic level the interests of states would remain identical or coterminous. Any *actual* conflict was to be properly seen either as a misunderstanding by the parties of their *real* interests or then arose from a deviant pursuit by somebody of their personal interests or those of their clan, as detached from the real (long-term) interest of their state. Under the 'harmony of interests', as described by its leading critic:

> [e]ach nation had its own special task for which its aptitudes fitted it, and the performance of this task was its contribution to the welfare of humanity. If all nations acted in this spirit, international harmony would prevail.[2]

The harmony of interests, applied in the world of sovereign states was – even in the somewhat caricaturised form presented by Carr – the home of various forms of inter-war legal idealism. It underlay, for example, a naturalist perspective that saw the world always already united by basic values, the principles of 'reason' or the 'nature' of humans that remained unchanging through space and time.[3] The task of international law was to enlighten states of those values and to direct their action into channels that would facilitate their attainment. In a non-naturalist vocabulary, it was expressed in the view that there was some will of the whole – the 'will

[2] E. H. Carr, *The Twenty Years' Crisis, 1919–1939: An Introduction to the Study of International Relations* (London, Macmillan, 2nd edn, 1946) 46.

[3] For an early example, see Alfred Verdross, *Die Einheit des recthlichen Weltbildes auf der Grundlage der Völkerrechtsverfassung* (Tübingen, 1923) and for a representative contemporary version, Christian Tomuschat, 'International Law: Ensuring the Survival of Mankind on the Eve of A New Century, General Course on Public International Law' (2001) 281 *Recueil des Cours de l'Académie de droit international* 63–72.

of the international community' – to which separate state policies should be made to conform.

The 'harmony of interests' was always dubious, however. It implied that if somebody were able – by whatever means – to grasp that common good or that general will, then there could be no plausible objection to having that person or institution rule the social whole, as this would be in the interests of the parts as well. Such a (Hobbesian) view was problematic in the way enlightened absolutism or real socialism are. But what is the alternative? Might it be possible to attain the general good in the absence of an 'ultimate' authority? This was achieved by the transformation of egoistic 'passions' to socially useful 'interests', as recounted by A. O. Hirschman, during early modernity. Owing to the loosening of the bounds of religion ('the viewpoint of the whole') it became increasingly unrealistic to expect that egoistic passions could be tamed by spontaneous altruism. Instead, it was suggested to check such passions by other passions, equally egoistic, but working in an opposite direction. In this way, they would simultaneously work for the good of the greatest number.[4] The history of capitalism (and international politics) can then almost be reduced to the single question of to what extent this process can be expected to take place spontaneously and what degree of involvement by an external regulator is needed.

What unites the 'harmony of interests' and the liberal (international relations) view is their assumption that the general good is the rightly understood good of each particular. They differ only in whether there is a spot (a person or an institution) that is able to seize it. For both, conflicts between states or between regimes emanate from problems of knowledge, not of political value, and are thus properly treated in scientific or economic vocabularies that seek to penetrate existing epistemic uncertainty. What would be needed, as a recent commentator puts this, is 'a coherent and disciplined theory', developed preferably through a 'social science methodology' that would possess 'sophisticated analytical techniques'.[5] Politics might of course intervene as ideology, irrationality or bad faith to complicate the calculus. But there would be no *fundamental* difference about the criteria to be applied. In the liberal (international relations) world, these would consist of techniques of social engineering that would

[4] Albert O. Hirschman, *The Passions and the Interests. Political Arguments for Capitalism before its Triumph* (Princeton University Press, 20th anniversary edn, 1997).

[5] Andrew Guzman, *How International Law Works. A Rational Choice Theory* (Oxford University Press, 2008) 187, 211.

persuade every actor of the 'rational' way to behave even when there is no sovereign to compel such behaviour.[6]

But why ought we to believe that there is a single 'rational' solution to every conflict – that is to say, a solution that would be rational for everyone in a certain situation – and that can be found by employing a specific 'methodology'? The answer is: we do not 'know' this in any clearly defined way. But we stick to the assumption because the alternative seems so problematic. If the clash of interests or values (or regimes) is not about knowledge but about radically incompatible preferences (including preferences about the method to be employed in resolving the conflict) – that is, if someone's interests can only be realised at the cost of someone else's – then no coordinating proposal or managerial decision can enjoy more than very weak authority, always amenable for contestation as ultimately favouring one regime over another without a valid justification. The 'general view' or the 'rational behaviour' will then appear as a grand name for just another preference with an epistemic status no higher than that of other preferences. It appears special only in that its proponents have been politically successful. Under this view, 'regime interaction' cannot be meaningfully reduced to technical coordination and the very suggestion that it can will appear as a linguistic strategy to make the speaker's preferences appear somehow natural because they are, for example, 'scientific' or 'methodological'. So phrased, there is no guarantee that everyone should agree in the end and that any eventual 'general view' would enjoy authority that would be distinct from the political power of its proponents.

B. Regime interaction in a world of states

'Regime interaction' captures themes from those older debates that concerned (and still concern) the interaction between states. As we have learned from international relations and international law, there are many ways in which states 'interact'. In the 1960s Wolfgang Friedmann famously juxtaposed the old view of relations he labelled the 'international law of coexistence' to a newer 'international law of cooperation', highlighting what he saw as a move from a confrontational juxtaposition under the conditions of the Cold War to a less conflict-prone world where states would be looking for increased cooperation in substantive areas

[6] For a manifesto in this regard, see Jack Goldsmith and Eric Posner, *The Limits of International Law* (Oxford University Press, 2005).

such as trade, technology and environment.[7] From a situation where hostile state-regimes were warily examining each other from behind a wall of fundamental political antagonism, content to coexist without major conflict, Friedman suggested, they were moving into a world where perception of shared interests would lead them to extend their hand across the Cold War divide.

Although the language of coexistence/cooperation has been firmly rooted in the analysis of the underlying conditions of the operation of international law,[8] the two nevertheless only mark a middle zone that is flanked by two more starkly juxtaposed alternatives of 'regime interaction' – namely 'war' and 'integration'. These two – war/integration – mark the limiting conditions of regime interaction between states: on the one side, complete alienation and absolute enmity, on the other, complete assimilation or identity. The vocabularies of international relations and international law (regime interaction in a world of states) have always been largely about how to live in the middle zone of reluctant or indifferent tolerance ('coexistence') and more or less enthusiastic pursuit of joint interests ('cooperation'). In conditions of war or integration international relations and international law are replaced by other vocabularies – the Clausewitzian consciousness of war's own rationality on the one hand, domestic law and the politics of national solidarity on the other.

International relations and international law are thus premised upon the assumption that states are able to interact within the grey zone between all-out war and complete integration. Indeed, much of the practice by the two disciplines is constituted by the effort to develop rules, techniques and strategies to fortify the middle zone against collapse over the margin, and to make life there as good as possible. But neither discipline has been content to assume that coexistence, cooperation or friendly competition would be attained spontaneously or that the actors were always acting bona fide. The degree to which motivations are selfish and cooperation is simply a name for not yet having developed the capacity for victory continues to be the object of polemics between more or less 'idealist' and 'realist' positions.

[7] Wolfgang Friedmann, *The Changing Structure of International Law* (London, Stevens & Sons, 1964).

[8] For a recent example, see Christian Brütsch and Dirk Leverkühl, 'Complex Legalization and the Many Moves to Law' in Christian Brütsch and Dirk Lehmkuhl (eds.), *Law and Legalization in Transnational Relations* (London, Routledge, 2007) 15–16.

C. 'Hegemony'

One conceptual tool that has been used to analyse the irreducibly political nature of tensions between actors engaged in ostensibly cooperative or competitive ventures has been that of 'hegemony'.[9] That notion may also be used to analyse the conditions under which functional regimes operate in political instead of technical terms. That the perspective offered by 'hegemony' is *political* means that it involves accepting that there is no such 'ultimate' or 'rational' ground in which conflicts between regimes and the right ways for actors to behave would *already* have been resolved so that the only remaining task would be the technical or epistemic one of finding the way to that resolution. It also involves accepting that there is *no regime-free way of describing their operation*, including taking a position on whether some form of interaction is closer to the functional alternatives of 'war' or 'integration' in a regime world, namely those of absolute alienation or absolute assimilation. As participants and analysts, we live in a world where it is always, to paraphrase the familiar story about turtles, 'regimes all the way down'.

Talk of 'hegemony' is of course common in international law and international relations.[10] The word is most frequently used as a general name for the predominance of some power over others – as in 'US hegemony'. It is usually understood not to involve any commitment as to the origin or nature of such power or its forms of expression, physical, ideological, economic or whatever. As a simple synonym for 'predominance', 'hegemony' is then employed in the context of discussions of 'equilibrium' or 'balance of power' as either their analytical opposite or then as an instrument for the bringing about, in the long run, of a cooperative system – or indeed of regimes – within which the types of equilibrium may again operate in a more limited sphere.[11] Indeed, in both of these versions, 'hegemony' has

[9] I have used this notion earlier in my essay, 'International Law and Hegemony: A Reconfiguration' (2004) 17 *Cambridge Review of International Affairs* 197–218.

[10] See especially Heinrich Triepel, *Die Hegemonie. Ein Buch von führenden Staaten* (Stuttgart, Kohlhammer, 1938), 4–6, defending the nature of 'hegemony' as a *legal* concept.

[11] For some typical discussions, see e.g. Michael W. Doyle, *Ways of War and Peace* (Norton, 1979) 143, 176–179 (discussing 'counterhegemonic balancing'); Ian Clark, *Legitimacy in International Society* (Oxford University Press, 2005) 227–229. Robert O. Keohane has famously developed a notion of 'hegemonic stability' according to which 'order in world politics is typically created by a single hegemonic power', also arguing that 'the formation of international regimes normally depends on hegemony'. See Robert O. Keohane, 'The Theory of Hegemonic Stability and Changes in International Regimes 1967–1977' in *International Institutions and State Power: Essays in International Relations Theory* (Boulder, Colorado, Westview Press, 1989) 74–100 and Robert O. Keohane, *After*

become a standard part of international relations 'realist' or 'institutionalist' discourse.

'Hegemony' is a loaded word. To claim that some entity is in a position of hegemony is often taken as a criticism, or at least the description of a problem calling for remedial – perhaps 'counter-hegemonic' – action. But I want to take my cue here from Gramsci, as updated by Laclau and Mouffe some years ago and use the notion as an analytical tool to examine the everyday phenomenon whereby some particular actor – in our case a regime – seeks to make its particular project or interest or pursuit seem the general project or interest.[12] Under this view, 'hegemony' describes what can also be called a universalisation strategy, the effort by some particular to appear as a representative of the universal. In the international world (but also in political life more generally), this is a commonplace. International actors typically enter the political scene by claiming to represent or to speak in the voice of the universal. Some such situations are quite obvious: think, for example, of verbal strategies in which the speakers invoke 'universal values' or claim to speak on behalf of the 'international community'.[13] The history of international law may easily be recounted as a development of successive universalisation vocabularies, such as those of 'Christianity', 'civilisation', 'modernisation', 'development' or 'rule of law' through which European powers have sought to describe European cultural items as universal features or objectives of social life.[14] But a universalisation strategy need not at all be so express on its surface. It may merely be about the 'right' or the 'correct' understanding of a rule or a policy, that is to say, an understanding that

Hegemony: Cooperation and Discord in the World of Political Economy (Princeton University Press, 1984) 31 and generally on the notion of hegemony 31–46.

[12] See especially, Ernesto Laclau and Chantal Mouffe, *Hegemony and Socialist Strategy* (London, Verso, 2nd edn, 2001) and Ernesto Laclau, 'Identity and Hegemony: The Role of Universality in the Constitution of Political Logics' in Judith Butler, Ernesto Laclau and Slavoj Žižek (eds.), *Contingency, Hegemony, Universality. Contemporary Dialogues on the Left* (London, Verso, 2000) 44–89; and Andreas Fischer-Lescano and Sonia Buckel, 'Emanzipatorische Gegenhegemonie im Weltrecht' in Regina Kreide and Andreas Niederberger (eds.), *Transnationale Verrechtlichung: Nationale Demokratien im Kontext globaler Politik* (Campus, 2008) 114–133.

[13] See, e.g. Michel Feher, *Powerless by Design: The Age of the International Community* (Duke University Press, 2000).

[14] I have discussed this in many places, for example, in 'International Law in Europe: Between Tradition and Renewal' (2005) 16 *European Journal of International Law* 113–124. For another discussion, see Immanuel Wallerstein, *European Universalism: The Rhetoric of Power* (New York and London, The New Press, 2006).

ought to be taken as *universally* right or correct.[15] In normal situations of international life the actors disagree on such matters, putting forward competing understandings and rival interpretations of the relevant rules or policies. These are situations that I like to call *hegemonic contestation* so as to highlight that what is at stake is not only what the general view is but *who is entitled to determine it*.

That hegemonic contestation is an everyday phenomenon follows from the fact that the universal has no authentic representative or a voice of its own. All we can see are particular actors making particular claims but insisting that those claims have universal validity, that they are not only right for the speaker (that is, they are not merely 'subjective values') but right for everyone else, too. Natural law provided a much-used universalisation vocabulary for most of Western political and legal history. To claim that some preference was valid as a matter of natural law was to insist that it was valid for 'all' because it was enshrined in (universal) human nature or human reason or indeed the frame of social life itself. When arguments about human nature, reason or the natural norms of human society started to become suspect – when they began to appear as mere smokescreens for the idiosyncratic preferences of the speakers – then other universalisation languages followed suit.

Legal formalism, for example, suggested that rules, when written into laws or treaties or arising from the behaviour of states ('customary law') would have the same (universal) meaning for all. And so much of the clash of universalisation vocabularies in the twentieth century – recent hegemonic contestation – has been about what should be the (universally) correct understanding of this or that rule or principle. But the 'turn to hermeneutics', imagining legal work as interpretation of rules, was never able to attain outcomes solid enough to serve as the basis for managerial decision-making. Recurring interpretative controversies undermined effective strategy.[16] Therefore the turn to managerial ideologies sometime in the 1990s; enlisting the help of economic, technical and scientific vocabularies seemed to bring certainty and solidity (i.e. universal validity) to the regime-world that techniques of interpretation lacked. Or to highlight the hegemonic interest in the process: it began to seem professionally more plausible to argue in the registers of institutional economics

[15] A hegemonic claim is not merely about the preferences of the speaker but embodies a professional-cultural *Weltanschauung*, see Fischer-Lescano and Buckel, 'Emanzipatorische Gegenhegemonie', above n. 12, 119.

[16] Duncan Kennedy, *A Critique of Adjudication (fin-de siècle)* (Harvard University Press, 1997).

or 'rational choice' so as to be taken seriously as an expert.[17] Adopting a technical vocabulary, one would appear to be speaking not only for one-self; one would be representing that which is true, as technical propositions are understood in the audiences committed to them. It is, after all, the point of a truth-regime to appear like no regime at all.

D. Hegemonic regimes

As I have observed elsewhere, the turn to 'regimes' in international law resulted from the fragmentation and deformalisation of the field. These manifested an increasingly technical understanding of global problems that required 'functionally specialised' instruments for their resolution. As a consequence, international law also began to appear in an instrumental light, as a tool in the toolbox of rule. In the struggle between politics and technique that has always been waged at international law's ideological heart, the pendulum swung with 'global governance' decisively towards the latter.[18] A new literature spread from political science faculties in the US to international relations and international law that was written in the vocabularies of political economy, governance and problem-resolution and focused on such questions as the design of international institutions and the effectiveness of alternative forms of transnational 'regulation'.[19] Treaties and customary law were discussed as optional instruments for the carrying out of managerial tasks, technical tools in the search for Pareto-optimal effects for particular 'issue-areas' of global governance.[20]

In the managerial consciousness, international law exists as an element in functional regimes whose point and purpose is well described by Robert O. Keohane:

> [Regimes] facilitate agreements by raising the anticipated costs of violating others' property rights, by altering transaction costs through clustering of issues and by providing reliable information to members. They thrive in situations where states have common as well as conflicting

[17] See, e.g. Andrew T. Guzman, *How International Law Works: A Rational Choice Theory* (Oxford University Press, 2008); Joel P. Trachtman, *The Economic Structure of International Law* (Harvard University Press, 2008).

[18] See my 'The Fate of International Law: Between Technique and Politics' (2007) 70 *Modern Law Review* 1–32.

[19] See, e.g. Judith L. Goldstein et al., *Legalization and World Politics* (MIT Press, 2001) and Brütsch and Lehmkuhl, *Law and Legalization*, above n. 8.

[20] I have critiqued this tendency in many places, most recently in my 'Miserable Comforters: International Relations as a New Natural Law' (2009) 15 *European Journal of International Relations* 395–422.

> interests on multiple, overlapping issues and where externalities are difficult but not impossible to deal with through bargaining.[21]

All the elements of the liberal 'harmony' are in place here, with the assumption the world is a place where everyone imagines themselves as egoistic but 'rational' calculators of their interests. What only needs to be added to this language is the sense of the increasing autonomy of the regimes as systems of interest in their own right.[22] In Keohane (and in this literature generally), states (or at least the US) still stand *outside* the regimes in a more or less hegemonic position. This overlooks the disaggregation of the state itself into yet another instrument of governance through which globally effective expert networks and systems of knowledge pursue their objectives.[23] Trade interests, environmental lobbies, human rights and security expert groups constantly intervene in states so as to make their preferences the states' preferences so as to open access to resources (such as government funds) or forums (such as intergovernmental institutions) to which only formal states have access. In the developed world, for example, parties in government represent increasingly sectoral interests and perspectives that are not only globally connected but defined in a thoroughly global process of interest-definition. A government is a collection of foreign policy, agricultural, environmental, financial, trade and development interests, each of which is defined in a global process so that 'Finland' or the 'United States' are often little more than names that represent local compromises between globally operative functional regimes of knowledge and interest.[24]

The crisis of representative politics in the West – the popular sense that the electoral parties offer no real alternatives – illustrates a widely shared sentiment that this has already happened and that political engagement in the sense of taking the nation's collective life in the hands of its citizens is somehow no longer possible. What would 'civic virtue' or positive

21 Keohane, *After Hegemony*, above n. 11, 97.

22 See Ingo Ventzke, 'International Bureaucracies from a Political Science Perspective – Agency, Authority and International Institutional Law' in Armin von Bogdandy et al. (eds.), *The Exercise of Public Authority by International Institutions: Advancing International Institutional law* (Heidelberg, Springer, 2009) 70–85.

23 As famously described by Anne-Marie Slaughter, *A New World Order. Government Networks and the Disaggregated State* (Princeton University Press, 2004).

24 See further, Stefan Oeter, 'Theorising the Global Legal Order – An Institutionalist Perspective' in Andrew Halpin and Volker Roeben (eds.), *Theorising the Global Legal Order* (Oxford, Hart Publishing, 2009) 61, 71–74 and Stefan Oeter, 'Prekäre Staatlichkeit und die Grenzen internationale Verrechtlichung' in Kreide and Niederberger, above n. 12, 90–113.

('Roman') liberty in a post-national constellation mean? Commitment to a constitution seems a lifeless substitute for the patriotism that once upheld the notion that collective futures could be politically determined – that is to say, that they were not the already-existing effects of knowledge-systems but matters of passionate and aesthetic reimagining, sometimes struggle, not something to be discovered but to be invented. In such a conception, whatever its historical dark sides, collective entities would not seek validation by espousing this or that type of global logic but by offering identities to the citizens that are not expected to remain stable over time (as citizens are reduced to passive recipients of welfare or security services) but to change in response to shared experiences. If there is frustration with the managerial politics of the West, it has at least something to do with the way it denies individual growth through participation in the formation of collective destinies.[25]

Whether or not this is a completely accurate description of the dilemmas of the domestic and international political world today, the point is that regimes such as the 'international trade system', the 'climate change system' or the 'security system' are all engaged in universalisation strategies, trying to make their special knowledge and interest appear as the general knowledge and general interest, a commonplace consciousness.[26] If they are successful, they will no longer appear to represent particular viewpoints at all but 'knowledge' in need of implementation everywhere. They have succeeded in becoming hegemonic. Their position has become the neutral position laying down the standard of normality against which alternatives will be assessed.

Concern over 'regime interaction' captures some of this. The new academic literature on global governance assumes the presence of a large number of transnational regimes, each of which has its special objectives, institutions, experts and ethos. They are needed because the 'new situation' can no longer be dealt with (managed) though traditional inter-state

[25] These are large themes that cannot be taken up here. The problem of democracy after nationalism is discussed in Jürgen Habermas, *The Postnational Constellation. Political Essays* (MIT Press, 2001). I have defended a view of civic activism in collective life in many places, most recently in 'Vocabularies of Sovereignty – Powers of a Paradox' in Hent Kalmo and Quentin Skinner (eds.), *Sovereignty in Fragments. The Past, Present and Future of a Contested Concept* (Cambridge University Press, 2010) 222, 239–242.

[26] See especially Gunther Teubner and Andreas Fischer-Lescano, *Regime-Kollisionen: Zur Fragmentierung des globalen Rechts* (Frankfurt, Suhrkamp, 2006); and Gunther Teubner and Andreas Fischer-Lescano, 'Regime-Collisions: The Vain Search for Legal Unity in the Fragmentation of Global Law' (2004) 25 *Michigan Journal of International Law* 999–1046.

cooperation. Creating economic prosperity, protecting the environment, seeing to the security of large populations, protecting human rights or making the world safe against international criminality require functionally specialised and technically up-to-date legal systems of global import, such as a world trade law system, networks of environmental treaties, transnational structures of cooperation between security experts, a global human rights movement and international institutions with criminal jurisdiction, among others.[27]

This literature accepts that the plurality of such regimes has produced new problems. They often address the same facts in different ways. Advancing free trade under a world trade regime may clash with objectives upheld by environmental or human rights regimes. Preferences valued within the latter may conflict with preferences of security regimes or of economic development. Some of this has had immediate legal articulations. May environmental values be recognised in the WTO dispute settlement system? Are security regimes to be interpreted in accordance with or as exceptions to the human rights treaties? If both human rights and humanitarian law regimes apply in a zone of conflict, which is to be given precedence? If a worldwide law of the sea regime enters into conflict with a regional economic integration regime, which one should have the final word? If the experts of the world food regime and the experts of the law of the sea regime are both competent in a matter concerning the regulation of fisheries, which group is to be given precedence?

The list of actual and potential regime-conflicts could be continued almost interminably. The theme of 'fragmentation' emerged to address them to the extent they were feared to lead to conflicting jurisprudence.[28] That danger did not greatly materialise, owing to the marginality of formal dispute settlement in the international world and the propensity of international lawyers not to accentuate the significance of formal overlaps. Techniques to resolve prima facie conflicts through ad hoc hierarchies created by legal practice are now laid out in the work by the International Law Commission on the 'Fragmentation of International Law'.[29]

[27] On the different ways to conceive systems of non-state legal expertise, see William Twining, 'Implications of Globalisation for Law as a Discipline' in Halpin and Roeben, above n. 24, 40–44.

[28] Martti Koskenniemi and Päivi Leino, 'Fragmentation of International Law? Postmodern Anxieties' (2002) 15 *Leiden Journal of International Law* 553–579.

[29] Fragmentation of International Law: Difficulties Arising from the Diversification and Expansion of International Law. Report of the Study Group of the International Law Commission, Finalized by Martti Koskenniemi, UN Doc. A/CN.4/L.682 13 April 2006 (Erik Castrén Institute Research Reports 21/2007, Helsinki, 2007).

But the problem is of a general nature and manifests itself above all in the daily operation of the regimes in blissful ignorance of each other and firmly committed to imposing their particular outlook on the world. Instead of through formal dispute settlement or legislation, however, regimes develop through the informal expansion of their vocabularies in academia and in bureaucracies and by occupying the position of dominant frameworks of thought and action, matrices for the identification of problems and thumb-rules for their resolution. They operate less as systems of formal commands than as broad cultural or professional orientations that do not respond to problems but act as mechanisms that make it possible to identify an aspect in the world as a 'problem' in the first place. As frameworks of thinking and 'regimes of truth' they operate beyond the consciousness of single individuals or collectives (such as professional groups). As autonomous social and epistemic wholes they end up creating something like limited or mini-sovereignties out of themselves.[30] The 'functional' character of such self-regulating structures as 'trade law', 'environmental law', 'human rights law' and so on, does not at all signify that they would work in view of a globally defined common good. It merely refers to their quality as mechanised producers of outcomes that are internally validated by their embedded hierarchies of preference – their structural biases.[31] They are functional for *themselves*, each seeking operative closure against the others even within the constitutional semantic of statehood and the international community.[32]

I have stressed the usefulness of perceiving the analogy – or better, identity – between problems of coordination that arose between sovereign states and those that arise between regimes. International lawyers are used to viewing 'sovereignty' as a decisive obstacle to the management of the state-world. This is so because – as Hans Kelsen once put it – to take sovereignty seriously is to adopt a point of view that is both solipsistic and

[30] For regimes as systems of knowledge and expertise, see, e.g. Ventzke, 'International Bureaucracies from a Political Science Perspective' above n. 22, 78–85.

[31] I have discussed this in *From Apology to Utopia: The Structure of International Legal Argument* (Cambridge University Press, reissue with a new epilogue, 2005) 600–615.

[32] For this obviously Luhmannian view, see further, e.g. Mathias Albert, 'Beyond Legalization: Reading the Increase, Variation and Differentiation of Legal and Law-Like Arrangements in International Relations Through World-Society Theory' in Brütsch and Lehmkuhl, above n. 8, 187–198. The classic here is, of course, Niklas Luhmann in Fatima Kastner, Richard Nobles, David Schiff and Rosamund Ziegert (eds.), *Law as a Social System* (Klaus Ziegert trans, Oxford University Press, 2004) (translation of the book first published as Niklas Luhmann, *Das Recht der Gesellschaft* (Frankfurt, Suhrkamp 1993)).

imperialistic simultaneously.[33] The sovereign state sees only its own needs and interests and acts so as to universalise them. While commentators have had no difficulty in understanding this in hegemonic terms (that is, to understand 'sovereignty' as political *par excellence*), they have failed to do so in regard to the identical process in a regime-world. Like states, functional regimes operate as clusters of interest and knowledge, and like states they act in solipsistic and imperial ways – they are coded so as to perceive only themselves and their own preferences and to translate those mechanically into the preferences of everyone.[34]

Moreover, a regime (unlike a state) has identity and purpose *only* as a special set of preferences and a type of knowledge that is organised as a system of experts and standard problem-solutions. Where the determination of state-preferences is often an arena of political controversy, regime-preferences are fixed usually in expert debates that refer back to discipline-internal (often scientific or technical but also more broadly cultural) criteria of validation that seldom articulate themselves in political terms. The reason for this is easy to understand. The authority of regimes and regime-experts is based on the scientific or technical nature of the expertise they represent. To depict *internal* conflicts among, say, environmental experts in political terms would undermine the authority of their shared form of expertise. Hence the virtual commitment of functional regimes to apolitical decision-making in solipsistic and imperial terms: after all, this is what it *means* for a regime to imagine itself in epistemic terms, as a regime of (scientific, technical, disciplinary) truth instead of political preference.

What happens when regimes 'interact' may thus not be amenable for technical management at all. If the regimes are both operationally closed (unable to view the external world apart from where it has been translated into their idiom) and expansive (that is, seeking to make that idiom the global Esperanto), then they are by definition hegemonic and every suggested coordination will appear as a strategic proposal either for conquest or alienation. In practice, expert groups competing for global influence know this very well. A few years ago a debate was waged between Ernst-Ulrich Petersmann, a recognised trade expert, and Philip Alston,

[33] Hans Kelsen, *Das Problem der Souveränität und die Theorie des Völkerrechts* (Tübingen, Mohr, 2nd edn, 1922).

[34] See further the works by Fischer-Lescano and Teubner, above n. 22. For a description of the effect of the expansion of technical regime-rationales on civil rights and freedoms, see Christian Hohmann-Dennhard, 'Wo bleiben die Bürger und ihre Rechte?' in Graf-Peter Calliess et al. (eds.), *Soziologische Jurisprudenz: Festschrift für Gunther Teubner* (Berlin, De Gruyter, 2009) 753–763.

an equally recognised expert in human rights, on whether the WTO ought to possess competence on human rights as well.[35] For Petersmann, only a globally effective trade system could guarantee an effective protection of rights, while Alston refused to give in to the 'merger and acquisition' of human rights by trade bodies. The nature of the debate and the stakes therein were easy to understand in political, hegemonic terms. For Petersmann, rights were always already translated into private exchanges and free trade so that expanding the latter will automatically strengthen the former; while for Alston, the heterogeneity of trade and human rights created the fear that if the latter were 'sucked into' the trade system, the result would end up supporting the preferences of trade lawyers instead of those of human rights lawyers.

The same problem emerges in the strategies of 'mainstreaming' human rights within areas such as (to take just two examples from projects in which I have been recently involved) development policy or in European Security and defence policy.[36] Mainstreaming is a technique of regime interaction: under it, regime A enters regime B so as to become a part of the latter's daily routine and self-understanding. Although this is usually discussed in terms of friendly cooperation and the pursuit of parallel and coterminous interests, in practice the matter is rarely so straightforward. In my two examples 'mainstreaming' raised the problem of whether the integration of human rights in development or security policy would actually end up advancing human rights or whether it would merely lead to co-option in support of policies dictated from developmental or security interests. There is seldom an easy answer to such a question. How the matter will turn requires complex strategic calculation that must begin with an assessment of the solidity of the preferences within both regimes: which one is more likely to be transformed by 'interaction'?[37]

One alternative to full integration or complete separation is the creation of regime hybrids such as 'sustainable development', 'human security' or 'corporate social responsibility'. Such hybrids involve an initial identification of conflicting preferences (environment/development, human rights/

[35] See Philip Alston, 'Resisting the Merger and Acquisition of Human Rights by Trade Law: A Reply to Petersmann' (2002) 13(4) *European Journal of International Law* 815.

[36] See Samuli Seppänen, *Possibilities and Challenges of the Human-Rights Based Approach to Development* (Helsinki, Erik Castrén Institute Research Reports, 2005), and Tiina Pajuste, *Mainstreaming Human Rights in the Context of The European Security and Defence Policy* (Helsinki, Erik Castrén Institute Research Reports, 2008).

[37] See my 'Human Rights Mainstreaming as a Strategy for Institutional Power' (2010) 1(1) *Humanity: An International Journal of Human Rights, Humanitarianism and Development* 47–58.

security, corporate profits/social interests) and the creation of a vocabulary and a platform and perhaps official texts through which the experts representing the respective regimes may wage their struggle for influence.[38] The hegemonic nature of that struggle is usually hidden by the way the relevant texts are written in the idiom of technical cooperation so as to avoid an open politicisation that would threaten the control of the process by the experts. As in the Petersmann/Alston situation, the experts themselves usually have a clear view of the political stakes in such hybrids – that is to say, the way any policy that will be adopted will advance one of the contrasting set of preferences at the cost of its competitor.

E. Strategic choices

In a world of hegemonic regimes, there is no 'innocent' or impartial, neutral terrain from the perspective of which regime interaction could be managed. Just as in the world of hegemonic states there was no such 'harmony of interests' that natural lawyers, inter-war legal idealists or liberal internationalists imagined that could be caught within some institution with universal jurisdiction (such as the UN). The interminable political conflicts within the UN illustrate the fact that in a world of limited resources all management involves deciding in favour of some and against other interests, the setting up of a hierarchy of values or pursuits that prefers some outlooks at the cost of others. Everybody enters 'regime interaction' like the representatives of states approach the UN: from the perspective of one's own preferences that are always already partial and contested or contestable but striving towards universal recognition. Who wins will be about hegemonic success; even the most reasonable reasons are reasonable only from the perspective of some system of reason.

There are of, course, vocabularies that seek to transcend the horizontal juxtaposition between equally partial regimes. The 'constitutionalisation of international law', public authority and administrative law have been referred to so as to imagine the decentralised wielding of global power in terms familiar to legal experts.[39] To the extent these efforts end up

[38] A partly similar discussion of regime hybrids (such as 'soft law' and 'sustainability') is in Inger-Johanne Sand, 'Hybrid law – Law in a Global Society of Differentiation and Change' in Graf-Peter Calliess et al., *Soziologische Jurisprudenz*, above n. 34, 871–886.

[39] See Jan Klabbers, Anne Peters and Ulf Geirstein, *The Constitutionalization of International Law* (Oxford University Press, 2009); Benedict Kingsbury, Nico Krisch, Richard B. Stewart and Jonathan Wiener (eds.), 'The Emergence of Global Administrative Law' (2005) 68 *Law and Contemporary Problems* 1–377; Bogdandy et al., *The Exercise of Public Authority*, above n. 22.

highlighting the *political* nature of the operation of functional regimes, and point to values such as democracy, transparency, accountability, inclusion and fairness, they imply a welcome corrective to the managerialist orientation of the regime-world. But as they lead into specific proposals, they become part of those struggles themselves: what should 'democracy', 'transparency' or 'accountability' *mean* in this or that institutional context? What structure of decision-making should it call for? Which criteria should be used to decide between alternatives? 'The struggle for world law is a struggle over the ruling opinion in world law.'[40]

Lawyers and constitutional and administrative law experts are also technical experts with their own distancing vocabularies, and the juridification of international politics that accompanies these suggestions has its well-known bright and dark sides. This is not to say that there might not be reason to support the 'turn to law', for example, as a counterhegemonic strategy against the turn to economics or to political science in global governance. But the real challenge is to bring the clash of regimes as systems of thought into the open and to address them by political means. The 'constitutional mindset' might be helpful to the extent that it is geared against the solipsism and imperialism of single regimes and to the extent it would support (in Kantian language) 'a moral politics' that refuses to make contestable choices seem natural by dressing them in the language of technique.[41] Its own institutional proposals (if it makes any), however, are no less hegemonic than those of its competitors.

Resisting permanent institutional hierarchies, it is hard to see what else global law could become than a *Koordinationsrecht*, as international law once was, a 'collision law' providing techniques for articulating and deciding conflicts between overlapping regimes. This is suggested both by the systems-theoretical perspective and the Study Group of the International Law Commission.[42] The alternative would always be the hegemony of a single regime, return to the harmony of interests and the enlightened absolutism of managerialism.

Under the hegemonic perspective, every effort to speak with a voice that rises above single regimes is a strategic manoeuvre and raises the question – coordination, yes, but under what conditions? In analysing this question, it is useful to distinguish between two positions – the position of a regime that

40 Buckel and Fischer-Lescano, 'Emanzipatorische Gegehegemonie', above n. 12, 129.

41 I have elaborated this theme in my 'Constitutionalism as Mindset: Reflections on Kantian Themes about International Law and Globalization' (2007) 8 *Theoretical Inquiries in Law* 9–36.

42 'Fragmentation of International Law', above n. 29, 250–256.

tries to become hegemonic and the position of the (weaker) regime seeking to resist this. The debate on trade and human rights juxtaposed a hegemonic trade regime with a human rights regime that felt itself threatened by integration. In the debates waged under the 'human rights approach to development' (HRBA), the challenge was to transform development priorities from being measured in macroeconomic terms by focusing on the needs of specific human groups. The danger was that the indeterminacy of the human rights preferences would in the process annihilate them as distinct from preferences for particular theories of development. In order to have influence, the human rights position needs to become an economic development position. Only through pragmatism and professionalism can human rights experts be taken seriously in development contexts. But in such a case would they still be *human rights experts?*[43]

In regime encounters, all actors are faced with an initial strategic question: should I prefer integration or separation? Integration might increase one's influence, open avenues to being heard and to having an impact on policy-making that would otherwise be out of reach. But it might also lead to co-option, lending support to policies one has little reason to support. It might actually lessen one's influence by diminishing one's credibility in the eyes of one's colleagues and (critical) outsiders. It also comes with a cost: great effort may be needed to develop the know-how in the substance of the target-regime without which no influence will be attained. That effort is lost from more straightforward activism. It is a necessary condition for influence in a human rights or a security regime that one learns to speak the langue of human rights or security – but learning these is hard work, and involves the risk that part of that learning might consist of the silent internalisation of the preferences that go with the new language.

Refusing to integrate and staying outside as a critic or a watchdog may often be the better strategic choice, for the harmonious functioning of a world of regimes is hardly an objective to be supported for its own sake. It all depends – or ought to depend – on what one's view of the world is: in an unacceptably unjust world, why should one contribute to its coherence or functional effectiveness? A colonialist or racist society is no better by the fact that its regimes work coherently; on the contrary. In a regime-world of strategic choices, there is thus always a prior, non-technical question to

[43] David Kennedy has discussed this in terms of the 'dance' between a humanitarian law expert and a military expert: in order to influence each other, each has to adopt the vocabulary of its counterpart and become a persuasive speaker in it – with the consequence that it may be impossible to distinguish the two from each other. *The Dark Sides of Virtue: Reassessing International Humanitarianism* (Princeton University Press, 2006) 266–272 and *passim*.

be asked that relates to the nature of the world in which one is acting. Is it a *good* world so that one has reason to work for its coherence and functional effectiveness? Or ought one rather contribute to its further fragmentation and possibly its transformation if not collapse? International lawyers often speak as if the smooth functioning of mainstream international institutions were an unmitigated good. This, as Kennedy has shown, is often an ideological or cultural choice that may actually contribute to the problems it hopes to resolve.[44]

The contribution of global regimes to the problems of violence and injustice in the world is anything but straightforward. So is the role of available strategies: integration in an existing regime through unthinking ideological commitment may be as much a problem as integrating as a strategically minded guerrilla warrior may be the right solution. Integration may reflect a wish to join the policy-making elites that generally *do* share the view that the present world (in which they have succeeded in attaining elite positions) is the best of all possible worlds – or it may reflect a well-thought-out strategy to move the regime in the direction of acceptable political choices. There is thus no a priori reason to be either for or against coordination. Parallel considerations affect the alternative of refusing to coordinate because one has no interest to ensure the smooth functioning of the whole. Refusal may lead to loss of influence – or it may enhance the critical power of what one has to say. It offers a principled stance but risks marginalisation. Which is the more likely result cannot be determined *in abstracto* but requires both strategic awareness and constant negotiation of what it is one actually wants to achieve in the world. But the matrix within which more or less intensive coordination should be contemplated can be easily sketched:

	Positive effects	Negative effects
Intensive coordination (integration)	Influence, prestige, professionalism	Assimilation, loss of identity and critical power
Weak or no coordination (separation)	Preserving critical voice, protecting values and principles	Exclusion, marginalisation, loss of influence, prestige and knowledge

[44] Ibid.

F. Regime interaction as political contestation

The vocabulary of regime interaction suggests that problems of global governance can be resolved by economic or technical means, in other words, that they are managerial problems. This hides their political nature – the way resolution allocates spiritual and material resources between human groups so that some groups will win at the cost of others while the criteria of allocation are subject to disagreement. Global governance is about the contestable use of global power; regimes are political projects and expert vocabularies manifestos. This takes away nothing from the complexity of the relationship between regimes of global expertise and the problems of injustice and violence in the world. We have no clear view of the causalities and our ability to evaluate the consequences of decisions made in the global 'centre' on the 'periphery' is limited. But there are two things on which we can be reasonably clear. One is that no single hierarchy of preferences or institutions is realistically available to producing good outcomes. Even if we had an agreement of what we would like to achieve – words such as 'peace', 'prosperity' and liberty come to mind – we are completely divided as to how we should get there. Second, however, the very notion of 'the good' is not only contested but we have no idea of how to measure the candidates. This incompatibility is expressed in the hegemonic struggle that some of its participants want to express in the jargon of 'regime interaction'. There is no objection to that jargon apart from that it pushes alternative vocabularies aside – namely such vocabularies as those of 'solidarity' and 'exploitation', to name just two, or those of faith and the nation.

Managerialism is not a solution. It is a problem. To deal with it could begin with the translation of its vocabularies, the languages of science, economics, technique – and law – in political terms. One way of doing this is to think of their expansive pursuits in hegemonic terms, as I have done here. This might undermine the propensity of such languages to present themselves as the global Esperanto in transmitting meanings that are universally shared. It would highlight the partial and contestable nature of the knowledge we have about the world. It would also draw attention to the genealogy of that knowledge: where has it come from? Whom does it support? What alternative knowledges are there? Vocabularies have histories that are tied with the genealogies of particular forms of rule. Gazing into the future in a problem-solving mode prevents asking the question about how it is that we are ruled by *these* languages, *these* men and women. Managerialism thinks of itself as a hill from which it is possible to see far. In truth it is a valley in which we always look in the same direction – and all the interesting questions lie behind our back.

INDEX

Lightning Source UK Ltd.
Milton Keynes UK
UKHW012156021218
333370UK00013B/149/P

9 781107 52178